ÉMILE ZOLA

ÉMILE ZOLA

F. W. J. HEMMINGS

SECOND EDITION

OXFORD

AT THE CLARENDON PRESS

1966

Oxford University Press, Ely House, London W. 1

GLASGOW NEW YORK TORONTO MELBOURNE WELLINGTON
CAPE TOWN SALISBURY IBADAN NAIROBI LUSAKA ADDIS ABABA
BOMBAY CALCUTTA MADRAS KARACHI LAHORE DACCA
KUALA LUMPUR HONG KONG

PRINTED IN GREAT BRITAIN

PREFACE TO
THE SECOND EDITION

SINCE this book was written, in 1951–2, more work has been
done on Zola than over the whole of the previous period since
his death in 1902. The body of relevant knowledge has grown
correspondingly, and as a result criticism has been able to focus on
aspects formerly neglected, ignored, or unsuspected. No one can
have read the contributions of MM. Guy Robert, Marcel Girard,
René Ternois, and Henri Mitterand, and of John Lapp, the Grants
father and son, and Martin Kanes in the United States, without
feeling a profound debt of gratitude for the way in which they have
renewed our understanding of the last great French novelist of the
nineteenth century. It would have been altogether wrong to bring
back into print what purports to be a general study of Émile Zola
without profiting from the work of these scholars especially and
of others too numerous to mention.

In revising this book for a new edition I have, besides, taken into
account what seemed to me justified criticisms on the part of those
who reviewed it when it first appeared; and, my own attitudes
having changed in some respects, I have taken the opportunity to
modify certain earlier judgements. While preserving the general
plan and framework of the book, I have added one chapter, re-
written certain others almost completely, and left none of them
entirely unaltered. Naturally I do not suppose that my revised
interpretations will command universal agreement any more than
did those I originally put forward; my aim has been to weigh up
all the new data that has been presented and to try and overlook
nothing of significance in retelling my story and reformulating
my views.

F.W.J.H.

Leicester, March 1965

CONTENTS

I

THE DREAMER AWAKES

IT must be counted among the odder ironies of literary history
that the first work of Zola's to be set up in print was an innocent little trifle about the metamorphosis of two medieval lovers
into sprigs of marjoram by a nursery fairy with wings of flame and
a crown of forget-me-nots.

The gulf between Zola in his early twenties, in a very real sense
the poet starving in the garret, and Zola only a few years later, the
bustling, prosperous pressman, gapes so wide that it hardly seems
possible to bridge it by any logically interlocking sections. An indefinite number of paradoxical confrontations can be made. In
1860 Zola's philosophy of life consisted in ignoring workaday
reality and feeding on daydreams—'Je détourne les yeux du fumier
pour les porter sur les roses, . . . parce que je préfère les roses, si
peu utiles pourtant'; seven years later a prudish critic will accuse
him of writing 'putrid literature', of wallowing in that very dung-
heap he had not been able to set his eyes on. In 1860 again, three
years after the appearance of *Madame Bovary*, Zola protested that
'le roman n'a pas que le but de peindre, il doit aussi corriger'; yet
six years later he will be ironical about a moral ending that he finds
in a novel by Louis Ulbach: Ulbach 'veut allier l'art et la morale.
Je ne puis qu'applaudir à cette excellente intention. J'ai des idées
diamétralement opposées. . . .' The letters he wrote just after
leaving school are rapturous about Chénier, Ronsard, Dante, and
the French Romantic poets; in an age of materialism, the poet has
a sacred mission: 'montrer à toute heure, en tout lieu, l'âme à ceux
qui ne pensent qu'au corps, et Dieu à ceux dont la science a tué la
foi.' In 1866, however, he will profess impatience at having to
review a packet of poetry books (even though, among them, was the
first issue of *Le Parnasse contemporain*); he has no time now for
poets—'pauvres gens qui se mettent l'esprit à la torture pour clouer
des mots dans le cadre étroit du vers'. What do people mean by
realism in art? he asked Cézanne in 1860. Painting farmyards

B

perhaps; but add a ray of sunshine and one of Greuze's village girls feeding the poultry and you will have provided the indispensable poetic touch. Ary Scheffer, 'that genius' who had died the previous year, 'était poète dans toute l'acception du mot, ne peignant presque pas le réel, abordant les sujets les plus sublimes, les plus délirants. Veux-tu rien de plus poétique, d'une poésie étrange et navrante, que sa *Françoise de Rimini*?' Little time would be needed for the young art-critic to smash the idols at whose altar he had worshipped. In his review of the 1868 exhibition Ary Scheffer will be named again, but in derision, as the very type of the painter who shirks the true aim of painting, which is to represent in line and colour the visible world, the material body, not the immaterial soul or any such cloudy emanation of poetic ecstasy.

So abrupt a transformation of outlook, so absolute a reversal of values, are easier to illustrate than to account for. How was it that even in early manhood Zola retained the candid idealism of adolescence? and what happened to cause this high-principled enthusiast to shed his illusions and make way for the brash, alert, ambitious journalist, later to develop into a burly builder of grandiose and immensely popular prose epics? Which, above all, was the real Zola? Was the latter stage the fundamental one, and has one to postulate the occurrence of some kind of psychological shock, analogous to the biological shock that determines the emergence of the insect from the chrysalis? Or was the final, settled shape merely a protective shell beneath which the lover of roses and of 'poésie étrange et navrante' continued to live and breathe, and now and then to utter some plaintive, discordant protest?

Two circumstances made Émile Zola's childhood an unusual one. He was the son of a foreigner; and his father died when he was not quite seven.

On his father's side he was of pure Italian stock. The line can be traced back to a great-grandfather, Antonio Zola or Zolla,[1] a native of Brescia who served as an infantry officer in the Venetian forces. All three of Antonio's sons became army officers in the service of the Republic; the second, Carlo (1752–1810), the novelist's grandfather, being in the engineers. Carlo appears to

---

[1] The name signifies in Italian 'clod of earth', a fact with which the novelist was acquainted and in which he took no little pride, to judge by his fondness for imparting it to visiting interviewers.

have contracted a first marriage, which was childless, with a young woman from Corfu; his second wife was Venetian, and the family he founded with her included a daughter and two sons, Marco and Francesco, both of whom took up engineering as a profession after graduating from the University of Padua. Francesco (born 1795), a man of restless ambition, left Venice in 1821 but remained in the service of the Habsburgs until 1830 when (possibly for political reasons) he went into permanent exile. He served in Algeria for little more than a year in the newly created Foreign Legion and then, having resigned his commission, set up in practice as a civil engineer in Marseilles. Here he conceived a grandiose scheme for improving and enlarging the harbour, and between 1836 and 1840 spent most of his time in Paris trying to interest the authorities in the project. And here, on 16 March 1839, he married, for 'her beauty and charm' as their son later said, a dowerless girl noticed as she was leaving church. Émilie Aubert was the daughter (born 1819) of a glazier domiciled in Dourdan (Seine-et-Oise). Émile Zola, the only child of this marriage, was born an hour before midnight on 2 April 1840 in a house in the Rue Saint-Joseph, formerly known as the Rue du Temps perdu. The house itself was said to stand on the site of a burial-ground in which had once been interred the mortal remains of Molière and La Fontaine. The literary auspices were more favourable than the novelist ever realized.

The son and grandson of Venetians, a boy whose father had spent a bare ten years on French soil before his birth, who was legally not even of French nationality,[1] whose first cousins (his aunt's daughter Marianna Petropoli and his uncle's son Carlo Zola) both spent their whole lives in Italy,[2] Émile Zola had his full share of the natural insecurity of a first-generation immigrant. This insecurity could only have been increased by the circumstance that his father, a far-sighted, gifted, energetic man, a man who might, had he lived, left a name to be mentioned alongside those of Brunel, de Lesseps, Eiffel, and others in that golden age of constructional engineering, the nineteenth century, died at the age of fifty-one, leaving uncompleted the first major project with which he was actively concerned.

---

[1] He became a naturalized French citizen on 31 Oct. 1862.

[2] They both tried to get in touch with him when, in 1877, he achieved European celebrity: knowing no Italian, he ignored their letters. But during his visit to Venice, 9–11 Dec. 1894, he met Carlo and it was then that he instituted researches into his family origins. See R. Ternois, 'Les Zola. Histoire d'une famille vénitienne', *Les Cahiers naturalistes*, no. 18 (1961), pp. 49–70.

This project was not the earlier scheme for a new harbour at Marseilles which, in spite of extensive lobbying of politicians, fourteen explanatory memoirs, a press campaign, and even an audience with Louis-Philippe, failed to secure government backing. Disappointed but in no way disheartened, Francesco Zola drew up a new plan to supply the perennially drought-plagued city of Aix-en-Provence with a water-supply by damming a mountain gorge some miles away and running a canal down from the artificial lake thus created. A company was floated, and in the winter of 1847 work was started. While supervising his labourers the engineer caught a chill, was put to bed in an hotel in Marseilles, and died of pneumonia shortly after, his body being carried back to Aix for burial. 'I can still picture myself,' Zola wrote almost at the end of his own life, 'a pale little lad, walking at the end of the long procession, through the streets crowded with people who had come to pay their last respects to the memory of their benefactor.'[1]

If the Venetian adventurer, whom his granddaughter was later to call 'une magnifique figure de roman, comparable à celle des grands capitaines de l'armée napoléonienne',[2] was indeed their 'benefactor', the people of Aix showed themselves singularly unappreciative of his benefactions. The Société du Canal Zola was allowed to go into liquidation; its assets were secretly acquired by one of the original promoters of the undertaking, who then refloated the company and constructed the canal according to the dead engineer's plans. The first shareholders lost their money and execrated the name of Zola; the widow, ill counselled, started a lawsuit but failed to secure compensation. From the time the head of the family died until, twelve years later, Émilie Zola and her son left Aix to return to Paris, the boy was living through at one remove the dispiriting experience of slowly encroaching poverty, a member of a household making do with less and less, moving from richer neighbourhoods to poorer, with the knowledge that there was little he could do to retrieve the situation and reverse the current of misfortune.

That these experiences played a part in moulding his character can hardly be doubted; that they were reflected in his later writings is demonstrable; but what precisely was the part they played, and where exactly they are reflected, are questions not easily settled. An early novel with no pretensions to literary merit, *Les Mystères*

---

[1] 'In the Days of my Youth', *The Bookman*, vol. xiv (1901), p. 344.
[2] Denise Leblond-Zola, *Émile Zola raconté par sa fille*, p. 10.

de Marseille, may well owe something to what Zola learned of the tricks financiers practise to fleece honest men: case-histories of such transactions, having little to do with the plot of the novel, may have been included to ease the peculiar resentment the author felt against such sharks. Scandalous profits made out of public works (the rebuilding of Paris under the Second Empire) constitute the most obvious theme of *La Curée*; there was, of course, a large basis of historical fact in the particular speculations Zola was denouncing here, but still, the choice of theme was significant. The ruin to which countless humble, unsuspecting shareholders are reduced when a large concern fails is depicted with painful intensity in *L'Argent*; possibly Zola was still smarting, in 1891, from the memory of the sour or desperate looks of his father's unsatisfied creditors in the streets of Aix forty years earlier. Balzac, his predecessor in this respect as in so many others, had exploited all these veins before him, of course, and when in due course Zola read *Illusions perdues* he would have recognized, in the section called 'Les Souffrances de l'inventeur', an episode having many analogies with his own father's unhappy experiences.

It has been suggested that what impressed Zola most was not his father's resourcefulness in the course of a chequered career, and near-success at the end of it, so much as his ultimate failure. The will to power that developed in the son was really the form taken by the desire to avoid repeating this failure himself.[1] Whatever truth there may be in this interpretation, we have still to explain how this 'will to power' developed so late in Zola, and why its development was preceded by a long period of quiescent withdrawal into a private world of gentle fantasy.

Zola never wrote the biography of his father which we know he was projecting in 1900.[2] If he had done so it is unlikely that it would have helped us appreciably to understand what his father represented for him in those formative years. We know that in 1868 he exerted himself, by means of a simultaneous press campaign in Paris and Aix, to secure recognition in the Provençal city of his father's work, for the ill-fated canal had been de-baptized and was then known no longer as the Canal Zola but as the Canal d'Aix. His agitation may have had some effect, for on 6 November 1868 the

[1] Angus Wilson, *Émile Zola, an Introductory Study of His Novels*, p. 3.
[2] A letter to Alfred Dreyfus, in which Zola thanks him for an offer of help in writing 'le livre que je rêve' about Francesco Zola, is dated 16 Feb. 1900.

municipal council voted in favour of naming one of the streets in Aix 'Boulevard Zola'.[1] Certainly Zola 'honoured his father' and required all others to do so: the piece of mud-slinging that he reacted against most violently at the time of the Dreyfus affair was a story concocted by an unscrupulous journalist to the effect that Francesco Zola's resignation from the Foreign Legion had been forced on him by the discovery that he was embezzling regimental funds. But in defending his father's achievements and his father's probity Zola was defending the name which he too bore, and in such instances his father was thought of simply as an extension of his own self.

Probably he never reached or attempted to reach a clear formulation of his private feelings towards his father. It was not necessary for him to do so, for he expressed them, if obliquely, in nearly every novel he wrote, almost until the end of his life. The Rougon-Macquart cycle was described in the sub-title as the 'history of a family', but within this family, and even outside it, it is hard to find a single *father* who discharges towards his children the bare minimum of a father's obligations. Often he evades them as Francesco had his, by dying prematurely. Silvère Mouret's father, in the first novel of the series, hanged himself for grief when his wife died. Grandjean, the father of the invalid child heroine of *Une Page d'amour*, died suddenly, just as had Émile Zola's, in an hotel in a great city. At the beginning of *Au Bonheur des Dames* the heroine, Denise Baudu, arrives in Paris with her two younger brothers to live with an uncle, their father having just died, leaving them unprovided for. In *Le Ventre de Paris* Florent and Quenu, half-brothers, are fatherless. Christine Hallegrain in *L'Œuvre* is an orphan; Pauline Quenu in *La Joie de vivre* has lost both her parents; Angélique in *Le Rêve* has been abandoned by hers. If the fathers live they prove, more often than not, useless as fathers. Lantier abandons his two infant boys and their mother at the beginning of *L'Assommoir*. Saccard, in *L'Argent*, rediscovers a bastard, begotten in an hour of drunkenness, who has grown up a criminal beyond redemption. The same Saccard has a legitimate family of which we see more in *La Curée*: it includes a son, Maxime, with whom he complacently shares mistresses and even, at the end, his wife Renée, Maxime's young stepmother. François Mouret, in

---

[1] See G. Robert, 'Une polémique entre Zola et le *Mémorial d'Aix* en 1868', *Arts et Livres*, no. 6 (1946), pp. 5–23.

La Conquête de Plassans, would seem that exception, a father devoted to his children, defending their interests if somewhat ineffectually when these are threatened by his wife's growing neglect of them; but he goes mad. Lazare Chanteau's father is a hopeless invalid. Nana's father, Coupeau, dies of drink. Sometimes the father is merely weak or foolish, and then the children turn against him: Fouan, in *La Terre*, suffers the fate of Lear, begrudged his bread by his children and finally turned out of doors; Josserand, martyred by the egoism of his wife and daughters, dies, in the last-but-one chapter of *Pot-Bouille*, 'avec simplicité. . . . Il avait passé inutile, il s'en allait . . ., étranglé par la tranquille inconscience des seules créatures qu'il eût aimées.'

It would be too simple to explain this consistent dismissal or degradation of the father-figure in the Rougon-Macquart novels by observing that Émile Zola had lost his father at too early an age to have experienced a normal, affectionate relationship within a family circle; for he was not an infant in arms at the time and besides, as he grew up, he had plenty of opportunity to observe among friends of his age the existence of such a relationship, and its genuineness. Rather, it seems that throughout his thirties and forties he was doing his utmost to avoid thinking of Francesco Zola; and hence, whenever he needed to represent a father in his fiction he showed him as being in all respects other than his own father had been: a wastrel, a debauchee, tainted in mind or body, senile, or a weakling. In only one respect could he portray a father like his own: by showing him dead, that is, absent and not to be reckoned with.

But if we turn to the novels written earlier, before Zola had taken the unconscious decision to repress the image he had formed of his father, we can find in one at least (*Madeleine Férat*) a remarkable delineation of a powerful father which is both a portrait and also a denunciation, only thinly disguised, of the author's own father. M. de Viargue had spent his youth outside France, as an *émigré*, and returned, after many years, with a foreigner's outlook. Though a wealthy landowner, he devotes his time and energies wholly to pure science—as Zola's father had to a form of applied science. Guillaume, the hero of *Madeleine Férat*, is his only son, whom M. de Viargue ignores and neglects, just as Francesco had withdrawn from his son—into the grave. He forbids Guillaume to train for a profession or to enter a career; and Zola had found himself, on the threshold of manhood, calamitously ill equipped for one; had his father lived, no doubt—and this thought could scarcely not have occurred to him—he would have been better prepared, better seconded at least. Finally, de Viargue destroys his life's work, smashing up his private laboratory, burning his notes, just before killing himself. In the same way Zola's father had died suddenly, leaving the work he was engaged on uncompleted and denying his son the fruit of his labours. The most significant touch of all, perhaps, is that the only chemicals to escape destruction are the phials of poison; Madeleine, the only woman Guillaume can ever love, finally commits suicide by swallowing one of these poisons.

Madeleine Férat is a poor novel but a most suggestive documentary aid to understanding the reasons for Zola's introspective adolescence, for the withdrawal into a fantasy world that characterized his inner life until about 1862. The novel is built on the idea of the unendurability and yet inescapability of reality, here equivalent to the unalterable past. Madeleine can never elude the consequences of having yielded, a virgin, to Jacques, however closely she subsequently feels herself tied to Guillaume by bonds of gratitude, affection, and esteem. Zola incarnated, in the otherworldly figure of the old Calvinist family servant Geneviève, the cruelty of this unrelenting inevitability of the past, which no change of heart and no virtuous resolutions can redeem. Geneviève has a disturbing habit of reading aloud those passages from the Old Testament in which Jehovah is shown as the vengeful and jealous deity, chastising bloodily his erring people; and her favourite maxim is: 'Dieu le Père ne pardonne pas.' In the concluding scene Geneviève enters the devastated laboratory to see Madeleine stretched dead on the floor and Guillaume insane, capering around her, and utters the concluding lines of the book: 'Dieu le Père n'a pas pardonné.'

For what irretrievable ancient guilt would Zola's father not forgive him? It is common enough, psychologists tell us—perhaps even normal—for small boys between the ages of three and six, particularly when there is no younger brother or sister in the family, to resent having to share their mother's affections with their father, and to develop an infantile jealousy which can crystallize in the usually unformulated wish that their rival might die. One may suppose that the six-year-old Émile had wished his father might conveniently disappear; a little too conveniently, magically, it must have seemed, his body is brought home on a shutter. But can one kill, even magically, with impunity? God and his father were now one: 'Dieu le Père ne pardonne pas.'

A portentous incident, occurring a little before this catastrophe, may have reinforced the small boy's uneasiness and confused sense of guilt. A Marseilles police report of 3/4 April 1845 records the committal of a twelve-year-old Algerian boy called Mustapha, 'domestique au service de M. Zola, ingénieur civil', accused of indecent conduct with his son Émile, aged five.[1] Zola himself, who was not particularly guarded in his allusions to his private life and to the experiences of his childhood, never referred to this episode, and it is possible that he suppressed the memory or else post-dated it. From certain remarks made in later life one is led to suppose that at school he underwent some kind of initiation into what was then called unnatural vice. In an article devoted primarily to the dangers of convent education for girls, he asked his male readers whether their own memories of boarding schools were not enough to make them hesitate about sending their daughters away from home. 'Souvenez-vous du collège. Les vices y poussent grassement, on y vit en pleine pourriture romaine. Toute association cloîtrée de personnes du même sexe est mauvaise pour la morale.'[2] And Edmond de Goncourt records a hesitant confession made by Zola one evening when the company was exchanging reminiscences about their schooldays. 'Moi . . . une jeunesse pervertie, dans un mauvais collège de province. Oui, une enfance pourrie! . . .'[3] The school he was referring to was the Collège d'Aix, which he entered at the age of twelve from a preparatory school.

'Au lycée, les attitudes gauches de Daniel, sa timidité d'orphelin, lui attirèrent les plaisanteries de ses camarades. Il fut profondé-ment blessé de ce rôle de paria. Ses allures en devinrent plus maladroites. Il resta solitaire. . . .' This passage from another of Zola's early novels, Le Vœu d'une morte, has the ring of autobio-graphical truth about it. The physical violence of which Guillaume, in Madeleine Férat, is the hapless victim at school may or may not

[1] The incident was unknown to Zola's earlier biographers; an historian engaged on researches in the police archives of Marseilles chanced on the report and hastened to publish it (see A. Chabaud, 'Un épisode inconnu de l'enfance d'Émile Zola', Mercure de France, vol. ccx (1929), p. 508). For a commentary by a professional psychologist, see J. Vinchon, 'Zola dîne avec les Goncourt', Æsculape, vol. xxxiv (1953), pp. 1-7.

[2] 'Au couvent', La Cloche, 2 Feb. 1870.

[3] Edmond and Jules de Goncourt, Journal . . . Texte intégral, vol. xi, p. 90 (entry dated 5 May 1876).

have been Zola's lot at first: Goncourt, again, records a lunch-time conversation during which Zola discoursed on 'les salauderies qui ont lieu dans les collèges de province et qui ont un coin de brutalité que ne présentent pas les brimades mignardes des collèges parisiens'.[1] Brought up by two cheerful, indulgent, and devoted women, his mother and grandmother,[2] Émile had a gentleness of manner which marked him off from the turbulent urchins who sat on the benches beside him. He was distinguished from them too by his northern speech, learnt at home, and perhaps by the slight lisp which he never fully conquered and of which Léon Daudet was later to make such cruel fun. Boys, as a tribe, will not tolerate the oddity or the outsider: they jeered at him, bullied him perhaps. Zola was to evoke them in La Confession de Claude: 'ces camarades, les méchants et les bons, qui étaient sans pitié, sans âme, comme tous les enfants. . . . Mes années de collège ont été des années de larmes. J'avais en moi la fierté des natures aimantes. On ne m'aimait pas, car on m'ignorait, et je refusais de me faire connaître.'

The boy was not so unbefriended as this passage suggests. The friends he was able to make remained his friends for years after. With Philippe Solari, who served him as model for Silvère, the boy-hero of La Fortune des Rougon, he was still on visiting terms well after the Franco-Prussian war; he devoted some well-intentioned lines in the press to one of Solari's sculptures exhibited in 1868. When he went to Marseilles in 1871 he founded a short-lived newspaper in association with Marius Roux, another old schoolfellow. His long friendship with Paul Cézanne is chronicled in all the histories of nineteenth-century art. It was chiefly in the company of Cézanne and another, more level-headed lad, Baptistin Baille, that Zola used to explore the countryside around Aix during holidays. There were bathing expeditions, shooting expeditions, or simply long tramps and long talks and frenzied declaimings from

---

[1] Journal . . ., vol. xiii, p. 27.

[2] His mother's unsentimental warmth of character and lively sense of humour come through admirably in the few letters of hers that have been published (see R. Walter, appendix to 'Zola et ses amis à Bennecourt', Cahiers naturalistes, no. 17 (1961), pp. 19–35, and the same author's 'Deux lettres inédites d'Émilie Zola à Gabrielle-Alexandrine Meley et à Émilie Zola', ibid., no. 22 (1962), pp. 280–3). Of his grandmother Aubert, who died in 1857, he left a slight but pleasing sketch in one of his articles in La Cloche: when the troops reinforcing the armies in the Crimea halted at Aix, she used to offer them wine and engage them in talk, delighted if she could find a soldier whose home was in her native Beauce.

a volume of verse tucked into one of the boys' pockets. Several of Zola's subsequent newspaper sketches were based on one or another of these memories and are to be read today in the section entitled 'Souvenirs' of the *Nouveaux Contes à Ninon*. Zola's most eloquent testimony to the 'harsh beauty' of Provence is to be found, however, in the preface to the original *Contes à Ninon*. When he composed these few pages, in October 1864, already some years had passed since his last visit to the south; they are tinged with nostalgia and the picture is idealized. He writes of a land 'grise et nue, entre les prairies grasses de la Durance et les bois d'orangers du littoral'. In this barren stretch he finds 'je ne sais quel air brûlant de désolation: un étrange ouragan de passion semble avoir soufflé sur la contrée; puis un grand accablement s'est fait, et les campagnes, ardentes encore, se sont comme endormies dans un dernier désir'. Already Zola is rendering nature—as he will, more blatantly and crudely, in *La Faute de l'abbé Mouret* and in *La Terre*—in terms of overheated erotic imagery. The mysterious Ninon of the title is at once the incarnation of Provence and the supreme projection of adolescent love-fantasies: she is significantly ambiguous even in her sex:

Tu étais femme, belle et ardente, et je t'aimais en époux. Puis, je ne sais comment, parfois tu devenais une sœur, sans cesser d'être une amante; alors, je t'aimais en amant et en frère à la fois, avec toute la chasteté de l'affection, tout l'emportement du désir. D'autres fois, je trouvais en toi un compagnon, une robuste intelligence d'homme, et toujours aussi une enchanteresse, une bien-aimée, dont je couvrais le visage de baisers, tout en lui serrant la main en vieux camarade. ... Ainsi tu réalisais le rêve de l'ancienne Grèce, l'amante fait homme, aux exquises élégances de forme, à l'esprit viril, digne de science et de sagesse.

Zola's best work, as we shall see, is irrigated by an underground current of private fantasies, some of them rosy wish-fulfilment, others dark and nightmarish terrors. It is therefore not idle speculation to attempt to trace and describe those that had their source in the daydreams of his boyhood at Aix and of his late teens, during the first years he spent in the capital. A few of these daydreams, transmuted but recognizable, are discernible in the more idiosyncratic of the pieces that compose the *Contes à Ninon*.

The first that was ever published, 'La Fée Amoureuse', was probably too the first that was written; it appeared in the Aix journal

La Provence in December 1859. In inspiration it connects distantly
with the *Lais* of Marie de France: it is a fairy-story with a conventional medieval setting, a frowning castle in which is confined a
beautiful sixteen-year-old damsel guarded by her uncle, a fierce
old warrior, and his retinue of men-at-arms. The inevitable handsome troubadour presents himself at the gates of the castle, gains
admittance, and steals the heroine's heart. The lovers are favoured
by 'la fée Amoureuse' whose wings have the property of hiding
them from prying eyes, and it is she who at the end, like one of
Ovid's river-gods, rescues them permanently from their persecu-
tors by changing them into two flowers with intertwining tendrils.
At the beginning of this chapter we referred to 'La Fée Amoureuse'
as 'an innocent little trifle'. Its innocence conceals a disabused
symbolism. The adult world is ugly, hostile, and inhibiting: the
wings of fantasy permit an occasional withdrawal, but ultimately
the solution is seen to lie in refusing the flesh-and-blood world and
escaping into the stillness of a non-animal, non-carnal form of life.

Two other stories were accepted in 1863 by a literary magazine
published at Lille, *La Revue du mois*. To the first, 'Le Sang', we
shall have occasion to allude later.[1] The second, 'Simplice', can be
interpreted as a transparent allegory of the situation Zola found
himself in during his first two or three years in Paris.

The decision to leave Aix had been taken by his mother at the
end of 1857 by which time all hope of securing a settlement of her
claims against the canal company had faded. There remained in
Paris one old friend of her husband's, a lawyer with some influence,
who might advise and help her. In February 1858, accompanied by
his grandfather (his grandmother had died three months before),
Émile Zola arrived at the capital in no mood of rapture; on the contrary it was, as he later admitted, 'une des plus cruelles déceptions
de ma vie. Je m'attendais à une succession de palais, et pendant
près d'une lieue, la lourde voiture roulait entre des constructions
borgnes, des cabarets, des maisons suspectes, toute une bourgade,
jetée aux deux bords. Puis, on s'enfonçait dans des rues noires.
Paris se montrait plus étranglé et plus sombre que la petite ville
qu'on venait de quitter.'[2] The moment of his arrival was, nevertheless, opportune: the old, semi-medieval city was on the point of

---

[1] See below, p. 193.
[2] 'Aux champs', *Le Capitaine Burle*; first published as an article in *Vestnik
Evropy*, Aug. 1878.

vanishing for ever under the pick-axes of Haussmann's demolition squads.

Zola had left Aix with his schooling uncompleted. Maître Labot, the family friend, recommended him to Nisard, then director of the École Normale Supérieure, and he was given a free place in the Lycée Saint-Louis. Later he was to recall the disappointment he experienced on discovering that, in competition with the precocious youngsters of Paris, he, who had been a prize-winner at Aix, acquitted himself indifferently here.[1] He formed no fresh ties and fell back on composing interminable letters to the friends he had left in the south, Cézanne and Baille. In November 1858 his health broke down; convalescence was slow, and at the end of the school year Zola failed his *baccalauréat*. His bursary was not renewed, and he found himself faced with the urgent need to secure a livelihood, without the least of the diplomas or certificates that might have helped him to employment. In the spring of 1860 he found a situation as copy-clerk; he was paid starvation wages and the work he was given was unspeakably dreary; he stuck it for two months only. Thereafter, privation supervened,

a life of dreadful want, of borrowings and debts, hunger and shabbiness, when I often had but one meal in the twenty-four hours, and that meal two sous worth of bread and two sous worth of cheese, or perhaps a few fried potatoes or some apples, or roast chestnuts bought at a street corner. And unable to obtain regular employment anywhere, mortified by constant repulses, robbed for a time of youthful confidence by my failure at my examinations, I led that life for two long years, ever wearing the one frayed coat that belonged to me, a coat which was at first black, but which in course of time became green and then almost yellow.[2]

This was the coat which, according to a story related by Paul Alexis in his biography and recorded by Edmond de Goncourt in his diary, he took off one cold night and gave to the girl he was living with to take to the pawnshop. Two days afterwards his trousers went the same way and Zola stayed in bed.

Cold and want had no power to overcome the defences sheltering him from the outside world, that world which would have nothing to do with him and which he despised in return. Goncourt goes on to quote Zola as saying that 'he was scarcely aware of the "jam" he was in, his head filled with an immense poem, "Genesis, Humanity, the Future". . . . He had never been happier than in those days,

[1] *Le Voltaire*, 19 Aug. 1879.   [2] 'In the Days of my Youth', p. 346.

destitute though he was.' Baille, a practical young man, could not understand this refusal to 'face facts', and the two were at logger-heads over this point. Zola wanted his friend to believe that his eyes were wide open: 'la réalité m'occupe tout le jour, . . . je ne rêve que pour me délasser.' Was he to be denied the right to withdraw into the inner world? 'Toute cette réalité présente me semble hideuse; je ne l'accepte que parce qu'elle s'impose. Combien je préfère mes instants d'espérance et de rêverie!' At times, Baille's arguments grate: 'Dans tout cela tu es le plus raisonnable, mais, franchement, tu es le plus mesquin. . . . La réalité est la réalité, et c'est déjà beaucoup; mais si de plus la réalité nous empêchait de rêver, le plus vite serait d'aller voir ce que nous garde le ciel.' Zola had no patience with Baille's constant talk about starting a career; already he felt privately that the only career for him would be that of the man of letters, but he knew too that there was no living to be made from writing—not at least from his kind of writing. All he wanted was a small situation to keep him from starving and leave him his evenings free for poetry and meditation.

He was moving, at this time, from one room to another round the Latin Quarter. In April 1861 he found himself stranded in a lodging-house of ill repute in the Rue Soufflot harbouring pimps, penurious students, and streetwalkers. Rowdy parties and free fights were common occurrences, and so were police raids. It was in this house that Zola wrote 'Simplice', and it was out of his memo-ries of this house that he was to write *La Confession de Claude*.

A few years later he used the name of the hero of his short story to sign certain newspaper articles, just as he used the name of the hero of his novel to sign others: a sufficient indication that both story and novel are in varying degrees transposed autobiography. Simplice is the young dreamer ill adapted to the real world. Son of a king, he irritates his father by refusing to join him in carousal, by saving the lives of the wounded in battle, and by fleeing the ap-proaches of court ladies. He is soon forgotten when he wanders off one day into an immense forest and never returns.

If the king represents, obviously enough, Francesco Zola (the contrast between Émile's examination failures and inability to make his way and his father's brilliant beginnings and unassisted career-making was no doubt a recent reinforcement of the guilt feelings of childhood), the forest is an equally obvious allegory of the world of fantasy into which Zola tried to escape from this overpowering presence. This world of fantasy is heavily erotic, and the forest is described, in a passage clearly premonitory of the pages later to be devoted to Le Paradou in *La Faute de l'abbé Mouret*, as one vast jungle of sexual yearning.

La mousse, ivre de rosée, s'y livrait à une débauche de croissance; les églantiers, allongeant leurs bras flexibles, se cherchaient dans les clairières pour exécuter des danses folles autour des grands arbres; les grands arbres eux-mêmes, tout en restant calmes et sereins, tordaient leur pied dans l'ombre et montaient en tumulte baiser les rayons d'été. L'herbe verte croissait au hasard, sur les branches comme sur le sol; la feuille embrassait le bois, tandis que, dans leur hâte de s'épanouir, pâquerettes et myosotis, se trompant parfois, fleurissaient sur les vieux troncs abattus. Et toutes ces branches, toutes ces herbes, toutes ces fleurs chantaient; toutes se mêlaient, se pressaient, pour babiller plus à l'aise, pour se dire tout bas les mystérieuses amours des corolles. Un souffle de vie courait au fond des taillis ténébreux, donnant une voix à chaque brin de mousse dans les ineffables concerts de l'aurore et du crépuscule. C'était la fête immense du feuillage.

As in *La Faute*, this flight of erotic fantasy is curiously and signifi-cantly elaborated in terms of wild vegetation. And as in *La Faute* again, as soon as sex becomes animal, catastrophe supervenes. In his sylvan wanderings Simplice glimpses the water-nymph of whom it has been predicted that both she and her lover will die of the first kiss they exchange. Simplice runs to join her, the forest throwing brambles and branches across his path to trip him and avert the fatal meeting. But the nymph catches sight of him, greets him as her beloved, and the forest gives way; the couple wander hand in hand until the first star shows, when they kiss and die.

The Pyramus-and-Thisbe or Hero-and-Leander myth can be explained as a characteristic expression of the inability of the adolescent to imagine beyond the consummation of his first love-affair; or else as the formulation of an acceptable imaginary punishment for subconsciously felt guilt. It matters little which explanation we adopt as an interpretation of 'Simplice'; what has to be noted is the persistence of the myth in Zola's work years after the cause might be expected to have disappeared. In *La Faute de l'abbé Mouret* (1875), Serge's love for Albine proves fatal to her. The ending adopted, after much hesitation, for *Le Rêve* (1888) was the sudden death of the heroine as she emerged from church after

the marriage ceremony.[1] The death of Benedetta in *Rome* (1896),
clasped for the first time in her lover's arms, is yet another variant
of the same fantasy. All these compulsive repetitions of the same
basic adolescent daydream, reappearing periodically in his mid-
thirties, mid-forties, mid-fifties, illustrate the extraordinary force
of the first vision which experience might overlay and temporarily
suppress but could never obliterate.

When he was writing 'Simplice' Zola was already caught up, or
was on the point of being caught up, in an experience which, much
more than the humiliation of failure and the chastening lesson of
poverty, was to lead him out of the phase of self-centred day-
dreaming and compel him to adjust himself to the demands of the
society into which he was born. *La Confession de Claude*, the first
part of which was written as early as 1862, chronicles this particular
crisis and summarizes its resolution.

Written, as its title demanded, in the first person (a style to
which Zola never reverted), and filled almost exclusively with
descriptions of vague and highly dramatized moods, *La Confession
de Claude* is unique among Zola's writings. It is by no means the
only thing of its kind in literature. The reader has an almost oppressive sense of having 'been here before'. Nearly every page
bears the imprint of Alfred de Musset, a volume of whose poetry
was usually taken along when Zola set off with his friends on those
boyhood shooting expeditions in Provence, where the infrequency
of game was an incitement to the study of literature. The language
echoes Musset's cadences and steals his similes; the themes—the
frailty of woman, the disillusion of high-minded youth—were
taken directly from *Lorenzaccio* and *La Confession d'un enfant du
siècle*. Zola cared so little to cover up his tracks that he took the very
name of the fifteen-year-old heroine of *Rolla* who affords Musset's

---

[1] In Zola's original plan for *Le Rêve*, Angélique was not to die: 'Je finis quand
les époux ressortent de l'église, la grand'porte de l'église large ouverte, et
donnant sur le monde. Là, je m'arrête. La fin du rêve, l'entrée dans la réalité'
(B.N. MS. *Nouvelles acquisitions françaises* 10323, fol. 232). But this symbolism
evidently left Zola unsatisfied. At a later stage in the plan he wrote: 'J'aimerais
mieux qu'elle mourût dans son triomphe. Cela est plus grand, plus pur, plus
éthéré. . . . A la sortie, au moment où elle va entrer dans la réalité, devant la place
ensoleillée, pleine de monde, la mort qui la prend. Elle ne peut que se hausser
jusqu'aux lèvres de Félicien, et elle lui met un long baiser sur la bouche (ce
baiser représente le mariage consommé) et elle meurt, satisfaite, ravie, emportée
dans la réalisation de son rêve, au moment où elle entrait dans la réalité. Cela
me paraît beaucoup plus grand et beaucoup plus touchant' (fols. 303, 305).
Admirers of Cocteau will recognize the *dénouement* of *Renaud et Armide*.

suicidal libertine his first and last taste of pure love, and gave it to the fifteen-year-old grisette who, before she dies, proves to Claude that love is not wholly a cheat.

But if the form and apparatus are counterfeit, there is nothing artificial, though there is much that is overdrawn, in the emotions they translate. Zola stated in his letter-preface that his whole theme was 'la lutte entre le songe et la réalité'. The opening chapter describes the impact of friendless city life on the country boy whose ideas of Parisian bohemianism have been founded on a literal interpretation of Murger's celebrated stories. The bookish un-realities with which his head is stuffed encourage him to try to repeat the experiment of redeeming the fallen woman, much as Hugo had described it in *Marion Delorme* and, more recently, Dumas in *La Dame aux camélias*. This abortive attempt provides the entire plot of *La Confession de Claude*. The book turns on the hero's struggle to win contact with his fellows: a struggle that failed with his chosen mistress, Laurence, and unexpectedly suc-ceeded with Marie, the mistress of a neighbouring student.

It was by no symbolic fiction that Zola thus represented his own illusion and disillusion. Claude's cohabitation with Laurence, and his poor attempts to teach the street-girl a sense of dignity and to set her to honest living and honest labour, appear to reproduce certain fumblings at reclamation made by Zola himself. He tells the story in a letter to Baille, without making it clear that the events concerned him personally; but, writing to Cézanne, he refers to his experience in more direct terms. 'Je sors d'une rude école, celle de l'amour réel', he declares, and after promising Cézanne, tan-talizingly for us, to tell him more about it when they meet, he adds: 'Je doute même de pouvoir te communiquer dans un récit de vive voix toutes les sensations douloureuses ou riantes que j'ai ressen-ties.' Further evidence for the authenticity of the whole episode is found in a letter written to the author of *La Confession de Claude* by a friend (G. Pajot) who was close to him at the time.[1] The same document provides us with the name of the unhappy drab, Berthe, who was Zola's first and very temporary mistress.

In the novel, as no doubt in life, the young idealist's failure to impose his idealism on the prostitute loosens his hold on idealism

---

[1] The letter, preserved in the Manuscript Department of the Bibliothèque Nationale together with hundreds of others received by Zola throughout his life, has been published by H. Guillemin, *Zola, légende et vérité*, p. 15.

altogether. His theories have to be abandoned since they do not fit reality, 'cette sublime réalité', he writes, 'qui nous vient de Dieu et que nous gâtons à plaisir par nos rêves. Nous sommes si maladroits à vivre que la vie en devient mauvaise.' His isolation had hunted him into a dream-world, and the dream-world was keeping him isolated from the real world. To break out of this painful circle, he must shake himself awake.

Je crains bien que nos rêves ne soient pas seulement des mensonges; je les sens petits et puérils en face d'une réalité dont j'ai vaguement conscience. Il est des jours où plus loin que les rayons et les parfums, plus loin que ces visions indécises que je ne puis posséder, j'entrevois les contours hardis de ce qui est. Et je comprends que c'est là la vie, l'action, la vérité, tandis que, dans le milieu que je me crée, s'agite un peuple étranger à l'homme, ombres vaines dont les yeux ne me voient pas, dont les lèvres ne sauraient me parler. L'enfant peut se plaire à ces amis froids et muets; ayant peur de la vie, il se réfugie dans ce qui ne vit pas. Mais nous, hommes, nous ne devons point nous contenter de cet éternel néant.

Claude's outward-turning vision settles first on the couple who live in the neighbouring apartment, Jacques and Marie; he is fascinated by the problems that their calm and ordinary existence presents. Here is a whole undiscovered, uncharted continent:

Ce monde est poignant, l'étude en est âpre, pleine de vertige. Je voudrais pénétrer dans les cœurs et dans les âmes; je suis attiré par ces femmes et ces hommes qui vivent autour de moi; peut-être, au fond, ne trouverai-je que de la fange, mais j'aimerais à fouiller le fond. Ils vivent une vie si étrange, que je crois toujours être sur le point de découvrir en eux des vérités nouvelles.

This exalted rhetoric is as clear a statement as we possess of the inner revolution that triumphed in Zola at the outset of his literary career, making him an ardent convert to objectivism and giving him his characteristic hatred of idealized presentations of the visible world. Because at this passage of his life the dreams had been useless and dangerous, therefore every subjective element and everything that smacked of the intangible must be energetically proscribed from art and thought. Because his dreams had been of pure spirits, therefore his drawings must be of vile bodies.

La Confession de Claude shows a consciousness of inner division no less remarkable in the lucidity with which it is described than in the intensity with which it is expressed.

Je sais et je vois, je m'aveugle et je rêve. Tandis que je m'avance sous la pluie, tandis que j'ai énergiquement conscience de tout le froid, de toute l'humidité, je puis, par une faculté étrange, faire luire le soleil, avoir chaud, me créer un ciel doux et tendre, sans cesser de sentir le ciel noir qui pèse à mes épaules. Je n'ignore pas, je n'oublie pas: je vis doublement. Je porte dans le songe la même franchise que dans les sensations vraies. J'ai ainsi deux existences parallèles, aussi vivantes, aussi âpres, l'une qui se passe ici-bas, dans ma misère, l'autre qui se passe là-haut, dans l'immense et profonde pureté du ciel bleu.

The future lay, he supposed, in the suppression of one of these two sides of his personality. But his later work was to show that this suppression was never complete, and that the 'faculté étrange [de] faire luire le soleil . . . sans cesser de sentir le ciel noir' was one that, happily, he never lost, though it was put to uses unimagined at this stage.

Provisionally, however, an attempt was to be made to concentrate attention on the external scene, to the neglect of internal fantasy-worlds. In the matter of living and loving, men and women and town and country must be taken as they are, and to a sane man they are richer and deeper so. The Claudes must learn that women from the streets are meant to be slept with and turned out into the streets again when one's pockets are empty or one's appetites satisfied. They cannot be made the subject of experiments in rehabilitation. The poet has no divine mission to set the world to rights. Evil is an illusion, 'une de nos inventions', says Claude when he has learnt wisdom, 'une des plaies dont nous nous sommes couverts'. Things are best left as they are and shown as they are.

The false sentimentalism of the end of *La Confession de Claude* ought not to make us miss the symbolic significance of the final tableau. In the same night Marie dies and Claude finds in himself the strength to break with Laurence. Afterwards he watches the rising sun from his window. 'Et moi, seul, en face de ce déchirement de la nuit, de cette naissance lente et majestueuse du jour, je me suis senti au cœur une force jeune, invincible, un espoir immense.' This sentence and the whole passage hint at the splendidly luminous endings for which *Germinal* and *La Débâcle* are justly famous. Here the dawn stands for the beginning of a new attentiveness in the author-hero to the tangible ocean of the living and to the scent of the perceptible winds that blow off it. The sleeper had awoken, the dreamer took his place among the watchers. Zola had turned a new leaf, and for many years he held it firmly pressed down.

II

TRIAL AND ERROR

No sooner had the strange new flesh-and-blood world opened out before him than Zola thought of rendering it in terms of art. This was before he had fixed on the eventual medium, prose. In July 1861 he hinted to Baille that he was busy on an essay which he intended to call 'On Science and Civilization in their relations with Poetry'. It was some years before he was able to publish it.[1] The importance of this essay is that it indicates a transitional stage in the development of his aesthetic speculation and, in particular, introduces for the first time an idea which in due course was to be given an immense extension: the idea of grafting on to literature recent scientific theories bearing on certain natural phenomena. Zola begins by examining the reasons why, in an age when science was making such conspicuous strides, poetry was lagging behind and refusing to take cognizance of the brilliant discoveries made in laboratory and observatory. 'Le poète . . . n'est poète selon l'esprit de nos temps qu'à condition de caresser les fables et de donner une interprétation éternellement fausse des phénomènes du monde extérieur.' Zola would like to see the naiads and the sylphs decently buried; 'plus de pleurs avec les cascades, plus de soupirs avec les brises. . . . Nous nous ferions savant, nous emprunterions aux sciences leurs grands horizons, leurs hypothèses si admirables qu'elles sont peut-être des vérités; nous voudrions être un nouveau Lucrèce et écrire en beaux vers la philosophie de nos connaissances plus étendues et plus certaines que celles de l'ancienne Rome.'

This document shows, incidentally, that Zola's reverential deference for 'science' was a thing of much earlier growth than is sometimes realized. In particular it demonstrably predates his reading of Taine (the first time we find Taine's name mentioned by Zola is in a letter to Valabrègue in August 1864). Zola's inspirer here was

---

[1] In *Le Journal populaire* (Lille), 16 Apr. 1864 and, in a somewhat modified form, in *La Tribune*, 25 Oct. 1868.

in all probability Michelet, in whose *L'Amour* he would not have failed to notice such a declaration as this: 'La science est la maîtresse du monde. Elle règne, sans avoir besoin de commander. L'Église et la Loi doivent s'informer de ses arrêts, et se réformer d'après elle.'

The aspiration to be a modern Lucretius faded when Zola renounced his ambitions to become the poet of his age. He had acquired, even before he left Aix, a remarkable facility for writing verse, and some pieces of his had even found their way into print: an ode, 'Le Canal Zola', had been accepted by *La Provence* in February 1859; towards the end of December 1861 he submitted a Lamartinian meditation entitled 'Doute' to a left-wing journal, *Le Travail*, on the staff of which Georges Clemenceau was serving his apprenticeship.[1] Zola was by that time nearing the end of his self-inflicted sentence of bohemian penury. In February 1862 he found permanent employment at last; he became an assistant in a publisher's bookshop. It was an opportunity to see and sometimes chat with a few of the literary notables of the day, and to observe how, in literature as in love, the facts were far less sublime, but no less enthralling, than the pictures he had doted on in his imagination. In any case, sublime or ignoble, the facts could not be blinked. After three and a half years of working in Hachette's, he had become worldly-wise. To Valabrègue, a budding young poet scribbling down in Aix, he wrote: 'Si vous saviez, mon pauvre ami, combien peu le talent est dans la réussite, vous laisseriez là plume et papier, et vous vous mettriez à étudier la vie littéraire, les mille petites canailleries qui ouvrent les portes, l'art d'user le crédit des autres, la cruauté nécessaire pour passer sur le ventre des chers collègues.' The poet, he discovered, was no prophet, no leader of men. Why write, unless your books sold? And poetry was not the stuff of best-sellers. The head of the firm insinuated this truth when the timid young employee in the parcels department left on his desk one Saturday evening the verse epic, 'L'Amoureuse Comédie', one of the fruits of his famished vigils in the garrets of the Latin Quarter. When Monday came Louis Hachette was kindly but unenthusiastic; he doubled Zola's wages, and told him there was a better market for prose. Zola took the hint and locked away the four or five thousand

---

[1] See H. d'Alméras, *Avant la gloire: leurs débuts* (1902), pp. 189–90. The text of 'Doute' has recently been transcribed from the manuscript and published (*Cahiers naturalistes*, no. 26 (1964), pp. 45–49).

lines of poetry he had composed. He hunted out a few of the shorter lyrics and had them printed in 1868 in *L'Événement illustré* as curiosities; the first of them was accompanied by an editorial note explaining this, and ending: 'Now we abandon him to the fury of the poets he has so ill-treated.'[1] In fact, the poets could not complain of harsh treatment at Zola's hands; rather, when he reviewed their productions for the press, it was pity that he extended to them for wasting their time on a difficult form of art for which in his opinion there was no audience. Without positively forbidding Valabrègue to go on writing verse, he advised him to arrive in Paris with a poem in his left hand and a novel in his right. 'Le poème sera refusé partout et vous le garderez comme une relique au fond de votre secrétaire; le roman sera accepté, et vous ne quitterez point Paris la mort dans le cœur. Tant pis si la Muse se fâche et si elle me garde rancune; je vous le dis en vérité, hors de la prose, point de salut.'

Zola's first book, the *Contes à Ninon*, was launched on the world —not by Hachette but by Lacroix—in 1864. It was accorded a polite welcome, but predictably created no sensation. The reception given to *La Confession de Claude* a year later was very different. Zola used the experience of the 'trade', acquired while he was acting as publicity manager for Hachette, to advertise himself persistently and with no false modesty. He wrote to leading critics soliciting reviews,[2] and also circularized newspaper editors with a notice, a *prière d'insérer*, which he probably composed himself:

L'auteur s'y révèle avec un talent étrange, fait d'exquise délicatesse et d'audace folle. On applaudira, on sifflera peut-être, ne pouvant rester froid devant ce drame plein d'angoisse et de terreur. Il y a dans l'œuvre une fierté indicible, une passion et une force qui annoncent un écrivain d'une rare énergie.[3]

These lines should not be read as the young author's considered opinion of his maiden novel: for this, his private correspondence

[1] Alexis published some specimens of Zola's poetry in his biography of his friend; they have been reproduced in the last volume (*Mélanges*) of Zola's *Œuvres complètes* (Bernouard edition).

[2] See R. J. Niess, 'An early Zola letter', *Modern Language Notes*, vol. lxix (1954), pp. 114–16 (letter to Édouard Fournier, literary editor of *La Patrie*). A short letter to Charles Deulin, begging him: 'tâchez d'en parler quelque part, où vous voudrez et comme il vous plaira', is dated 14 Nov. 1865: see *Quo Vadis*, vol. v (1952), pp. 103–4.

[3] Quoted in J. C. Lapp, 'The critical reception of Zola's *Confession de Claude*', *Modern Language Notes*, vol. lxviii (1953), pp. 459–60.

provides a surer indication. He deprecated Valabrègue's excessive enthusiasm for *La Confession de Claude*:

il est faible en certaines parties, et il contient encore bien des enfantillages. L'élan manque par instants, l'observateur s'évanouit, et le poète reparaît, un poète qui a trop bu de lait, et mangé trop de sucre. L'œuvre n'est pas virile; elle est le cri d'un enfant qui pleure et se révolte.

But (he goes on to say), judging solely by the impact it has made, he can call it a success:

aujourd'hui, je suis connu, on me craint et on m'injurie; aujourd'hui je suis classé parmi les écrivains dont on lit les œuvres avec effroi. Là est l'habileté.... L'habileté, pour moi, ne consiste pas à mentir à sa pensée, à faire une œuvre selon le goût ou le dégoût de la foule. L'habileté consiste, l'œuvre une fois faite, à ne pas attendre le public, mais à aller vers lui et à le forcer à vous caresser ou à vous injurier.

It would be wrong to speak of cynicism, or even showmanship, in these words which reveal one of the most abiding of Zola's preoccupations: how to get himself talked about, without at the same time sacrificing one iota of his independence or originality. He could conceive of no greater misfortune for a creative artist than to fail to make his impact; for him Cézanne, whatever his genius might be, remained a misunderstood genius, and therefore in a real sense suffered diminishment. It is perhaps regrettable that Zola should have felt compelled to dissipate so much energy in the pursuit of literary celebrity or, in default of celebrity, of notoriety; but early experiences had, as we have seen, withered the serenity of his self-confidence, so that to be discussed became for him the only credible confirmation of the value of his activity. 'Le tout est de remuer les foules', he once wrote to his Dutch admirer Van Santen Kolff. 'L'indifférence seule tue.' Possibly it was less the contemporary public he needed to impress than his absent father from whom, precisely because of his absence, he could never wring the approval that he needed to expunge the vaguely remembered, deeply implanted infantile guilt. But if his father's name, thanks to him, rang through the length and breadth of the land, then perhaps he might win forgiveness. Thus it was certainly in obedience to no impulse of smug self-satisfaction that he told the same Dutch correspondent in 1880, in answer to a request for his address: 'Il suffit de mettre sur une enveloppe: Émile Zola, France, pour que cela m'arrive.' 'Émile Zola, France' on an envelope meant that his apprehensions were quieted, that he had gained sufficient stature to overawe an obstinate ghost. Not that the struggle could cease even then; for he still had to hold the attention of his fickle public and, when it seemed at the end of the century to be wavering, to recapture it by an act of resounding defiance which set the whole world ringing once more with his name.

The scandal caused by *La Confession de Claude* was only in part due to the audacity of certain bedroom scenes—though this was enough to make difficulties with the printer and, after the book was published, to provoke a police inquiry. The authorities decided not to prosecute: the work, though unchaste, was not obviously subversive.[1] But the critics were taken aback by the contrast between the apparent otherworldliness, the pastoral charm of the *Contes à Ninon* and the grim slum drama of *La Confession*. Zola was named in Gustave Vapereau's *Année littéraire* for 1866 as specializing in 'le roman d'antichambre et d'alcôve: peintures indiscrètes'. He was more amused than annoyed by the label.[2]

The reputation he was acquiring was not, however, of the kind wanted in an employee by a staid family firm like Hachette's; in addition, the office hours he worked were long,[3] and he needed some leisure if he was to follow up his initial success. He felt, a little prematurely perhaps, that the time had come when he could stand on his own feet.

At the end of January 1866 he had resigned his position at Hachette's, sacrificing the salary of 200 francs a month that went with it. He did not suppose that he could support himself, his mother, and the young woman, Alexandrine Meley, who had shortly before joined their establishment, on the royalties Lacroix paid him—which amounted to 30 centimes per copy sold of *La Confession de Claude* out of an edition of 1,500 copies. Novelists, he realized, could pay their way and reach a wide public only if they could get their books accepted as serial stories by newspaper editors, who bought them at a fixed rate of 15 centimes a line.

[1] The confidential report addressed by the public prosecutor to the Garde des Sceaux (Attorney-General) has been discovered and published: see G. Vauthier, 'Émile Zola et *la Confession de Claude*', *La Révolution de 1848*, vol. xxiii (1925), pp. 626–30, and A. Zévaès, 'A propos de *la Confession de Claude*: Émile Zola et le parquet impérial', *Nouvelles littéraires*, 3 Mar. 1934.

[2] See his review of Vapereau's almanac, *L'Événement*, 27 Apr. 1866.

[3] 8.30–11.30 and 1–6, Saturdays included. See his letter of 18 Apr. 1864 to Géry-Legrand, published by C. Bellanger, *Les Cahiers naturalistes*, no. 26 (1964), p. 29.

Ponson du Terrail, that inexhaustible spinner of yarns and king of *feuilletonistes*, who had devotees all over Europe, was a power not to be underrated. Granted that his literary gifts were negligible, that he was no more than 'un équilibriste dansant sur la corde raide d'une intrigue', wrote Zola in a review of his *Cosaques à Paris*,[1] even so, 'nous ne pourrons lui refuser ce je ne sais quoi qui fait lire ses ouvrages avec emportement par une notable partie du public. . . . On ne peut dédaigner l'écrivain qui tient dans sa main les émotions de deux ou trois cent mille hommes.' Zola's next two novels, *Le Vœu d'une morte* and *Les Mystères de Marseille*, were written with an eye to instalment publication, and he made no bones about admitting as much. 'Il ne m'est pas permis comme à vous de m'endormir', he wrote to Valabrègue again, a little tartly, 'de m'enfermer dans une tour d'ivoire, sous prétexte que la foule est sotte. J'ai besoin de la foule, je vais à elle comme je peux, je tente tous les moyens pour la dompter. . . . Il est bien entendu que je vous abandonne *les Mystères de Marseille*. Je sais ce que je fais.'

Serial stories were published along the bottom of French newspapers. Zola, however, started by inserting his prose halfway up the page: his career as a journalist began before he left Hachette's, and continued with very little intermission for the next fifteen years.

It was in the space of Zola's lifetime that the national daily press, in its modern form, came into existence. Its rapid growth corresponded with an increasing demand for inexpensive reading-matter, but there were also technical and economic reasons for the development—improvements in printing processes, the extension of telegraphic services, and above all, the use of revenue from advertisements to finance cheap newspapers with big circulations. A new industry was created, and Zola was among its early recruits.

Le Petit Journal, for which he began writing in 1865, was the first of these cheap newspapers in France. It was then only two years old, but had already reached a circulation of 200,000, considered phenomenal in those days. In 1867 rotary presses, another innovation, were installed to deal with the huge number of copies that had to be printed off daily. Founded by a Jewish banker, the paper was designed, by its contents as much as by its price, to attract the maximum of readers. Zola knew this, and half apologized to Valabrègue for his association with so frankly mercantile a venture; but, as he said, the 20 francs he earned for his weekly

[1] *L'Événement*, 1 Sept. 1866.

article were a welcome addition to the salary Hachette paid him, and, he added: 'Je considère aussi le journalisme comme un levier si puissant que je ne suis pas fâché du tout de pouvoir me produire à jour fixe devant un nombre considérable de lecteurs.' At a later date, when he had left Hachette's, and depended for his livelihood on free-lance work alone, he wrote to the same friend: 'Je compte bien ne jamais déserter entièrement le journalisme, qui est le plus grand moyen d'action que je connaisse.' This anticipation was justified: although Zola ceased regular contributions to newspapers and periodicals after 1881, he never wholly discarded this valuable 'means of action', remaining, for instance, more accessible than most men in his position to interviewing reporters.

At Hachette's Zola had met Bourdin, the son-in-law of one of the press lords of the day, Henri de Villemessant. Villemessant's flair for promising novelties and novelty-mongers was legendary. The staff of *Le Figaro*, over which he presided, was in perpetual flux, Villemessant throwing out old collaborators with as little formality as he brought in new ones. He had a gracious habit, little copied since no doubt, of signifying dismissal by making a present of an ornamented walking-stick to the journalist who was no longer fulfilling expectations. One day towards the end of 1865 Bourdin started telling Zola about a subsidiary newspaper his inexhaustible father-in-law was on the point of launching. Bourdin had found himself designated as literary editor of the new organ, *L'Événement*, and relished the prospect so little (for he was already in charge of the same department in *Le Figaro*) that he was delighted to stand down when Zola offered himself for the job. The young man went to Villemessant with a bold new scheme: he would not be content with reviewing books as they appeared—his idea was to get in touch with authors and publishers before the new books were put on sale and to commit certain agreed indiscretions, giving synopses and occasionally printing extracts while the book was still in proof. Zola's feature, which he called 'Livres d'aujourd'hui et de demain', was thus, if not the father, then a collateral ancestor of the well-known 'Books to Come' column in our own leading literary weekly.[1]

The venture (which was short-lived, for in the year of its birth *L'Événement* was swallowed up by *Le Figaro*, when the parent

[1] See Zola to Bourdin, 22 Jan. 1866. L. W. Tancock, in *The Modern Language Review*, vol. xlii (1947), pp. 43–57, has published a study of the contents and significance of the first part of this article series.

undertaking changed from being a bi-weekly to a daily paper) testifies to Zola's increasing alertness in what he undoubtedly regarded as purely business matters. He was developing a professional's nose for the 'scoop'. Among his first letters to the Goncourts were two anxious requests to be allowed to see the proofs of their book *Idées et sensations* before it was published. 'Plus j'arriverai avant les autres, et plus je vous serai reconnaissant', he wrote with disarming candour. The brothers sent him what he wanted and had no reason to regret it: Zola published extracts from the book in *L'Événement* (24 April 1866) and composed a eulogistic article for *Le Salut public*, a Lyons paper with which he was also collaborating, the following month. When occasion arose, he did not even trouble to obtain the author's permission to print fragments of works in the press. At the end of 1868, as he was correcting the final proofs of his novel *Madeleine Férat* in the printing-house of Poupart-Davyl, his eye lighted on another packet of proof-sheets lying on the table. Glancing through them, he recognized the style of Victor Hugo, and realized he was reading the first chapter of the master's much-heralded new novel, *L'Homme qui rit*. He was alone in the room. His first impulse was to put the bundle in his pocket. But a more prudent course recommended itself; since he might be surprised if he started to copy the pages, he went through them carefully, committing them to memory as he read. On 4 January 1869 he started a new series of 'Livres d'aujourd'hui et de demain' in *Le Gaulois* by announcing *L'Homme qui rit* (which was not to appear until 20 April) and printing parts of what he remembered.

Zola put no more value on his free-lance journalism than it warranted; only a small portion of it did he later consider fit to be collected and published in book form. In the company, particularly, of his seniors Flaubert and Edmond de Goncourt he was careful to belittle these fugitive and hastily written sketches. Those high priests of the written word looked wryly on such prostitution of their ideals. But they had private incomes. In a famous conversation with Flaubert, recorded by Goncourt, Zola pleaded his indigence in mitigation of these 'écritures misérables'. And it was with tremulous embarrassment that he admitted, in a letter to Flaubert, to being a correspondent of the Marseilles paper *Le Sémaphore*: 'c'est une de mes petites hontes cachées'.

At the time this attitude was not in the least insincere. In an article on the Goncourts published in *Le Gaulois* on 22 September

1868, Zola voiced a wistful envy of the brothers' financial independence. 'A notre époque, il n'est pas permis aux pauvres diables d'être
des artistes. Les gens qui vivent de leur plume sont de misérables
ouvriers livrant un article comme un cordonnier livre une paire de
bottes: l'art n'a rien à voir dans cette branche du commerce contemporain.' But this plaintive note was struck at a moment when
his journalistic commitments were beginning to be a burden, and
when his dream was to free himself from them—at least temporarily
—so as to concentrate on preparing and launching the Rougon-
Macquart series of novels.

Once he was out of the wood, he gave it as his considered opinion
that journalistic work was an excellent schooling for the young
writer, an indispensable agent of natural selection. 'Qu'on me cite
donc un écrivain de race qui ait perdu son talent à gagner son pain
dans les journaux, aux heures difficiles du début. Je suis certain,
au contraire, qu'ils ont puisé là plus d'énergie, plus de virilité, une
connaissance plus douloureuse, mais plus pénétrante, du monde
moderne.'[1] Whatever the general truth of this pronouncement, it
was undoubtedly valid for Zola himself. 'Writing for the papers'
gave him the needed illusion of multiple contacts with those
strangers, his fellow men; it probably induced in him the lifelong
habit of regular daily output without which the sheer mass of his
achievement would be inconceivable; and lastly it trained him to
see instinctively the issues that required discussion, the problems
that demanded ventilation. Harry Levin is no doubt right in suggesting that, in this respect at least, Zola and Dickens have a good
deal in common, not only in their careers but in the way their
careers influenced their art.[2]

His book reviews for L'Événement commanded far less attention,
in 1866, than did the series of articles he published on the official
art exhibition that year. He had begun to frequent the café Guerbois, the rendezvous of the future school of impressionist painters,
in February. Some of the habitués were already old friends: Pissarro,
who had been a fellow student of Cézanne's when the latter was
attending the Académie suisse in 1861; and Bazille and Monet
who in 1865 were sharing a studio which Zola would sometimes

---

[1] 'L'Argent dans la littérature', Le Roman expérimental, p. 146. (My page references to Zola's works should be taken in all cases to refer to the Bernouard
edition (1928–9).) 'L'Argent dans la littérature' was first published in the
Russian periodical Vestnik Evropy, Mar. 1880.
[2] The Gates of Horn (1963), p. 350.

visit in the company of Cézanne or Pissarro. Pissarro and Bazille were regular guests at the Thursday evening gatherings that Zola inaugurated when he set up house with Alexandrine Meley. Cézanne had also introduced him to the young landscape painter Antoine Guillemet, and he had met Duranty, the art-critic and novelist, during business hours at Hachette's. All these men were in the habit of dropping in at the Guerbois, particularly during the winter evenings when the light faded early, and in addition Zola was able to listen here to Degas, a formidable debater, Renoir, sceptically amused at the vehemence of his companions, Fantin-Latour, another art-critic Philippe Burty, the Belgian Alfred Stevens, the American Whistler. Only Cézanne, temperamentally unsociable, and Manet, rather older than the others and already a somewhat aloof figure, stayed away; but Guillemet took Zola that winter to visit Manet in his studio, see the canvases he was working on, and hear from his lips the story of his artistic apprenticeship.

Talk among these young and struggling painters ran principally, it may be surmised, on their chances of having their submissions accepted by the hanging committee in the spring; or, if their pictures were rejected, on the possibility of the establishment of a *salon des refusés* such as had been, by imperial command, set up in 1863, on which occasion Manet had scandalized nearly everyone with his *Déjeuner sur l'herbe*. Zola, stimulated by his friends' withering sallies against the academicians, and by the stories they retailed about the inner politics of the art world, begged Villemessant to let him 'write up' the exhibition. The newspaper editor agreed, foreseeing a scandal but not the dimensions it would take. The exhibition was due to open on 1 May; Zola published his first two articles in advance, on 27 and 30 April; they were devoted not to the artists but to the committee of old and respected painters who had been given the unenviable task of selecting the few hundred pictures to be exhibited among the thousands sent in. The young art-critic's impudence staggered the readers of *L'Événement*: the jury was denounced almost to a man as a bevy of traditionalists bent on stifling all innovation, and its members were presented singly as weak-eyed nonentities, shameless intriguers, or tired old fogeys. Some of these worthies protested apoplectically to Villemessant; one of them wanted to fight a duel with Zola; the wisest pretended to be amused. The fledgling critic, unperturbed, brought out his fourth article which was devoted entirely to Manet; but

Manet was one of the artists whose works had been excluded from the exhibition Zola was supposed to be reviewing. The bewilder-. ment of Villemessant's readers turned to indignation and a steep drop in circulation made him regret not having had the exhibition covered by a more respectful reporter. Zola was allowed to publish his fifth article ('Les Réalistes au Salon') in which Monet alone was wholeheartedly praised (for the sake of his portrait of Camille Doncieux in a long green dress), and his sixth ('Les Chutes') which contained some surprising reservations about the arch-realist Courbet, accused of making concessions to curry favour with the academic critics. Then he was told to finish the series. His last article, 'Adieux d'un critique d'art', was as defiant as those that had preceded it. He recalled and reiterated some of the formulae he had used before: 'Ce que je cherche surtout dans un tableau, c'est un homme et non pas un tableau'; 'faites vrai, j'applaudis; faites individuel, j'applaudis plus fort'; 'j'ai plus souci de la vie que de l'art'. He asserted that his defence of Manet was deliberate and justified: 'J'ai défendu M. Manet, comme je défendrai dans ma vie toute individualité franche qui sera attaquée. Je serai toujours du parti des vaincus. Il y a une lutte évidente entre les tempéraments indomptables et la foule. Je suis pour les tempéraments et j'attaque la foule.' And he ended by reciting the catalogue of his sins: to have been logical in his preferences; to have required power and originality in a work before he would admire it; to have pointed out that the old masters were masters because they were possessed of vigorous and forceful temperaments; to have predicted oblivion for the fashionable artists of the day; to have dared to disagree with the fashionable critics of the day; and wantonly to have hurt the feelings of many respectable people in his disinterested search for truth. 'En un mot, j'ai fait preuve de cruauté, de sottise, d'ignorance, je me suis rendu coupable de sacrilège et d'hérésie, parce que, las de mensonge et de médiocrité, j'ai cherché des hommes dans la foule de ces eunuques.'

There is no denying the vigour and originality with which Zola urges the supremacy of just those two qualities in art. It was a fortunate chance that it should have been precisely Manet—and, moreover, the Manet of the 1860's, of *Le Déjeuner sur l'herbe* and *Olympia*—who stood in need of a champion at this juncture, for there was something in the harshness of his vision which could fairly be called vigour, something in the strangeness of his compositions which was unmistakably original, especially when set along-side the empty conventionality of Cabanel, Gérome, Meissonier, and the other academic idols of the day. The peculiar mixture of crudeness and elegance that characterizes these canvases could credibly be attributed to Manet's temperament, 'un tempérament sec, emportant le morceau' as Zola described it, referring to the absence of transition passages between the patches of colour.

The question has from time to time been raised how far Zola had merely constituted himself the mouthpiece or interpreter of his artist friends.[1] The vehemence with which he expressed his views is some guarantee of the sincerity with which he held them; in addi-tion, he went out of his way to claim sole responsibility for them, notably at the end of the foreword written for the re-edition of the articles in pamphlet form which was published later in the year. Apologizing for bringing his 'ideas' before the public a second time, he declared: 'J'ai foi en elles, je sais que dans quelques années j'aurai raison pour tout le monde. Elles sont à moi, bien à moi — et je les crie de toutes mes forces.' Zola's approach to painting lacked subtlety; it was, in spite of the visits to studios and art galleries in Cézanne's company, not nourished on a lengthy course of medita-tion on the artist's problems and aims. Above all, it was less catholic than he imagined: delicacy of touch, insidiousness, the poignancy of tired and drooping lines made little appeal to this searcher after 'men in the throng of eunuchs'. Zola consistently underestimated Degas, for instance. But his instincts were on the whole remarkably sound; Cézanne was practically the only painter of his generation whose future greatness he failed to divine; he never mistook mere illustration for artistic achievement, nor virtuosity for accomplish-ment. And his unswerving faith in the rightness of his judgement ensured that he never softened his assertions with prudent reserva-tions. There is an honest forthrightness about his art criticism, endearing, refreshing, or exasperating, according to the tastes and prejudices of the reader.

The literary criticism he was writing at about the same time seems in comparison thin and lacks incisiveness: the formulae he uses merely anticipate or repeat what he applied with far more fire

[1] By F. Doucet, *L'Esthétique d'Émile Zola et son application à la critique* (1923), p. 344; and, more recently, by Hélène and Jean Adhémar, 'Zola et la peinture', *Arts*, 12–18 Dec. 1952. The authors of this article are categoric: Zola 'fut ren-seigné par ses amis, dont il est l'écho'.

to Manet's art. 'Une œuvre est simplement une libre et haute manifestation d'une personnalité, et dès lors je n'ai plus pour devoir que de constater quelle est cette personnalité', he wrote flatly, reviewing the Goncourts' *Germinie Lacerteux*. A new volume of poetry from Victor Hugo he insists on regarding simply as 'le produit logique, inévitable, d'un certain tempérament mis en présence d'un certain sujet'. Zola finds himself, inevitably, judging the personality, the 'temperament', in preference to the work itself: he specifically denies the possibility of using literary criteria to evaluate literary products. 'Le beau n'est fait ni de ceci ni de cela: il est dans la vie, dans la libre personnalité; une œuvre belle est une œuvre vivante, originale, qu'un homme a su tirer de sa chair et de son cœur.'[1] At this rate sincere self-expression is the *summum bonum*. But Zola is very apt to suppose that sincerity is the same as honesty, and that honesty consists of showing the world as it is—or as it seems to the critic. In the book reviews contributed to *L'Événement* he repeatedly gives short shrift to works of pure imagination and reserves his praise for any book which seemed to show powers of observation in the writer. On 7 April 1866 he had to give account of two novels from the same press: the first, by a certain d'Amézeuil, was called *Les Amours de contrebande* and bore the sub-title *Scènes de la vie réelle*; the second novel was Alfred Delvau's *Le Grand et le Petit Trottoir*. Zola asked ironically whether the printer had not affixed the sub-title to the wrong book. 'Où l'auteur a-t-il donc vu la vie réelle, pour la décrire comme il le fait? Ça! la vie réelle! M. d'Amézeuil ignore qu'il faut une main forte et puissante, lorsqu'on veut prendre des réalités dans ses mains et les jeter tout debout au milieu du public.' Having finished the book, he reread a few pages of *Madame Bovary*: 'On m'avait promis une histoire réelle, il m'en fallait une.' Delvau's book, on the other hand, pleased him: the author obviously had first-hand information about the underworld he was describing, and his characters were real characters—'pas de poupées pleines de son et d'étoupe, des personnages de chair et d'os, dont le sang et les larmes coulent'. A month after this Zola returned to the charge in discussing a collection of short stories (Camille Dutripon's *La Tante Capitaine*) which, from the description he gives of them, seem to have been fairly similar to his own

---

[1] These quotations are taken from *Mes haines* (1866), a collection of essays some of which had appeared in the Lyons newspaper *Le Salut public* or in *La Revue contemporaine*, while others had found no editor disposed to print them.

Contes à Ninon. But Zola was not, he says, amused. 'Je suis très difficile pour les œuvres de pure imagination, n'ayant pu encore comprendre la nécessité du rêve, lorsque la réalité offre un intérêt si humain et si poignant.' This sentence gives the clue to Zola's attachment to realism: he did not turn to it because it was the newest fashion in literature, nor because of the noisy successes its adherents occasionally won; as it has been suggested already, the appeal of the new formula consisted in the opportunities it gave for closer contact with the humanity whom hitherto he had held too much at arm's length.

The final revelation of the possibilities of realism came with the discovery of Balzac. At the end of 1866 Zola was inexpressibly flattered to receive an invitation to address the Congrès scientifique de France, meeting that year at Aix. Unable to attend in person, he sent his speech through the post. It comprised an astonishingly erudite survey of the development of the novel from the earliest Greek specimens down to the nineteenth century.[1] The lecture culminated in an enthusiastic presentation of Balzac, with whose aims and methods Zola proclaimed himself rapturously in agreement. Balzac, the congress members were told, is

l'anatomiste de l'âme et de la chair. Il dissèque l'homme, étudie le jeu des passions, interroge chaque fibre, fait l'analyse de l'organe entier. Comme le chirurgien, il n'a ni honte ni répugnance, lorsqu'il fouille les plaies humaines. Il n'a souci que de vérité, et étale devant nous le cadavre de notre cœur. Les sciences modernes lui ont donné pour instrument l'analyse et la méthode expérimentale. Il procède comme nos chimistes et nos mathématiciens; il décompose les actions, en détermine les causes, en explique les résultats; il opère selon des équations fixes, ramenant les faits à l'étude de l'influence des milieux sur les individualités. Le nom qui lui convient est celui de docteur ès sciences morales.

In assuming, after Balzac, these new functions, the modern novelist finds himself discarding others that were formerly considered his province.

Il ne s'agit plus d'inventer une histoire compliquée d'une invraisemblance dramatique qui étonne le lecteur; il s'agit uniquement d'enregistrer des faits humains, de montrer à nu le mécanisme du corps et de

---

[1] Parts of it have been reproduced as an appendix to *Le Roman expérimental* (Bernouard edition); but the most interesting portions (those from which I have taken my quotations) were first given by G. Robert, 'Trois textes inédits d'Émile Zola', *Revue des Sciences humaines*, fasc. 51 (1948), pp. 181–207.

l'âme. L'affabulation se simplifie; le premier homme qui passe est un héros suffisant; fouillez en lui et vous trouverez certainement un drame simple qui met en jeu tous les rouages des sentiments et des passions.

In these preparatory years, it is clear that Zola was thinking hard about the nature and technique of the art he had chosen. *Thérèse Raquin* in 1867 and the novel that followed it after twelve months, *Madeleine Férat*, cannot be fully appreciated except in the light of these meditations; they must be seen as experiments in a new realism—new, at all events, in the path of Zola's development, but one that leads back to Balzac and the positivist gospel. In these two works the young writer can be watched trying his hand at objective presentation of invented characters, the difficult feat that his other great forerunner, Flaubert, had toiled to achieve. Zola, of course, was far from succeeding at the first attempt. But he seems to have seen where and why he failed, and afterwards to have resolutely recast his method in order to come closer to grips with the problem. *Thérèse Raquin* and *Madeleine Férat* are not blind alleys from which Zola was obliged to retrace his steps; they are stages in the steady progression that led him up to the peaks of attainment, *L'Assommoir* and *Germinal* and *La Terre*, where the dispassionate objectivity of the artist is almost perfectly balanced by his passionate involvement in the creative act.

The test by which we may most readily judge the objectivity of a work of fiction is a negative one: the reader should be unable, simply by studying the text in front of him, to draw any conclusions about the author's sympathies or antipathies, his creed or his philosophy. Flaubert, just about the time when Zola was meditating *Thérèse Raquin*, put this ideal into words in one of his letters: 'Un romancier, selon moi, n'a pas le droit de donner son avis sur les choses de ce monde. Il doit, dans sa vocation, imiter Dieu dans la sienne, c'est-à-dire faire et se taire.' Zola, in a later essay on Flaubert, elaborated this principle which he had no doubt heard many times, differently worded, on the master's lips. The passage reflects a point of view to which Zola had probably not fully progressed in 1867; but it was the logical terminus of a process that was already well under way.

Le romancier naturaliste affecte de disparaître complètement derrière l'action qu'il raconte. Il est le metteur en scène caché du drame. Jamais il ne se montre au bout d'une phrase. On ne l'entend ni rire ni pleurer avec ses personnages, pas plus qu'il ne se permet de juger leurs actes.

C'est même cet apparent désintéressement qui est le trait le plus distinctif. On chercherait en vain une conclusion, une moralité, une leçon quelconque tirée des faits. Il n'y a d'étalés, de mis en lumière, uniquement que les faits, louables ou condamnables. L'auteur n'est pas un moraliste, mais un anatomiste que se contente de dire ce qu'il trouve dans le cadavre humain. Les lecteurs concluront, s'ils le veulent, chercheront la vraie moralité, tâcheront de tirer une leçon du livre. Quant au romancier, il se tient à l'écart, surtout par un motif d'art, pour laisser à son œuvre son unité impersonnelle, son caractère de procès-verbal écrit à jamais sur le marbre. Il pense que sa propre émotion gênerait celle de ses personnages, que son jugement atténuerait la hautaine leçon des faits. C'est là toute une poétique nouvelle dont l'application change la face du roman.[1]

Measured against this standard of objectivity, *Thérèse Raquin* can hardly be said to qualify as a product of the 'poétique nouvelle'. The author betrays in all kinds of question-begging touches the moral assumptions on which his book is based. Granted, these assumptions are truistic and would be subscribed to unresistingly by the great majority of his readers. For their own comfort they could be counted on to agree with him that adultery is a violation of the moral law, and that 'crime never pays'. But by the manner in which he shows his two central characters committing adultery and perpetrating a crime, Zola ceases to be the detached 'metteur en scène'; he cannot conceal the repugnance he feels for them, however scrupulously he analyses the attendant circumstances of their adultery and crime. It emerges, for instance, when he comments, after describing Thérèse's feelings at the beginning of her liaison with Laurent—'elle savait qu'elle faisait le mal'; or when after the murder of her husband, of which she was an accomplice, she has a nervous breakdown which conveniently passes as the effect of the shock of bereavement—'la nature', remarks Zola, 'aidait à la *sinistre comédie* qui venait de se jouer'; or when, right at the end, just before their double suicide, Laurent and Thérèse 'pleurèrent, sans parler, songeant à la *vie de boue* qu'ils avaient menée et qu'ils mèneraient encore, s'ils étaient assez lâches pour vivre'. The claim that Zola made in the preface to *Thérèse Raquin*: 'J'ai simplement fait sur deux corps vivants le travail analytique que les chirurgiens font sur les cadavres', cannot really be allowed: the sermonizing follows too pat on the analysing.

[1] *Les Romanciers naturalistes*, pp. 109-10.

In this preface, written in April 1868 for the second edition (the first had sold out after four months), Zola was principally concerned to defend himself against the charges of immorality which certain critics had brought against him. A violently hostile article had appeared, under the title 'La Littérature putride' and above the signature of Louis Ulbach, in *Le Figaro*, 23 January 1868. *Thérèse Raquin* was elegantly described in this review as 'une flaque de boue et de sang' and of the author it was said, rather cruelly: 'M. Zola passe pour un jeune homme de talent. Je sais, du moins, qu'il vise avec ardeur à la renommée.' Ulbach also asserted: 'il voit la femme comme M. Manet la peint, couleur de boue avec des maquillages roses', and here, if one discounts the discourtesies, it must be acknowledged that Ulbach hit on very nearly the right formula to describe what Zola at any rate intended to do: to realize with the pen what the painter of *Le Déjeuner sur l'herbe* had achieved with his brush. This canvas too had been called wanton by those who limited their attention to the subject.

> La foule . . . y a vu seulement des gens qui mangeaient sur l'herbe, au sortir du bain, et elle a cru que l'artiste avait mis une intention indécente et tapageuse dans la disposition du sujet, lorsque l'artiste avait simplement cherché à obtenir des oppositions vives et des masses franches. . . . La femme nue du *Déjeuner sur l'herbe* n'est là que pour fournir à l'artiste l'occasion de peindre un peu de chair.

So Zola had written in his longest and most considered apologia for Manet.[1] And in rejecting, in the preface to *Thérèse Raquin*, the accusation of immorality, he conducts his defence along the same lines as he had used to acquit Manet of this charge.

> Je me suis trouvé dans le cas de ces peintres qui copient des nudités, sans qu'un seul désir les effleure, et qui restent profondément surpris lorsqu'un critique se déclare scandalisé par les chairs vivantes de leur œuvre. Tant que j'ai écrit *Thérèse Raquin*, j'ai oublié le monde, je me suis perdu dans la copie exacte et minutieuse de la vie, me donnant tout entier à l'analyse du mécanisme humain, et je vous assure que les amours cruelles de Thérèse et de Laurent n'avaient pour moi rien d'immoral, rien qui puisse pousser aux passions mauvaises. L'humanité des modèles disparaissait comme elle disparaît aux yeux de l'artiste qui a une femme nue vautrée devant lui, et qui songe uniquement à mettre cette femme sur sa toile dans la vérité de ses formes et de ses colorations. Aussi ma

[1] 'Une nouvelle manière en peinture: Édouard Manet', *Revue du XIX*^e *siècle*, 1 Jan. 1867. See Zola, *Salons*, ed. Hemmings and Niess, p. 96.

surprise a été grande quand j'ai entendu traiter mon œuvre de flaque de boue et de sang. . . .

There is much that is ingenuous, just as there is much that is revealing, in this line of defence. In creating Thérèse, whatever he implies, Zola was copying no model, nude or draped; he was copying a phantasm of his own brain. It is true that the seed of the story was an actual occurrence, reported in the press at the time, in the *commune* of Gordes (Vaucluse): a farmer's wife and a married horse-dealer, exasperated by the checks to their adultery represented by their respective spouses, plotted to dispose of them by poison. This proved difficult, but on Christmas night 1861 the farmer was shot dead. The horse-dealer was arrested and confessed to the crime, without, however, implicating his accessory, though a little later she too was brought to justice, some letters having been found in which she had incited her lover to commit the murder.[1] The events were used by Adolphe Belot and Ernest Daudet to construct a serial thriller (*La Vénus de Gordes*) published in 1866. Zola adapted it in his turn, first in a short story, 'Un Mariage d'amour', published in *Le Figaro*, 24 December 1866, and finally in *Thérèse Raquin*. He made two changes. In his version, the troublesome husband met his death by drowning; and—by a more original twist—the criminals were not caught, but were punished none the less by the workings of their own conscience or, as he preferred to put it, of their disordered nerves. The story of Fortunée Auphante and her lover Denante, whether read in a newspaper six years previously or, as is more likely, in an already fictionalized version by two fellow writers, could at the most have confirmed Zola in the belief that some passionate people will go to the lengths of homicide to encompass their desires—that, in fact, the 'brute humaine' does exist as a species. But to say that Fortunée posed for his portrait of Thérèse is only true in the limited sense that it can be claimed Antoine Berthet posed for Stendhal's portrait of Julien Sorel.

The analogy between the realism of *Thérèse Raquin* and the realism of the painters is, then, on this account alone highly specious. In his preface Zola makes a further comparison between what he was trying to do in his novel and what is done in the dissecting theatre by the anatomist. He declared unashamedly that he

---

[1] See L. Mandin, 'Les Origines de *Thérèse Raquin*', *Mercure de France*, vol. ccxcvii (1940), pp. 282–98.

had no intention of creating 'characters', of writing about normal
human beings with normal moral scruples. 'Dans *Thérèse Raquin*,
j'ai voulu étudier des tempéraments et non des caractères', he
writes. There is a beast in man, and it is this beast alone that
interests him.[1] 'Thérèse et Laurent sont des brutes humaines, rien
de plus.... L'âme est parfaitement absente, j'en conviens aisément,
puisque je l'ai voulu ainsi. ... Je n'ai eu qu'un désir: étant donné
un homme puissant et une femme inassouvie, chercher en eux la
bête, ne voir même que la bête, et noter scrupuleusement les
sensations et les actes de ces êtres.' He then continues with the
sentence we have already quoted: 'J'ai simplement fait sur deux
corps vivants le travail analytique que les chirurgiens font sur des
cadavres.' Ever since Balzac's Desplein (in *La Messe de l'athée*) it
was of course accepted that every surgeon was bound to be a
materialist and an agnostic, one who, never having come across the
soul in the tissues he incised, dismissed its existence as an un-
necessary hypothesis, preferring to regard human behaviour as no
more than a set of complicated responses to physical stimuli.

One does not ask of the particular creed or philosophy that a
novelist adopts whether it is sensible or even tenable, but simply
whether it enables him to write original and impressive works. In
the case of *Thérèse Raquin* it has to be admitted that in deciding to
study 'temperaments' rather than 'characters', Zola was prevented
by his materialism from imparting to his pair of passionate male-
factors the kind of human appeal which is normally a necessity if
a novelist is to compel his reader's interest. They suffer from being
too passive in the current of physiological necessity that sweeps
them along. And this passivity impairs their vitality. To give the
illusion of reality, the characters a novelist invents must not appear
to be utterly at the mercy of their own 'temperaments': few of us

---

[1] Zola had used the phrase 'la bête humaine' in his earlier novel, *Le Vœu d'une
morte*. Daniel, whose sense of honour at one point forces him to act as inter-
mediary between the girl he loves and his close friend Georges whom she wishes
to marry, experiences a pang of bitter regret which Zola expresses in the sentence: 'Alors, la bête humaine se réveilla au fond de son être, et il eut une crise
effrayante de désespoir et de folie.' This was in 1866. In two, at least, of his book
reviews that year he used the term, and on both occasions to commend the
novelist concerned. Jules Claretie's *Un Assassin* evoked the comment: 'Je frémis
lorsqu'on me présente la bête humaine dans toute sa violence' (*L'Événement*,
26 Feb.), and in a favourable notice of Hector Malot's *Victimes d'amour* he wrote
that the author 'passe le tablier blanc de l'anatomiste et dissèque fibre par fibre
la bête humaine étendue toute nue sur la dalle de l'amphithéâtre. Et ici la bête
humaine est vivante . . .' (*Le Figaro*, 18 Dec.).

are thoroughgoing fatalists, and we do not recognize our fellows in beings who have no hand at all in the guiding of their destinies. If a novelist is ruled by materialism, at least he must not ascribe to flesh and blood the properties of stocks and stones. For all that, *Thérèse Raquin* has found readers by the thousands ever since it appeared in 1867. We have hitherto been considering only Zola's stated intentions; and it is noteworthy that he hardly presents himself at all in this preface as a novelist. He is a painter, or he is a surgeon, or a scientist.[1] In fact, if his book has gripped the imagination of generations of readers, this is because of its qualities as a novel, that is, of a piece of fiction bathing in a specific atmosphere which has the property of arousing a specific response.

This atmosphere is not in the least 'realistic' in the sense of being composed of elements recognizable in our experience of everyday life. Sainte-Beuve, in a letter to Zola about his book, criticized it on the score that these recognizable elements were not reproduced, that, for instance, in his description of localities he had overstepped the bounds of 'average truth'; Sainte-Beuve objected in particular to the opening passage in the book in which a certain Paris street is presented as having 'l'aspect sinistre d'un véritable coupe-gorge'. The critic was familiar with the little lane that Zola was describing, and he protested that, for him, it was no more than a little lane, with nothing sombre or sinister about it. Ten years after Sainte-Beuve's death Zola published the gist of this criticism and humbly —but quite unnecessarily—admitted its justice: 'Il est certain', he wrote, 'que dans *Thérèse Raquin*, les choses sont poussées au cauchemar, et que la vérité stricte est en deçà de tant d'horreurs.'[2] Now it is quite clear that if Zola had eschewed the horrors, if he had been the kind of realist he thought he ought to be, if he had not given his work the 'nightmarish' qualities which he deplores here, *Thérèse Raquin* would have hardly risen above the level of an ingenious thriller and would be deservedly forgotten today.

The dreadful intensity, the primitive violence in the expression of passion that one finds in *Thérèse Raquin* are notes which will be struck again and again in Zola's mature work: they are sounded here for the first time. The risk of hysterical overstatement is

[1] 'Mon but a été un but scientifique avant tout' (Préface). Cf. also, in a later article protesting against the official ban on the sale of the book by hawkers: '*Thérèse Raquin* est une étude de savant' (*La Tribune*, 9 Aug. 1868).

[2] *Documents littéraires*, p. 226. Sainte-Beuve's letter will be found in his *Correspondance*, vol. ii, p. 314.

always present but always avoided. Realism is, of course, forgotten, and replaced by a lurid impressionism which transports a thoroughly unlikely story into a sphere of dark poetry where Zola joins hands with Poe, Hawthorne, and a certain Dickens.[1] These are the words, for instance, in which a shop-assistant addresses her lover, a local government clerk:

J'ignore comment je t'aimais; je te haïssais plutôt. Ta vue m'irritait, me faisait souffrir; lorsque tu étais là, mes nerfs se tendaient à se rompre, ma tête se vidait, je voyais rouge. Oh! que j'ai souffert! Et je cherchais cette souffrance, j'attendais ta venue, je tournais autour de ta chaise, pour marcher dans ton haleine, pour traîner mes vêtements le long des tiens. Il me semblait que ton sang me jetait des bouffées de chaleur au passage, et c'est cette sorte de nuée ardente, dans laquelle tu t'enveloppais, qui m'attirait et me retenait auprès de toi, malgré mes sourdes révoltes. . . .

To lay bare the germ of physical cruelty which lies hidden at the heart of erotic passion, turning it into what is too glibly called a 'love–hate relationship', was perhaps not Zola's conscious intention in *Thérèse Raquin*; but a passage such as this is a pertinent gloss on Baudelaire's dictum: 'Il y a dans l'acte de l'amour une grande ressemblance avec la torture ou avec une opération chirurgicale.' In the same way, when circumstances deny Thérèse and Laurent the opportunity to satisfy their violent passion for one another, they put everything into a handclasp which seems meant more as a laceration than a caress: 'Ils auraient voulu, mutuellement, emporter des lambeaux de leur chair, collés à leurs doigts.'

Lust and violence, or perhaps one should say (since lust and violence are here one) lust and death, execute an infernal *pas-de-deux* throughout, beginning with Thérèse's clandestine evening visit

[1] It is less the role of François (the cat) that suggests Poe (Mandin, loc. cit., argues unconvincingly in favour of regarding *The Black Cat* as an inspirational source), than certain descriptions of Mme Raquin's feelings when paralysis prevents her from denouncing her niece and Laurent as murderers: 'Son esprit était comme un de ces vivants qu'on ensevelit par mégarde et qui se réveillent dans la nuit de la terre, à deux ou trois mètres du sol; ils crient, ils se débattent, et l'on passe sur eux sans entendre leurs atroces lamentations.'—'Ses sensations ressemblaient à celles d'un homme tombé en léthargie qu'on enterrerait et qui, bâillonné par les liens de sa chair, entendrait sur sa tête le bruit sourd des pelletées de sable' (ch. xxvi: cf. *The Premature Burial*). For possible reminiscences of *The Scarlet Letter* and of *Dombey and Son* (Mrs. Clennam) in *Thérèse Raquin*, see R. J. Niess, 'Hawthorne and Zola—an influence?', *Revue de Littérature comparée*, vol. xxvii (1953), pp. 446–52, and S. Atkins, 'A possible Dickens influence in Zola', *Modern Language Quarterly*, vol. viii (1947), pp. 302–8.

to Laurent's lodgings (the only such visit she ever pays). It is then that 'l'idée de mort, jetée avec désespoir entre deux baisers' first occurs to them—the idea of murdering Thérèse's husband Camille who is also Laurent's closest friend. The murder is plotted, successfully executed, and successfully passed off as an accident. Before Thérèse's widowhood becomes a legal fact, however, it is necessary that Camille's body should be found. Laurent takes to dropping in at the morgue during his lunch hour to inspect the corpses drawn from the Seine, and in his extraordinary thirteenth chapter Zola outdoes Jules Janin in his account of this eery institution. The murderer is, for instance, fascinated one day by the naked body of a young girl who had hanged herself for love. 'Laurent la regarda longtemps, promenant ses regards sur sa chair, absorbé dans une sorte de désir peureux.' He notices that he is not the only one who seeks this queer gratification: there is a well-dressed young woman, veiled, wearing gloves, exuding an aura of expensive perfume, who stands rapt in front of the plate-glass behind which is exhibited the sturdy body of a mason killed in falling from some scaffolding. 'La dame l'examinait, le retournait en quelque sorte du regard, le pesait, s'absorbait dans le spectacle de cet homme. Elle leva un coin de sa voilette, regarda encore, puis s'en alla.' These illustrations of the perversion which has since been given the name of necrophilia are entirely gratuitous, as far as the narrative is concerned; their function is clear: to 'pousser les choses au cauchemar', in the words Zola later used.

The full nightmare starts in chapter xvii and increases in violence and horror for the remainder of the book. Camille's horribly decomposed corpse is eventually recognized by his murderer. The death is duly registered, and Laurent and Thérèse are at liberty to marry. But prudence obliges them to delay and, besides, their ardour has queerly ebbed. Fifteen months after the crime, though nothing hinders them now from resuming their liaison, they feel no inclination to do so. The slightest bodily contact now makes them recoil: 'Lorsqu'ils échangeaient une poignée de main, ils éprouvaient une sorte de malaise en sentant leur peau se toucher.' They decide to marry none the less: it seems absurd to have risked the guillotine for nothing. But the very night after they have reached this decision, each is made sleepless by recurrent dreams of the drowned man. Laurent's nightmare is particularly horrific: he sees himself walking through the streets to the shop in the Passage du Pont-Neuf, climbing the back stairs as he used to, scratching at Thérèse's bedroom door. But in the doorway, instead of his eager mistress, stands Camille, not as he was in life, but as Laurent had seen him in the morgue, dreadfully disfigured, his flesh green, his tongue black; with arms outstretched, he grins at Laurent in ironic welcome.

Zola proceeds to develop episodes of grisly horror when the wretched pair, once married, find themselves haunted by hallucinations of the living corpse of their victim who seats himself on an armchair between them, lies between them in bed, jealously squeezes his ice-cold, clammy flesh against their shrinking limbs to keep them apart. What monstrous shapes in the deep caverns of the novelist's unconscious bodied themselves forth in these appalling scenes it is hard to imagine. Venus is a ghoul in *Thérèse Raquin*; but it is clear that the work is directly affiliated to the apparently harmless 'Simplice' of a few years before: the nymph and her ravisher who die of their first kiss suggest an obstinate association in Zola's mind between carnal love and death[1] which, recurrent down to *La Bête humaine*, provides the dark side to the equally persistent and ultimately triumphant faith in the justification of sexual union as the victorious initiator of new life.

The sources of *Madeleine Férat*, the next of Zola's novels to be published, are just as personal as those of *Thérèse Raquin* but more obviously autobiographical. It is important to note that the book was an expanded version of a play apparently written in 1865 (under the title *La Madeleine*) but separately refused by two theatre managers to whom Zola proposed it at that time. Guillaume, the hero of the novel, represents a side of Zola examined in the previous chapter—that side which he seems to have more or less successfully transcended or suppressed after 1865: the shy, shrinking dreamer, asking only to be allowed to contract out of active life, but being forced by circumstances to deal with situations that clamour for drastic resolution. Guillaume's only way of dealing with situations is to run away from them; his one desire—never satisfied except temporarily—is for tranquil forgetfulness, a kind of death-in-life: 'une existence morte, exempte d'événements, faite d'un sentiment unique', his wife's unfailing, reassuring affection.

---

[1] 'La volupté même, chez Zola', as Camille Lemonnier was to remark, 'se couronne des fleurs noires de la Mort.' Quoted by Maurice Le Blond, 'Sur Émile Zola', *Mercure de France*, vol. cvi (1913), p. 18.

At school Guillaume is bullied (as Zola had been), mocked at as a bastard, that is, a child without a true father, as Zola had suffered for being a child without a living father. And, just as Zola did, he takes refuge in a daydream, and the same sort of daydream as Zola did, if one may regard 'Simplice' as its transcription: a fantasy involving an impenetrable forest, streams of running water, and a fairy, a nymph, or a boy companion, the obligatory complement of adolescent escapism:

il se perdait au fond du songe sans fin d'une passion imaginaire dans laquelle il se jetait en entier, à jamais. Et il rêvait alors une solitude bénie, un coin de terre où il y avait des arbres et des eaux, où il était seul à seul en compagnie d'une chère passion; amante ou camarade, il ne distinguait pas bien . . . quelque bonne et douce fée qui resterait toujours près de lui; et plus tard, lorsque des désirs vagues commençaient à battre dans ses veines, il avait repris ce songe sous les arbres du parc, aux bords des eaux claires, remplaçant la fée par une amoureuse, courant les taillis, avec l'espoir de rencontrer sa chère tendresse à chaque détour des sentiers.

Madeleine, whom he meets in a shabby hotel in Paris, is, he decides, the girl of his private dream. But Madeleine has a past, of which he guesses nothing and which she, believing it buried beyond recall, refrains from disclosing to him. A medical student had befriended her, she had become his mistress in spite of her fundamental indifference to him; after a few months of cohabitation he had left her to go overseas and had been reported drowned on the voyage.

If Guillaume is a self-portrait it is at least arguable that Madeleine represents the woman with whom Zola chose, probably at the end of 1865, to link his life.[1] We are, and shall probably remain, ill-informed about the origins and early life of Alexandrine-Gabrielle Meley. Her biography has been written by a godson and second cousin who, although he saw a great deal of Mme Émile Zola in her late middle age, never heard from her lips how her early life had been spent: it was a period she preferred to remain silent about.[2] Her parentage is established by her birth certificate: she was born in Paris, the illegitimate daughter of a seventeen-year-old

---

[1] A copy exists of *La Confession de Claude* inscribed in Zola's hand on the fly-leaf: 'A ma chère Gabrielle, en souvenir du 24 décembre 1865'.

[2] A. Laborde, *Trente-huit années près de Zola. Vie d'Alexandrine Émile Zola* (1963).

mother and an eighteen-year-old father, who did not remain together. Edmond-Jacques Meley, a hatter, married when his little
daughter was nine years old; her mother, Caroline Wadoux, contracted a marriage a year later; the certificate shows she was at that
time a florist by trade. She died, however, six months after this
marriage (in September 1849), and what happened to Alexandrine
then is a matter for pure speculation. She may have lived for a
while with her father and stepmother; but her relations with them
seem to have been unhappy—they were not present when her
marriage to Émile Zola was celebrated in 1870. The balance of
probability is that she found a home with a sister-in-law of her
mother's, also a florist, and was apprenticed to this trade. Those
who knew her closely remarked that she was unusually knowledge-
able, for a woman bred in the city, about horticulture, and it is
worth observing, perhaps, that flower-sellers figure not infrequently
in her husband's novels: in *Les Mystères de Marseille*, in *Le Ventre
de Paris*, and above all in *L'Assommoir*, where there is a detailed
description of the work and working conditions of girls employed
in making up bunches of cut flowers for sale.

Such girls were not, if one is to believe Zola's account in *L'Assommoir*, invariably proof against the temptations of the city streets.
Alexandrine Meley was in her mid-twenties when Zola met her;
never having had, as a child, a normal home life, reaching womanhood in the climate of relaxed moral standards that obtained in the
early Second Empire, possessed of undoubted beauty, she would
have needed exceptional strength of will to have stayed chaste. It
is, of course, idle to speculate how many adventures she had and
with what men: all that can be said is that she remained relatively
honest—she was no Berthe. But the man she settled down with and
eventually married was one who, judging from certain of his early
letters and from *La Confession de Claude*, had spent his own adolescence sustained by obsessive dreams of a virgin bride.

Probably he entered into his union with Alexandrine with his
eyes open; possibly he regretted it a little later; and it is at any rate
conceivable that an unexpected encounter with an earlier lover of
Alexandrine's precipitated the personal crisis which he dramatized
and at the same time sought to resolve in *Madeleine Férat*. There
is a tradition that Zola met his future wife through Paul Cézanne;[1]

[1] John Rewald, the principal authority on the relations between Cézanne and
Zola, asks us to attach a limited credence to this story. 'It is believed that Cézanne

some biographers have gone further and assumed that Cézanne was the lover who relinquished the handsome girl to his friend. But there is really no shred of evidence in support of this hypothesis which seems to be based on a shaky deduction from the supposed autobiographical nature of *Madeleine Férat*. The most that can be said is that the choice of theme may have been prompted by certain half-suppressed pangs of retrospective jealousy in Zola: but of whom, we cannot know for certain.[1]

What is quite certain is that on a more deliberate level the story was written to illustrate a theory about female psychology which Zola found in a book too readily accepted as an authoritative statement of scientific findings. This book, one of the bibles of his youth, was Michelet's *L'Amour*. *Madeleine Férat* was a striking particular instance of the general 'truth' that Michelet had enunciated in these categoric words: 'La femme fécondée une fois, imprégnée, portera partout son mari en elle. Voilà qui est démontré. Combien dure la première imprégnation? Dix ans? vingt ans? toute la vie? Ce qui est sûr, c'est que la veuve a souvent du second mari des enfants semblables au premier.'[2] What Zola asks us to believe is that a woman, having once cohabited with a man, remains tied to him by indissoluble physiological bonds, even though her affection for him has been destroyed, and even though, having been long abandoned by him, she has placed her trust and her hopes of happiness in another man who cherishes her and who has given her a child; that the child will inherit the facial characteristics of the first lover, although begotten by the second; and that the woman, if she meets her first lover again, will be quite incapable of resisting him once he makes a gesture to take her back.

introduced them to each other, but nothing definite is known about it' (*The Ordeal of Paul Cézanne*, p. 33). In his edition of Cézanne's *Correspondance*, in a footnote to a postscript at the bottom of a letter to Zola written from Aix, 30 June 1866, in which Cézanne sends his respects to 'Gabrielle', Rewald observes: 'Le romancier l'aurait connue vers 1862–1864 chez Cézanne.'

[1] As J. C. Lapp points out in *Zola before the Rougon-Macquart* (1964), the theme of the hero's betrayal in love by his closest friend occurs in nearly all these early novels: in *La Confession de Claude* the narrator loses Laurence to Jacques, in *Le Vœu d'une morte* Jeanne, with whom Daniel is in love, marries Georges, and, of course, in *Thérèse Raquin* Camille regards Laurent (who is to kill him and take his wife) as his boon companion.

[2] *L'Amour* (1858), pp. 325–6. On the question of Zola's debt to Michelet, see M. Cressot, 'Zola et Michelet. Essai sur la genèse de deux romans de jeunesse: *La Confession de Claude*, *Madeleine Férat*', *Revue d'Histoire littéraire de la France*, vol. xxxv (1928), pp. 382–9, and Lapp, op. cit., pp. 121–4.

Not all these postulates are absurdly improbable. It is, perhaps, only the second of them that puts any strain on normal powers of belief, if it is understood that the reference throughout is to certain women only, not to the whole sex. Still, they are novel notions. Zola's mistake is that, instead of relegating them to a preface or an appendix, he insists on introducing them into the body of the novel by way of author's commentary. It is as though he were so anxious lest the reader put the wrong construction on his heroine's behaviour and emotions that at every turn he must provide the proper explanation. Madeleine, when she becomes Jacques's mistress, 'ne pouvait comprendre encore les conséquences terribles de ce don. L'avenir lui échappait.' But Zola does not intend that this future should escape us: he maps it all out in advance for our benefit. A spell is being cast over Madeleine during the year she spends with Jacques. 'Elle ne l'aima jamais avec passion; elle reçut plutôt son empreinte, elle se sentit devenir lui, elle comprit qu'il prenait une entière possession de sa chair et de son esprit. Maintenant, il lui était devenu inoubliable.' When Jacques sails away to the East his friend Guillaume, knowing nothing of Madeleine's earlier entanglement, becomes her protector; but when he suggests marriage she recoils at first, instinctively, 'comme si elle ne se fût pas appartenue et qu'elle se fût déjà trouvée en la possession d'un autre homme'. Then Jacques returns, and the crisis is reached as Madeleine feels drawn back to him by an irresistible fascination. Zola devotes (in his ninth chapter) three pages to a careful and detailed explanation of the phenomenon of impregnation, and the circumstances in which it is particularly liable to function. All this elucidation is supplied by Zola; Madeleine herself is quite unaware of the forces that are governing her behaviour. 'Elle ignorait les fatalités de la chair qui lient parfois une vierge à son premier amant, d'une façon si étroite, qu'elle ne saurait ensuite rompre ce mariage de hasard, sous peine de ne plus commettre qu'un long adultère.'

These 'fatalities of the flesh' take the place, in *Madeleine Férat* as in *Thérèse Raquin*, of the more acceptable environmental determinism which, in *Madame Bovary*, allowed Flaubert to show a heroine who is human even though her disastrous career is perhaps, as her husband resignedly remarks at the end, 'la faute de la fatalité'. *Thérèse Raquin* and *Madeleine Férat* are fate tragedies in which the mysterious 'laws of physiology' take the place of the ancestral curse that powers certain dramas of the German Romantics, of the Erinyes that hunt the protagonist of a Greek tragedy, or of Hardy's 'President of the Immortals'. The two novels have many of the incidental characteristics of such works. There is much play, with dramatic irony and the tempting of providence. Guillaume, for instance, when an adolescent, tells his friend Jacques: 'Je n'aimerai jamais qu'une seule femme, et je l'aimerai tant que je défie le sort de troubler nos tendresses.' Mme Raquin is constantly uttering prophetic truths unawares: her daughter-in-law, to conceal her liaison with Laurent, is glacial in her dealings with him in front of others, and Mme Raquin apologizes to the young man on her behalf: 'Je la connais; son visage paraît froid, mais son cœur est chaud de toutes les tendresses et de tous les dévouements.' After the murder, when it is suggested to Mme Raquin that Laurent should marry Thérèse, the appeal she makes to him is charged with unconscious irony: 'Oui, oui, mon ami, épousez-la, rendez-la heureuse, mon fils vous remerciera du fond de sa tombe.'

The two books are filled with coincidences in which the finger of fate is visible. When Laurent starts visiting the Raquins he paints Camille's portrait; but he is as unskilful a draughtsman as he is a colourist, and in the picture 'le visage de Camille ressemblait à la face verdâtre d'un noyé; le dessin grimaçant convulsionnait les traits, rendant ainsi la sinistre ressemblance plus frappante'. A long time afterwards, when Camille has in fact met his death from drowning, this portrait glowers at Laurent and Thérèse from their bedroom wall, and they shrink back, thinking they are looking at their victim's ghost. In the other book the whole plot rests on the sinister chance that the first woman Guillaume meets and falls in love with in Paris is the former mistress of his dearest friend; he and Madeleine become lovers in the same room, in a country inn, where she used to spend nights with Jacques. This is a coincidence not essential to the plot of the book, but it strikes at the outset the note of predestination that is sustained throughout. The coincidence is repeated once again when, in a hotel at Mantes, Madeleine and her husband find themselves in a bedroom which she had shared with Jacques years before; one of the servants remembers her, and she herself discovers the place on the mantelpiece where she can still read the sentence she once traced with an inky finger: 'J'aime Jacques.' The culminating scene of the book exceeds coincidence, trespasses into the realm of the occult, and is explicable only as supernatural chastisement: Madeleine, at the moment when she finally abandons herself to Jacques, hears the clock striking noon; when she returns home she finds her sick child had died at noon.

The 'fatalities of the flesh' deny the characters any chance of making moral choices, or even exerting their will to any noticeable extent. Laurent is not troubled by any pangs of remorse after he has murdered Camille, or rather, 'ses remords étaient purement physiques. Son corps, ses nerfs irrités et sa chair tremblante avaient seuls peur du noyé. Sa conscience n'entrait pour rien dans ses terreurs, il n'avait pas le moindre regret d'avoir tué Camille.' Similarly Madeleine Férat is not faced with any moral conflict when she has to choose between Jacques and Guillaume. For Guillaume she feels strong affection, gratitude, and a kind of maternal compassion; nothing attracts her to Jacques except what Zola calls 'physiological fatalities', and when finally she yields to the invincible physical magnetism of her first lover, it is the animal in her who takes charge. 'Elle obéit à son étreinte comme un cheval qui reconnaît les genoux puissants d'un maître.'

In short, it is scarcely possible to regard *Thérèse Raquin* and *Madeleine Férat* as objective presentations of any recognizable reality. They are, in different ways, stories with a high content of interpolated subjectivism; and their psychology, thickened into 'physiology', derives from doctrines to which one would hardly expect a writer professing adherence to scientific realism to attach belief: Fate, and the all-powerful 'temperament', or the irresistible force of 'impregnation'. The books differ from the 'Gothic novel' of the eighteenth century only in that the supernatural, externalized as ghosts and bugaboos by Horace Walpole and Mrs Radcliffe, is seated by Zola in his characters' nerves, in their blood, in their genital organs.

Zola, in his beginnings, had the humility of those marked out for great achievements. These two novels to which he had devoted such loving care were, he realized, only a trial of his powers; and they were not exempt from errors. He had sent a copy of *Thérèse Raquin* to the critic whose views he most admired at this time, Hippolyte Taine, with the request that he might review it in the *Journal des Débats*. Taine turned a deaf ear, but wrote the young author a long letter full of pertinent and valuable criticism, the burden of which was that Zola ought to aim at social panoramas rather than private dramas:

un livre doit être toujours, plus ou moins, un portrait de l'ensemble, un miroir de la société entière; il faut à droite, à gauche des biographies, des personnages, des indices qui montrent le grand complément; les antithèses de toutes sortes, les compensations, bref l'au-delà de votre sujet. Let his models be Balzac and Shakespeare: 'Vous avez fait une œuvre puissante, pleine d'imagination, de logique, et très morale; il vous reste à en faire une autre qui embrasse plus d'objets et ouvre plus d'horizons.' Taine reverted to the same point in a later letter, this time devoted to *Madeleine Férat*.

Si le roman a pour objet la peinture des mœurs contemporaines, il faut avouer que ces maladies morales, ces cauchemars persistants, ces dominations de l'instinct charnel et de l'idée fixe sont rares. Le trait dominant depuis 1789 est celui qu'a montré Balzac: la volonté qui à force de persévérance et d'intelligence aboutit à une œuvre. Le plébéien fait son chemin, par de bons ou mauvais moyens, parfois en se ruinant le corps et en détraquant ses nerfs, et sans arriver au vrai contentement. N'importe, il agit et produit. A mon sens, l'avenir du roman consiste dans l'histoire de la volonté combattante et victorieuse à travers le pêle-mêle social et les défaillances. Vous avez le sentiment de la vérité, et je crois qu'en jetant les yeux autour de vous comme moi vous reconnaîtrez celle-là.

Much of the essential programme of the *Rougon-Macquart* series, which Zola embarked on as soon as *Madeleine Férat* was published, is implicit in these admonitory lines: the abandonment of domestic histories for sociological studies, the elevation of Balzac to the status of the great master and predecessor, the reinstatement of the human will, especially when exerting itself in the struggle for power, wealth, or fame. Taine's advice to avoid the exceptional case in favour of the typical was less easy to put into practice: it was precisely 'ces maladies morales, ces cauchemars persistants, ces dominations de l'instinct charnel et de l'idée fixe' that stimulated Zola's creative genius because they found their echo in his own neuroses and obsessions.[1]

Taine, himself the materialist and arch-determinist, did not suggest that Zola should broaden his views about the complexity of human motivation, and so Zola saw no reason why he should not

---

[1] The full text of Taine's two letters is given in J. C. Lapp, 'Taine et Zola: autour d'une correspondance', *Revue des Sciences humaines*, fasc. 87 (1957), pp. 319–26.

continue to subscribe to that corollary of materialism, the limitation of behaviour to the bare response to physiological stimuli and inherited disposition. But he was sensitive to the danger of this simplification: the rich arabesques of human life become reduced to the few bare strokes of animal existence; the machinery of the individual being then too rudimentary for self-propulsion, characters have to be driven and guided by external impulse; and the work of art in consequence becomes skeletonized. It was imperative to reintroduce density and elaboration, qualities indispensable to the novel, but at the same time not to sacrifice the concept of the *brute humaine*, the *bête humaine*, which was to be his original contribution to literature. Zola decided that this could be done only by multiplying his characters, by cramming his books with a swarming menagerie of the two-footed animals. There are eight characters named in *Thérèse Raquin*, and about the same number in *Madeleine Férat*; there will be over thirty in *La Fortune des Rougon*, and in this matter Zola went from strength to strength.

Besides this, he would endeavour to provide in his novels that 'miroir de la société entière', that 'peinture des mœurs contemporaines' that Taine had urged on him. There would be an end (for the time being) to private catastrophes and closet dramas; individual tragedies would be representative of vast social movements, the founding and falling of empires, the warring of classes, the march of industry, and the countermarch of religion. This in itself would help to eliminate the subjective virus, for the novelist will rely more on impartial inquiry about public affairs than on personal interpretation of private concerns. And if a particular 'scientific' theory is buried still in the substructure of the work, he must choose it among those which call for no detailed exposition, no dogmatizing.

The way was clear for the *grandes machines* about which Zola talked excitedly to the Goncourts one evening towards the end of the year 1868.

III

BLUEPRINT FOR A LIFE'S WORK

MEETING Zola on his first, triumphal visit to London, Henry James noted the impression he had of the great author 'fairly bristling with the betrayal that nothing whatever had happened to him in life but to write *Les Rougon-Macquart*'. This was just after the famous chronicle had been completed, and five years before Zola took up the fight for truth, justice, and the rehabilitation of Captain Dreyfus, 'the act', to quote James further, 'of a man with arrears of personal history to make up, the act of a spirit for which life, or for which at any rate freedom, had been too much postponed, treating itself at last to a luxury of experience'.[1]

Zola's life-history is, in fact, a very simple one, revolving on the publication of the *Rougon-Macquart* volumes and the publication of his belief in the innocence of Dreyfus. It is not a life that lends itself easily to dramatization; perhaps this is why Zola has received more than his fair share of attention from the writers of *biographies romancées*.

If his first ventures had taught him anything, it was, as we have seen, that the particular kind of fictional art he was gifted for could not be realized unless he broke away from the conventional dimensions of the novel and the conventionally limited character-plot. But however necessary the shift to large-scale work, his courage and confidence in setting aside twenty-five years of his life solely for the execution of a vast, carefully planned undertaking were little less than heroic. There have been other instances of writers devoting a lifetime to a single literary project, but seldom, if ever, has devotion been so single-minded. The *Comédie humaine* was not preconceived by Balzac as a coherent whole. The composition of *Faust* spanned Goethe's long life, but it did not by

---

[1] *The House of Fiction*, p. 224. James made much the same remark in a letter to R. L. Stevenson, written from London during Zola's stay there. See the *Letters*, ed. Lubbock, vol. i, p. 215.

any means totally absorb it. For sheer determination and purposefulness there had been few events in recorded literature to match the twenty-volume series of *Les Rougon-Macquart*, and subsequently there has been perhaps nothing that can be put beside it except *A la recherche du temps perdu*.

To have ventured this gigantic wager, in which the chances against him were time with its accompanying hazards sickness and death, the risk of losing popularity and livelihood, and the possibility of his own discouragement, something more was needed than the conviction that he was better at painting mural frescoes than miniatures. There was that in Zola which made hugeness and comprehensiveness come more naturally than daintiness and selection. He had the collector's instinct and the architect's brain.

Both were symbolized in his house at Médan, purchased with some of the thousands that *L'Assommoir* earned him. Inside, the visitor was bewildered by an indescribable medley of miscellaneous pieces of furniture and *objets d'art*, for Zola was the junkshop dealer's natural victim; contemporary prints of the interior of the house show well this concentration of bric-à-brac. Outside the house the builders were seldom idle, adding and elaborating under Zola's personal direction. Médan was *Les Rougon-Macquart* edited in bricks and mortar and upholstery.

He was himself quite conscious of his encyclopedic instinct; there were occasions when he had to fight it down, having embarked on a study for which the mass of material available threatened to waterlog him. Involved in the preparatory work for *La Débâcle*, he made this revealing complaint: 'J'ai toujours, comme nous disons, les yeux plus grands que le ventre. Quand je m'attaque à un sujet, je voudrais y faire entrer le monde entier. De là, mes tourments, dans ce désir de l'énorme et de la totalité, qui ne se contente jamais.' Details, to his mind, became artistically effective only through accumulation and repetition; the isolated, pregnant, illustrative particular was foreign to his conceptions. He explained this temperamental bias as a search for originality, in a conversation with Edmond de Goncourt when *Les Rougon-Macquart* were in their infancy. Flaubert, he said, had exhausted one vein, 'les analyses des infiniment petits du sentiment'; the Goncourts themselves had pursued to the uttermost 'l'analyse des choses artistiques, plastiques et nerveuses'; he, Zola, would have to be content with what was left and make his mark by 'la quantité des volumes, la puissance de la création'. Under this assumed modesty lurks the pride of one who senses the quality and value of his own genius. For Zola had no false modesty. Jules Vallès recalled how he first met him, in 1864 inside Hachette's bookshop, and how they talked together of the future. At one point Zola looked at him and asked point-blank: 'Sentez-vous que vous êtes une force?' Vallès could not remember what answer he gave, but he did not forget Zola's next words, uttered without emphasis, as if simply stating a fact: 'Moi, je sens que j'en suis une.'[1]

This sense of power meant that he never shied from an undertaking because of its size. This had been so since the beginning. In his rhyming days his bent had been epic, not lyric, and the heroic couplets had been marshalled in their thousands. There is indeed a strange analogy between those ill-starred poems and the mountainous prose of the riper man. In 1860 he confided to Baille his scheme for a poem in three cantos to be called 'La Chaîne des êtres'. The first part would be concerned with the past (from the creation of the world to the creation of man); the second would describe the present (man's history from his creation onwards); and the third would embrace the future—Zola was going to anticipate the higher species that would succeed *homo sapiens* in the unbroken chain of evolution. 'Ainsi donc, au premier chant, savant; au second, philosophe; au troisième, chantre lyrique.' What strikes us in this concept is not its originality (Zola had been reading Chénier as well as Darwin, and the arrangement of 'La Chaîne des êtres' is copied from the plans and fragments that have survived of Chénier's epic 'Hermès'), but the persistence of this threefold development in the grouping of the later novels. The *Rougon-Macquart* series is indeed an evocation of the past, since the Second Empire which was its setting had passed away before even the first volume came out; and in writing it, Zola prided himself in being 'un savant'. *Les Trois Villes*, the trilogy that followed, is set in present time and is concerned with the solution of problems of social philosophy. And finally, the unfinished tetralogy *Les Quatre Évangiles* looks into the future and is lyrically optimistic.

Of course Zola never contemplated, at the outset, a total of twenty-seven volumes in three groups, following time forward from the early nineteenth to the late twentieth century, and following human progress upward from economic servitude to intellectual

[1] Vallès, 'Dickens et Zola', *Le Voltaire*, 11 Feb. 1880.

emancipation. There is not even any evidence that he realized how his life's work does fit into the framework of a poem he dreamed of in youth; sudden death denied him the opportunity of the illuminating backward glance. But the connexion cannot be overlooked now: it points to the presence of a spiritual pattern in the man.

In 1868 and 1869 he envisaged only ten novels;[1] but from the very start they were conceived as pivoting on the fortunes of a single family, which would be representative of 'le vaste soulève-ment démocratique de notre temps; partie du peuple, elle montera aux classes cultivées, aux premiers postes de l'État, à l'infamie comme au talent'. This focus on a family was the saving limitation on the work, its cohesive element too, and its originality.

Familiarity with the 'saga' or *roman-fleuve* of more recent times tends now to obscure the boldness of Zola's design. But the mul-tiple novel, as it had been practised up till then, had confined itself to single lives, men and women ageing, perhaps, but not being re-placed. The co-ordinating element in such novel-clusters was no more than a specific historic setting—the Restoration and the July Monarchy for Balzac's *Comédie humaine*, the seventeenth century for Dumas's 'musketeer' novels, the Revolution and the First Empire for Erckmann-Chatrian's *romans nationaux*. The innova-tion intended in *Les Rougon-Macquart* was to show the successive flowering of three, four, even five interlinked generations, to con-struct vertically down a genealogical line, not simply horizontally over a social superficies. As he promised his publisher, Lacroix, in the general plan he submitted in 1869, he would not only 'étudier tout le second Empire, depuis le coup d'état jusqu'à nos jours', but he would also 'étudier dans une famille les questions de sang et de

---

[1] Those that he had originally projected were:

1. *La Fortune des Rougon*.

2 and 3. *La Curée* which united the subjects of what were originally conceived as two separate novels, viz., 'la vie sotte et élégamment crapuleuse de notre jeunesse dorée', and 'les spéculations véreuses et effrénées du second Empire'.

4. *Son Excellence Eugène Rougon*.

5. *La Faute de l'abbé Mouret*.

6. A war novel, originally intended to be about the Italian campaign of 1859. *La Débâcle* dealt, of course, with the Franco-Prussian War which had not been fought when Zola's first plans were drawn up.

7. *L'Assommoir*.

8. *Nana*.

9. *L'Œuvre*.

10. *La Bête humaine* (but cf. p. 239, below).

milieux'. In the first article he would still be an historian; in the second a student of embryology and physiology.

Balzac's generation and Zola's were only forty years apart, but in the interval a gospel had been proclaimed in the name of science. Sainte-Beuve's celebrated exclamation on first reading *Madame Bovary:* 'Anatomistes, physiologistes, je vous retrouve partout!' had announced the invasion of the novel by scientific values. Balzac's *études* had been the comments on the times of the Catholic monarchist that he was; Zola trusted that for his part he would be inspired merely by the dissector's zeal to analyse and understand. In a kind of *aide-mémoire* called 'Différences entre Balzac et moi' he reminded himself that his work would be 'moins sociale que scientifique', and added: 'Je ne veux pas comme Balzac avoir une décision sur les affaires des hommes, être politique, philosophe, moraliste. Je me contenterai d'être savant, de dire ce qui est en en cherchant les raisons intimes.'

Since any novelist is primarily interested in human beings, the novelist who is also a scientist goes to work in the belief that human behaviour can be reduced to a limited number of fixed laws just like the behaviour of stars or atoms; the research-worker needs only to make enough observations to deduce the laws. This had been the teaching of Hippolyte Taine, with whose works Zola became rapidly familiar:[1]

Que les faits soient physiques ou moraux, il n'importe, ils ont toujours des causes; il y en a pour l'ambition, pour le courage, pour la véracité, comme pour la digestion, pour le mouvement musculaire, pour la chaleur animale. Le vice et la vertu sont des produits comme le vitriol et le sucre,[2] et toute donnée complexe naît par la rencontre d'autres données plus simples dont elle dépend. Cherchons donc les données simples pour les qualités morales, comme on les cherche pour les qualités physiques.

One of the few authorities cited by Taine in his *Introduction à l'histoire de la littérature anglaise,* which contains this famous

[1] 'C'est vers l'âge de vingt-cinq ans que j'ai lu [Taine] et, en le lisant, le théoricien, le positiviste qui est en moi s'est développé. Je puis dire que j'ai utilisé dans mes livres sa théorie sur l'hérédité et sur les milieux et que je l'ai appliquée dans le roman' (Zola, in an interview with Louis Trébor published in *Le Figaro,* 6 Mar. 1893 and quoted by Martineau, *Le Roman scientifique d'Émile Zola,* p. 75.) It was in *L'Événement,* 25 July 1866, in a review of a new edition of the *Essais de critique et d'histoire,* that Zola proclaimed himself Taine's 'humble disciple'.

[2] Zola used this phrase as an epigraph for *Thérèse Raquin.*

determinist text, was Prosper Lucas; and it may have been Taine's footnote that led Zola to consult Lucas's *Traité de l'hérédité naturelle,*[1] unless Michelet's mention of the same work in *L'Amour* had already encouraged him to do this. It is easy today to dismiss Dr Lucas's book as a rash and eminently unscientific raid into regions even now largely unexplored; but Taine's reputation stood high, and Zola may be pardoned his uncritical adoption of Lucas's theorizings in consideration of the weighty recommendation Lucas had received.

It is impossible to say whether a reading of Lucas inspired Zola to choose the laws of heredity as the ones his novels would demonstrate, or whether, having decided that all his main characters would have a common family origin, he thought of using the *Traité de l'hérédité naturelle* to provide the veneer of scientific authenticity. It is the problem of the hen and the egg. But at any rate he acknowledged later that he had been well guided in fixing on heredity as the fabric of his fiction, for it had the advantage of being one of the most fluid of sciences; the tentativeness of the experts' conclusions lessened the risk that the layman would perpetrate absurdities. In *Le Roman expérimental* he defined the function of the naturalist novelist: 'accepter strictement les faits déterminés . . . puis, là seulement, devant l'inconnu, exercer notre intuition et précéder la science, quittes à nous tromper parfois, heureux si nous apportons des documents pour la solution des problèmes.' Thus it will be permitted to the novelist to venture hypotheses about questions of heredity and the influence of social environment on the individual, because such problems have not yet been resolved and docketed by the scientists, and in those confines 'nous préparerons les voies, nous fournirons des faits d'observation, des documents humains qui pourront être très utiles'.

Heredity, besides being a conveniently unsettled branch of knowledge, held out brilliant promise to the artist. In *Thérèse Raquin* and *Madeleine Férat* the subordination of characters to physiological laws had intensified the drama of the action and the relentlessness of the sweep towards catastrophe. The drawback had been that these laws were far-fetched and not popularly acknowledged; and in consequence the novelist had had to instruct his reader in them and drill him into accepting them. That heredity

[1] Full title: *Traité philosophique et physiologique de l'hérédité naturelle dans les états de santé et de maladie du système nerveux,* 2 vols., 1847-50.

in some ways influences individuality is, on the other hand, a truism: 'like father, like son' rates as one of the most commonplace of proverbs. To the artist in Zola, heredity was a substitute for old-fashioned Fate, the Spinner of the Homeric sagas, and a better substitute than the theories of temperament or of impregnation.

Prendre avant tout une tendance philosophique [he noted], non pour l'étaler, mais pour donner une unité[1] à mes livres. La meilleure serait peut-être le matérialisme, je veux dire la croyance en des forces sur lesquelles je n'aurai jamais le besoin de m'expliquer. Le mot force ne compromet pas. Mais il ne faut plus user du mot fatalité qui serait ridicule dans dix volumes.

These preliminary notes,[2] which Zola threw down on paper to clear his head and order his thoughts, and where we see him freed from the anxiety to carry his point which is responsible for much of the *naïveté* of his published theory, are an effective answer to those of his critics who, like Anatole France, mocked him for 'his genealogy of the Rougons [which] is no less fabulous and no more scientific than the genealogy of Huon de Bordeaux or Mélusine'. It is clear that Zola, in his original conceptions at any rate, never entertained the remotest illusion that his work would be 'true' in the sense that the findings of a geneticist observing the offspring of white, grey, and piebald mice are true. The common belief that he laboured under this misconception was fostered by the risky analogy he drew at a much later stage between the scientist's methods of work and the novelist's. But the private 'declaration of intent' made in 1868-9 suggests that Zola considered the reliability of his 'scientific' authority to be of small account; far more important was the fillip that the theorizings of the authority could give to the imagination of the artist. Zola believed in Lucas about as much, perhaps, as Virgil in Venus, and a little less than Shakespeare in ghosts and witches. But having committed himself to the assumption that Lucas knew what he was talking about, Zola kept constantly in mind the need to build consistently on that basis. In literature, truthfulness (or realism) is practically equivalent to

---

[1] Zola first wrote here 'une force', and crossed the word out.

[2] Viz. 'Notes sur la marche générale de l'œuvre', 'Notes générales sur la nature de l'œuvre', and 'Différences entre Balzac et moi'. They are preserved in manuscript in the Bibliothèque Nationale (*Nouvelles acquisitions françaises* 10345, fols. 1-15), and have been published as an appendix to the Bernouard edition of *La Fortune des Rougon*, in H. Massis, *Comment Émile Zola composait ses romans*, and elsewhere.

plausibility or verisimilitude. So, he noted, 'avoir surtout la logique de la déduction. Il est indifférent que le fait générateur soit reconnu comme absolument vrai. . . . Mais lorsque ce fait sera posé, lorsque je l'aurai accepté comme un axiome, en déduire mathématique-ment tout le volume, et être alors d'une absolue vérité.'

The first service Lucas rendered Zola was to stimulate his imagination where it was least active—in the invention of human types. The notes he made on the *Traité de l'hérédité naturelle* and certain other medical books show that the last thing he had in mind to do was to disentangle the main drift of the specialist's argument. He looked on these treatises as repositories of information, collec-tions of strange and suggestive cases of mental and nervous aber-ration; these could be usefully worked into the *Rougon-Macquart* novels, thus dispensing him from creating by his unaided imagina-tion the types of degeneracy he required, or drawing them from his limited field of observation.

In the second place, Lucas's classifications helped Zola to keep tags on his numerous characters. All in all, thirty direct descendants of Adélaïde Fouque, the progenetrix of the Rougon-Macquart family, are mentioned by name and in some degree characterized in the novels. Each had to be distinct and at the same time recog-nizably an offshoot from the same stock. The various categories of 'bequest-types' established by Lucas assisted Zola in this intricate work. Certain individuals inherited the preponderance or totality of the characteristics of either father or mother: Lucas's term for this exclusive resemblance was *election*; or there might be *mixture*, separate elements being inherited from both father and mother, either by *fusion*, *dissemination*, or *soldering* (the details of what was meant are unimportant); or finally there could be *combination*, where elements bequeathed by both parents combined chemically, as it were, to form an apparently new type. It is evident that Lucas did not so much deduce imaginary 'laws' of heredity as classify the results of laws he could not formulate. What determined the parti-cular 'bequest-type' of a child at conception was still wrapped in mystery. The system was, therefore, ideal for Zola's purposes: there could be no argument to prove that it was impossible or inherently unlikely that François Mouret and Marthe Rougon, for instance, should produce three such dissimilar children as Octave, Serge, and Désirée; while by assigning each of them to one of Lucas's categories he guaranteed the plausibility (the 'realism') of this fictitious consanguinity. Octave, if we turn up the family tree, is a case of *élection du père*, Serge of *mélange dissémination*, and Désirée of *élection de la mère*. The choice of 'bequest-type' was left to the artist, while the scientist vouched for the authenticity of his conclusions. The 'scientific veracity' of the *Rougon-Macquart* novels amounts to no more than that; but that was quite enough for the novelist's purposes. The outcome was, as it happened, precisely the reverse of what Zola hoped and expected: his books did not help science appreciably, but science, or what passed as science, acted on the creative artist as a stimulant and rubber-stamped his inventions.

By a further improvement on the earlier novels, the author was content, most of the time, to leave the esoteric jargon in his notes; in the finished product, the characterization of any particular member of the family was done without puzzling technicalities. It is only *Le Docteur Pascal* that is cluttered up by Lucas's undigested hypotheses.

Moreover, Zola did not overstrain the scientific scaffolding by putting all the weight on one plank. Following Taine's formula, he gave quite as much prominence to environment as to race (or heredity). The analysis he offers (in *La Curée*) of the character of Sidonie, the elder daughter of Pierre Rougon, is a clear instance. Her brother Saccard notes that

elle était bien du sang des Rougon. Il reconnut cet appétit de l'argent, ce besoin de l'intrigue qui caractérisait la famille; seulement, chez elle, grâce au milieu dans lequel elle avait vieilli, à ce Paris où elle avait dû chercher le matin son pain noir du soir, le tempérament commun s'était déjeté pour produire cet hermaphrodisme étrange de la femme devenue être neutre, homme d'affaires et entremetteuse à la fois.

The hereditary streak is sometimes of hardly any practical account: environment seems all-powerful. Would Gervaise Macquart have turned into a drunken old harridan without the misery of her life and the example of her husband?—surely the intemperance of her father and mother provided no more than an innate disposition to alcoholism which might just as well not have been there? Would her daughter have turned prostitute without the corrupting influences of the street and especially without the total disorganization of her home? Allowance must, of course, be made for the hereditary freak of exceptional sexual magnetism and the hereditary thirst for enjoyment—but to these Zola attributes far less importance, in *L'Assommoir* and *Nana*, than he does to environmental factors. Alone in the series, *La Bête humaine* introduces a character entirely at the mercy of his poisoned ancestry. In the other novels the influence of the family is not allowed to show itself too nakedly, its very presence remains shadowy. Each novel is primarily concerned, not with one or the other aspect of the legacy of evil in the Rougon-Macquart stock, but with one or other of the worlds which fit together as a panorama of the Second Empire.

It is remarkable, too, how disunited this family is. Its various members, unlike the Forsytes, rarely assemble and hardly ever co-operate. Except for the first novel of the series, which is a kind of prologue played with a full complement of actors before the main action begins, and the last (*Le Docteur Pascal*), most of the novels introduce only one member of the family as hero or heroine. If he or she has relations with another member (Lisa Macquart with her nephew Claude in *Le Ventre de Paris*, Saccard with his brother Eugène in *L'Argent*) the relations are not intimate. Only Félicité, who has merely married into the Rougons, has any sense of family pride or corporate ambition. It is a family without any solidarity, whose particles, in fact, act on each other by repulsion, so that it is quite in the order of things that when two first cousins marry (Marthe Rougon and François Mouret in *La Conquête de Plassans*) the wife should drive her husband mad. Brothers separate, sister turns her back on sister, sons and fathers forget each other or never meet, opulent daughters let their mothers starve to death—to say nothing of the orphans whose recurrence has already been commented on. It is a family of individuals, and Zola studied it in its individuals, seldom as an entity.

This centrifugal effect was precisely what he needed for the impression he wanted to give of the Second Empire, a period of energy recklessly dissipated, of ferocious disregard for human values. The men of the Second Empire were like famished invaders pouring into a besieged city and scattering to pillage it. To quote once more from his preliminary notes:

Mon roman eût été impossible avant 89. Je le base donc sur une vérité du temps: la bousculade des ambitions et des appétits. J'étudie les ambitions et les appétits d'une famille lancée à travers le monde moderne, faisant des efforts surhumains, n'arrivant pas à cause de sa propre nature et des influences, touchant au succès, pour retomber. . . . Le moment est trouble. C'est le trouble du moment que je peins.

The words apply with greater force to the Rougon branch than to the Macquarts; uppermost in Zola's mind when he wrote them were the novels he intended to write first: *La Fortune des Rougon, La Curée, Son Excellence Eugène Rougon*. The Rougons are the *parvenus*, the despoilers, the pack fathered by Pierre in whose face, even when he was a boy, 'on lisait déjà l'ambition sournoise et rusée, le besoin insatiable d'assouvissement, le cœur sec et l'envie haineuse d'un fils de paysan, dont la fortune et les nervosités de sa mère ont fait un bourgeois'. The illegitimate branch of the family is split in the first generation between the son and daughter of Macquart the hard-drinking smuggler. Although Antoine Macquart, the son, shares the spoils with Pierre Rougon after the crushing of the republican insurrection, very few of his descendants benefit from the new régime. They suffer in varying degrees from their vitiated origin, descending as they do from a vagabond tippler and a woman with insanity in her family who is herself insane most of her life. Thus they cannot, on the whole, compete in the struggle for existence; they sink and the waters close over them. It is from among the Macquarts that Zola will pick the uncultured heroes and heroines of his low-life tragedies which are the peaks of the *Rougon-Macquart* range: *L'Assommoir, Germinal, La Terre, La Bête humaine*, and *La Débâcle*. Lastly, there are the Mourets, the younger stem of the Macquart line, descended from Pierre's half-sister Ursule. They too bear within them the germ of madness and debauchery that spells their doom; but by the chance of beginning on a higher social plane they do not sink into the lower depths as do the children and grandchildren of Antoine Macquart. Octave Mouret is, in fact, the most successful in a worldly sense of all the Rougon-Macquart progeny.

This family, the vertebral column of his immense work, was created by Zola all of a piece; before he started, he named each member and placed them all on the family tree,[1] each with a few brief notes showing how the individual temperaments were derived from their parents, grandparents, and from further back still. And round each one there began to crystallize the particular social study in which he was to play the central part. Zola's original hope had

[1] Only five characters (Victor Saccard, Angélique, Jacques and Jacques-Louis Lantier, and Louiset, Nana's son) are not entered on the original family tree printed at the beginning of *Une Page d'amour*; they were included in the second family tree, in *Le Docteur Pascal*.

been to complete his ten novels within five years. But he overjudged his powers, and he could not foresee the initial frustrations, the outbreak of war and the bankruptcy of his first publisher. And further, the scheme widened as he progressed. In the end it took him a quarter of a century to write twenty novels, about 10,000 pages of fine print.

If it is remembered that during these twenty-five years Zola found time, in addition, to keep up regular contributions to several periodicals, to publish three volumes of short stories, to write four plays produced in Paris theatres,[1] and collaborate in the dramatization of several of his novels, his achievement looks even more impressive; and Zola never, at any stage of his work, had resort to the services of an amanuensis, as did Stendhal, Dostoevsky, and other less prolific writers than he. So gigantic an output could have been obtained only by a gross abuse of physical powers—the means by which Balzac kept up his tremendous production—or by unflagging, unbroken application.

The latter was Zola's way. Experience taught him that a regular routine suited his temperament better than fitful, volcanic activity. The maxim which he caused to be inscribed in his study at Médan —nulla dies sine linea—was obeyed almost to the letter: he worked all the year round, at Paris, Médan, and in the various resorts where he spent the summer months when he became rich enough to afford holidays. He would get up every morning at nine o'clock, and by ten he was sitting at his desk. For the next three hours he wrote steadily, covering from three to five sheets of quarto paper in this time.[2] When he was engaged on the early novels of the series, he used sometimes to work in the afternoons too; but this was only so as to fulfil his journalistic commitments, from which he freed himself after 1881. The rest of his day was arranged just as

---

[1] Thérèse Raquin (1873), Les Héritiers Rabourdin (1874), Le Bouton de rose (1878), and Renée, written by Zola 1880–1, but not produced until 1887. See L. A. Carter, Zola and the Theater (1963).

[2] The daily stint seems to have increased towards the end of his working life. 'Il affirmait aujourd'hui', Goncourt wrote in his diary, 6 June 1878, 'qu'il faisait trois pages dans ses bons jours, deux dans ses mauvais.' Three pages was also the figure Zola quoted to De Amicis (Ricordi di Parigi (1879), p. 258). In 1898, however, though the hours of work remained unaltered, output had increased. In the diary Zola kept during the first weeks of his exile in England, one entry reads: 'Aujourd'hui, à dix heures, j'ai commencé à écrire mon roman Fécondité. J'ai travaillé jusqu'à une heure, et j'ai fait mes cinq pages réglementaires' (Pages d'exil, ed. C. A. Burns, Nottingham French Studies, vol. iii (1964), p. 45).

uniformly. A copious lunch and the siesta that followed occupied him until three in the afternoon. Reading the papers and dealing with his correspondence filled the next hour, and from four till half past seven he took exercise. Dinner and after-dinner conversation filled the evening; towards ten o'clock Zola went upstairs to bed, though he often read there till one in the morning.

He was equally methodical in organizing the writing of each novel, and very ready to explain his method—though not always with complete frankness—to anyone interested. Shortly after *L'Assommoir* had made him a public figure he talked to two journalists, one French (Félicien Champsaur) and one Italian (Edmondo de Amicis) whose accounts[1] were substantiated or corrected by later writers.[2] Since 1952 a start has been made on a systematic study of Zola's process of literary composition.[3] The material for this study is exceptionally abundant, for Mme Zola saw to it that not only the original manuscript of each novel was preserved, but also the often bulkier mass of paper constituted by the preliminary drafts and the voluminous 'documentation'.

Zola's first step was always to draft what he called, for *Le Ventre de Paris* and all succeeding novels, the *ébauche*. Zola's *ébauches* are unique documents, the exact equivalent of which exists for no other major writer: they allow us as close a view as we are likely to be granted of a creative imagination at work. Occasionally, before setting pen to paper, he had settled in his own mind broadly how the story would run; but more often he had reached no firmer decision, when he started to write the *ébauche*, than that this or that member of the Rougon-Macquart family would play a principal

---

[1] Champsaur, *Les Hommes d'aujourd'hui*. No. 4. *Émile Zola* (1878); De Amicis, op. cit.

[2] See in particular the chapter 'Méthode de travail' in Alexis, *Émile Zola, notes d'un ami*; Toulouse, *Enquête médico-psychologique . . .*, pp. 268 ff.; Eugène Clisson, 'Un nouveau livre d'Émile Zola', *L'Événement*, 8 Mar. 1889.

[3] The time is perhaps not quite ripe for a synoptic account of Zola's *méthode de travail*, though one has been attempted by Guy Robert in chap. iii of his *Émile Zola: principes et caractères généraux de son œuvre* (1952). It is probable that the 'method' was less rigorously uniform than has been supposed, and investigation must proceed along the lines of patient analysis of the process of composition for each novel taken separately. Here again, Guy Robert has blazed the trail in his study '*La Terre*' *d'Émile Zola: étude historique et critique* (1952). Subsequent monographs of the same type have included N. O. Franzén, *Zola et 'la Joie de vivre'* (1958); R. B. Grant, *Zola's 'Son Excellence Eugène Rougon'* (1961); E. M. Grant, *Zola's 'Germinal'* (1962); and M. Kanes, *Zola's 'La Bête humaine'* (1962).

part in the novel. Hence it is not surprising that the *ébauches* vary considerably in length: that of *La Faute de l'abbé Mouret* consists of fifteen sheets only, that of *L'Assommoir* of sixteen, whereas for *Germinal* he covered just under a hundred and for *L'Argent* just over a hundred sheets. The end in view was, of course, a workable plot; but, reading the *ébauches*, the impression one has is of the invention of character rather than of plot, of the author summoning his dramatis personae from the wings, giving each his cue and his part. That the completed novels emerged with their characteristically solid construction was due to the care Zola took, right from the beginning, to 'trouver un lien entre les personnages', to use a phrase that occurs time after time in the *ébauches* in one form or another. And each character had to typify, embody, or represent some aspect of his theme. Only in certain instances did Zola allow himself the pleasure of introducing characters marginal to the story, characters whom he called 'la fantaisie du livre': Marjolin and Cadine in *Le Ventre de Paris*, Bazouge in *L'Assommoir*, the Charleses in *La Terre*. Normally the characters, being strictly functional, remained strictly under control, subservient to the plot or, more properly, to the *idea*, the dominant theme.

Another significant feature of the *ébauches* is the degree of repetition to be found in them, especially, of course, in the longer ones. At intervals of ten or twenty pages Zola will run over the same scene or situation, the same idiosyncracy attaching to a particular character, the same snatch of dialogue even, often in almost the same words, but occasionally with the addition of some small detail. It was, no doubt, a means of mentally 'developing', in a photographic sense, the scene in question. The whole *ébauche* may have had no other real function: where for another novelist a few hours or days of quiet concentration would suffice, he could do nothing unless his pen was covering the paper, resolving immediately each stroke of the imagination into words. The process was one of fixation: out of a thousand possible combinations, that which he recorded was, by the mere fact of being recorded, authorized; thereafter he had no need to depart from it.

This is not to say that he did not occasionally change his mind in the course of writing the *ébauche* and discard some vicissitude settled on earlier; or else introduce, perhaps at quite a late stage, a change of emphasis which could affect the entire design of the embryonic novel. He might or might not note his reasons for these alterations; usually he gives no explanation, or an inadequate one. He was, after all, writing for no eyes but his own, and for the most part we are reduced to guessing his motives. Changes of this kind were often made after he had proceeded to the later stages of the preparatory work, for he was continually returning to the *ébauche*, rereading it, adding to it, deleting, until the time had come when he judged he was ready to start writing the actual novel.

Drawing up a list of characters was apparently the next task. There was a sheet for each, down to the most episodic, including even, on occasion, animals: the name heads the sheet, then follow particulars of the character's age, state of health, past history and antecedents, moral qualities. Zola took every precaution to ensure that none of his characters should escape from his control and develop in unforeseen directions; these precautions were not always sufficient, of course, since he remained, almost against his will it seems, an imaginative writer.

Once he had a clear picture of the contents and shape of his novel, Zola started collecting the information needed to give verisimilitude to his setting and background. Some of this work was done in his own study: pen in hand he leafed through whatever books occurred to him as being the most reliable factual sources. But he never engaged in the concentrated, exhaustive course of reading that Flaubert set himself to accomplish before writing *Salammbô* or *Bouvard et Pécuchet*; and the notes he took were fragmentary and sometimes misrepresented the contents or argument of the books he read. These researches were supplemented by personal investigations, where possible and desirable, and by private inquiries made of friends who had specialist knowledge (Gabriel Thyébaut, for instance, was always applied to whenever Zola needed to have a point of law explained to him). But to arrive at the facts was not his real concern; he wanted simply not to be 'caught out' distorting the facts. Documentation was, as one commentator has expressed it, *la bonne conscience de Zola*.[1] Turning the pages of a medical treatise or a work of political economy, he scanned it above all to see whether it corroborated the guesses he had hazarded when drawing up the *ébauche*. Of course it did occasionally happen that the information collected at this stage forced him to modify a decision reached earlier, and some slight

---

[1] M. Bernard, 'Émile Zola et son époque', *Cahiers français d'information*, 1 Oct. 1952.

adjustment of plot or character was effected. More frequently, if an inconvenient fact presented itself, Zola set himself to circumvent it or even ignored it completely. He may have pretended, in the 1880's, that documentation was basic to his method of composition; in the mid-1890's, after *Les Rougon-Macquart* had all been published, he admitted that it had been ancillary and that he never allowed any discovery he might make in the course of his researches to interfere with what he conceived to be an artistic necessity of the novel he was working on. In this, he claimed, he was following the example of the greatest artist of all:

> Lorsque Flaubert, après de longs mois d'enragée poursuite avait enfin réuni tous les documents d'une œuvre, il n'avait plus pour eux qu'un grand mépris. J'ai ce mépris complet, les notes ne me sont que des mœllons dont un artiste doit disposer à sa guise, le jour où il bâtit son monument. J'use sans remords de l'erreur volontaire, quand elle s'impose, par une nécessité de construction.[1]

Next, when his documentation had been completed—or at least taken as far as he was prepared to take it—Zola proceeded to establish what he designated as the *plan* of the novel. Referring back to the *ébauche* and the notes on the characters, he decided where he was to introduce each character and how the incidents and situations were to be distributed and graded through the novel. At this point too the contents of each separate chapter were determined; as a general rule, he preferred to divide his books into a few long chapters instead of a great number of short ones, in spite of the fact that the novels were almost invariably serialized in daily papers which could print only a fraction of each chapter in one issue.[2] In the last stage of all, in the *plan définitif*, the haphazard accumulation of details in each chapter underwent a rearrangement

---

[1] 'Les Droits du romancier', *Le Figaro*, 6 June 1896; reprinted in *Nouvelle Campagne*.

[2] Zola—and his friends—were continually deploring this method of instalment publication. 'Si j'osais,' he wrote when *L'Assommoir* was appearing *en feuilleton*, 'je mettrais une annonce ainsi conçue: "Mes amis littéraires sont priés d'attendre le volume pour lire cette œuvre." ' Some form of pre-publication was customary in those days, as much in France as in England, and provided the novelist with an important source of income; and the unsavoury reputation of Zola's writings denied him entry into a periodical review which could print longer instalments. Only *Le Rêve* and *Le Docteur Pascal* were so published; and even so, the management of *La Revue hebdomadaire* received so many complaints from subscribers about the latter novel that they issued their magazine for a while in dual form, sending to the more susceptible of their readers copies in which the offending work was replaced by one less scandalizing.

in accordance with the literary effect aimed at and, where necessary, certain details which were found to be out of place were transferred to other parts of the book. It is likely that this fuller plan was drawn up in respect of each chapter immediately before that particular chapter was written. The *plan définitif* thus reads like a précis of the finished work; but the manuscript version of the novel is much more than a mere expansion of this synopsis. In the heat of actual composition touches were introduced that had not been foreseen; above all, the creative imagination finally took charge and life was breathed into the dry bones of the plan. In the end, despite the extraordinary care with which everything was arranged and calculated, the finished work was much more than an admirable specimen of craftsmanship. The same 'method' in the hands of a lesser artist would never have resulted in *L'Assommoir*, *Germinal*, or *La Terre*: Charles Reade, to take but one example, undertook personal investigations (visiting prisons, for instance, before writing in 1853 *It is never too late to mend*) long before Zola did; in his use of indexed files of newspaper cuttings he seems to have been even more systematic than Zola. But Reade's books are no more than the highly competent products of a technician of the novel who was stirred by a powerful social conscience.

Zola evolved his 'method' less in obedience to a necessity of art than in response to a private need. An inherent distrust of his powers inhibited him from plunging into a new work, as Stendhal appears to have done, with little notion beforehand where it would take him. Zola needed to know where he was going. He set about each novel in much the same way as an artist in oils might start by tracing with a charcoal pencil the outlines of the figures he proposes to paint: the term *ébauche* is, after all, a borrowing from the vocabulary of the painter. Documentation corresponds broadly to the sketches in an artist's notebook, some of which he will use in his pictures, others not. The colours go on in layers; the finishing of details is left to the end. Once more, Zola's affinities with his friends in the studios are clearly apparent. And, as we shall see, the qualities of the works themselves are in some degree pictorial; it is not for nothing that the most penetrating study so far made of *Germinal* starts from a consideration of the colour-symbolism used by Zola in this masterpiece.[1]

[1] M. Girard, 'L'Univers de *Germinal*', *Revue des Sciences humaines*, fasc. 69 (1953), pp. 59–76.

Though it might seem that Zola, with his stage-by-stage approach to the business of writing a novel, aimed to reduce the craft of fiction to an almost mechanical technique, it yet remains obvious that this technique would have availed him nothing had it not been that he possessed, to the degree he did possess them, the gifts of imagination, vision, and a sense of artistic balance and direction, and employed them at all stages of the work. These gifts were not destroyed or even impaired for being harnessed. In other writers, for whom the evolution of a masterpiece is better performed in the mind, or for whom a book grows like a living organism under their pen as they write, it might prove fatal methodically to foresee and overcome in advance each difficulty, as Zola did. This means no more than that the nature of Zola's art was different from theirs. He was able to contemplate the work he was engaged on with greater detachment than Balzac or Flaubert, who were sometimes so deeply immersed in the novel they were writing that they were literally convinced, for the time being, of the reality of their characters and the incidents they were inventing. Zola wrote his novels as an architect builds a cathedral: not stone by stone, but deciding before even the ground is cleared how deep his foundations must be laid, how many buttresses will be needed to shore up the walls and how many pillars should be raised to support the roof, and how high the spire is to rise. When one tries to describe the salient features of the great novels, it is understandable that architectural similes should spring most readily to the mind: solidity of foundation, balance, and symmetry, ascending and descending lines, vistas, patches of light and shadow, and, above all, hugeness of dimension.

IV

POLITICS

WHEN Zola decided that the Second Empire would be the
setting for his novel series, he assumed he would be writing
a contemporary chronicle. But before even the first volume
had appeared the Empire crashed in the thunder of Prussian cannon
and the flames of the Commune, and when the dust from the ruins
had settled he discovered that events had turned him into the
historian of a vanished society.

To preserve the contemporaneity of the series it would have been
sufficient to modify the plan by extending the time-scale into the
early years of the Third Republic. He decided against this largely
on artistic grounds. The crushing finality of the Franco-Prussian
War was a fifth act which history itself seemed to be proposing to
the dramatist. He made it the subject of the last-but-one novel of
the series, but the shouts of soldiers moving off to the front and of
chauvinistic crowds cheering are heard at the end of several of the
others: *Nana*, *La Terre*, *La Bête humaine*. The very pattern that the
train of events provided him with—'a convulsive rise followed by
a sickening collapse' in Martin Turnell's phrase[1]—corresponded
closely with that of the careers of certain types that cried out to be
included: the Financier, the Courtesan, the Politician.

Nevertheless, it would have been more convenient for the
novelist if Prussia had attacked and defeated France in 1880
instead of 1870. As he admitted naïvely to an interviewing journalist: 'Je prévoyais 1870, mais . . . la chute est venue plus tôt que
je ne le supposais. J'avais établi l'âge de mes personnages, et je
comptais, en quelque sorte, développer leur existence au prorata de
la mienne. Mes personnages "se sont cassé le nez" contre 1870. . . .'[2]
Clearly, the mere eighteen years to which he found himself confined seriously cramped the development of five successive generations. Certain careers, that of Nana, for instance, became meteoric

---

[1] *The Art of French Fiction*, p. 114.
[2] F. Xau, *Émile Zola* (1880), p. 51.

to an incredible degree if one is a stickler for chronology: she would have been only eighteen when she died! When he came to write *L'Œuvre*, the hero of which had figured as a seven-year-old boy in *L'Assommoir* and as a youth between sixteen and nineteen in *Le Ventre de Paris*, he decided that he would have to intercalate a couple of years or more in Claude Lantier's life and, moreover, place the later episodes under the Third Republic—though he might hope, by suppressing all mention of dates, that the fact would not be noticed. His decision to 'cheat' is recorded in the preliminary notes for *L'Œuvre*: 'Si mon roman commence tout de suite après [*le Ventre de Paris*], en 1862, il a donc 20 ans. — Mais il me faudra tricher, je lui donnerai de 22 à 24; et cette fois, je suis décidé à dépasser 1871, à mener Claude jusqu'à 35 ans au moins, sans préciser les dates. . . .'[1]

More serious is the objection that *Les Rougon-Macquart*, written under the Third Republic and dealing with the Second Empire, are of necessity products of the archivist's researches and not, as true works of realism should be, the results of direct personal observation. As Jules Lemaître commented happily, on the appearance of one of the later novels of the series: 'M. Zola is bringing back to life the men of bygone ages. He is very nearly writing historical novels—just like Walter Scott, shame on him!'[2]

The historical aspect of *Les Rougon-Macquart* is not at all, of course, that of the *Waverley Novels*, which mostly deal with a past already well buried and mummified when the books were written. Zola's history was recent history, the past time of his series overlapped the present time of his readers, the events to which he alluded and which on occasion he related had been 'current events' within living memory. Mallarmé, in a letter to Zola, put the point well, and singled out what was essentially new in Zola's handling of the historical novel. He was commenting on *Son Excellence Eugène Rougon* which, he said, marked the point where the novel borders on history, superimposes itself on history completely and stakes out for itself all the anecdotal side, the passing and the chance event; the historian of the future will simply have to sum up a few conflicts of ideas, etc., while the portentous little fellows who fancied themselves to be

---

[1] B.N. MS. *Nouv. acq. fr.* 10316, fol. 219.

[2] Lemaître, *Les Contemporains*, 4ᵉ série (1890), p. 272. Georges Pellissier made the same objection to *L'Argent* when it appeared: 'Ce que fait actuellement M. Zola, c'est, à proprement parler, de l'archéologie . . .': *Essais de littérature contemporaine* (1893), pp. 201–2.

something bigger than mascots of policies all at once find themselves the prey of the novelist. What a sudden and unexpected acquisition for literature, which the English call Fiction!

With the exception of *La Faute de l'abbé Mouret*, all the *Rougon-Macquart* novels of Zola's early period (up to the writing of *L'Assommoir*) incorporate to some extent the 'anecdotal side, the passing and the chance event' of the national scene between 1851 and 1871. They would be better described as political than historical novels since, to all except the youngest members of the French public during the years in which they were published, the revolutions, wars, bomb-throwings, and financial scandals that Zola recalled still appeared primarily in a political light. And among these early novels two—the first (*La Fortune des Rougon*) and the sixth (*Son Excellence Eugène Rougon*)—are almost exclusively political; the latter, indeed, bore the sub-title (when published in instalments in *Le Siècle*): *Scènes de la vie politique*.

A writer of political novels incurs certain well-known risks. Being too near events to see them in their proper proportions, he is liable to distort their appearance. Also—this is graver—he will find it hard to avoid being swayed by notions of the equity of one social-political process and the iniquity of another. But if he allows this to happen, the detachment necessary for objectivity will be imperilled, and with it realism—in the sense in which realism was understood in the nineteenth century. Not only this, but he will limit the universality of his appeal by alienating the sympathies of that section of his readers which backs whatever policy he condemns. 'La politique', observed Stendhal in a celebrated aside in *Le Rouge et le Noir*, 'est une pierre attachée au cou de la littérature, et qui, en moins de six mois, la submerge.... Cette politique va offenser mortellement une moitié des lecteurs, et ennuyer l'autre qui l'a trouvée bien autrement spéciale et énergique dans le journal du matin.' The aesthetic doctrine of impartiality, which Flaubert and the 'art for art's sake' movement had consecrated, and to which Zola at least honestly aspired in his first period, yields, in this sense, art for the many, not art for the few.

The *tour de force* of writing, under the Empire, a novel relating without partisanship the historical events leading to its foundation had been achieved by Flaubert in his *Éducation sentimentale*, just before Zola started his series. Zola wrote of it, in *Les Romanciers naturalistes*, as 'le seul roman vraiment historique que je connaisse, le seul, véridique, exact, complet, où la résurrection des heures mortes soit absolue'. Flaubert's drastic recipe for impartiality had been to cover republicans and conservatives alike with obloquy: the first are shown as brawling demagogues, the second as vindictive egoists, and both as addicted to the vice Flaubert endured least calmly—stupidity. The result is a dispiriting picture of wasted effort, so that on the political as well as on the personal plane the impression is of machinery threshing furiously in a void and seizing up with the heat of its own friction. This was the picture Flaubert desired to give, his artist's vision of modern life; it was poles apart from Zola's.

Nothing, perhaps, separated the two friends more than the attitude of each to the present and the degree of hope with which each looked into the future. 'Quand j'affirmais mes croyances au vingtième siècle,' wrote Zola after Flaubert's death, 'quand je disais que notre vaste mouvement scientifique et social devait aboutir à un épanouissement de l'humanité, il me regardait fixement de ses gros yeux bleus, puis haussait les épaules.' Flaubert's works, from *Madame Bovary* to *Bouvard et Pécuchet*, are all dominated by a note, growing more strident with the years, of savage contempt for the bourgeois ideology of his day; a contempt which is desperately nihilistic, for Flaubert's aristocratic fastidiousness shrank from the egalitarian society which Zola saw was the only practical substitute. It has been said that Flaubert painted 'a society in the unmaking'.[1] *Les Rougon-Macquart* show a society not indeed 'in the making', but a society 'going to pieces'; the pieces remain, and out of them can be rebuilt a better world.

The 'Notes sur la marche générale de l'œuvre' make it clear that Zola intended, from the very beginning, to sweeten his work with a limited dose of social optimism.

Il faut *absolument* remarquer ceci: je ne nie pas la grandeur de l'effort de l'élan moderne, je ne nie pas que nous puissions aller plus ou moins à la liberté, à la justice. Seulement ma croyance est que les hommes seront toujours des hommes, des animaux bons ou mauvais selon les circon-stances. Si mes personnages n'arrivent pas au bien, c'est que nous débutons dans la *perfectibilité*. Les hommes modernes sont d'autant plus faillibles qu'ils sont plus nerveux et plus impatients. C'est pour cela qu'ils sont plus curieux à étudier.

[1] 'Une société qui se défait': Albert Thibaudet, *Gustave Flaubert* (1922), p. 120.

Zola had a further aim, from which in later years he fell increasingly away. Although the artist might allow himself to be guided by certain beliefs about general tendencies, these beliefs ought not to be caught up into a tight net of religious or political dogmas. He may show humanity marching towards the light, but he may not say: 'This path is the right one, this and this other lead back to darkness.' As he wrote further on in the 'Notes':

Il est bien entendu que je mets à part la discussion de l'état politique, de la meilleure façon de gouverner les hommes religieusement et politiquement. Je ne veux pas établir ou défendre une politique ou une religion. Mon étude est un simple coin d'analyse du monde tel qu'il est. Je constate purement. C'est une étude de l'homme placé dans un milieu social, sans sermon. Si mon roman doit avoir un résultat, il aura celui-ci : dire la *vérité humaine*, démonter notre machine, en montrer les secrets ressorts par l'hérédité, et faire voir le jeu des milieux. Libre ensuite aux législateurs et aux moralistes de prendre mon œuvre, d'en tirer les conséquences et de songer à panser les plaies que je montrerai.

This was the first synthesis Zola constructed to reconcile the two trends of his nature: the artistic and the reforming. The artist foresaw shipwreck unless he steered a straight course through the cross-currents of rival political programmes; the reformer in him pleaded that if he failed to throw all his gifts, and his artistic talent in the first place, into the struggle to establish freedom and justice, he would be guilty of betrayal. Hence the compromise by which the artist would point out where the social shoe pinched, leaving it to the professional politician to do the cobbling. It was an uneasy and a short-lived compromise. In time the reformer in Zola was bound to see that the 'legislator' was shirking his duty, or rather conceived his duty as being to safeguard the interests of the class he represented, not to give practical shape to the ideals of humanitarians like Zola. When this happened the situation had to be reviewed.

At the stage we have reached, however, the division between art and political life is fairly clear. Zola, in the first half-dozen novels of his series, is the sympathetic historian of the lost cause of republicanism and the censorious annalist of the triumphant autocratic régime. But any semblance of crusading is absent from the books. He hoped he was an observer merely, an honest witness submitting testimony for a judicial inquiry which might one day be held.

As far as his private opinions were concerned, Zola was a man of fairly advanced political principles without, at this period, any set convictions. He could probably be best described as a reforming radical. It is said that back in the days when he was Hachette's employee, his chief returned him his short story 'Sœur des pauvres' as unsuitable for publication in the children's magazine for which it had been commissioned. 'Vous êtes un révolté, M. Zola', said the publisher with a frown. To have smelt subversion in this thin tale is proof certainly of a very delicate nose—more delicate, in fact, than that of the police: for when the authorities were considering whether *La Confession de Claude* did not render its author liable to prosecution for indecency, the report on his 'political reliability' was quite reassuring. 'Il n'a pas d'opinion politique tranchée' wrote the Public Prosecutor, 'et son ambition paraît avant tout littéraire.'[1] Be that as it may, almost as soon as he became conscious of political issues, Zola had shown himself an 'anti-establishment man'. In the early sixties he was a sympathizer with the small left-wing groups who were debarred from expressing their hostility to the authoritarian régime of the day except through the medium of semiclandestine sheets whose existence was perpetually at the mercy of a court order prohibiting further publication.[2] The last and longest piece in the *Contes à Ninon* is, in part, a Voltairian satire of quite outstanding boldness, considering when it was written, in which the foreign and domestic policy of Napoleon III is subjected to witty and damaging criticism.[3] When the Emperor published his *Histoire de Jules César*, Zola composed a review-article which none of the newspaper editors whom he approached dared to print; he inserted it instead in his miscellany, *Mes haines*.[4]

At the same time he was not—nor would he ever be—a 'party man'. However strongly he sympathized with the political aims of the opponents of the imperial régime, he was never prepared to tolerate the propagation of these aims in works which purported to be literary. A novel published by André Léo (under the pseudonym Mme Champseix) in 1866 was spoiled for him by 'une sorte de

---

[1] See above, p. 24.

[2] The *Revue du progrès*, suppressed in 1862, and *Travail*, a fouriérist organ. Zola had contacts with the editorial staff of both these papers; see M. Girard, 'Positions politiques d'Émile Zola jusqu'à l'affaire Dreyfus', *Revue française de science politique*, vol. v (1955), p. 507.

[3] I have examined in some detail this aspect of 'Les Aventures du grand Sidoine et du petit Médéric' in 'Les Sources d'inspiration de Zola conteur', *Les Cahiers naturalistes*, nos. 24–25 (1963), pp. 41–43.

[4] See Zola's letter of 17 July 1865 to Géry-Legrand, editor of the *Journal populaire de Lille*; and his recollections of the affair in *La Cloche*, 4 Sept. 1872.

tendance humanitaire à faire des sermons politiques, à propos des passions et des sentiments de ses personnages'; in reviewing the book, he expressed the fear that 'les libéraux qui ont lancé l'auteur, n'aient pas vu l'artiste en lui, mais simplement le penseur dévoué à la cause d'un certain parti . . .'. The line between art and political propaganda cannot be too firmly drawn. 'Je ne suis pas un disciple de l'art pour l'art', Zola continues. 'Seulement, j'aime bien qu'un roman soit un roman. . . . Rien ne me paraît encombrer un drame comme une pelletée de politique ou de science sociale jetée au beau milieu de l'action.'[1] This position is close to—if not identical with—Stendhal's in the famous passage where he likens the intrusion of politics in a novel to letting off a pistol in a concert hall; and it does not imply that Zola, any more than Stendhal, was tepid or timorous in his views. But such remarks did not endear him to the politicians of the left, and Zola needed all his credit with an old friend, the art-critic Théodore Duret, to get himself on to the staff of *La Tribune*, a socialist paper in which he was to make his name as a fearless and provocative political journalist.[2]

La Tribune was one of several opposition papers founded to take advantage of a liberalizing measure passed on 11 May 1868 which repealed or relaxed the earlier draconian press laws. In joining the staff of this paper Zola had chiefly in mind the need to increase his earnings; he may have felt a little out of place in a team in which, as he would later say, only he and the office-boy were not proposing to stand for parliament at the next elections.[3] But if one reads the articles Zola wrote for *La Tribune* and for a paper of similar political complexion, *La Cloche*, during the last two years of the Second Empire,[4] one can hardly mistake the note of authentic indignation with which he denounces the crimes of the 'hommes du Deux Décembre' and the continuing oppressiveness of an unpopular régime. An entry the Goncourts made in their diary on 13 December 1868 has prompted doubts about the good faith with which these pieces were composed: Zola is on record as bewailing the 'articles

[1] *L'Événement*, 9 Apr. 1866.

[2] See his letters to Duret, 19 June and 19 July 1868.

[3] Zola intended to depict this circle in *L'Argent*, as his preliminary notes for this novel show: 'Voir si je ne pourrais pas prendre *la Tribune* où tous étaient candidats, sauf le garçon de bureau et moi' (B.N. MS. *Nouv. acq. fr.* 10268, fol. 417).

[4] A representative selection has been published by Martin Kanes, *L'Atelier de Zola, textes de journaux 1865–1870* (1963). See also, by the same author, 'Zola, Pelletan, and *La Tribune*', *P.M.L.A.*, vol. lxxix (1964), pp. 473–83.

infâmes, ignobles . . . que je suis obligé de faire à *la Tribune*, au milieu de gens dont il me faut prendre l'opinion idiote'. But it is important to remember that this was the first occasion Zola had met the brothers; he sincerely admired their work, he knew they were staunch conservatives, and he wanted to make a good impression; hence the apologetic tone he felt obliged to adopt in talking to them.

There is, in fact, a close relationship between the themes Zola treated in newspaper articles just before the collapse of the Empire and those he introduced into *La Fortune des Rougon* and *La Curée*, of which the first was written, and the second partly written, while Napoleon III was still on the throne. The very word chosen for the title *La Curée* is one the journalist was as fond of applying to this historical period as the novelist:

Si jamais siècle demande un Juvénal, c'est, à coup sûr, notre siècle, non qu'il soit plus mauvais que les autres, mais parce que la rapidité des fortunes y a singulièrement développé les appétits. Depuis une vingtaine d'années, nous assistons à la plus féroce curée qu'on puisse voir.[1]

Ah! quelle curée que le Second Empire! Dès le lendemain du coup d'état . . . ils ont mis les mains aux plats, en plein dans la sauce, mangeant goulûment, s'arrachant les morceaux de la bouche. Ils se sont rués à la satisfaction de leurs appétits, avec un emportement de bête, et lorsqu'ils ont été gorgés, ils ont mangé encore. Ils mangent toujours. . . .[2]

The word signifies, strictly, the portion of an animal given to the hunting pack after the head and hide have been removed. Zola introduced, at the conclusion of the seventh chapter of *Son Excellence Eugène Rougon*, a piece of fairly obvious symbolism in showing, after a hunt at Compiègne, the entrails of a stag being thrown to the hounds in full view of the court.

Les chiens se ruèrent, se vautrèrent, sur les débris; leurs abois furieux s'apaisaient dans un grognement sourd, un tremblement convulsif de jouissance. Des os craquaient. Alors, sur le balcon, aux fenêtres, ce fut une satisfaction; les dames avaient des sourires aigus, en serrant leurs dents blanches; les hommes soufflaient, les yeux vifs, les doigts occupés à tordre quelque cure-dents apporté de la salle à manger. . . . Et, en bas, les chiens achevaient leurs os. Ils se coulaient furieusement les uns sous les autres, pour arriver au milieu du tas. C'était une nappe d'échines mouvantes, les blanches, les noires, se poussant, s'allongeant, s'étalant comme une mare vivante, dans un ronflement vorace. Les mâchoires se hâtaient, mangeaient vite, avec la fièvre de tout manger.

[1] *Le Gaulois*, 19 July 1869.   [2] *La Cloche*, 13 Feb. 1870.

Zola may well have remembered the poem written by Auguste Barbier with the same title (*La Curée*) after an earlier seizure of power, in 1830. This polemical piece ends with a similar allegorical picture: France (or perhaps the fallen monarchy) is represented by a dying boar, and those that profited by the revolution are the hounds, 'chiens courants et limiers, et dogues, et molosses', who tear the carcase of the noble beast to pieces.

In the very centre of his vision of the Second Empire was this image of ravening beasts, this eighteen-year-long orgy. The economic historian may talk of the great material prosperity of the era, of booming trade, rising incomes, the steady accumulation of capital wealth. Zola saw it all as a vast champing of tireless jaws, a stuffing of infinitely capacious bellies, a disgusting and mannerless blow-out. The first three novels of the cycle in particular may be thought of as constituting an enormous prose gloss on certain violent satires in Hugo's *Châtiments*: 'Joyeuse Vie, On loge à la nuit', or the 'Chanson' that begins:

> Courtisans! attablés dans la splendide orgie,
> La bouche par le rire et la soif élargie. . . .

La Fortune des Rougon tells how the founders of the family, living in the provinces, lined their pockets at the cost of a little bloodshed in 1851; *La Curée* how their greedy son came to Paris and, a few years later, grabbed his million by taking advantage of a wave of frenzied speculation on properties due for demolition; while *Le Ventre de Paris*, set in the hey-day of the Empire, shows an entire population of satisfied tradespeople waxing fatter and fatter on an inexhaustible supply of carbohydrates, as cooped and mindless as battery-hens.

It is well known that the Second Empire was founded by a small and energetic group profiting from the dissensions and inaction of the monarchist reactionaries, the republican socialists having raised too many enemies against themselves to hope for survival. For his first novel Zola transported the decisive events that took place in Paris to the conveniently more compact theatre of Plassans, which is the Aix-en-Provence of his boyhood. Plassans is a town in which the conservative elements outnumber the radical ones; but the conservatives are divided into two self-contained, mutually suspicious groups, the nobility ('dead men finding life tedious', as Zola sums them up) and the middle classes, secretly smarting under the disdain in which the gentlefolk hold them. It is the Rougons' diplomatic triumph, related in *La Fortune des Rougon* and its sequel *La Conquête de Plassans*, to persuade the aristocrats and bourgeois to unite and crush the enemies of both, the working people.

It is an unsavoury story, and Zola's design is obvious: he wishes to show the inglorious origins of imperial rule. He does this both by exposing the pettiness, cruelty, and cowardice of the champions of Bonapartism, and by throwing a halo of martyrdom round the heads of the militant republicans doomed to extinction. The Rougons he describes as 'une famille de bandits à l'affût, prêts à détrousser les événements'. Pierre Rougon and his wife Félicité have had their appetites sharpened by years of frustrated ambition; what they hope to fish out of these troubled waters are a lucrative post under the government for him, and the awed respect of their fellow townsmen for both of them. They 'jump the band-wagon' on the advice of their elder son Eugène, who is secretly working in Paris for the coming seizure of power.

The insurrectionary danger that threatens Plassans is largely a manufactured scare, a red terror arranged between Pierre Rougon and Antoine Macquart to afford a pretext for the white terror that follows. Macquart is a beer-parlour orator who, out of a grudge he bears his half-brother, breathes fire and slaughter against all men of property and passes as the most bloodthirsty of republicans. Zola is half apologetic for blurring thus the clear division between sheep and goats. 'Chaque parti a ses grotesques et ses infâmes. Antoine Macquart, rongé d'envie et de haine, rêvant des vengeances contre la société entière, accueillit la république comme une ère bienheureuse où il lui serait permis d'emplir ses poches dans la caisse du voisin, et même d'étrangler le voisin, s'il témoignait le moindre mécontentement.'

The true spirit of the Republic, valiant but pathetically defence-less, is represented by the pair of lovers, Miette Chantegreil and Silvère Mouret. Miette, who in the first chapter takes the red flag and places herself at the head of the insurgents, is, as the author himself declares, 'la vierge Liberté'. When a bullet goes through her heart in the hour of defeat, this death epitomizes the political crime that has been committed: it is symbolic of the butchery of the first and greatest of the ideals of the French Revolution.

Silvère is a more realistically observed character. His uncle

Pascal Rougon, learned in the mysteries of heredity, can discern in his 'sublime madness' a sub-form of the nervous hysteria of the boy's grandmother Adélaïde Fouque. He is the type of half-taught socialist who believes blindly in the golden age that the revolution will usher in. 'Ce fut un naïf, un naïf sublime, resté sur le seuil du temple, à genoux devant des cierges qu'il prenait de loin pour des étoiles.' An odd volume of Rousseau is enough to turn his head; he had hailed the proclamation of the Republic with beatitude, but his mood changes to ferocity as soon as the counter-revolution sets in. Yet when he draws the blood of an enemy of the people (accidentally knocking out a gendarme's eye) he is horror-stricken and rushes back to his grandmother's house. Silvère is a type common enough during the '48 rising and later: for Le Ventre de Paris Zola merely remodelled his creation, giving Pierre Florent a little more education but the same half-gentle, half-violent visionary fervour, evaporating at the first thought of bloodshed.

Zola might justifiably claim, in this the maiden novel of the series, to have avoided the aesthetic fault of advocating a specific course of political action, and to be offering nothing more than 'un simple coin d'analyse du monde tel qu'il est'. His sympathies are with the republicans—there can be no question of that; but (save for Miette, a symbolic figure) he paints them as human, subject to fatigue, discouragement, and error. His dislike of the conservatives is equally apparent: they are treacherous, egoistic, and comically faint-hearted; but they are not monsters, even though in the eyes of the scientist Pascal they are nearer the animal state than the human. On the whole, La Fortune des Rougon reads as a satire of man's folly in ever hoping to establish, by violent political action, the ideal society. Save for the heroic but misled exceptions, men are too self-seeking to be effective agents of their own communal betterment.

The first book of the series is not one of the greatest, and certainly not one of the easiest to read. It is perplexing chiefly, it seems, because of the curious juxtaposition of two entirely different time-scales. The actual events narrated cover no more than a week. But this brief space of time is set against the background of a long stretch of history. Zola begins by relating in detail and at length how the woodcutters' yard (used by his two pathetic young lovers as a trysting-place) had, thirty years previously, been a cemetery, though for an even longer space of time no one had been buried there, and it had become a jungle. In his second chapter he gives us the life-story of Adélaïde Fouque, which takes us back into the eighteenth century (she was born a year before Napoleon I, in 1768). One of the difficulties Zola did not succeed in solving in *La Fortune des Rougon* was how to digest into the work the huge amount of preparatory matter necessary for the understanding of the remaining nineteen novels of the series. A whole regiment of actors, members of the family in the first three generations, are introduced, their biographies sketched out, and their characters summed up, but they are given, in most cases, no significant part to play.[1] These interpolations cause the action to grind down to an absolute standstill in the second, third, and fourth chapters (there are seven in all). In the fifth chapter the action has barely started up again when Zola introduces a new and lengthy digression—the idyll of the loves of Miette and Silvère, a charming episode which one can understand appealed vastly to Turgenev,[2] but which, since it is a 'flash-back', can with difficulty be justified in the economy of the book.

La Fortune des Rougon was written in the summer of 1869. *Le Siècle* agreed to publish it, but was in no hurry to begin, and there was near on a year's delay before serialization was started. Zola had begun work on *La Curée* when war broke out, and the Empire whose bloody origins he had narrated dissolved abruptly in the smoke of battle. A new republic came into being.

The outbreak of hostilities did not affect Zola as deeply as it might have: as the only son of a widow he was exempted from military service. But his career as a writer suffered a hiatus. At the beginning of September 1870 he took his wife (he had got married on 31 May that year) and his mother as far away from the fighting as he could, down to Marseilles. His principal worry was how to

---

[1] Curiously, the cast of characters is smaller in the first edition of the novel than in the edition published by Charpentier in 1872. In revising his book Zola made mention of a number of members of the Rougon-Macquart family whom he intended to introduce into novels not foreseen in the original, eight- or ten-part series. Thus, in the first edition of *La Fortune des Rougon* Antoine Macquart and Fine have only two children, Gervaise and Jean; in the later editions we encounter a third, Lisa, who was destined, of course, to figure largely in *Le Ventre de Paris*. Only one child (a son) is spoken of in the first edition as having been born to François and Marthe Mouret; this number was increased to three (Octave, Serge, and Désirée).

[2] Turgenev invited the author to read the *puits mitoyen* passage at one of Mme Viardot's *soirées*. Zola recalled the occasion years later in a letter to Élie Halpérine-Kaminsky (see *Correspondance*, p. 789).

make ends meet, the revenue from his journalism having dried up: *La Cloche*, on the staff of which he was serving, had suspended publication on 18 August. In order that they might 'occupy their time usefully' as he put it, but also, no doubt, in order that he might turn an honest penny, he suggested to his old friend Marius Roux that between them they should found a new daily to be called *La Marseillaise*. It had a brief existence before being taken over by an older paper.[1] Even before it ceased to appear Zola realized he must try another tack: he undertook the cross-country journey, slow and difficult in time of war, from Marseilles to Bordeaux where the provincial government had its seat, arriving there on 12 December. His letters to his wife and mother who had remained in Marseilles give a good impression of his worried state of mind.[2] Lodgings were hard to come by, the weather was bad, he did not like Bordeaux, and he was bored, having nothing to do. Also, there was the perpetual anxiety whether the two women he had left behind would manage on the money they had until he secured a salaried post. His hope was that the contacts with republican politicians he had made formerly in the offices of *La Tribune* and *La Cloche* would help him to the sub-prefecture of Aix-en-Provence: to return to this city as chief administrative officer would surely lay his father's ghost. Instead, Roux wrote to him that his ill-wishers at Aix had been circulating the story that he was being sought by the police for evading military service. The post was, in any case, not in the gift of his patrons; and Zola loathed soliciting favours. 'Quel triste métier je fais, en tendant la main à la République! Attendez donc que ces gens-là soient balayés, et moi je me retrouverai debout.' But the necessitous cannot afford to be nice. He accepted, with relief, the offer made by a venerable but uninfluential ministerial figure, Glais-Bizoin, to engage him as private secretary. His employer pulled what strings he could to have him nominated at Bayonne—without success. His candidature for the sub-prefecture of Castel-Sarrasin (Tarn-et-Garonne) was equally unlucky: the holder of the post, an obscure Parnassian poet called Delthil, reacted energetically to the intimation of his displacement,

---

[1] H. Mitterand (*Zola journaliste*) thinks it lasted from 27 Sept. to 16 Dec. 1870. In spite of extensive research no copy of any issue of *La Marseillaise* has ever come to light.

[2] They have been published by H. Mitterand, 'Émile Zola à Marseille et à Bordeaux de septembre à décembre 1870', *Revue des Sciences humaines*, fasc. 98–99 (1960), pp. 257–87.

came to Bordeaux, pleaded his case, and kept his job.[1] However, on 19 February 1871 Zola was able to resume journalism, with a series of reports for *La Cloche* on the activities of the Constituent Assembly; when the Chamber moved to Versailles, he returned to Paris, continuing to act as parliamentary correspondent until 3 August 1872.[2]

At Versailles one day he was pointed out to another newspaper-man, Ernest Alfred Vizetelly, later to be the principal translator of his works into English.

It was an artist of *L'Illustration* who first called my attention to Zola, saying derisively: 'You know!—the man who believes in Manet.' I looked, and the impression that I have retained is one of a pale, shabby, silent, and observant individual, with a curiously misshapen nose,[3] by which on sundry subsequent occasions I recognized him. There, at Versailles, he was always very quiet and unobtrusive, speaking little and learning a great deal, with the air of one who found the political turmoil of the time rather hard to understand.[4]

Zola's unassuming and attentive demeanour misled Vizetelly: he understood only too clearly the struggle for power, position, and the crude rewards of office, which the parliamentary manœuvres he was reporting disguised but thinly. The insight gained in these eighteen months served him in excellent stead when he came to write, some three years later, *Son Excellence Eugène Rougon*.

The book is, however, less a study of political life than of one outstandingly powerful political figure. The guiding intention was, as Zola wrote at the beginning of the *ébauche*: 'étudier l'ambition dans un homme, l'amour du pouvoir pour le pouvoir lui-même, pour la domination.' In the text of the novel he characterized Rougon as having

un amour du pouvoir pour le pouvoir, dégagé des appétits de vanité, de richesses, d'honneurs. D'une ignorance crasse, d'une grande médiocrité dans toutes les choses étrangères au maniement des hommes, il ne

---

[1] Glais-Bizoin's letter to the Préfet of Bordeaux, desiring him to appoint Zola at Bayonne, has been preserved (B.N. MS. *Nouv. acq. fr.* 24519). On the other episode, see L. Deffoux, 'Émile Zola et la sous-préfecture de Castelsarrasin en 1871', *Mercure de France*, vol. cxci (1926), pp. 336–46.

[2] This long series of articles ('Lettres de Bordeaux' and 'Lettres de Versailles'), has been republished by J. Kayser, under the general title *La République en marche* (2 vols., 1956).

[3] This was the famous 'nez bifide' seized on by most contemporary caricaturists.

[4] E. A. Vizetelly, 'Some recollections of Émile Zola', *Pall Mall Magazine*, vol. xxix (1903), p. 63.

devenait vraiment supérieur que par ses besoins de domination. Là, il aimait son effort, il idolâtrait son intelligence. Etre au-dessus de la foule où il ne voyait que des imbéciles et des coquins, mener le monde à coups de trique, cela développait dans l'épaisseur de sa chair un esprit adroit, d'une extraordinaire énergie. Il ne croyait qu'en lui, avait des convictions comme on a des arguments, subordonnait tout à l'élargissement continu de sa personnalité. Sans vice aucun, il faisait en secret des orgies de toute-puissance.

Zola was at one and the same time fascinated and repelled by his creation. He gave him that pharisaic 'hatred of literature' which he feared was the distinguishing mark of the administrator.[1] There is a bitterly satirical account of a stormy interview between Rougon during one of his spells of power and a newspaper editor who is publishing a realist novel in instalments.

> Votre feuilleton est odieux. . . . Cette femme bien élevée qui trompe son mari, est un argument détestable contre la bonne éducation. On ne doit pas laisser dire qu'une femme comme il faut puisse commettre une faute. . . . Cette malheureuse a-t-elle des remords à la fin ?
> Le directeur porta la main à son front, ahuri, cherchant à se souvenir.
> — Des remords ? non, je ne crois pas.
> Rougon avait ouvert la porte. Il la referma sur lui, en criant:
> — Il faut absolument qu'elle ait des remords! . . . Exigez de l'auteur qu'il lui donne des remords!

Rougon is responsible for the most sinister crimes. His return to power follows a bomb-outrage against the Emperor in which fifty bystanders lost their lives; Rougon had been forewarned of the conspiracy, and deliberately refrained from reporting it so that the ministry that had supplanted him might be overthrown. Later he has an innocent man arrested brutally—the shock kills him—in order that his sister, one of Rougon's clients, might inherit.

Yet Eugène Rougon is the hero of the novel, a figure impressive by his one positive quality, his strength. The book is weakened by the unreality of the world it describes (Zola had no first-hand acquaintance with the ruling circles of the Second Empire and his researches could be no substitute for direct experience); but it has considerable momentum, provided by the drama of the conflict between the masculine strength of Eugène and the feminine machinations that undermine him. These are personified in

---

[1] Cf. 'La Haine de la littérature', *Le Voltaire*, 17 Aug. 1880, subsequently reprinted in *Le Roman expérimental*.

Clorinde, one of the least credible of Zola's women, a hazily drawn
adventuress of melodrama. But it is really his own supporters who
encompass his defeat, whose greed exhausts his credit and hunts
him from office.

Zola concentrates the venom of his satire of political life on those
little men that surround his hero, worrying him in his disgrace,
cowering before him and flattering him when he recovers power,
deserting him when he returns to the wilderness, rallying when he
triumphs afresh: Delestang, a nonentity with an imposing presence;
Du Poizat, who worked with Rougon from the beginning to push
the Prince-President on to the throne; Kahn, a deputy engaged in
shady financial transactions; Colonel Jobelin, angling for promotion in the army; Bouchard, angling for promotion in the civil
service; and D'Escorailles, whom Rougon enjoys patronizing
simply because his family is one of the most ancient in Plassans,
and this reversal of roles relieves an old itch of inferiority still felt
by the all-powerful minister, who had once been a disregarded
notary vegetating in the sleepy old town.

To judge by *Son Excellence Eugène Rougon* and by its provincial
counterpart *La Conquête de Plassans*, Zola's notions about the art of
government as practised in his time were excessively simple. Control
and power were vested in a few unscrupulous men—Rougon in the
one book, Faujas in the other—loving control for its own sake and
power for the exhilaration of exercising it. Around and beneath
was a medley of 'fools and rascals', dupes and profiteers, the essential pedestal for the master but an unstable one, which sooner or
later must crumble beneath his feet. The strong are supported by
the weak for so long as the strong can infuse their strength into the
weak. It is the antithesis, habitual in Zola, of the male and the
female principles, the male spurning the female but in the long run
at her mercy; Faujas is destroyed by Marthe just as surely as
Eugène falls through Clorinde.

The formula was too diagrammatic to correspond with reality.
Statecraft cannot be reduced to a game of beggar-my-neighbour,
having no bearing on the lives of the millions who, in a modern
state, eat or starve, are clothed or go ragged, are enlightened or
remain locked in superstition, live content or die despairing, largely
in consequence of decisions made at ministerial meetings and implemented in government offices. Zola's world of politics functions
in a void. The millions whom it ought to affect provide merely a

POLITICS 85

holiday crowd to gape at gay imperial processions. Once only in *La Curée* are we allowed a glimpse of the workmen who are actually operating the transformation of Paris which is one of the main subjects of the book. In the last chapter a commission is inspecting some property in the process of demolition, and one gentleman wonders at the housebreakers' disregard of danger. He is answered by another member of the commission, a doctor: 'Bah, c'est l'habitude. Ce sont des brutes.'

After *Son Excellence* Zola began his 'novel of the working class', *L'Assommoir*. Here the fact of social suffering, evaded in the earlier books, is stated with an emphasis that leaves nothing to be desired. But *L'Assommoir* is not a political novel,[1] because there is no attempt to lay at anyone's door the blame for the degradation of the masses. The book demonstrated that the impartiality of the realist need not exclude a sense of social wrongs; but it also showed that, if the rules of realism were to be observed, and the artist were to refrain indefinitely from intervention and conclusion, then the social formula he reached would always be short of one term or the other. Either the oppressed would be shown without the oppressors, or the exploiters without the classes they exploit.

Zola overcame the difficulty once only in his career: in *Germinal*. There, the formula he settled on to avoid a crude siding against social tyrants was to exonerate them of the intention of tyranny, even though he could not overlook its reality. The *rentiers* in *Germinal* are naïvely unaware that their privileged comfort is founded on the blood and sweat of the miners; the manager class is a powerless agent of the abstract monster 'capital', which Zola relegates carefully to the shadows. By these means no one set of characters is shown to be unjust, though the fact of injustice is painfully evident; and so the appearance of impartiality is maintained, precariously but all the same convincingly.

This juggling feat was not repeated. Zola's logic eventually demanded that a verdict of Guilty should be returned against someone or something, even if only against a social system. Once he took it on himself to act the juryman, however, his artistic integrity was of necessity compromised. This is what happened in *Paris* and in

---

[1] 'Le roman de Gervaise n'est pas le roman politique, mais le roman des mœurs du peuple; le côté politique s'y trouvera forcément, mais au second plan et dans une limite restreinte': *ébauche* of *L'Assommoir*, B.N. MS. *Nouv. acq. fr.* 10271, fol. 172.

the last three novels he wrote; and it partly explains why *Paris* and the *Évangiles* rank increasingly lower as literature. The course Zola took killed little by little the great artist that he was; but if he had remained bleakly impartial the effort might well have chilled his generous heart. Like Tolstoy he was a victim of the age he lived in. The pure serenity of certain great literary figures is perhaps largely a product of the atmosphere of unquestioned social traditions in which they lived out their lives.

V

THE ROMANTIC SURVIVAL

LACROIX, Zola's first publisher, was able to bring out only the first two volumes of the *Rougon-Macquart* series before he went bankrupt. This business failure was catastrophic for Zola, who almost despaired of finding another publisher. Eventually Georges Charpentier came to the rescue and undertook to publish the unwritten novels, laying, by this act, the foundations of a lasting friendship with the author and of a prosperous future for the firm he had inherited from his father shortly before.

Charpentier had not acted solely on his own initiative. The interesting part of this episode is that it should have been the ageing Théophile Gautier who, consulted by Charpentier, advised him strongly to take the step. Thus the irony of circumstance willed it that Zola, who thought he had cut himself free from his romantic affiliations when he reached man's estate, and who continued to pursue romanticism with whips of scorn in all his critical articles, found himself indebted to a veteran of the 'battle of *Hernani*' for the financial backing that enabled him to tide over his early period of neglect and obscurity. Moreover, the recommendation was made because Gautier thought he recognized in the author of *La Fortune des Rougon* a disciple of his own school. 'It is a Master who comes to us,' he told Charpentier enthusiastically, 'with his prophetic Z, like Z. Marcas and Balzac himself.' Then he added, with an ironical smile: 'Tell him from me not to lay the romanticism on too thickly.'[1]

[1] We have this anecdote on the authority of Gautier's son-in-law, Émile Bergerat (*Souvenirs d'un enfant de Paris*, pp. 400–1). The account that Bergerat goes on to give of the visit of thanks Zola paid to Gautier would seem to be a fabrication: see M. Dreyfous, 'Théophile Gautier et Émile Zola', *Bulletin de l'Association Émile Zola*, no. 7 (1912), pp. 251–3.

By his reference to Z. Marcas, Gautier was probably thinking of these lines in the opening pages of Balzac's short story: 'Ce Z qui précédait Marcas, qui se voyait sur l'adresse de ses lettres et qu'il n'oubliait jamais dans sa signature, cette dernière lettre de l'alphabet offrait à l'esprit je ne sais quoi de fatal. . . . Ne voyez-vous pas dans la construction du Z une allure contrariée? Ne figure-t-elle pas le zigzag aléatoire et fantasque d'une vie tourmentée?'

This is the first hint of the paradoxical legend that Zola, the quintessential naturalist—naturalism being but realism multiplied by itself—was nothing but a romantic born out of his time. The legend was propagated by his friends and used as evidence against him by his enemies; in the end he acknowledged resignedly that there was a good deal of truth in it. 'Il est certain', he wrote to an Italian admirer, 'que je suis un poète et que mes œuvres sont bâties comme de grandes symphonies musicales. . . . Je trempe dans le romantisme jusqu'à la ceinture.'[1]

Flaubert, in a letter thanking him for a presentation copy of *Mes haines*, finished his compliments with the parting thrust: 'And I maintain you are a splendid romantic. In fact, it's just for that that I like and admire you.' We may wonder how the author received this jolting slap in the back, he who had written in the concluding pages of this very book, *Mes haines*: 'Je suis fou de réalité, et je demande à toute œuvre . . . la vérité humaine, la vérité des passions et des pensées.'[2]

Maupassant, in what was primarily an apologia for Zola and his school,[3] wrote of him: 'son of the romantics, a romantic himself in the way he deals with everything, he has an inborn tendency to create poems, an urge to enlarge and magnify, to use living creatures and inanimate objects as symbols'; and Maupassant's observation served the turn of Zola's detractors, who detected in it a damning admission of inconsistency between Zola's doctrine and his practice. Brunetière, thundering from the pulpit of the *Revue des Deux Mondes*, proclaimed that 'the more he preached *naturalism*, the more he reverted to romanticism, from which he sprang, incidentally, and in which he will end his days'; Émile Faguet dismissed him disdainfully as 'a minor romantic, who would have cut a very small figure . . . round about 1830'; and Anatole France observed archly in his column in *Le Temps*: 'It is at Médan that the last of the romantics lurks in hiding.'[4]

The meaning of the over-used word depended, of course, on the user. As a term of opprobrium in the arsenal of hostile critics it

[1] Letter to Giuseppe Giacosa dated 28 Dec. 1882, published by R. Ternois, 'Zola et Giacosa', *Cahiers naturalistes*, no. 15 (1960), pp. 605–18.

[2] *Mes haines*, p. 184. Flaubert's remark was occasioned by the reissue of the book by Charpentier in 1879.

[3] 'Émile Zola', *Revue bleue*, vol. xxxi (1883), pp. 289–94.

[4] Brunetière, 'La Banqueroute du naturalisme', *Revue des Deux Mondes*, 1 Sept. 1887; Faguet, *Zola* (1903), p. 17; France, *Le Temps*, 6 Mar. 1887 (a review of Abel Hermant, *Le Cavalier Miserey*).

signified that Zola was no innovator, that his campaign for naturalism was a storm in a tea-cup, and that he was nothing but a belated devotee of an outworn creed. If Gautier's remark had reference only to *La Fortune des Rougon*, it is safe to say that he was equating romanticism with sentimentalism, and had in mind chiefly the idyll between Miette and Silvère; but it is curious that Brunetière later singled out this book as the only one in the series in which he could detect 'some shadow of naturalism'. Flaubert's comment was made in all friendliness; it betokened recognition of a quality he had long ago observed in himself, and which he named variously 'lyricism', 'exuberance', or, coining new words to describe it, as the passion for *'gueulades, hurlades'*. The writer loses control of his imagination, which gallops up into the skies of the ideal, of perfect form and the pure idea, leaving far below him the ploughed fields and the drabness of reality.

Maupassant's meaning is open to no doubt. He was all the more alive to what he called Zola's 'romanticism' because it was a feature entirely absent from his own writing. Maupassant was a more consistent realist than Zola. His prostitutes are never anything but prostitutes, never, like Nana, mystical embodiments of the corruption of slumland spilling over and infecting the cultivated classes. His low-grade civil servants are actual samples of what might be met in government offices, and never take on inflated proportions, like Josserand in *Pot-Bouille*, a sort of tragic Lear without even a kingdom to divide among his daughters. Maupassant's article on Zola coincided with the publication of *Au Bonheur des Dames*, which carried to its climax the career of Octave Mouret, started in *Pot-Bouille*. When, a couple of years later, Maupassant wrote, in *Bel-Ami*, his own version of the story of the modern *homme à bonnes fortunes*, he did not risk covering Zola's ground. The saga of Georges Duroy is not really comparable with that of Octave Mouret. In Maupassant's book the intention is simply to depict the rise to prosperity of a handsome scoundrel with little but his dash to help him; in Zola's two novels the centre of gravity is not the adventurer himself, but certain impersonal entities that owe their oppressive presence solely to the artist's vision: the block of flats in *Pot-Bouille*, the great modern universal store in *Au Bonheur des Dames*. From the point of view of a sober observer like Maupassant they are bound to appear exaggerations; they are transformed into symbols of the rottenness of the *bourgeoisie* or the savage depersonalized conflict between old-fashioned shop-keeping and modern commerce. In the mixture of authenticity and artificiality that composes even the most 'realist' of fictions, it is the artificial element that is responsible for what is most characteristic and vital in Zola's writing.

Leaving on one side questions of form and style, there are two directions in which an artist like Zola with a powerful imagination will tend to break loose from the discipline of representing things as they are. He may create characters that are not normal—not typical, that is, of the class of which they are supposed to be specimens; or he may inject into natural objects the human emotions that agitate his characters, or even load them with a significance that escapes his characters and is discoverable only by the artist himself, until he communicates his discovery to the reader.

The very conception of *Les Rougon-Macquart* forbade the employment of 'normal' types, for the characteristic of the whole family was that an initial flaw made all the descendants of Adélaïde Fouque more or less morbid, abnormal individuals. That Zola saw this necessity from the very start is made clear by a paragraph in the 'Notes générales sur la nature de l'œuvre'.

Il y a deux genres de personnage, *Emma* et *Germinie*, la créature vraie observée par Flaubert, et la créature grandie créée par les de Goncourt. Dans l'une l'analyse est faite à froid, le type se généralise. Dans l'autre, il semble que les auteurs aient torturé la vérité, le type devient exceptionnel. Ma *Thérèse* et ma *Madeleine* sont exceptionnelles. Dans les études que je veux faire, je ne puis guère sortir de l'exception; ces créations particulières sont d'ailleurs plus d'un artiste, ce mot étant pris dans le sens moderne. Il semble aussi qu'en sortant du général, l'œuvre devient supérieure (*Julien Sorel*); il y a création d'homme, effort d'artiste; l'œuvre gagne en intérêt humain ce qu'elle perd en réalité courante. Il faudrait donc faire exceptionnel comme Stendhal, éviter les trop grandes monstruosités, mais prendre des cas particuliers de cerveau et de chair.

It is worth observing that Zola here makes Stendhal, not Balzac, his model. Both these predecessors had dealt in 'exceptional' characters; but Balzac's creations nourish within themselves the seed of madness that makes them exceptional, while Stendhal's heroes and heroines are made to behave extraordinarily by the stresses of their environment. It is particularly the early *Rougon-Macquart* novels that are richer in the Stendhalian type of character than the Balzacian. Later, Zola showed himself able to give credibility to the born monstrosity, as well as the monstrosity conditioned by environ-ment. In *La Curée* (1872) Saccard is a reckless speculator, cor-rupted simply by the great opportunities that tempt him; in *L'Argent* (1891) he reappears, but this time as a kind of financial mystic, a Gobseck working in the open, with an odd streak of genuine philanthropy traversing his crazy dreams.

Saccard on his second appearance is a more grandiose and, from the point of view of the novelist's art, a more complete and suc-cessful creation. In *La Curée* he interested the author far less than did the heroine, Renée; the book, in fact, took shape in Zola's mind as a 'new Phèdre'.[1]

Renée, however, sprang from the brain of a determinist novelist, not from the imagination of a tragedian steeped in Hellenic (and perhaps Jansenist) ideas of predestination. No ancestral curse hangs over her, compelling her to incest against her will. She is the daughter of an honourable member of the magistrature and would never have been given in marriage to a man of Saccard's reputation but for an accident: she had been outraged by an unknown man, and Saccard, recently widowed, accepted her in consideration of her dowry.[2] This unusual start to married life, and the whirl of pleasure into which her husband plunges her, set up strains within her which prove finally fatal.

There was an opportunity here for the analysis in depth of a tragic figure driven in one direction by the instincts implanted by her upbringing and in another by the temptations which a licentious society throws across her path. Renée might have been a second, though a different, Emma Bovary: she has all Emma's indistinct yearnings for what she cannot apprehend, though her discontent arises from satiety, not frustration. There are touches, indeed, that recall Flaubert's book a little too obviously. Renée, like Emma, is harried by creditors; a distasteful admirer (M. de Saffré in *La Curée*, the notary Guillaumin in *Madame Bovary*) offers to help settle the debt; and when Renée rejects the proposition, in a des-perate surge of pride, she uses exactly the same formula as Emma: 'Je ne suis pas à vendre.' Yet Renée is a colourless and insubstantial heroine compared with Emma. Zola never succeeds in 'getting

---

[1] 'Décidément, c'est une nouvelle *Phèdre* que je vais faire': *ébauche* of *La Curée*, B.N. MS. *Nouv. acq. fr.* 10282, fol. 298. Zola included in his preparatory notes a synopsis of Racine's play (fol. 374).

[2] A closely similar incident was used by Zola in one of the least successful of his short stories, 'Nantas', which was published in 1879.

inside her'. We wonder at her, we do not understand her; she remains as alien as some distant Punic princess. The novelist reports the drift of her thoughts, he describes in broad outline her moods; but he never conveys to us the fragile texture of her thinking, the shifting patterns and dissolving colours of her moods. His method is altogether different from Flaubert's; he works from outside, by referring his heroine's mortal dilemma to objects and the qualities of objects; these are made to signify, or externalize, stresses that are really within Renée herself.

Her life falls into two parts: a sheltered girlhood (evoked in flashbacks) and a noisy, shameless womanhood, and these two successive phases are made concrete for us by her two abodes: her father's house in the Île Saint-Louis, and the flat in the rue de Rivoli into which she moves when she marries Saccard and where she stays until he builds the monstrous house in the Parc Monceau which is the main setting of the action. The Hôtel Béraud keeps for her all the associations of childhood. Zola describes it as gaunt, sunless, and chilly, even in summer. He concentrates attention on the interior courtyard, paved with stone slabs, where, immediately in front of the porch, one sees a carved lion's head from whose half-open jaws a stream of ice-cold water gushes into a drinking-trough green with moss. 'Là, au fond de cette cour fraîche et muette comme un puits, éclairée d'un jour blanc d'hiver, on se serait cru à mille lieues de ce nouveau Paris où flambaient toutes les chaudes jouissances, dans le vacarme des millions.' Zola's symbolism calls for no very subtle interpretation: the chilliness, the silence, the wintry pallor of this island house, contrasting with the heat and clamour of the city, point to Renée's past which is in conflict with her present. On the two occasions (chapters v and vii) when, later in the novel, she returns on a visit to her father's house, Zola reminds us again of the courtyard and its 'humidité morne de cloître', its 'froideur de cloître': the cloister suggests the sheltered, safe life, but also the puritan values, continence and self-denial, which are in opposition to the unbridled excesses of the neo-pagan Second Empire.

Life in the rue de Rivoli is characterized by noise, turmoil, fever, lawlessness. 'Les portes y battaient toute la journée; les domestiques y parlaient haut; le luxe neuf et éclatant en était traversé continuellement par des courses de jupes énormes et volantes, par des processions de fournisseurs, par le tohu-bohu des amies de Renée,

des camarades de Maxime et des visiteurs de Saccard.' Maxime,
Saccard's son, is still a schoolboy; when they move to the new house
in the Parc Monceau he is a young man, and Renée discovers, or
imagines she will discover, the 'jouissance rare, inconnue' that she
has been looking for, in an affair with her pretty, languid, and cor-
rupt stepson. Images of heat abound particularly in this part of the
novel, when, for instance, Renée is shown crouching in her sitting-
room over an enormous fire which numbs her consciousness of
sin and shame.

Elle grelottait, il lui fallait des brasiers ardents, une chaleur suffocante
qui lui mettait au front de petites gouttes de sueur, et qui l'assoupissait.
Dans cet air brûlant, dans ce bain de flammes, elle ne souffrait presque
plus; sa douleur devenait comme un songe léger, un vague oppresse-
ment, dont l'indécision même finissait par être voluptueuse. Ce fut ainsi
qu'elle berça jusqu'au soir ses remords de la veille, dans la clarté rouge
du foyer, en face d'un terrible feu qui faisait craquer les meubles autour
d'elle, et lui ôtait, par instants, la conscience de son être.

There is an extraordinary and notorious scene at the end of chapter
iv in which Maxime and Renée are shown making love in the damp,
airless heat of the conservatory beyond the windows of which the
private park can be seen frost-bound under the moon—

des bouquets d'arbres aux fines découpures noires, des pelouses de
gazon blanches comme des lacs glacés, tout un paysage mort, dont les
délicatesses et les teintes claires et unies rappelaient des coins de gravures
japonaises. Et ce bout de terre brûlante, cette couche enflammée où les
amants s'allongeaient, bouillaient étrangement au milieu de ce grand
froid muet.

Dante, it must not be forgotten, had been one of Zola's favourite
poets; his lovers are, he writes at this point, plunged 'en plein enfer
dantesque de la passion . . . [goûtant] l'inceste, comme le fruit
criminel d'une terre trop chauffée, avec la peur sourde de leur
couche terrifiante'. Renée, it can be said, creates her own hell-fire
in advance of damnation.

One of the childhood memories connected with the Hôtel Béraud
which she recalls at the end, when humiliation has broken her
spirit, is of two grey woollen dresses with a red chequer design
which their aunt had made one Christmas for her sister and her.
The two little girls were delighted at first; but the long
sleeves and high collars drew teasing comment from the other
children at the convent school and Renée, during play-time, had

rolled up her sleeves and tucked down her collar. Zola's unquestioningly conventional morality picked once more on a symbolic contrast between Renée's overdressed childhood and her
décolletage as a woman of high fashion after her marriage. The
equation established between nudity and evil, which will be exploited afresh in *Nana*, is recurrently underlined in *La Curée*.
Statues of naked goddesses, caryatids, or simply decorations on the
façade, are a feature of Saccard's new house seen from outside;
and inside, at the foot of the staircase, on two marble pedestals,
stand two half-naked gilt-bronze nymphs holding five-branched
candelabra. On the particular evening on which the story opens,
when Renée comes down to dinner, her gown creates a mild
sensation among the *blasé* guests.

Décolletée jusqu'à la pointe des seins, les bras découverts avec des
touffes de violettes sur les épaules, la jeune femme semblait sortir toute
nue de sa gaîne de tulle et de satin, pareille à une de ces nymphes dont
le buste se dégage des chênes sacrés; et sa gorge blanche, son corps
souple, était déjà si heureux de sa demi-liberté, que le regard s'attendait
toujours à voir peu à peu le corsage et les jupes glisser, comme le vête-
ment d'une baigneuse, folle de sa chair. Sa coiffure haute, ses fins cheveux
jaunes en forme de casque, et dans lesquels courait une branche de lierre,
retenue par un nœud de violettes, augmentait encore sa nudité, en
découvrant sa nuque que des poils follets, semblables à des fils d'or,
ombraient légèrement.

Renée is described, in the course of the novel, in three different
evening dresses of which this, the hamadryad costume, is the first.
Each time she gives a stronger impression of wearing nothing. We
see her at a ministry ball at which her brother-in-law Eugène
Rougon is present. 'Elle s'était décolletée avec un tel mépris des
regards, elle marchait si calme et si tendre dans sa nudité, que cela
n'était presque plus indécent.' *Décolletage* is expressly connected
here with the durability of the régime: the minister 'sentait cette
gorge nue plus éloquente encore que sa parole à la Chambre, plus
douce et plus persuasive pour faire goûter les charmes du règne et
convaincre les sceptiques'.[1] On her final appearance—this is on the
evening when Saccard discovers the adultery between his son and
her—she is wearing the costume of a Tahitian girl:

[1] Zola had introduced this idea already in one of his contributions to *La Cloche*
(21 Feb. 1870): 'Les Épaules de la marquise', reprinted in the *Nouveaux Contes à
Ninon*. The shoulders of the unnamed court-lady in this sketch are 'l'enseigne
vivante des charmes du Second Empire . . . le blason voluptueux du règne'.

un maillot couleur tendre, qui lui montait des pieds jusqu'aux seins, en lui laissant les épaules et les bras nus; et, sur ce maillot, une simple blouse de mousseline, courte et garnie de deux volants, pour cacher un peu les hanches. Dans les cheveux, une couronne de fleurs des champs; aux chevilles et aux poignets, des cercles d'or. Et rien autre. Elle était nue.

There is this difference between Renée and Nana, that the actress undresses to drive to insanity and destruction the cohort of her male admirers, whereas the heroine of *La Curée* damages no one but herself by the exposure of her body. She is no *femme fatale*. Zola had planned at first that she should end by eloping with a lover; then he imagined her confronting Saccard and Maxime and castigating them for their loose morals. In the final version, however, he wisely chose a crushing instead of a flamboyant dénouement. Saccard pretends not to have noticed her in Maxime's arms. He contents himself with a banker's draft for a hundred thousand which she has signed. Theseus, far from calling down the wrath of the gods on Hippolytus, asks him for a light for his cigar, and walks out of the room arm in arm with him. And Phaedra is left to stare at herself in her wardrobe mirror, feeling, for the first time, shame at her nakedness. 'C'étaient ces gens-là qui l'avaient mise nue. Saccard avait dégrafé le corsage, et Maxime avait fait tomber la jupe. Puis, à eux deux, ils venaient d'arracher la chemise. . . . Pas de sang sur le tapis, pas un cri, pas une plainte. C'étaient des lâches. Ils l'avaient mise nue.'

Renée is, then, like Emma Bovary again, more sinned against than sinning. Literally, she 'follows false gods'. The obsessive nudity motif is linked by Zola with a more particularized theme —one which, again, will be encountered in *Nana*—that of the reapparition in modern times of the paganism of ancient Greece, but debased, cheapened, made vulgar. Renée suppresses the guilt she feels at sharing herself between husband and stepson, by evoking classical mythology to justify a purely hedonistic code of values: 'elle finissait par croire qu'elle vivait au milieu d'un monde supérieur à la morale commune, où les sens s'affinaient et se développaient, où il était permis de se mettre nue pour la joie de l'Olympe entier.' There are hints at bogus classicism in the details of Saccard's mansion, apart from the caryatids already mentioned. The gatehouse, for instance: 'le concierge habitait un élégant pavillon, qui rappelait vaguement un petit temple grec.' A silver centrepiece on the dinner table represents 'une bande de faunes

enlevant des nymphes', while the two silver candlesticks consist
each of 'un satyre courant, emportant sur l'un de ses bras une
femme pâmée, et tenant de l'autre une torchère à dix branches'.
That the subject of both these *objets d'art* should be rape is, given
that Saccard chose or commissioned them, appropriately sinister.
In her drawing-room, which is papered and upholstered in yellow,
Renée, with her yellow hair, is twice compared to Diana; in the
conservatory, however, she becomes a different creature—but also
a creature of ancient fable—the Sphinx. There is a black marble
statue of a sphinx among the tropical plants and at one point,
making love to her there, Maxime sees this 'dark idol' immediately
behind her, above her shoulders: 'Renée avait la pose et le sourire
du monstre à tête de femme, et, dans ses jupons dénoués, elle semblait la sœur blanche de ce dieu noir.' It is principally Rénee who
affords Zola pretexts for evoking classical antiquity, and invariably
as a period of high heathen wickedness, compared with which the
licentiousness of the Second Empire was mere crapulous debauchery. She prevails on Maxime to initiate her into the night-
life of Paris (at a period when such revels were attended only by
women of the lowest class), and afterwards confesses to him how
disappointed she had been:

> Je m'imaginais des choses prodigieuses, des festins antiques, comme
> on en voit dans les tableaux, avec des créatures couronnées de roses, des
> coupes d'or, des voluptés extraordinaires. . . . Ah! bien oui. Tu m'as
> montré un cabinet de toilette malpropre et des femmes qui juraient
> comme des charretiers. Ça ne vaut pas la peine de faire le mal. . . . Le
> mal, ce devrait être quelque chose d'exquis, mon cher. . . . C'est une
> affaire d'éducation, comprends-tu?

Of classical education, of course.

The guying, deliberate or involuntary, of ancient myths is yet
another aspect of this degenerate neo-classicism. A series of
tableaux vivants, representing the legend of Echo and Narcissus, is
the principal entertainment at the fateful *soirée* when Renée's liaison
with Maxime is discovered. One of the most popular of Offenbach's
operettas in the sixties was *La Belle Hélène*, a burlesque which, as
we know from his journalism, revolted Zola's musical and dramatic
taste;[1] he refers to it in the text of *La Curée* (Renée picks out the

---

[1] 'J'aboie dès que j'entends la musique de mirliton de M. Offenbach. Jamais
la farce bête ne s'est étalée avec une telle impudence . . .' etc.: *L'Événement
illustré*, 6 June 1868.

catchy tunes on her piano) and contrasts it tacitly with a work of truly classical inspiration in the account he gives of Renée's reactions to *Phèdre*. She recognizes her own story and the closeness of her situation to that of Racine's heroine, but at the same time measures the distance that separates her sordid intrigue from the ancient drama. 'Phèdre était du sang de Pasiphaé, et elle se demandait de quel sang elle pouvait être, elle, l'incestueuse des temps nouveaux. . . . Aurait-elle la force de s'empoisonner, un jour? Comme son drame était mesquin et honteux à coté de l'épopée antique!' In the end Renée dies, prosaically, of meningitis, leaving debts to the tune of a quarter of a million, which her father pays.

There is of course another—but to modern readers probably less interesting—side to *La Curée*: that which presents the specific social scandal that gave the novel its title, the building of Saccard's fortune on extravagant indemnifications paid to property owners in Paris when the compulsory demolition orders were made to enable the new boulevards to be driven through the city. This sociological aspect is linked to the symbolic in no very hard-and-fast way, and this is perhaps one of the weaknesses of the book. In addition, Zola's moral assumptions in *La Curée* are, after all, a little puerile. It is difficult to agree that moral evil is contingent on a low neck-line, or even that sleeping with one's stepson in a centrally heated conservatory represents the depth of human depravity. In his next novel, *Le Ventre de Paris*, Zola was more successful in effecting a proper juncture between the symbolist (or 'romantic') and the sociological (or 'realist') strands in his work, and also in finding, and discussing, a moral issue of somewhat deeper import: the ignoble depths to which the average, 'decent', middle-class family man (and woman) will stoop if their comfort and domestic peace are threatened.

'Quels gredins que les honnêtes gens!' The remark with which Claude Lantier, an important but largely inactive commentator in *Le Ventre de Paris*, sums up the whole sticky treachery of the main characters provided Zola with an unusually epigrammatic conclusion to his novel. The events that have evoked the comment were set in train by the clandestine return to Paris of a republican wrongfully deported to Devil's Island after the *coup d'état* of 1851. During his exile his half-brother, a pork butcher, has been growing steadily richer and fatter as the Empire prospers and brings prosperity to its meek supporters. Pierre Florent can neither square his conscience with the tacit acceptance of a guilty régime, nor adjust his temperament to this atmosphere of stewing plenty. He begins an amateurish conspiracy, is pounced on by the police, and deported once more.

The most original creation in the book is Lisa Quenu, *née* Lisa Macquart, the elder daughter of the ferocious old drunkard of Plassans whom we met in *La Fortune des Rougon*. She is, wrote Zola at the beginning of the *ébauche*, 'une honnête femme'. But, he added, 'honnête, il faut s'entendre. Je veux lui donner l'honnêteté de sa classe, et montrer quels dessous formidables de lâcheté, de cruauté, il y a sous la chair calme d'une bourgeoise.' A respectable woman, yes: 'une femme chaste, économe, aimant son mari et ses enfants, tout à son foyer, et qui sera socialement et moralement un mauvais ange flétrissant et dissolvant tout ce qu'il touchera.'[1] Zola had originally thought of making her commit one or two really shameful deeds: she was to deprive her poorer sister Gervaise of her means of livelihood out of mere pique; or she was to plant a compromising letter to ensure her brother-in-law is put away. In the end he changed his mind: 'je ne lui prêterai aucune mauvaise action. Je la montrerai honnête, et pire peut-être qu'une coquine.'[2] Gervaise was finally given no part in the novel; and Florent is denounced by others. Lisa has a strong sense of what is due to her husband's brother though she dislikes him. At one point, however, she is driven beyond endurance. Florent lodges at the top of their shop and she has seen his room piled high with red flags in preparation for the insurrection. Fearful lest her husband should be compromised if there were a police raid, she calls a cab, drives to the *préfecture*, and tells her story. She is given to understand that the police are already fully informed, and a packet of anonymous letters, in which she recognizes the handwriting of all her neighbours and even her own apprentice, is handed to her to read. She emerges shaken:

> Ce qu'elle sentait de plus net, c'était l'inutilité de sa démarche. Son mari ne courait aucun danger. Cela la soulageait, tout en lui laissant un remords. . . . En somme, ce n'était pas elle qui avait livré Florent. Cette pensée qui lui vint brusquement, l'étonna. Aurait-elle donc commis une méchante action, si elle l'avait livré? Elle resta perplexe, surprise d'avoir pu être trompée par sa conscience.

[1] B.N. MS. *Nouv. acq. fr.* 10338, fol. 49.
[2] Ibid., fol. 88.

This is the nearest Lisa ever gets to questioning her own motives. She soon banishes these importunate doubts, however: she had not been moved by mercenary considerations in going to the police, and at any rate she had written no anonymous denunciations. Lisa's morality is that of the decent French *bourgeoise* of her time: honesty is a matter of making sure your money is lawfully come by, and beyond that, if you can persuade yourself that your neighbours have more on their conscience than you, then you really have nothing you can reasonably reproach yourself with. Zola lets the inadequacy of these principles speak for itself.

He understood Lisa, in a sense sympathized with her, and she emerges as the most convincing of his feminine characters before Gervaise in *L'Assommoir*. Florent, by contrast, the other central figure in *Le Ventre de Paris*, remains obstinately opaque. After his harrowing ordeals in the penal colony and during his escape, he is quite simply bemused when suddenly surrounded by the warmth, the comfort, the self-assurance, the round faces, and the round bellies in his brother's household. He tells his story hesitantly, and as though it concerned not him but another, listened to by Quenu, Lisa, their small daughter Pauline, and the apprentice, for whom all this is so far from their own experience that they are almost incredulous and at all events scandalized; Lisa in particular. Could there be men who go without food?

On mange toujours, plus ou moins. . . . Il faudrait des misérables tout à fait abandonnés, des gens perdus. . . .

Elle allait dire sans doute 'des canailles sans aveu'; mais elle se retint, en regardant Florent. Et la moue méprisante de ses lèvres, son regard clair avouaient carrément que les gredins seuls jeûnaient de cette façon désordonnée. Un homme capable d'être resté trois jours sans manger était pour elle un être absolument dangereux. Car, enfin, jamais les honnêtes gens ne se mettent dans des positions pareilles.

Florent's terrifying experiences, the march through the trackless jungle, threatened with a hundred deaths from snake-bite or yellow fever, from drowning in quagmires or being devoured by alligators, all this is literally unimaginable to the pork butcher's wife; and making what sense she can of the whole lamentable episode, she tells her brother-in-law that he ought to be ashamed of wandering about the country like a tramp, and that it is high time he started behaving as a man of his age, social class, and education should behave. Surprisingly, Florent submits to being lectured to and even acquiesces in the good sense of Lisa's homily; the rich odours of the kitchen, the warm atmosphere of good living, are enough, it seems, to abolish the thought of the ideal for which he had sacrificed himself and which, one supposes, had sustained him in the midst of his sufferings in Guiana.

Florent is the first intellectual we have met in *Les Rougon-Macquart*: he will have a number of successors—Lazare in *La Joie de vivre*, Souvarine in *Germinal*, Sigismond Busch in *L'Argent*, Maurice Levasseur in *La Débâcle*, and of course Pascal Rougon in the last volume of the series. They are none of them convincing, none even very interesting, and in this domain Zola has been easily outdistanced by many a lesser novelist than he.[1] We have only to consider *Le Ventre de Paris* to see why. The enormous importance Zola gave—partly for doctrinal reasons but mostly because it accorded with the natural bent of his imaginative processes—to environment, 'le milieu qui complète et détermine l'homme', hampered him when he tried to deal with a figure who, having an intense inner life, must be supposed more impervious than most to the pressure of the external world. The real Florents can be convinced only by evidence or argument. In the scene we have evoked, Florent's mind is changed not by the soundness of Lisa's views but by her radiant good health—and by the smell of the blackpudding cooking.

Elle avait raison sans doute. Elle était si saine, si tranquille, qu'elle ne pouvait vouloir le mal. C'était lui, le maigre, le profil noir et louche, qui devait être mauvais et rêver des choses inavouables. Il ne savait plus pourquoi il avait résisté jusque-là. . . . Il était pénétré par cette odeur de cuisine, que le nourrissait de toute la nourriture dont l'air était chargé; il glissait à la lâcheté heureuse de cette digestion continue du milieu gras où il vivait depuis quinze jours. C'était, à fleur de peau, mille chatouillements de graisse naissante, un lent envahissement de l'être entier, une douceur molle et boutiquière.

The swamping of mind by matter leaves Florent with little real substance; but in the novel as a whole, and particularly where the lesser characters are concerned, the supremacy of the world of phenomena—colours, shapes, and above all smells—imposes itself on the reader with a force which overwhelms all but the most refractory. It is not merely that Zola shows us people in thrall to their environment; they merge with it, they become mere

[1] From Vallès to Sartre. See V. Brombert, *The Intellectual Hero* (1962).

extensions of the objects surrounding them, or the objects become mere extensions of them: it is all one. The bunches of flowers in a flower-seller's baskets are integrated with her moods: 'Ses bouquets gardaient ses méchantes humeurs et ses attendrissements; il y en avait de hérissés, de terribles, qui ne décoléraient pas dans leur cornet chiffonné; il y en avait d'autres, paisibles, amoureux, souriant au fond de leur collerette propre.' A young fruit-seller's sexual charm seeps into the peaches and plums she offers for sale: 'C'était elle, c'étaient ses bras, c'était son cou, qui donnaient à ses fruits cette vie amoureuse, cette tiédeur satinée de femme. Sur le banc de vente à côté, une vieille marchande, une ivrognesse affreuse, n'étalait que des pommes ridées, des poires pendantes comme des seins vides, des abricots cadavéreux, d'un jaune infâme de sorcière. Mais elle, faisait de son étalage une grande volupté nue.' In the cheesemonger's three gossips are exchanging slander about their neighbours: here, the foul emanations from the cheeses on a hot day both accord with and to some extent provoke the nastiness of the women's innuendos.

The whole action of *Le Ventre de Paris* is set either inside the Central Markets or in the neighbouring streets; only once are we taken outside, to a market garden beyond the city boundary, an alimentary canal through which food is injected into the 'belly of Paris', the Market itself. The book is the first of those in which a construction of steel, glass, bricks, and mortar is galvanized by Zola's creative power into an autonomous life that transcends and absorbs those of the men and women living beside and beneath it. 'L'idée générale est: le ventre,' he wrote on the first sheet of the *ébauche*, 'le ventre de Paris, les Halles, où la nourriture afflue, s'entasse, pour rayonner sur les quartiers divers; — le ventre de l'humanité, et par extension la bourgeoisie digérant, ruminant, cuvant en paix ses joies et ses honnêtetés moyennes.' Fatness is everywhere, the ruddy plumpness of shameless good health. The market women are drawn in rotund curves, mere quivering bellies and bosoms. Lisa displays to the world 'sa belle face tranquille de vache sacrée'. When Florent first encounters the Quenus, father, mother, and little daughter, he sees them as 'superbes, carrés, luisants; ils le regardaient avec l'étonnement de gens très gras pris d'une vague inquiétude en face d'un maigre'. For Florent is 'maigre comme une branche sèche' and can never put on flesh. The incompatibility between him and his half-brother's family is an aspect of the eternal war between the Fat and the Thin,[1] as Claude Lantier points out to the spare-framed revolutionary. 'Pour sûr, dit-il, Caïn était un gras et Abel un maigre. Depuis le premier meurtre, ce sont toujours les grosses faims qui ont sucé le sang des petits mangeurs. . . . Voyez-vous, mon brave, défiez-vous des Gras.' When he gives in to Lisa's insistence that he should 'become respectable', Florent accepts a post as market inspector. But the corpulent vendors take an instinctive dislike to him and make his job intolerable, so that in the end he repents having abjured his old republican idealism. In a sort of fevered vision he sees the vast covered markets at night as a collection of bloated, snoring, sweating hussies: 'vautrées au fond de l'ombre, toutes nues, en sueur encore, dépoitraillées, montrant leur ventre ballonné et se soulageant sous les étoiles.'

In *Le Ventre de Paris*, overloaded as it is with symbolism and choked with fantasticated description, the poet and myth-builder in Zola all but elbow out the plodding registrar of everyday fact. He undertook painstaking research into the statutes regulating the markets (braving, in the doing of it, the suspicious stares and uncivil rebuffs of the police officials he questioned). He gave proof of exemplary conscientiousness in rising before dawn to watch the market-gardeners cart their produce into the city. Yet in spite of these pledges to realism, the picture Zola achieved in *Le Ventre de Paris* of the *quartier des Halles* can be called realistic only in the sense that Renoir's swelling beauties are admitted to be so. It could only have been by a sharpening of the senses to the point of uselessness as instruments of normal perception that Zola arrived at such disturbing impressionism. No eye but his was ever so dazzled by an array of carrots and lettuce in the sunlight, or could have rendered a display of peaches, apricots, apples, and pears in terms of a still-life seraglio, 'des rougeurs de seins naissants, des épaules et des hanches dorées, toute une nudité discrète, au milieu des brins de fougère'. The presence of Claude Lantier, the young art student, sanctions only occasionally these vivid canvases. In no other novel does Zola show quite so clearly his affinities with the rising school of painters whose revelation of the colourful variety of modern city life was ushering in a new epoch in French art. If red and gold, the red velvet hangings and the gilt ornaments of Saccard's mansion, appear to be the symbolic dominants of *La Curée* (red for lust, gold

[1] The first translation into English of *Le Ventre de Paris* was entitled *The Fat and the Thin*.

for greed),[1] the chromatic riot in *Le Ventre de Paris* is such that no single colour can be said to give the characteristic tone of the book: rather it is the indigestible medley of pigments in the great palette of the Central Markets that conveys with suffocating force the impression of an enslaved and gluttonous populace, ferocious only when its feeding-trough is threatened.

An oft-noted peculiarity of Zola's career as a novelist is his tendency to interpose a quiet, monochrome composition between two violent, highly coloured ones. *La Conquête de Plassans*, coming after *Le Ventre de Paris* and before *La Faute de l'abbé Mouret*, is a controlled work, written seemingly in strict conformity with realist conventions, and separating two gorgeously romantic rhapsodies: much as the quiet B flat symphony was composed by Beethoven after a stirring Eroica and before the portentous Fifth. Like *La Fortune des Rougon* it is a Balzacian work, having certain similarities in particular with *Le Curé de Tours*: the Abbé Faujas repeats the Abbé Troubert—both ambitious and austere priests whose scheming proves successful, and who owe their success in part to the spell they manage to cast over the woman in whose house they are lodging (Mlle Gamard in Balzac's story, Marthe Mouret in Zola's).

Nothing could be gentler—and, it must be confessed, more uncharacteristic of Zola—than the opening scenes of *La Conquête de Plassans*, in which François and Marthe Mouret are shown in their home, surrounded by their children and fussed over by the cantankerous old servant Rose; there is a general atmosphere of contentment and well-being, the master of the house (for whom, exceptionally, Zola had an actual model, Paul Cézanne's father the banker)[2] ruling more by his habits of sarcastic pleasantry than by sternness. Into this quiet refuge come the priest Faujas, his mother, and a little later his sister and her husband. They arrive as lodgers; they stay to wreck the settled tranquillity of their hosts, and end by perishing when the house is burned down by Mouret, driven mad by the religious hysteria his wife has succumbed to under the influence of Faujas.

Seen as a piece of social history, the book can be described as a

---

[1] 'Dans l'histoire naturelle et sociale d'une famille sous le second Empire, *la Curée* est la note de l'or et de la chair': opening lines of the preface of *La Curée*. This aspect of the symbolism of the novel has been excellently analysed by H. Petriconi, *Das Reich des Untergangs*, pp. 42–48.

[2] 'Prendre le type du père de C. goguenard, républicain bourgeois, froid, méticuleux, avare' (B.N. MS. *Nouv. acq. fr.* 10280, fol. 19).

restrained, factual account of the 'conquest' of a provincial town for the cause of Bonapartism by a priest entrusted with this mission by the authorities in Paris. The religious mania that infects Marthe and breaks up her family is incidental to this political struggle. Here, in all likelihood, Zola was relying on the Goncourts' study, in *Madame Gervaisais*, of a woman falling into imbecility in her pursuit of mystic transports.[1] Except in the concluding chapters, Zola is hardly being himself in *La Conquête de Plassans*, which is perhaps why it has never been a favourite with his public: it had sold fewer copies, by the end of his life, than any other volume of *Les Rougon-Macquart*.

Yet the climax of the book is as stirring as any Zola invented. Flaubert told him so, and added: 'La peur vous prend comme à la lecture d'un conte fantastique, et vous arrivez à cet effet-là par l'excès de la réalité, par l'intensité du vrai!' This testimonial from the master of realism should have consoled the author; but though Flaubert does justice to the effects Zola obtained, he fails to give a complete account of their source.

The insanity of François, and the hysterical fits of Marthe which bring on this insanity, give the impression of being realistically, quite 'clinically' observed, to use a term then fashionable. But this madness cannot be considered in isolation. Both husband and wife are descended from Adélaïde Fouque, and it is this absent octogenarian, and even more the grey buildings of the lunatic asylum that houses her, which, presiding over the drama of the Mourets, signpost the escape route from realism. Antoine Macquart, now the 'reformed wolf', is installed near the asylum to watch over his mother; his words to Marthe, when she is already touched by her nervous disorder, stir the reader with the sense of huge shadows lying behind and before. 'Quand je m'asseois à cette place, en face de cette grande coquine de maison, je me dis souvent que toute la clique y viendra peut-être un jour, puisque la maman y est.' The prophecy does in a sense come true, years later, when, in a memorable scene in *Le Docteur Pascal*, members of four generations are assembled in Adélaïde's cell: her son, Antoine Macquart; her

---

[1] At the same time, Zola's misgivings about the effects of a religious education on women of nervous disposition appear to have been genuine; he voiced them notably in an article published in *La Cloche* on 8 May 1872, a little before *La Conquête de Plassans* was put in hand. A related topic (the dangerous hold a confessor can acquire over a female penitent) was the subject of another article in the same paper, 8 Sept. 1872.

grandson, Pascal Rougon; his niece and nephew, Clotilde and Maxime; and Maxime's son Charles, the last puny offshoot of the condemned tree.

The madhouse breaches the closed circle of naturalism, and through the gap we glimpse distant vistas of an eternal pattern working itself out beyond nature and rational comprehension. By the accent he puts on apparently gratuitous details, the artist draws the eye to this opening, suggests to the mind correspondences of retribution and recompense which no strictly realist approach would have discovered.

La Faute de l'abbé Mouret, published in the spring of 1875, must be accounted the least realist of all Zola's works, and the most lyrical because the most personal. Symbolism runs riot and is hard to disentangle, harder still to make sense of. We have already noticed the starting-point in one of the *Contes à Ninon*, 'Simplice'.[1] The pattern of this story, the youth who escapes from his own world into a virgin forest where he meets and loves a nymph to whom his love is fatal, underlies in a broad sense the novel; but there are significant modifications. Serge Mouret, the counterpart of Simplice, is a priest, and so his love for Albine is sacrilegious in a sense inapplicable to the earlier *conte*. For many years Zola's imagination had been working round the question of priestly celibacy which had, in the Romantic era, led Lamartine to weave the pathetic legend of Jocelyn and Laurence and Hugo to create the awesome figure of Frollo, the cleric in *Notre-Dame de Paris* who is tormented by lust for Esmeralda. One of the very first books Zola ever reviewed was Gaston Lavalley's *Aurélien*, which touched on this theme.[2] He gave an unsympathetic account of Barbey d'Aurevilly's *Un Prêtre marié* in *Le Salut public* (10 May 1865), and in *L'Événement* (5 July 1866) drew his readers' attention to a reprint of the seventeenth-century *Traicté du célibat des prestres* by Urbain Grandier which, however, the editorial policy of his paper forbade him to discuss. Finally, there was Ernest Daudet's novel *Le Missionnaire*; the terms in which Zola reviewed this work in *Le Gaulois* (3 Feb. 1869) indicate the direction in which he thought he might break fresh ground when the time came for him to deal with this somewhat hackneyed subject:

Le prêtre amoureux de la créature, se débattant dans les fièvres chaudes de la passion, sentant son cœur se gonfler et faire éclater les

[1] See above, p. 15.   [2] *L'Écho du Nord*, 19 July 1864.

vœux qui le lient, est un héros dont les luttes poignantes et profondément humaines ont tenté bien des romanciers contemporains. A vrai
dire, cette grande figure de la chair révoltée et combattue a été jusqu'ici
pauvrement traitée. Les écrivains qui l'ont mise en œuvre en ont fait une
arme pour ou contre le catholicisme; selon moi, il faudrait l'étudier,
l'analyser sans parti pris, comme un cas humain d'un curieux intérêt.

This programme was not really implemented in *La Faute de l'abbé
Mouret*. Serge is not a case of 'la chair révoltée et combattue' since
he breaks his vows, as it were, in a state of innocence; having lost
his memory, his vestments exchanged for the loose clothing of a
convalescent, his tonsure hidden under a growth of new hair, he
must be exonerated at least from the fault of consciously rejecting
the demands of the religious life he had embraced.

Another small but significant change was that the forest of
'Simplice' becomes in *La Faute* a walled garden. This garden or
park, with the small lodge adjoining it, is the sole theatre of action
for the whole of the second of the three parts of the novel. Pascal
Rougon, who is Serge's uncle and his doctor, had the young priest
transported there during an attack of brain-fever brought on by
the austerity of his life, and left him to be nursed by the young girl
Albine who has scarcely ever stirred from its precincts. It is a garden
which has been allowed to run wild for decades and in which
exotic plants proliferate over lawns and drives. Such abandoned
estates did, it seems, exist in the part of the country where Zola
spent his boyhood: Paul Alexis mentions one, on the road from Aix
to Roquefavour, and Zola himself devoted one of his 'chroniques'
in *La Tribune* to describing another, discovered one hot afternoon
near the banks of the Durance.[1]

The situation of a young man and a girl isolated in a secret
garden and awakening to love suggested immediately to the novelist
the parallel with the second and third chapters of Genesis. He
made his intentions perfectly plain by calling the garden 'le
Paradou'. His preliminary notes show that the adaptation of the
story of Eden and the Fall was deliberate and carefully planned.
'C'est la nature qui joue le rôle du Satan de la Bible,' he wrote;
'c'est elle qui tente Serge et Blanche [i.e. Albine] et qui les couche
sous l'arbre du mal par une matinée splendide. . . . Je calque le

---

[1] *La Tribune*, 24 Oct. 1869. le bain, a short story by Zola first published in
La Renaissance artistique et littéraire, 24 Aug. 1873, has as its setting the
neglected pleasure garden in the grounds of a country house.

drame de la Bible, et à la fin je montre sans doute Frère Archangias apparaissant comme le dieu de la Bible et chassant du paradis les deux amoureux.'[1] But this modernization of an ancient myth involved a revision of interpretation so thorough that Zola can properly be said to have stood the Book of Genesis on its head.[2] For the act of love (corresponding to the eating of the apple) performed by his new Eve and Adam beneath a tree which is less the 'arbre du mal' than the Tree of Life, is surely not meant to be regarded by the reader as a transgression. Serge and Albine are complying with the natural law, the only law that Zola consciously and willingly recognized. The shame that Albine subsequently experiences is thus totally inappropriate.[3] 'Cachons-nous, cachons-nous', she cries. 'Elle cueillait, le long des haies, des verdures dont elle cachait sa nudité. . . . Elle lui dit à voix basse, d'un air d'alarme : Ne vois-tu pas que nous sommes nus ?' The scriptural reminiscence jars altogether with what might be called the thesis of La Faute de l'abbé Mouret, but it was allowed to stand, clearly, because it accorded exactly with the equivalence Zola habitually establishes, and which we have noted particularly in La Curée, between nudity and sinfulness. A fundamental ambiguity in Zola's attitude to sexual love emerges here. Virginity was, he considered, an antinatural state; continence if long continued in leads to monstrous growths in the imagination of the continent: there is an example ready to hand in Archangias, the abstinent friar who is foulmouthed in his denunciation of fornication. And yet the consummation of love, in all Zola's early novels from La Confession de Claude to La Faute de l'abbé Mouret, is invariably presented as at best a sad compromise, at worst a crime, and is usually attended by the sniff of brimstone to come.

This repulsive and stony-hearted Archangias, who drags Serge out of Le Paradou and back to his presbytery, leaving the gentle Albine to pine away and finally take her life, represents, Zola says, Jehovah. And why not? Archangias is God the Father, Zola's

---

[1] B.N. MS. Nouv. acq. fr. 10294, fol. 3.
[2] Phillip Walker ('Prophetic myths in Zola', P.M.L.A., vol. lxxiv (1959), pp. 444–52) writes of the 'irony, not to say sarcasm, underlying the repetition of the Biblical story' in La Faute de l'abbé Mouret. But there is nothing in the ébauche to show that this irony was intentional, or even that Zola was aware of it.
[3] This point has been vigorously made by R. B. Grant, 'Confusion of meaning in Zola's La Faute de l'abbé Mouret', Symposium, vol. xiii (1959), pp. 284–9.

father, for ever glowering in one of the darker recesses of his mind, with arm upraised in a gesture of prohibition or menace. *La Faute de l'abbé Mouret* must be read as yet another dramatization, after *Madeleine Férat*, of his unexpunged childhood guilt.

Zola was a personal artist to a greater degree than it suited him to admit. He would have liked the novel to be reduced to 'des notes prises sur la vie et logiquement classées'; the work of art was to be 'un procès-verbal, rien de plus; elle n'a que le mérite de l'observation exacte, de la pénétration plus ou moins profonde de l'analyse, de l'enchaînement logique des faits'.[1] The inventions of the imagination were to be proscribed and art was, somehow, to be distilled out of the bald facts.

How was this to be done? In 'documentation' he had, he thought, a discipline that he could rely on. Documentation was not merely a guarantee of authenticity, it was a brake applied to the wheels of runaway fancy. And so we may watch Zola stationed outside the mansion of the chocolate-millionaire Menier, at the entry to the Parc Monceau, and taking notes on the strength of which he might describe 'realistically' the residence of Saccard, in *La Curée*; then hurrying off to the Jardin des Plantes to view the conservatory there, which was to be the model for his hot-house. To please him Flaubert, who had been received at Compiègne in the old days, mimicked the Emperor's gait and talk, and the impression was carefully consigned to the pages of *Son Excellence Eugène Rougon*. Over the preparation of *La Faute de l'abbé Mouret* Zola took more trouble than ever. Alexis tells us that

for many months his desk was piled high with nothing but books of devotion. All the mystical part of the work, notably what concerns the cult of the Virgin, derives from his reading of Spanish jesuits. Many borrowings, almost word for word, were taken from *The Imitation of Christ*. The documentation for [Serge's] years in the seminary was obtained verbally from an unfrocked priest. Finally, on several consecutive mornings, in the little church of Sainte-Marie des Batignolles, the few pious women who attended early mass were edified by the presence of a man sitting in a corner, missal in hand, following the slightest movements of the priest so attentively that he might have been taken to be rapt in contemplation.

According to the same authority Zola did not only resort to gardeners' catalogues to equip himself for the descriptive passages

[1] *Le Roman expérimental*, pp. 197, 102.

in the second part, but went to the length of attending horticultural shows.

There is something a little pathetic in this expenditure of effort for results which are so little in proportion. No one would turn to *La Curée* for an historical account of the speculative fury which transformed the face of Paris in the days of Baron Haussmann; no one today reads *Le Ventre de Paris* in search of information about the growth and internal policing of the Central Markets. Whoever wished to investigate such matters would be better advised, if no more reliable source was available, to consult just those books that Zola drew on, *Les Comptes fantastiques d'Haussmann* by Jules Ferry or the relevant chapter in Maxime du Camp's *Paris, sa vie et ses organes*. And one has no need to be a great respecter of the religious life to decide that Serge Mouret, in spite of the indiscretions of a renegade priest, is far from being a typical specimen of the *genus abbatis*.

La Faute de l'abbé Mouret was described by Maupassant in his 1883 essay on Zola as 'a kind of poem in three parts', and by Huysmans in his pamphlet *Émile Zola et 'l'Assommoir'* (1880) as not a novel at all, properly speaking, 'but rather a love-poem and one of the finest poems I know'. Both these critics had been anticipated by Taine who wrote to Zola on receiving his presentation copy: '*La Faute de l'abbé Mouret* transcends the tone and the proportions of the novel; it is a poem . . . it reminds one of a piece of Persian poetry, of the intense and dazzling dreams of Heine, of passages in the Hindu epics.' Finally Zola appears to have accepted the verdict. He had long rejected verse, but his vision remained a poet's. Certain formulae used in the *ébauches* of later novels are significant: *Nana* started in his imagination as 'le poème des désirs du mâle', *Au Bonheur des Dames* as 'le poème de l'activité moderne', *La Terre* as 'le poème vivant de la terre'. It is not enough to say that the romantic poet survived in Zola: little of him that is worth having could have existed if the poet had died.

VI

VOX POPULI

IN the summer of 1875, Zola's wife needing to recover her strength after one of her periodical bouts of ill health, the couple went to stay at Saint-Aubin-sur-Mer, a resort on the Normandy coast. The novelist, an inlander all his life, was much stimulated by this first prolonged experience of the sea. He wrote to Alexis, who had found and booked them a cottage:

Nous avons ici des temps superbes, des tempêtes, des jours de grand soleil, des nuits de Naples, des mers phosphorescentes, le tout coup sur coup, brusquement. Jamais je n'ai vu un changement de décor plus varié. Par le temps gris, la mer est d'une immensité grandiose. Je commence à comprendre le pays que je trouvais d'une laideur abominable. Je prends des notes, à chaque nouvel aspect de la mer, pour un grand épisode descriptif d'une vingtaine de pages que je rêve de glisser dans un de mes romans.

The novel in question must have been *La Joie de vivre*, which he did not begin writing for another seven and a half years. This was Zola's way: the rapidity with which he brought out a new book often concealed a long period of conscious and subconscious gestation. The writing of *L'Assommoir*, to which he addressed himself immediately the summer holidays were over, is another instance of the same thing.

In the list of ten novels drawn up for his publisher's benefit before Zola had even invented the name Rougon-Macquart, there figures, as the seventh, 'un roman qui aura pour cadre le monde ouvrier. . . . Peinture d'un ménage d'ouvriers à notre époque, drame intime et profond de la déchéance du travailleur parisien sous la déplorable influence du milieu des barrières et des cabarets.'[1] All the time he was writing the earlier novels of the series Zola kept turning the idea over in his mind, and now and again noting down scenes which he might be able to introduce. A half-page of jottings which probably, to judge from the handwriting, were made shortly

[1] B.N. MS. *Nouv. acq. fr.* 10303, fol. 60.

after the war, itemizes many of the features and incidents incorporated in the finished novel: scenes to be situated in a laundry, women looking for their menfolk in the public houses; there are four lines summing up a feast given by the laundress, with the windows wide open so that the passers-by can join in the fun, which show that the main movements of chapter vii of *L'Assommoir* were fixed by the author several years before it was written down. This particular sketch is headed 'Roman ouvrier. — Le roman aux Batignolles'. The district which was originally intended to be the setting of his working-class novel was in fact where Zola had his home at the time, and these notes clearly record the typical street scenes he might have witnessed at any time of the day or night. It is probable that he was led to choose a laundress's establishment for Gervaise because the ironing of linen was one of the few kinds of manual labour which was conducted in full view of the bystander; Degas's famous series of paintings (which slightly antedate *L'Assommoir*) was identically inspired.

'J'ai longtemps vécu parmi le peuple', he wrote in answer to a working-class correspondent's appreciative letter about *L'Assommoir*. 'J'étais très pauvre et je l'ai vu de près. C'est ce qui m'a permis de parler de lui sans mensonge.' Memories, dating back to the early sixties, of the slum tenements he had been forced to take rooms in at this period offered him ample material for his account of the living conditions of the lower classes. One of his mother's brothers, Adolphe Aubert, was a house decorator periodically unemployed, and later a concierge at no. 2, place Saint-Michel; when Émile was eleven he and his mother, during a four-month visit to Paris, lodged with this family which included a little girl, Anna, a cousin who later appears to have gone to the bad, perhaps rather in the way that Anna Coupeau (Nana) was to in *L'Assommoir*. And, as we have seen, Alexandrine's antecedents were purely working-class.[1]

It is certain that Zola had accumulated sufficient material to write *L'Assommoir* earlier than he did, and we may wonder why he should have shied off this promising subject for so long. The idea of a sincere portrayal of an artisan family was, as he had grasped at

---

[1] Cf. E. Lepelletier, 'Les débuts d'Émile Zola', *Écho de Paris*, 1 Oct. 1902: 'Avec son beau-frère ouvrier dans le bâtiment, sa belle-sœur travaillant en journée, et sa belle-mère débitante de vins, Zola a eu sous les yeux le décor et les personnages de *l'Assommoir*.' Lepelletier's information cannot all be correct, however: Zola never knew his mother-in-law who, as has been noted, died when Alexandrine was still a girl.

the start, a boldly original one. The proletarian proper is almost totally absent from *La Comédie humaine*;[1] George Sand's working-class characters were charming fictions; Flaubert had not then written 'Un Cœur simple'. There had been, of course, *Germinie Lacerteux*: this, the most notorious of the Goncourts' novels, had been the first study of the lower classes by masters of realism, and the authors had justified their audacity in a preface which Zola doubtless read as an invitation to the scientist and social historian that he conceived himself to be, to embark on wider exploration of this almost virgin territory. It was not altogether by chance that one of Zola's 'holiday tasks' at Saint-Aubin was a long essay on the Goncourts in which the authors of *Germinie Lacerteux* are extolled for having given a new social class a place in serious literature.

There are many reasons why Zola should have shelved his working-class novel for so many years. With the reaction that followed the 1871 rising in Paris, it was not altogether safe for a novelist to draw attention to the plight of the proletariat, even if his attitude was strictly non-political. Repressive laws such as that passed in March 1872, making it a penal offence to belong to the Workers' International, were still in force; and it was not until 1879 that the *communards* were amnestied, and not until 1880 that the workers had recovered cohesion sufficiently to group themselves in a party. Then there were certain purely literary difficulties confronting Zola. All the previous novels, except perhaps *La Faute de l'abbé Mouret*, had been tethered to precise historical events or processes; but *L'Assommoir* was not to be contingent in this manner. Except for a passing reference to the street-fighting ensuing on the December seizure of power, and another, towards the end of the book, to the new streets and buildings which had changed the face of Paris during the course of the Second Empire, there is little in the novel of the 'colour of the times'. Lantier's rude remarks about the person of the Emperor, and the police-sergeant Poisson's dignified defence of the head of the state, are typical of men of their stamp under any form of government. *L'Assommoir*

---

[1] Balzac was aware of the existence of the working-man, 'l'ouvrier, le prolétaire, l'homme qui remue ses pieds, ses mains, sa langue, son dos, son seul bras, ses cinq doigts pour vivre', and describes his condition in a few vivid paragraphs in the first chapter of *La Fille aux yeux d'or*; he even introduced into *Pierrette* 'un jeune homme âgé d'environ seize ans, et dont la mise annonçait ce que la phraséologie moderne appelle si insolemment un prolétaire'. But this appears to be as far as his investigations took him.

was in a general sense a 'modern' novel, but it was not specifically an account of a particular aspect of the social scene during the reign of Napoleon III.

This was no fault; on the contrary, its generality gave the formulation wider currency; but with *L'Assommoir* Zola had to abandon one of his original specifications, the strict localization of the *Rougon-Macquart* novels in the period of which they were supposed to be a chronicle. And once he had relinquished the rigorously historical standpoint he did not try to regain it; among the later novels only *L'Argent*, *La Débâcle*, and possible *L'Œuvre*, can be described as scenes from the pageant of the Empire.

In *L'Assommoir* too, for the first time, chronological sequence between the novels is broken. It is the novel of Gervaise Macquart; and her son, Claude, had already been given an important part to play in *Le Ventre de Paris*. Here again a precedent was established: the novel of Jean Macquart, *La Terre*, appeared later than *L'Œuvre*, *Germinal*, *La Joie de vivre*, and *Nana*, the novels in which his nieces and nephews figure as principals. A methodical planner, Zola was bound to feel some uneasiness in making the river of time flow upstream.

Having set aside these small scruples, however, he went to work in a fury. Beside the sea, he pondered his plan, and wrote to his publisher that he was 'enchanted' with its simplicity and energy. He was back in the capital on 4 October and spent the next few days (until the 10th, when he started writing the novel) choosing the precise setting for his story and familiarizing himself with its layout. Zola always drew a line, however thin at times, between reality and fiction, and in fact there never was a gin-palace situated where he set down the infamous establishment of le père Colombe, at the corner of the Rue des Poissonniers and the Boulevard Rochechouart. But the streets described in *L'Assommoir* exist still, for the most part, in the area stretching back behind the Gare du Nord, though some of them have been rechristened; and the aspect and atmosphere of this quarter seem to have changed very little in the intervening eighty years. The overhead railway running above the boulevard in front of the Hôpital Lariboisière, which he helped to build, is perhaps the only landmark which Coupeau, were he to return today, would fail to recognize.

L'Assommoir was Zola's first indisputable masterpiece. He was to write two or three books which might be considered more overwhelming, but he was never to compose a more perfect work of art. Sheer artistic perfection was not something Zola often came within reach of—perhaps he seldom even strove seriously after it; and among all his books *L'Assommoir* alone is proof against the acid of purely formal criticism. Politicians and moralists have assailed it, but judges of literature, unless their judgement was tainted by morality or politics, have hardly diluted their admiration by a single serious qualification.

L'Assommoir proved that Zola could, at his best, construct a novel as well as Flaubert and better than any other of his predecessors or contemporaries. None of the earlier novels had been to anything like the same degree so purposefully and economically built. By comparison, they sprawl and bulge; they do not sweep up to their culmination, they distract by subsidiary outgrowths. But *L'Assommoir* has a classic simplicity of line which was not incompatible with the complexity and density of a work of realism.

This line coincides with the fortunes of Gervaise. Zola had, indeed, originally intended to call his novel *La Simple Vie de Gervaise Macquart*. Beginning at ground-level, with her desertion by Lantier, it mounts steadily through the second, third, fourth, and fifth chapters. If her prosperity shows no indication of decline at this point, however, the blight of decay has already set in. Her husband Coupeau's accident, the habits of idleness which his convalescence induces in him, the financial burden Gervaise shoulders by nursing him at home, these threats to her happiness manifest themselves even before it is crowned by the attainment of her dearest ambition, to set up in business on her own. In chapter v, which shows Gervaise completely contented, generally liked by her neighbours, and highly respected by the tradesmen, Zola placed a small episode which marks the first wavering in this ascendent line. It is an afternoon in June, hot out of doors, hotter still in the laundress's shop. Gervaise's three assistants are busily ironing, and Gervaise is counting out soiled garments to a washerwoman. 'Elle s'était assise au bord d'un tabouret, se courbant en deux, allongeant les mains à droite, à gauche, avec des gestes ralentis, comme si elle se grisait de cette puanteur humaine, vaguement souriante, les yeux noyés. Et il semblait que ses premières paresses vinssent de là, de l'asphyxie des vieux linges empoisonnant l'air autour d'elle.' Her husband enters the shop, the worse for drink. Indulgent as usual, she tries to get him to go and lie down, but he is obstinate, and she goes on telling out the washing. It piles up round her like a sea; and Coupeau, stumbling in it, insists on embracing her in front of the others. 'Elle s'abandonnait, étourdie par le léger vertige qui lui venait du tas de linge, sans dégoût pour l'haleine vineuse de Coupeau. Et le gros baiser qu'ils échangèrent à pleine bouche, au milieu des saletés du métier, était comme une première chute, dans le lent avachissement de leur vie.'

After this precarious zenith the curve descends, gradually at first, then more steeply. First it is Coupeau, who takes to drinking spirits when wine no longer satisfies him; then it is the return of Virginie, a reminder of bad old days, which heralds the reappearance of her former lover, Lantier; he and Coupeau strike up a dangerous friendship, and Lantier is invited to take a room in their flat; inevitably the evening comes when he makes Gervaise his mistress again. Her own increasing carelessness begins to lose her custom. Coupeau, seldom sober, strains her dwindling resources. Finally she has to give up her shop and move into a small, dark apartment at the top of the house.

This stage is reached in the tenth chapter: the decline nicely balances the ascent. And, as if to measure the distance covered, Zola notes a strange hallucination that Gervaise's nerves give her one day shortly after her move.

Un jour, se penchant, elle eut une drôle de sensation, elle crut se voir en personne là-bas, sous le porche, près de la loge du concierge, le nez en l'air, examinant la maison pour la première fois; et ce saut de treize ans en arrière lui donna un élancement au cœur. La cour n'avait pas changeé. . . . Mais elle, à cette heure, se sentait joliment changée et décatie. Elle n'était plus en bas, d'abord, la figure vers le ciel, contente et courageuse, ambitionnant un bel appartement. Elle était sous les toits, dans le coin des pouilleux, dans le trou le plus sale, à l'endroit où l'on ne recevait jamais la visite d'un rayon. Et ça expliquait ses larmes, elle ne pouvait pas être enchantée de son sort.

The line of development, after briefly maintaining itself at this low level, takes a sudden further plunge and pitches downwards into the nether depths. Zola had toyed with the idea of some frightful ending. Gervaise was to find Lantier in bed with her rival, and empty a bottle of acid over their bodies. Lantier, maddened with the pain, was to drag Gervaise by the hair into the courtyard and when Goujet tried to intervene, engage in a fearful duel with the smith. Then Lorilleux, Gervaise's brother-in-law, was to kick her as she lay on the ground, and this brutal assault was to end her life. Wisely, he rejected this melodrama. It was not in Gervaise to revolt; she accepts Lantier's desertion, and having sold her shop to Virginie who has supplanted her, is glad to come and scrub the floor for her under the indifferent eye of her former lover. Already she has taken to drink in imitation of her husband. Her daughter, Nana, tired of blows and of going supperless to bed, leaves home and starts her career as a *fille galante*. Gervaise herself endures the final humiliation of being driven on to the streets by hunger. The end is a drawn-out agony. Coupeau dies raving in a padded cell. She perishes slowly, in idiocy, of hunger and cold, so neglected that the neighbours know she is dead only when the smell attracts their notice.

There is nothing sinuous in this line, nothing to deflect its steady rise and inexorable plunge. Zola supported it on huge chunks of chapters, after his custom. Each is solidly massed round one or two central episodes, so that if it had been the fashion in the French novel, as it was in the English, to give titles to chapters, these would have imposed themselves almost automatically: 'Le Lavoir', 'La Maison de la rue de la Goutte d'Or', 'La Noce', and so forth. The seventh chapter is outstanding in its unity and fullness, being through its fifty pages entirely taken up with the narrative of a gargantuan feast Gervaise gives on her name-day, beginning with the choice of guests and menu and ending with the vision of the cat walking on to the table and finishing off the goose while the diners are snoring where they sit or lie.

The complete control which Zola maintains over his effects, and the assurance with which he graduates and gears them, are signs of the mastery which inborn gifts and practice had given him over his art.

Though *L'Assommoir* is superior to the novels that had preceded it, it is not essentially distinct from them. We find in it the same over-exuberant vision of reality which gives their peculiar quality to *La Curée, Le Ventre de Paris,* and the others; there had been no departure from the earlier technique, only a more balanced and maturer application of it.

Zola's habitual use of symbolism to impose an artificial pattern on the meaninglessness of reality can be observed in *L'Assommoir*, but it is not disconcertingly obtrusive, as in some of the other novels. The colour of the waste water that runs from the dyer's workshop across the yard of the tenement house varies according to the state of Gervaise's fortunes; this is the pathetic fallacy, but in a minor degree, so that it enters into the fabric of the book without standing out in a hard knot. Bazouge, the perpetually drunken undertaker's assistant, stands outside real life, a blear-eyed wizard casting a malignant spell over Gervaise in her hour of contentment and seeing it worked out at the end as he had prophesied;[1] but if exception is to be taken to Bazouge, on the grounds that he conflicts with the unexciting banality of ordinary fact, the same objection would have to be brought against the blind beggar who haunts Emma Bovary in her decline, and the sinister moujik with his sack over his shoulder of whom Anna Karenina dreams and who rides the train that crushes her to death. In *L'Assommoir* Zola did not strip his subject down to the 'unvarnished truth': had he done so he would probably not have achieved a great work of literature. Zola left it to his disciples to make the experiment, with what jejune results anyone can discover by reading such a book as Huysmans's *Sœurs Vatard* (another study of the Parisian working classes which followed *L'Assommoir* after an interval of two years, and 'the best and only true naturalist novel', in Remy de Gourmont's judgement). Whatever he might publicly proclaim, Zola intuitively realized that art was not photography, and that bare realism was too constricted a formula.

As in *Le Ventre de Paris*, we can watch, in *L'Assommoir*, things of brick and metal starting into a species of independent sub-life and groping with deadly tentacles after the living whom they dwarf and devour. Again, it is symbolism, a transcending of reality by the artist who, outside his polemical works, was never a doctrinaire of realism. The distillery with its adjoining tavern has often been quoted as the materialization of the curse of drink; but in fact Zola gives it relatively little prominence, and only when Gervaise is tempted to drown her miseries in alcohol (chapter x) does the still come to life: Zola compares it to 'quelque sorcière qui lâchait goutte à goutte le feu de ses entrailles'. Less noticed has been Zola's use of the huge apartment house to symbolize the demoralizing promiscuity of slum life. The house impresses the reader as a giant sponge, alive itself and peopled by swarms of existences, right from

---

[1] The undertaker was, in any case, regarded with a sort of superstitious horror by the lower orders in France at this period. Zola founded one of the *Nouveaux Contes à Ninon* ('Mon ami Jacques') on this popular aversion to the *croque-mort*.

the moment when it first confronts Gervaise, 'surprise de cette énormité, se sentant au milieu d'un organe vivant, au cœur même d'une ville, intéressée par la maison, comme si elle avait eu devant elle une personne géante'. Some years pass before she goes to live in the block, but when she does, 'il lui semblait faire quelque chose de très hardi, se jeter au beau milieu d'une machine en branle, pendant que les marteaux du serrurier et les rabots de l'ébéniste tapaient et sifflaient, au fond des ateliers du rez-de-chaussée'.

These are elements in *L'Assommoir* which hint at a more significant universe than that visible to the mere observer, but they are neither numerous enough nor sufficiently disturbing for the book to be classed as allegorical fantasy or sombre rhapsody or indeed as anything but realistic fiction. It is rooted in ordinary life by the characters; their environment is not allowed to stifle them by its brooding presence, and there is nothing about them but what is redolent of human nature. Admittedly, it was human nature at its least polished and least subtle: this is perhaps why Zola managed it so well. His unlettered toilers, whose native spontaneity has not been trimmed or refined by any life of the mind, were the ideal caryatids of the kind of monumental art which it was in him to construct. The worst that can be said is that there is a certain lack of substance in Goujet, with his tearful, platonic admiration of Gervaise and his filial piety. But Goujet was a concession to philanthropists who believed in 'the deserving poor'. The rest of them—Coupeau, gay and friendly, until his accident breaks his nerve and alcohol poisons his character; Lantier, the unscrupulous and irresponsible plunderer, the Lorilleux, soured by avarice, and Mme Lerat, with her would-be scabrous innuendoes: all these and all the others are firmly planted, brightly if crudely coloured; their remarks are unprompted, their movements unrehearsed; the food and drink they consume with such gusto go to build real flesh and bone inside them.

In particular, Gervaise is for Zola a unique achievement. She is not a type, which is why she has not broken loose and become self-subsistent like Becky Sharp or Sarah Gamp. But Zola gave her an imperishable local presence, and Gervaise is one of those figments of the imagination which for many book-lovers retain a more authentic existence than most of the people they have daily dealings with.

She was conceived under the sign of pathos, yet never was there a more discreet and purified pathos than this. She has what virtues she can and what ambitions she may; but her best virtue—simple good-heartedness—is the soft spot through which circumstance wounds her mortally, and her modest demands of life are cruelly rejected, one by one and one and all. 'Mon Dieu! je ne suis pas ambitieuse, je ne demande pas grand'chose', she had told Coupeau when he was courting her in her younger days.

Mon idéal, ce serait de travailler tranquille, de manger toujours du pain, d'avoir un trou un peu propre pour dormir, vous savez, un lit, une table et deux chaises, pas davantage. . . . Ah! je voudrais aussi élever mes enfants, en faire de bons sujets, si c'était possible. . . . Il y a encore un idéal, ce serait de ne pas être battue, si je me remettais jamais en ménage; non, ça ne me plairait pas d'être battue. . . . Et c'est tout, vous voyez, c'est tout. . . .
Elle cherchait, interrogeait ses désirs, ne trouvait plus rien de sérieux qui la tentât. Cependant, elle reprit, après avoir hésité:
— Oui, on peut à la fin avoir le désir de mourir dans son lit. . . . Moi, après avoir bien trimé toute ma vie, je mourrais volontiers dans mon lit, chez moi.

This unassuming programme is turned upside down—by bad luck, as Gervaise thinks, but really by the merciless pressure of the social environment, as the determinist, Zola, knows. In her old age (she ages rapidly) she cannot find work, she starves or eats refuse, she sleeps on filthy straw. Her daughter prostitutes herself, her husband ill-treats her. And she dies like a pariah-dog.

By moving us as deeply with his recital of Gervaise's disillusions as any tragic poet with the history of kings stricken by blindness and brought to beggary, Zola proved that, contrary to the classical doctrine, the aesthetic potentialities of a catastrophe do not vary directly with its magnitude. The fall of a sparrow is, in the artist's eyes, as pregnant with pity and terror as the fall of a conqueror. Balzac had invested the bankruptcy of a scent-manufacturer with the tragic pomp of the direst disasters. *L'Assommoir* was a further milestone, after *La Grandeur et la décadence de César Birotteau*, along the path that led from the literature of feudalism to that of the age of the common man.

Only one or two of Zola's more discerning readers, among them Mallarmé,[1] saw this overriding quality which is what ultimately

[1] Mallarmé wrote to Zola, after reading *L'Assommoir*: 'Voilà une bien grande œuvre; et digne d'une époque où la vérité devient la forme populaire de la

confers greatness and permanence on *L'Assommoir*. The book startled and shocked many, but, judging from the comments uttered in the press, for reasons we should now be inclined to dismiss as secondary. Two points were chiefly fastened on, for praise or blame: the style the novel was written in; and the social-political intentions of the author.

There is a story that Zola, arriving late for a dinner appointment, excused himself by explaining that he had been revolving in his mind how he was to write the narrative part of his book. While waiting for his bus, the expression that Lantier would have used in the circumstances flashed into his mind: *Je fais le poireau sur le trottoir*. It came to him as a revelation: everything in the book must be shown through the minds of the characters, and expressed in their words. 'Il ne faut pas que l'atmosphère qui les entoure soit telle que je la vois, mais bien telle qu'ils la voient eux-mêmes. Ce n'est donc pas dans mon langage d'écrivain que je dois la décrire, mais dans le leur, dans la langue qu'ils parlent.'[1]

To a realist writer it was self-evident that his characters should be made to speak as did their real-life counterparts. Zola learned the workmen's colloquialisms from conversations overheard in the streets and behind tavern doors; he also studied certain dictionaries of popular speech, although it has been established[2] that he used them in the main merely to remind him of a vocabulary which he had already thoroughly assimilated aurally. As he explained in his preface, it was 'un travail purement philologique'. But his sense of artistic cohesion was troubled by the prospect of having to juxtapose in his novel two distinct styles—a familiar, racy one for dialogue, and a stylized, neutral one for recitative. It was a problem that had given Flaubert much anxiety while he was composing *Madame Bovary*. 'Ce que j'écris présentement', he had complained to a correspondent, 'risque d'être du Paul de Kock si je n'y mets une forme profondément littéraire: mais comment faire du dialogue trivial qui soit bien écrit?' Flaubert's solution is implicit in his grumble: the book as a whole was to be supremely well written,

beauté! Ceux qui vous accusent de n'avoir pas écrit pour le peuple se trompent dans un sens, autant que ceux qui regrettent un idéal ancien; vous en avez trouvé un qui est moderne, c'est tout.'

[1] See J. Patin, 'Du "Bœuf nature" à la "table des beylistes"', *Le Figaro*, 7 Dec. 1930.

[2] By M. Cressot, 'La Langue de *l'Assommoir*', *Le Français moderne*, vol. viii (1940), pp. 207–18.

and what dialogue there was would have to harmonize with the rest. In practice Flaubert avoided directly reporting conversation as often as he could.

Zola's solution was diametrically opposed; for him, the vulgarity of his characters' speech was to be extended over the whole of the work. It is true, of course, that there is a world of difference between the mannered provincial middle-class types that inhabit *Madame Bovary* and the tough Parisian artisans in *L'Assommoir* whose language, if monotonous, was often picturesque and invariably sinewy.

However, Zola's reversal of his friend's method is enough to explain Flaubert's peevish reception of the book, or rather, of the odd instalments he read at first in *La République des Lettres*. 'Zola devient une précieuse à *l'inverse*' he wrote to Turgenev. 'Il croit qu'il y a des mots énergiques, comme Cathos et Madelon croyaient qu'il en existait de nobles. Le *Système* l'égare.'[1] This was a hasty judgement (Flaubert was fairer when he had had a chance to read the book in volume form).[2] Zola's only 'system' was to maintain the unity of tone. In a reply to Albert Millaud, who had assailed the book with vigour in *Le Figaro*, Zola pleaded: 'Vous me concédez que je puis donner à mes personnages leur langue accoutumée. Faites encore un effort, comprenez que des raisons d'équilibre et d'harmonie générale m'ont seules décidé à adopter un style uniforme.'

The effect of his decision went further than these purely technical considerations suggest. The book itself had, from the very start, been intended as a study of the repercussions of environment —an evil environment—on a typical victim of that environment. Gervaise was that victim. 'Une nature moyenne' Zola called her, 'qui pourrait faire une excellente femme, selon le milieu. *L'étude du milieu sur une femme ni bonne ni mauvaise.*'[3] This environment was

---

[1] The same observation was made apparently independently by Henri Houssaye, in his damning review of *L'Assommoir* for *Le Journal des Débats*: 'M. Zola, qui méprise assurément la littérature de l'hôtel Rambouillet, est, lui aussi, un précieux, un précieux d'un genre tout particulier: le précieux de l'ordure.'

[2] He recommended it heartily to Mme Roger des Genettes: 'Connaissez-vous *la Fille Élisa* [Goncourt's novel about a prostitute, which was just out]? C'est sommaire et anémique, et *l'Assommoir* à côté paraît un chef-d'œuvre, car enfin il y a dans ces longues pages malpropres une puissance réelle et un tempérament incontestable' (letter dated 2 Apr. 1877).

[3] The words occur in the section of the preparatory notes entitled 'Personnages': B.N. MS. *Nouv. acq. fr.* 10271, fol. 122.

to an important degree composed of the other inhabitants of slum-land, the gossiping housewives for whom Gervaise's ascent to respectability and subsequent decline to destitution is a natural subject for endless envious commentary or jubilant *Schadenfreude*. Zola adopts the language of these aproned gossips, and with it their moral standpoint, head-shaking or shoulder-shrugging as the case may be. The result looks very like moral neutralism and in fact *L'Assommoir* has been attacked for this, in what is surely the most searching critical examination of the novel so far conducted.[1] Gervaise, it is claimed,

becomes so much a conditioned part of her milieu that she can only properly be described in its own colloquial terms. We get not appraisal, but the impression of a forced withdrawal from the attempt at appraisal; we witness a gradual retreat by the novelist, a handing over of his role to a succession of appropriate narrators. The novel is a dramatized admission, and demonstration, of the impossibility of an absolute moral judgement. . . .

and is therefore, the critic implies, of limited value. In effect what is being said here is that Zola did not take up the same attitude towards his material as did George Eliot. But, of course, to have done so would have been quite inappropriate. Hetty and Gwendolen Harleth are products of their environment as Gervaise Macquart was of hers. The spiritually well-nourished, Protestant origins of these heroines permitted, even encouraged, development of the faculty of moral discrimination which, even when they ignore it, makes us, and the author, value them. The starved child-mother, daughter of drunkards, uprooted from her province and abandoned to fend for herself in a city where no one cared if she lived or died, is a different creature altogether, set in altogether different conditions. That Zola, in order to enter into her and convey to us the savour of her life, by a device of style which helped him to a new vision shut himself and us up in the same world as she inhabits and forgot there were other worlds, is perhaps, after all, proof of transcendent human charity.

Moreover there is, in *L'Assommoir*, an 'absolute moral judge-ment', but it is passed on absentees.

Three years before he wrote his novel Zola published an indig-nant article in a newspaper which, a few days later, was suppressed

---

[1] Ian Gregor and Brian Nicholas, *The Moral and the Story* (1962). The quota-tion that follows is taken from p. 77.

by government order because of an even more inflammatory contribution of his. A deputy of the right had referred to the workers as a drunken rabble, and Zola made the obvious point (obvious now, but novel then) that if their wages went on drink, their employers were to be blamed for underpaying and overworking them. 'Quand l'homme est changé en machine, quand on ne lui demande plus que le rôle d'un engrenage ou d'un piston, il faut lui tolérer le vin, le vin qui rend puissant, qui met du cœur au ventre. Si les salaires étaient plus élevés, si une journée n'avait pas douze heures, il se boirait moins de litres dans les faubourgs.' Then, addressing the ruling classes, Zola told them that if the worker loses hope and self-respect, 's'il glisse, s'il roule à l'ivrognerie, c'est votre faute. . . . Il entre au cabaret, il prend la joie qu'il a sous la main, il en abuse, parce que vous lui fermez l'horizon et qu'il a besoin d'un rêve, fût-ce le rêve de l'ivresse.'[1]

These lines enshrine the unexpressed moral argument of *L'Assommoir*. But since the argument was unstated in the novel, however clearly it was implied, Zola came under the fiercest of attacks from the political champions of the working classes. The book was denounced by Charles Floquet as 'un pamphlet ridicule dirigé contre les travailleurs et forgeant ainsi des armes pour la réaction'. Arthur Ranc, in exile in Brussels, published there a booklet entitled *M. Émile Zola et 'L'Assommoir'* in which he concluded that 'M. Zola est un bourgeois, bourgeois dans le mauvais sens du mot. Il a pour le peuple un mépris de bourgeois, doublé d'un mépris d'artiste faisant de l'art pour l'art, d'un mépris néronien.'[2]

Zola answered these reproaches in a long and interesting letter addressed to the editor of *Le Bien public* and published in its literary supplement, *La Vie littéraire*, on 22 February 1877. Zola's arguments are those he had often used before: given a social evil (here, the drunkenness, promiscuity, and illiteracy of the lower classes) one begins by analysing the causes of this evil. This is what he had done in *L'Assommoir*. 'Je ne suis qu'un greffier qui me défends de conclure. Mais je laisse aux moralistes et aux législateurs le soin de réfléchir et de trouver les remèdes.'

The reception of the book by the 'moralists and legislators' must have made Zola wonder whether this partitioning of responsibilities

[1] *Le Corsaire*, 17 Dec. 1872.
[2] Quoted by Zévaès, *Zola*, pp. 63–64.

was ever likely to work satisfactorily. No one seemed to draw the obvious conclusions which he proceeds to spell out in the next paragraph of this letter: build more schools, abolish overcrowding, raise the level of wages, and reduce the hours of work. Conservative politicians used *L'Assommoir* simply as evidence that the lower strata of society were unfit to vote.[1] Socialist politicians were indignant because Zola appeared to be providing just this evidence which could ruin their hopes of building up a strong party of the left. It seemed that it was not enough, then, simply to imply the need for extensive, costly, and in many ways revolutionary social reforms: the need would have to be urged, and urged in the pages of his novels. But this meant a complete break with the aesthetic of impartial statement that Zola had inherited from Flaubert.

Zola made this break, hesitantly at first, but more and more unmistakably with the years. As we pass from *L'Assommoir* to the *romans à thèse* of his last period, Zola's sense of the social responsibilities of the writer can be observed growing steadily more acute until, in the end, he seems to have become so weighed down by responsibility that he can no longer write.

The process would never have started if *L'Assommoir* had not been so widely discussed and universally read. Its success took him by surprise. Just before publication date he suggested to Charpentier that if they were patient they might be able to sell between five and six thousand copies in time. In the event, *L'Assommoir* ran through its 38th impression before the end of the year (1877), and the hundred thousandth copy was sold in 1881. And, of course, the earlier novels benefited from this soar in Zola's stock. It had almost seemed that literary critics had agreed on a deliberate policy of silence where Zola was concerned: with few exceptions, none of them took note of any of the first six *Rougon-Macquart* volumes as they appeared. Flaubert was infuriated by this cold-shouldering. 'Jusqu'à quelle profondeur de bêtise descendrons-nous?' he asked George Sand rhetorically in 1874. 'Le dernier livre de Belot s'est

---

[1] Armand Lanoux (preface, Pléiade edition of *Les Rougon-Macquart*) quotes from the 1878 edition of Larousse's famous encyclopedia (*Grand Dictionnaire universel du XIXe siècle*) which included, even at this date, an entry devoted to Zola. His novel was here judged to play into the hands of the reactionaries: 'Les ennemis de la République y pourraient trouver une arme contre le suffrage universel; car s'il y a parmi le peuple beaucoup d'hommes semblables aux principaux personnages de *l'Assommoir*, on est forcé de convenir que de tels hommes paraissent peu dignes d'exercer des droits politiques.'

vendu en quinze jours à huit mille exemplaires, *la Conquête de Plassans* de Zola à dix-sept cents en six mois, et il n'a pas eu un article!' Zola would have infinitely preferred invective to this studied neglect.[1]

But the boycott broke down after *L'Assommoir*, and for twenty years (until the odium he incurred over the Dreyfus Affair permitted it to be partly reimposed) remained in abeyance. Zola became the most discussed writer in France; he had the ear of the entire reading public, unmarried girls of good family apart.

A contemporary Englishman gave a graphic if perhaps exaggerated account of the excitement aroused by the appearance of a new Zola novel in those days. It was 'a boulevard event looked forward to for days previously. On the mornings of publication huge piles of the yellow-backed volumes may be seen heaped up on the stalls of the booksellers, and by noon the boulevard is flecked by yellow spots as people hurry along, each holding in his hand the eagerly purchased volume.'[2]

Popularity, of course, was materialized in a rain of gold. Until shortly before, Zola had been quite a poor man. A fairly detailed account of his financial position at the beginning of 1875 is to be found in one of the letters which Turgenev wrote to Stasyulevitch when he was arranging for Zola to start contributing articles to Stasyulevitch's periodical, *Vestnik Evropy*.[3] Zola, it appears, was receiving a subsidy of 6,000 francs a year (£240 at the rate of exchange in those days) from his publisher Charpentier in lieu of royalties; this was a long-standing arrangement made at Zola's own request after the war. He was earning a few extra sums by freelance journalism but, as Turgenev said, 'Zola, working from morning to night and living very modestly and even poorly, can hardly make ends meet'—a statement which it is not hard to accept, for Zola not only had to support his wife and mother, but had to renew bills issued in his name at the time of Lacroix's bankruptcy, not to

[1] A paragraph in Zola's essay on Musset in *Documents littéraires* seems to refer as much to his own case as to that of the poet he is discussing: 'En France, le fait s'est répété pour tous les hommes de grand talent qui grandissent isolés, sans appartenir à une coterie. Quand un nouveau venu paraît gênant, on se contente de ne jamais prononcer son nom, quel que soit le chef-d'œuvre qu'il produise. De cette façon on espère que le public l'ignorera et que, de désespoir, il cessera peut-être de produire.'

[2] Sherard, *Émile Zola* (1893), p. 118.

[3] The letter (dated 13 Mar. 1875) is given in Lemke, *M. M. Stasyulevitch i ego sovremenniki . . .*, vol. iii, p. 51.

speak of debts incurred before the war during bouts of unemployment.

It is true that after 1875 his position improved considerably, for Stasyulevitch paid him rather more than 500 francs a quarter for his articles, while in 1876 he accepted the post of dramatic critic on *Le Bien public* at a salary of 6,000 francs a year. His appointment with the Marseilles paper *Le Sémaphore* continued, and all told he must have been earning something more than 15,000 francs (£600) annually, which in those days was a comfortable income.

However, the success of *L'Assommoir* turned Zola into a rich man, and incidentally put Charpentier on his feet. The publishing house was in no very flourishing state before 1877, and, as his partner later revealed, Charpentier had every reason to feel relieved when Zola at last produced a best-seller.[1] He generously cancelled his first contract with Zola and began paying him royalties of 50 centimes a copy; and since in the summer of 1877 (*L'Assommoir* was published at the end of February) his novels were already selling between 2,500 and 3,000 copies a month, these royalties alone rapidly amounted to an extremely handsome income. In addition, newspapers began paying him larger sums for the right to serialize his novels, and to publish other products of his pen (he accepted 18,000 francs in 1880 from *Le Figaro* for fifty-two weekly articles). Specialist publishers sought his agreement for illustrated editions, foreign publishers treated with him for translation rights, theatre managers paid him for stage adaptations of the novels. It has been estimated that, by the mid 1880's, Zola was half-way on the road to being a millionaire.[2]

The rewards of *L'Assommoir* were a visible sign that the author had at last emerged from the wilderness and made contact with humanity—with humanity's broadest reaches. With this book Zola came to be regarded as the novelist of the common people, writing in their language and about their lives. Only a little before this triumph he had morosely declared at Edmond de Goncourt's dinner-table that he would always be a 'pariah' for the public, repeating this word four or five times. From now on that risk was not to be reckoned with; but there were other risks, for favour takes toll no less than ostracism.

[1] Dreyfous, *Ce qu'il me reste à dire*, p. 303.
[2] See Lanoux, *Bonjour Monsieur Zola*, p. 184.

VII

THE FLESH AND THE DEVIL

THERE are large tracts of Zola's writing which can profitably be approached along the lines he himself suggested when he defined the work of art as a section of nature seen through the medium of a temperament. 'Temperament' is a loose enough term; still, it is fairly clear, for instance, that in *Le Ventre de Paris* Zola set out to see and then render accurately the life of the Paris markets, but that his vision and rendering were strongly affected by certain inborn tendencies: a love of vivid colouring, a leaning towards allegories and symbols, a bent for anthropomorphism, and so forth. These were so many factors preventing him from achieving an objective presentation of life and nature; or, looked at in a different way, these were the sources of the peculiarly Zolaesque illumination shed over the scenes he observed. The four novels that were published in succession to *L'Assommoir* and which we have now to consider show the same discrepancy between purpose and result. They all in some degree distort instead of copying reality; but this time not by reason of the author's 'temperament' so much as of the temporary pressure on him of certain questions, of one question above all.

Une Page d'amour, *Nana*, *Pot-Bouille*, and *Au Bonheur des Dames* all deal, in the last resort, with the same problem: the disruptive force of the passion of love. It was a subject that had hardly concerned Zola since he had started on his great undertaking. The early novels of the *Rougon-Macquart* cycle deal, on the whole, with other themes. 'Il est inutile', he wrote in his preliminary 'Notes générales', 'de s'attacher sans cesse aux drames de la chair. Je trouverai autre chose,—d'aussi poignant.' *La Curée*, *La Conquête de Plassans*, and *L'Assommoir* are all studies of the disintegration of a family. But in the first book it is not primarily Renée's depravity but Saccard's gold-fever that leads to this disaster; *La Conquête de Plassans* has, properly speaking, no love-plot at all; while in *L'Assommoir* love—Coupeau's, and then Goujet's, for Gervaise—is clearly subordinate to the main theme which is, as Zola described it himself, 'la déchéance fatale d'une famille ouvrière, dans le milieu empesté de nos faubourgs', in which 'le relâchement des liens de la famille, les ordures de la promiscuité' will be simply an end-product.

The case of *La Conquête de Plassans* is particularly instructive. Originally Zola had planned that the priest who comes to lodge with the Mourets should make Marthe his mistress. In the first half of the *ébauche* Zola sketches out a novel which would have given Faujas something of the complexion—if not the stature—of Tartuffe. After due consideration he changed his mind. 'Je pense qu'il faut modifier le sujet ainsi qu'il suit', he wrote. 'D'abord faire Faujas chaste. Il n'est que dominateur et non sensuel. . . . C'est un ambitieux, rien de plus. Je ne lui donnerai donc aucun désir devant Marthe. Il la pétrit comme une cire molle pour ses projets.' Marthe will be attracted to him, and he will recognize this. 'Mais il s'en défend. Il *use* seulement de cet amour, pour venir à bout de ses projets. Lui, dit que les hommes chastes sont seuls forts.'[1] Faujas, in this as in other respects, resembles his patron Eugène Rougon. This hero of a later novel also remains always master of his own desires. He is violently attracted to Clorinde Balbi, who would willingly marry him; but as a wife she would be of no help to him in his political career, though as a mistress, she might. There is, in *Son Excellence Eugène Rougon*, a scene where he tries to assault her in a stable, and is held at bay by her expert use of a riding-crop. When she leaves, he throws himself on a sofa, and after ten minutes of silent struggle he regains self-control. He makes no further attempt to approach Clorinde, and instead marries her off to one of his creatures.

Paul Alexis was the first of several commentators to suggest that Eugène Rougon, in the novel to which he gave his name, was in some respects a self-portrait of the author.[2] Eugène's ability to do without women is perhaps one of the points of resemblance; for Zola had his theory—which he shared, incidentally, with Flaubert—about the need for continence in creative artists.

Clorinde avenges herself on Eugène for his rejection of her, and uses her attraction on other men, including the Emperor, to have

[1] B.N. MS. *Nouv. acq. fr.* 10280, fols. 29, 31.
[2] Alexis, *Émile Zola, notes d'un ami*, p. 105; Lepelletier, *Émile Zola, sa vie, son œuvre*, p. 73; R. B. Grant, *Zola's 'Son Excellence Eugène Rougon'*, p. 90.

him thrown out of office; but essentially her manœuvres are political, and the novel remains, as we have seen, a political novel, not a study of sexual intrigue.

In *Une Page d'amour*, however, the intrinsic destructiveness of the passion of love becomes, for the first time, the principal theme of a novel by Zola. 'Voici ce que je désirerais comme sujet', he wrote at the beginning of the *ébauche*. 'Une passion. De quoi se compose une grande passion. Naissance de la passion, comment elle croît, quels effets elle amène dans l'homme et dans la femme, ses péripéties, enfin comment elle finit.' But Zola remembered enough school Latin to know what this word meant; and, after sketching out a possible plot, he wrote further: 'Mon sujet devient celui-ci: . . . *la passion* dans le sens de la *souffrance*, les quelques joies aiguës et les déchirements profonds: *un calvaire*.'[1]

There is a curious and revealing slip of the pen in these preparatory notes. Zola wrote: 'Étudier dans le ménage ces trois figures: la femme, l'amant, le mari, l'enfant.'[2] The three figures he mentions first—wife, lover, and husband—are of course the conventional actors in what might fairly be called the 'classical' triangle situation: treated in the comic mode in *Georges Dandin*, for example, and in the tragic in *La Princesse de Clèves*. By adding the child, Zola was adding the typical complication of modern adultery which Molière and Mme de Lafayette had, for reasons of economy or seemliness, excluded. Nevertheless, in intention and design, *Une Page d'amour* was a work in which the virtues and the values of classicism were if possible to be reinstated. '*Faire l'histoire générale* de l'amour en notre temps', he wrote. 'Tout le mérite devrait être dans le côté *général* de l'œuvre. Il faudrait que tout le monde s'y reconnût.' The conflict within the heroine was to be a moral conflict: just as Mme de Clèves found herself divided between her duty as a wife and her passionate inclinations as a woman, so Zola's heroine was to find her longing to be loved at variance with her obligations to her child. Mme de Lafayette, spending relatively little time on the thoughts and feelings of M. de Clèves and M. de Nemours, had concentrated her analytical powers on displaying the agonized struggle in the mind of her princess; in the same way Zola decided

---

[1] B.N. MS. *Nouv. acq. fr.* 10318, fols. 491, 503.
[2] Ibid., fol. 492. S. Lemm, who quotes the passage in which this sentence occurs, corrects without comment: 'Étudier dans le ménage ces *quatre* figures . . .' (*Zur Entstehungsgeschichte von Émile Zolas Rougon-Macquart . . .*, p. 27.)

that his lover's emotions would be indicated merely in his words and actions, 'tandis que je sonderai et analyserai Agathe jusqu'aux dernières fibres'. Finally, the drama would be kept as simple as possible, which again is in accordance with classical prescripts. 'L'important, je m'en aperçois, ne serait pas de multiplier les faits; mais de les fixer et de les élargir.'

Zola departed from the schema of *La Princesse de Clèves* by choosing as his protagonist an unattached woman, while the lover is a married man. Hélène Grandjean (the name Agathe, used in the *ébauche*, was changed presumably because it had been used in *La Curée* for Saccard's first wife) is a young widow living alone in Paris with her small daughter Jeanne, who emerges finally as the true third member of the triangle; and just as M. de Clèves's death ultimately drives Mme de Clèves and M. de Nemours apart, so Jeanne's death will end matters between Hélène and the doctor, Deberle, with whom she falls in love. Jeanne is intelligent, precocious, but not strong. It is a sudden illness of hers that brings Deberle on to the scene. He and Hélène drift into a sentimental attachment and, after wrestling with their scruples for the greater part of the book, become lovers. Meanwhile Jeanne, a morbidly susceptible child, is suffering intensely from her mother's transfer of affections to an outsider. In the end she dies of a chill caught when Hélène is out of the house keeping an assignment, and this shock breaks the tie between the lovers. The doctor returns to his wife and Hélène marries an older, stolid admirer.

Zola saw clearly enough that his story would be neither exciting nor exalting. 'Tout cela manque un peu de grandeur', he remarked a little doubtfully in the *ébauche*. He had gone down to L'Estaque to compose his book, in the summer and autumn of 1877, and wrote from there to Edmond de Goncourt telling him that *Une Page d'amour* would provide a striking contrast to *L'Assommoir*, a contrast which he claimed was intentional. 'Cela fera opposition, et l'on va me classer parmi les romanciers honnêtes. Par parti pris, je travaille pour les pensionnaires, je me fais plat et gris.' Flat and grey are the right adjectives. His mistake was to choose a situation which gave no scope for his particular gifts as a novelist. He had noted that he was proposing to 'étudier l'amour naissant et grandissant comme j'ai étudié l'ivrognerie' (in *L'Assommoir*); but love, though it may be an intoxication, and even an obsession, can never be an addiction. The kind of effect a novelist can study when he is dealing with a character in love is—as Proust has demonstrated exhaustively—self-discovery, deepening self-knowledge. Zola's insight was never of the quality or penetration that would allow him to make this kind of exploration. The pages he devotes (in the fifth chapter of the second part, for instance) to Hélène's meditations as she sits by her window looking out over Paris, are painful proof of this shortcoming. Only after the act, in the flood of sensual satisfaction which succeeds the contentment of a craving long held in check, does she become a little convincing.

The book is rescued from dullness, however, by the study of the child's jealousy. (*Une Page d'amour* is, incidentally, one of the few books of Zola's in which children are given any important part to play: we can find in it a quite charming account of a children's party, where good manners break down under the stress of frank appetites, and a dance turns quickly into a stampede; elsewhere, Jeanne's play with her dolls is a delicate piece of observation on the part of a man who was not yet a father.) Jeanne, in addition, affords the means whereby a minor matrimonial peccadillo shifts to a tragic major key. The child's possessive passion for her mother fights desperately against the wave of sexual passion which momentarily sweeps Hélène off her feet. In the end, when the wave recedes, Jeanne is discovered dead from exhaustion.

If the novel is neo-classical in inspiration and design, there is more than a dash of romantic convention in its theme, that of love the destroyer, which reaches back to Byron, probably through Zola's boyhood idol Musset (the Musset of *On ne badine pas avec l'amour*). But this theme is blended with a powerful admixture of an ingredient which Musset never thought to introduce: puritanism.

Hélène is a granddaughter of Adélaïde Fouque through her mother Ursule Macquart who married the hatter Mouret. Her elder brother is the François Mouret of *La Conquête de Plassans*, her younger brother the boy Silvère whose execution is recorded at the end of *La Fortune des Rougon*. She has a relatively balanced temperament herself: she has more of the Mourets than of the Macquarts in her make-up. (Her daughter's hypersensitivity is due, Zola explains, to her being a throw-back to her great-grandmother, the hysteric now in an asylum near Plassans.) Hélène is presented, at the outset, as irreproachably virtuous, proof, she thinks, against all weaknesses. She is a stranger to passion, her husband never having stirred her though he adored her; but she has observed its ravages in others—her father, for instance, hanged himself for grief when her mother died.

Love steals in upon her with the seductive scents of springtime, with the discreet suggestions of a romantic novel, with the secret looks of sympathy exchanged with the doctor during social calls and professional visits. She experiences the fascination of an emotion she has never fully known, a fascination which Zola loosely connects with the lure of the vast, unknown human ocean of Paris, described under different conditions five times in the book, in the fifth chapter of each of the five parts.[1] All the same, her moral principles, and the thought of Jeanne, might have triumphed over temptation, had it not been for the contagious flightiness of Deberle's wife, Juliette. She overhears talk between Juliette and a certain young dandy who is paying his addresses to her; she listens to another of Juliette's friends retailing scandal about the guests at dinner.

Dans ce monde digne, parmi cette bourgeoisie d'apparence si honnête, il n'y avait donc que des femmes coupables? Son rigorisme provincial s'étonnait des promiscuités tolérées de la vie parisienne. . . . L'adultère s'embourgeoisait là d'une béate façon, aiguisé d'une pointe de raffinement coquet.

The revelation leads directly to Hélène's sinning (the vocabulary of the moralist is almost unavoidable) and to retribution, which is swift. *Une Page d'amour* is a book with a moral, or at any rate with moralistic overtones; not the kind of novel to be expected from the pen of the man who had in earlier years held up the amoralist Stendhal as an example to a tiresomely didactic Dumas fils, bidding him remember: 'L'œuvre du romancier doit cesser où commence celle du moraliste.'[2]

The eighth novel of the *Rougon-Macquart* series is thus remarkable for a sudden intensified exteriorization of Zola's concern about sexual passion, that incalculable, incomprehensible, explosive force; and with it went, this time, a readiness to put his reader—and through him, society at large—on their guard.

[1] The geometrical stiffness of these regularly recurrent passages was selected for attack by critics when *Une Page d'amour* appeared. In *Le Roman expérimental* (p. 189) Zola dealt with these objections, explaining that the idea of writing 'un roman dont Paris, avec l'océan de ses toitures, serait un personnage, quelque chose comme le chœur antique' had haunted him for many years. Racine, it is worth remembering, introduced the chorus in *Athalie* at the end of the first four of his five acts. Was this the 'chœur antique' that gave Zola his idea?

[2] *L'Événement illustré*, 4 July 1868.

One or two explanations occur why Zola's manner should have undergone this kind of change at just this moment in his career. To begin with, it was a period when he was living increasingly in the company of fellow novelists. Before the war, and in the years immediately after it, Zola's friends, the men with whom he discussed questions of *métier*, were mainly painters, sculptors, or art-critics: Cézanne, Guillemet, Solari, Coste, Duret, Béliard, to mention only the most important.[1] One may be fairly sure that these discussions ran mainly on the representational aspect of art, excluding the spiritual or moral significance of what was represented. One of the chief endeavours of the Impressionists was, in fact, to escape from the tyranny of the subject, to show that a still life can sometimes stir the emotions more than a portrayal of the butchery of Sardanapalus's concubines. For Renoir, flesh posed a problem in chromatics, for Degas, the female body was a challenge to render stance and attitude.

The novelist nourishes his art on many things that the painter passes over. Nine-tenths, at least, of all novels, from *Daphnis and Chloe* to *The Brothers Karamazov*, have dealt with the subject of erotic passion. It was, therefore, not entirely the club-room atmosphere of the *dîner des auteurs sifflés*[2] that caused the conversation to veer round so frequently to the topics of women and love (with a licence that made the waiters' hair bristle, according to Zola). These writers were comparing notes about the staple material of their books past and to come; they were talking shop.

For Zola, who had until then given love as little place in his books as in his private life, this inexhaustible speculation about the same subject, now serious, now bawdy, varying from the refinements of Turgenev to the enormities of Flaubert, must have been something like a revelation. It is possible that we are in the presence here of a literary influence springing from unrecorded words, but quite as powerful as if it had had a textual origin.

The moralizing trend which is apparent in *Une Page d'amour* and which becomes more and more pronounced in *Nana* and

---

[1] Thus, in respect of the last-named (a minor landscape painter who exhibited with the Impressionists in 1876), see the letter Zola wrote him from Paris on the eve of the siege of the *Communards* by the Versailles troops (5 Apr. 1871). This letter, which is concerned with fundamental aesthetic principles, is unfortunately not included in Zola's *Correspondance*; it was published by J. Patin in *Le Figaro*, 20 June 1931.

[2] See below, p. 160.

Pot-Bouille had a different source, traceable to the reception given to *L'Assommoir*. The cry of immorality had been raised by a host of readers before the serialized version had proceeded beyond the first chapter; the punishment that Gervaise visits on Virginie's bare buttocks was the signal for so general an uproar that the editor of *Le Bien public*, in which the book was appearing, was compelled before long to stop its publication. Zola was moved by these charges of indecency to go back over his novel from a new point of view: was it, or was it not, an immoral work? He put his conclusion, which was also his defence, in the preface: *L'Assommoir* was 'de la morale en action, simplement'. *En action*, that was to say, implicit. It is easy to see that once started on this train Zola was in grave danger of running into didacticism. Each bold exploration of the 'seamy side' would be vindicated, not now by insisting on the artist's freedom of choice, but by pleading the moralist's freedom of inquiry.

Nana, as everyone knows, is Zola's *Roxana* or his *Fanny Hill*, but it is not a licentious or even a titillating work. To call it an austere one may be to make too much of Zola's earnestness; but this earnestness is unmistakable. Brunetière missed the point when he refused to acknowledge the seriousness of Zola's moral intentions because, as he said, no one could credit that 'Nana's smallpox would ever outweigh in the estimation of an unhappy lower-class girl all the attractions of freedom, pleasure, and luxury which [the author] depicts so freely'. In the first place, if Zola's novel had been intended as a tract for distribution in reformatories, one imagines he would have had Nana die of an illness more appropriate to her occupation than smallpox, her contraction of which is as arbitrary a stroke of fate as is Mme de Merteuil's infection with the same disease at the end of *Les Liaisons dangereuses*. *Nana* was not written to be read by 'lower-class girls'; of this there is no better proof than the ironical passage in the book itself, in which Nana, leading the idle life of a kept woman, reads a novel about . . . a prostitute: 'et elle se révoltait, elle disait que tout cela était faux, témoignant d'ailleurs une répugnance indignée contre cette littérature immonde, dont la prétention était de rendre la nature; comme si l'on pouvait tout montrer! comme si un roman ne devait pas être écrit pour passer une heure agréable!' The truth is that Zola wrote *Nana* for the Brunetières of society; his heroine personifies a threat to the security of the upper middle classes; all unconsciously she is an avenging angel sent forth by the oppressed and neglected dwellers of slumland. To put his intentions beyond any doubt, Zola provided within the text of the novel the key to his symbolism, in the form of a summarized article supposedly written by a journalist, Fauchery, under the heading 'La Mouche d'or'. Here we read that Nana is the biological product of a diseased ancestral line and the social product of mean streets and stinking hovels. 'Avec elle, la pourriture qu'on laissait fermenter dans le peuple, remontait et pourraissait l'aristocratie. Elle devenait une force de la nature, un ferment de destruction, sans le vouloir elle-même, corrompant et désorganisant Paris entre ses cuisses de neige.' At the end of his article Fauchery introduces the comparison with the fly: 'une mouche couleur de soleil, envolée de l'ordure, une mouche qui prenait la mort sur les charognes tolérées le long des chemins, et qui, bourdonnante, dansante, jetant un éclat de pierreries, empoisonnait les hommes rien qu'à se poser sur eux, dans les palais où elle entrait par les fenêtres.'

From the beginning of the novel to the end, this is the theme to which Zola sticks. Wherever Nana goes she wreaks destruction, and always among the 'pillars of society'. She is the most expensive of whores, consequently the powerful, the wealthy, and the highborn are her only possible prey; she maddens them, ruins them, drives some of them to suicide, others to dishonour, and in the meantime shows considerable ingenuity in devising ways of humiliating them. One evening she invites to dinner the four men who are at the time more or less concurrently her lovers, imposing on them as fellow guest a tawdry prostitute with whom she has remained on good terms ever since, as ragged children, they used to play together in the streets of the slum area where they were born and bred. To the embarrassment of the gentlemen in dinner-jackets, Nana insists on evoking at table the various lamentable scenes that we remember from *L'Assommoir*; and when Count Muffat timidly protests: 'Ce n'est pas gai, ce que vous racontez là', she rounds on him indignantly: 'Je crois bien que ce n'est pas gai! . . . Il fallait nous apporter du pain, mon cher.' Her mother was a washerwoman, her father drank himself to death, and it is now her sovereign pleasure that they all listen to her family history. 'Les yeux sur la table, tous quatre maintenant se faisaient petits, tandis qu'elle les tenait sous ses anciennes savates boueuses de la rue de la Goutte d'Or, avec l'emportement de sa toute-puissance.'

Muffat is a chamberlain at the Imperial court. In showing his abject enslavement to Nana, Zola overreached himself: Muffat is so utterly dominated that he fails to come to life; he moves through the novel making the automatic gestures of a hypnotic subject; but for the moment, it is not with Zola's artistic errors that we are concerned. Muffat represents titled respectability; in the palace of this modern Circe he becomes, quite literally, a brute beast on all fours. Nana, in a spurt of sadism, rides him round the room like a horse, and afterwards she makes him act the dog and fetch her handkerchief in his teeth. The incident has nothing to do with 'observed reality'. Nearly all Zola's 'documentation' for *Nana* was, as might be expected, second-hand, and this particular detail comes from a curiously unlikely source—Jacobean melodrama. It is a transcription of a scene in Otway's *Venice Preserv'd* which Zola had read in Taine's *Histoire de la littérature anglaise* at least twelve years before.[1]

The passage that follows, however, is apparently Zola's own invention (although Otway's Senator Antonio is also honoured by a kicking from his mistress). Nana demands one day that Muffat should visit her dressed in his official uniform, wearing full regalia.

Emportée de l'irrespect des grandeurs, par la joie de l'avilir sous la pompe officielle de ce costume, elle le secoua, le pinça, en lui jetant des: 'Eh! va donc, chambellan!' qu'elle accompagna enfin de longs coups de pied dans le derrière; et, ces coups de pied, elle les allongeait de si bon cœur dans les Tuileries, dans la majesté de la cour impériale, trônant au sommet, sur la peur et l'aplatissement de tous. Voilà ce qu'elle pensait de la société! C'était sa revanche, une rancune inconsciente de famille, léguée avec le sang. Puis, le chambellan déshabillé, l'habit étalé par terre, elle lui cria de sauter, et il sauta; elle lui cria de cracher, et il cracha; elle lui cria de marcher sur l'or, sur les aigles, sur les décorations, et il marcha. Patatras! il n'y avait plus rien, tout s'effondrait. Elle cassait un chambellan comme elle cassait un flacon ou un drageoir, et elle en faisait une ordure, un tas de boue au coin d'une borne.

The moralist, here, is clearly coupled to a poet, and the poet seems to be taking charge. While we may not doubt that Zola's intention was to issue a solemn warning against licensed prostitution and private vice among the leaders of a nation, we cannot doubt either that *Nana* mercifully exceeds this limited brief. The

[1] He paraphrased the scene (attributing it, by a slip, to Shakespeare) in an article in *La Tribune*, 6 Dec. 1868, and after the war, in a different article in *La Cloche*, 14 July 1872.

novel, as it develops, becomes a tremendous phantasmagoria in which an opulent and cultured civilization is shown sinking through vulgarity and debauchery to enervation and ultimate dissolution. Nana herself presides over and accelerates this ruin. She is an infinitely more impressive figure than Huysmans's Marthe or Goncourt's Élisa, who were merely realistic. She has the advantage over Laclos's Marquise de Merteuil and Balzac's Madame Marneffe in being more depersonalized, hence more timeless. Zola writes of her, at the climax of her career, as standing alone, 'avec un peuple d'hommes abattus à ses pieds. Comme ces monstres antiques dont le domaine redouté était couvert d'ossements, elle posait les pieds sur des crânes'—a simile which shows that at such moments Nana must be classed as one of the innumerable variants of Mario Praz's 'fatal woman'. She descends from the Ekhidna of Leconte de Lisle:

> Mais ceux qu'elle enchaînait de ses bras amoureux,
> Nul n'en dira jamais la foule disparue.
> Le Monstre aux yeux charmants dévorait leur chair crue,
> Et le temps polissait leurs os dans l'antre creux.

She is one of the reincarnations of Flaubert's Ennoïa, in *La Tentation de Saint Antoine*, and the older man's enthusiasm on reading this, the last of Zola's novels he was to see, is understandable.[1] 'Nana', he wrote to the author, 'tourne au Mythe, sans cesser d'être réelle. Cette création est *babylonienne*. Dixi.'

Though not a composite character, she has, as Flaubert implied, two aspects: the mythical and the real. There is the Nana who, as Martin Turnell expresses it, is 'the creation of the frenzied eroticism of the age, a projection of the collective neurosis in its sexual form';[2] and there is the other Nana who, as Zola himself noted in the *ébauche*, underlining the words, is 'bonne fille malgré tous les malheurs qu'elle cause', and again, surprisingly perhaps: 'le personnage sympathique, se donnant, mais en bonne enfant, inconsciemment.'[3] *Bonne fille, bonne enfant*: Henry James can seldom have written a more unjust review than that he published

---

[1] The day *Nana* was published, Flaubert read it right through, starting at ten in the morning and finishing at half past eleven at night. See his letters dated 15 Feb. 1880 to his niece Caroline, to Georges Charpentier, and to Zola himself.

[2] *The Art of French Fiction*, p. 162.

[3] B.N. MS. *Nouv. acq. fr.* 10313, fols. 212, 227.

on *Nana*,[1] in which he dismissed Zola's heroine as 'the brutal *fille*, without a conscience or a soul, with nothing but devouring appetites and impudences'. Her impudences are excusable, given the lack of dignity of her clients. At the racecourse Nana points to the grandstand, filled with royalty and court officials, half of whom she has had in bed with her. 'Vous savez, ces gens ne m'épatent pas, moi!' she comments to the little crowd of admirers round her landau. 'Je les connais trop. Faut voir ça au déballage! . . . Plus de respect! fini le respect!' Her appetites are not really 'devouring', for all the fortunes she runs through; she is simply unimaginably extravagant, plundered, besides, by servants she cannot control. But she is not mercenary. At one stage, she leaves her rich protector to go and live with a comedian to whom she has given her heart; and returns to Muffat only when this man, Fontan, having stripped her of her savings, turns her out of doors. She gives herself to a youth who has nothing but his pocket-money, because she finds his boyish devotion irresistible; Zola put in her mouth a famous saying attributed to one of the *cocottes* who served him as model: 'Je ne puis refuser ça à mes amis pauvres.' And as for her conscience, when finally it is brought home to her what disasters she has heedlessly caused, she bursts into a paroxysm of tears.

Ils diront ce qu'ils voudront, ce n'est pas ma faute! Est-ce que je suis méchante, moi? Je donne tout ce que j'ai, je n'écraserais pas une mouche. . . . Ce sont eux, oui, ce sont eux! . . . Jamais je n'ai voulu leur être désagréable. Et ils étaient pendus après mes jupes, et aujourd'hui les voilà qui claquent, qui mendient, qui posent tous pour le désespoir. . . . Nom de Dieu! ce n'est pas juste! La société est mal faite. On tombe sur les femmes, quand ce sont les hommes qui exigent les choses. . . .

Nana never properly understands (but who does, who can?) the chemistry that draws men to her, the unrelenting chemistry of desire, and indeed there is a horrid mystery in the demonic sexual attraction she exerts. When she first appears on the stage, playing the part of Venus in a burlesque operetta, she conquers the theatre public not by her acting, which is pitiable, nor by her singing, which is atrocious, nor even by her beauty, but by 'autre chose', as the impresario Bordenave had predicted: 'quelque chose qui remplace tout'. When the curtain goes up in the third act and discovers her naked,

[1] In *The Parisian*, 26 Feb. 1880; reprinted in *The House of Fiction* (1957), pp. 274–80.

il n'y eut pas d'applaudissements. Personne ne riait plus, les faces des hommes, sérieuses, se tendaient, avec le nez aminci, la bouche irritée et sans salive. Un vent semblait avoir passé très doux, chargé d'une sourde menace. Tout d'un coup, dans la bonne enfant, la femme se dressait, inquiétante, apportant le coup de folie de son sexe, ouvrant l'inconnu du désir. Nana souriait toujours, mais d'un sourire aigu de mangeuse d'hommes.

Nana is what a more light-hearted age called 'a woman of plea-sure'; but the impression Zola gives us is that it is anything but pleasure that her lovers find in her embraces. The book is streaked with pain, thick with suffocating horror, for what unwittingly he was dramatizing in *Nana* was his own ineradicable disgust of the sexual act. It is significant that all allusions to sensual delights of the obviously carnal sort are rigorously excluded. The fiercest concupiscence here is the concupiscence of the eye, and the most troubling scene in the book is that in which Muffat watches his perverse mistress posturing naked in front of a glass, oblivious of him. It is true that Céard had given Zola the scenario of this episode, which the novelist even toned down a little: for his friend had described the woman as wearing mauve stockings, boots and nothing else; Nana is at least totally nude. Again, in Céard's sketch the lover reclines on a sofa smoking cigarettes and paying scant attention to the woman; but Muffat stares at Nana in agonized concentration. The blend of abhorrence and attraction that he feels repeats the emotions of Claude, in Zola's maiden novel, when he first sees Laurence: she is in bed with a fever, sleeping, and has tossed off the sheet, exposing the upper part of her body. 'Cette poitrine brutalement découverte m'a fait rougir', writes Claude, 'et m'a mis au cœur une telle angoisse que j'ai cru en pleurer. . . . Mes impressions avaient un charme si étrange que je ne puis aujourd'hui les comparer qu'à la sainte horreur qui m'a secoué le jour où j'ai vu un cadavre pour la première fois.' It is not of death that Nana's naked body puts Muffat in mind of, but of damnation: 'Il songeait à son ancienne horreur de la femme, au monstre de l'Écriture, lubrique, sentant le fauve.' Muffat is, admittedly, a religious maniac of a sort, but it is not difficult to see that, for the moment, he speaks for the author; once more we have Zola's characteristic identifica-tion of the unclothed female form with absolute moral evil, and the no less characteristic compulsion that drove him to stage the classic *voyeur* situation, with the woman either unconscious of, or oblivious of, her nudity, and the scene impressing itself on us through the thoughts and morose imaginings of the man watching her.[1]

Zola destroyed Nana in the last chapter of the book which Flaubert called *michelangesque* and which sent the author to bed for three days 'avec douleurs nerveuses abominables' by way of reaction when he had terminated it.[2] This chapter is, in itself, a marvel of the novelist's art. Nana, returning from a tour of the east, had caught smallpox from her baby boy whom she went to see immediately on her return; for she was a doting mother and whenever possible—which was seldom—took Louiset about with her. A fellow actress, a constant rival but an old friend none the less, Rose Mignon, had her taken to a room in the Grand Hôtel, and nursed her through the last. Zola shows us Mignon standing outside the hotel with a growing group of men collected round him, while the women are upstairs in the dead-room with Rose. The cowardice of the male is thus discreetly illustrated: none of her former lovers dare, for fear of catching the infection, go up to her room and take a last look at her; there is no question, in *Nana*, which is the weaker sex, in every respect. The talk both in the street outside and in the hotel room runs on Nana's past exploits, those known, those that can only be guessed at; and on war with the Prussians, which has just been declared. There is the sense of an epoch that has ended. Finally the women, frightened by a sudden stench, cease their chat and leave the room, Rose last of all, locking the door behind her. Only then, on the last page of all, when the stage is quite empty, does Zola show us Nana.

Nana restait seule, la face en l'air, dans la clarté de la bougie. C'était un charnier, un tas d'humeur et de sang, une pelletée de chair corrompue, jetée là, sur un coussin. Les pustules avaient envahi la figure entière, un bouton touchant l'autre; et, flétries, affaissées, d'un aspect grisâtre de boue, elles semblaient déjà une moisissure de la terre, sur cette bouillie informe, où l'on ne retrouvait plus les traits. Un œil, celui de gauche, avait complètement sombré dans le bouillonnement de la

---

[1] There are other occurrences in *Madeleine Férat* (see J. C. Lapp, 'Zola et *la Tentation de Saint Antoine*', *Revue des Sciences humaines*, fasc. 92 (1958), pp. 513–18), and, after *Nana*, in the first chapter of *L'Œuvre*, where Claude Lantier contemplates the uncovered torso of Christine Hallegrain as she lies asleep. In this scene, however, the man is conscious only of aesthetic pleasure, and proceeds to sketch the girl's breasts, working fast before she wakes up; the erotic element in the *voyeur* situation is thus minimized if not totally dispelled.

[2] Letter to Céard, in *Vingt messages inédits de Zola à Céard*, ed. A. J. Salvan, p. 11.

purulence; l'autre, à demi ouvert, s'enfonçait, comme un trou noir et gâté. Le nez suppurait encore. Toute une croûte rougeâtre partait d'une joue, envahissait la bouche, qu'elle tirait dans un rire abominable. Et, sur ce masque horrible et grotesque du néant, les cheveux, les beaux cheveux, gardant leur flambée de soleil, coulaient en un ruissellement d'or. Vénus se décomposait.

Zola killed his mysterious, simple-minded, terrifying, pitiful heroine, it might be said in self-defence, defiling her in the flesh which was her pride. But he could not kill in himself the puritanical horror of carnal excess that Nana personified. In his next novel the denunciation of the erotic peril was just as vehement, though less high-pitched.

A letter written to Céard while he was working on *Pot-Bouille* (24 August 1881) shows that Zola fully realized that he was once more composing a work in a minor key. 'Mon roman n'est décidément qu'une besogne de précision et de netteté. Aucun air de bravoure, pas le moindre régal lyrique.' He goes on to ask the pertinent question whether—at any rate in his case—a writer's best work is not achieved when he is driven by passion. 'Si un de mes livres reste, ce sera à coup sûr le plus passionné.' And this part of the letter ends with the suggestive statement: 'j'appelle [*Pot-Bouille*]: mon *Éducation sentimentale*.'

L'Éducation sentimentale was Zola's favourite among Flaubert's novels. He saluted it with a lyrically appreciative review in *La Tribune* when it appeared, and ten years later wrote another long article about it in *Le Voltaire* in an attempt to break down the obstinate indifference of the reading public to this masterpiece.[1] He concluded that it had been ignored because it was too truthful, and the truth is always frightening. But according to Zola this, its essential quality, was what drew him to it with a kind of envious, despairing admiration.

A mon sens, tous nos livres, que nous croyons vrais, sont à côté de celui-ci des œuvres romantiques, des opéras arrangés pour le spectacle et la musique. Lui seul a le développement large de la vie, sans que jamais l'effet soit exagéré, en vue d'un agrandissement de l'ensemble. . . .

Tous nos romans sont des poèmes à côté de celui-là; il a beau traiter

[1] *La Tribune*, 28 Nov. 1869; *Le Voltaire*, 9 Dec. 1879. I have attempted a comparative study of these two articles (neither of which was reprinted in the *Œuvres critiques*) in 'Zola and *L'Éducation sentimentale*', *Romanic Review*, vol. l (1959), pp. 35–40.

d'une grande passion inassouvie, de cet amour de Frédéric pour Mme Arnoux, si pur, si profond; il ne ment jamais, il dit les choses et rien au delà des choses, tandis que, nous autres, nous allons très souvent plus loin que les choses, pour augmenter nos effets, mettre nos personnages en lumière, enlever une finale à grand orchestre. . . . Voilà le modèle du roman naturaliste, cela est hors de doute pour moi. On n'ira pas plus loin dans la vérité vraie, je parle de cette vérité terre à terre, exacte, qui semble être la négation même de l'art du roman.

Reading *Pot-Bouille*, we are bound to agree that the author appears to have done his utmost to ensure that it could not be classed among the 'opéras arrangés pour le spectacle et la musique'. But in literature the truth cannot be secured by the simple process of eliminating falsehood. Zola's professed intention was to depict the life and manners of the Parisian middle classes as, in *L'Assommoir*, he had depicted those of the lower classes. His qualifications for the task were, however, minimal, for at this stage in his life he had probably mingled less with professional people than he had with the manual workers who had served him as models for his 'proletarian' novel. There were only two middle-class homes in which he and his wife were familiars: the Daudets' where they met mainly writers, and the Charpentiers' who largely entertained painters: and it was not painters and writers he was describing in *Pot-Bouille* (they were reserved for *L'Œuvre*). Some of his younger friends with jobs in the civil service moved in the right circles, and Zola leaned heavily on them for his 'documentation'. The preparatory notes include twenty pages in Zola's handwriting, headed 'Notes de Céard et d'Huysmans', which appear to be a record, in staccato and highly abbreviated form, of the confidences of these two: possibly he got them talking one evening at Médan.[1] For once there is a good deal of justice in the criticism that Goncourt made of the book and which he excised from the version of his diary published during his lifetime: 'C'est fait, ce *Pot-Bouille*, avec des racontars de disciples, sans une scène observée d'après nature, sans une parole entendue.'[2] One of the disciples in question, Huysmans, was bold enough to write to Zola after the book was published and tell him he had not succeeded in catching the tone of conversation of middle-class ladies; and Brunetière criticized *Pot-Bouille* on exactly the same grounds when he reviewed it, concluding,

[1] B.N. MS. *Nouv. acq. fr.* 10321, fols. 306–25.
[2] Entry dated 17 Feb. 1882.

correctly, that the book was not a product of observation, and that Zola had not sketched a portrait so much as a caricature of the *bourgeoisie*.

It would seem, then, that he fell far short of the 'vérité vraie . . . vérité terre à terre, exacte' that he had so admired in Flaubert's great novel; for in assessing the realism, in the narrowest meaning of the word, of a novel purporting to mirror a phenomenon so transitory as the manners and speech of a given class in a particular era, we are bound to rely on the testimony of contemporaries.[1] There is, however, another sense in which *L'Éducation sentimentale* and *Pot-Bouille* can reasonably be linked. In their treatment of the theme of love both books exhale the same odour of stagnancy, the impression being, if anything, stronger in *Pot-Bouille*, for there are occasional patches of freshness in Flaubert's novel, and the disconcerting final page suggests that there is at least one fleeting moment in life when love is new and enrapturing. *Pot-Bouille*, however, aims solely at bringing out the mortal flatness and mono- tony of sexual pleasure (if the word 'pleasure' can properly describe the joyless urge that tumbles these men and women into bed with one another). There is no age of innocence, when inexperience confers a deceptive lustre to love: even the children in the society that Zola depicts mimic their parents' adulterous embraces. Marri- ageable and undowered girls know by heart the technique of husband-catching by conduct balanced nicely between shameless provocation and decent reserve, and are tormented by having to sham the innocence they no longer possess. Virginity is but the initial capital with which each new-comer to the marriage-market is expected and encouraged to speculate.

There is only the ghost of a plot in this book. Nothing ever happens, or what happens is never anything that has not happened before. A couple of husbands have jealous suspicions, but the first is persuaded that the compromising letter he had found was intended for a servant-girl, and the other is prevailed upon to take

[1] From the standpoint of today's reader, of course, the 'realism' in the sense of the historical reliability of *Pot-Bouille* is a minor consideration. The point has been well put by Lionel Trilling: 'We do not ask whether Zola's representation of the bourgeoisie is accurate or even if it is justified. We read his book for the pleasure of its fierce energy, for the strange pleasure we habitually derive from the indictment of the human kind. The work has a reality beyond anything that might be proved of the Parisian middle class of 1882, it has the reality of the author's rage and disgust with human inadequacy' (*A Gathering of Fugitives*, p. 17).

his wife back in the flurry caused by the timely expiry of his father-in-law. There are wrangles about unpaid dowries, which peter out, hagglings about a legacy, which come to nothing. A respected magistrate, deserted by his mistress, retires to the lavatory and puts a bullet through his head; but he does not succeed—much to his wife's disappointment—in ending his life. The tedious aridity of the book—aptly exemplified by the repetition, in the last chapter, of a reception narrated in the fifth, with the same musical entertainment, the same surreptitious flirtations—purposes to demonstrate the eternal uniformity of lust.

Lust is, indeed, the level above which, in *Pot-Bouille*, passion never rises. There is a systematic animalization of everything connected with sex, not excluding maternity: the account of the unaided confinement of Adèle, the servant who gives birth to an illegitimate child begotten on her by one or other of her masters, and immediately murders it, is the culminating horror of this dusky book. For the rest, adultery is shown to be so furtive and unexhilarating an activity that the reader finds himself wondering how anyone can be brought to indulge in it. The characters in *Pot-Bouille* make love with the dreary application of a chain-smoker lighting his successive cigarettes.

The setting Zola used for most of the action of *Pot-Bouille* was a 'respectable' apartment-house in a residential district of Paris. Two tribes live in this house: in front, the middle-class tenants; behind, and under the roof, the servants in their kitchens and sleeping-quarters. The masters, except for occasional snarls, remain outwardly on terms of decorous mutual esteem; it is left to the servants to supply devastating comment on their depravity. On one occasion Octave Mouret, the nominal hero of the novel, and the young married woman who is his mistress, Berthe Vabre, overhear this scandal-mongering. Zola's purpose in recording the scene will be apparent from a brief summary of it.

Octave is using the room of one of the maids while she has a day off, since Berthe is afraid to visit him in his own room. She arrives shortly before the servants get up to begin their day's work. Then the two lovers are forced to listen to a rancorous exposure of the vice and promiscuity rampant in the house, as the maids gossip in raucous voices from window to window, stopping occasionally to empty refuse into the yard. Berthe's own private affairs come under this review, and there is nothing the pair can do to stop the torrent of derisive and foul-mouthed abuse. 'Ils restaient, la main dans la main, face à face, sans pouvoir détourner les yeux; et leurs mains se glaçaient, et leurs yeux s'avouaient l'ordure de leur liaison, l'infirmité des maîtres étalée dans la haine de la domesticité. C'était ça leurs amours, cette fornication sous une pluie battante de viande gâtée et de légumes aigres!'

In *Nana* sexual passion had been a raging elemental force, out of which poetry could still be wrought. In *Pot-Bouille* this gaudy splendour is gone, to be replaced by the authentic greyness of realism. *Pot-Bouille* is nevertheless written with the same moralizing fervour as the preceding book; there is not a trace of *gauloiserie* in these unending cuckoldries, and sexual indulgence is shown to be just as grave a menace, although here it saps a society at its base, whereas in *Nana* it had pulverized it with thunderbolts from above.

Zola fought, and lost, an unusual kind of lawsuit in connexion with the serialized publication of *Pot-Bouille*. The name he had originally chosen for his magistrate (the same who tries to blow out his brains) was Duverdy. It happened that there was a barrister at the Court of Appeal at Paris who bore the same name and had a certain facial resemblance to the fictional character. Moreover, he had recently stood for election to parliament, and some of his bills had been posted at Médan. His action in applying for an injunction against Zola's using his name surprised no one but Zola.

In the course of the hearing, plaintiff's counsel argued that the translation of his client into *Pot-Bouille* was defamatory because the book was an obscenity. This imputation aroused Zola to an indignant protest, which he made public in a letter to A. de Cyon, editor of *Le Gaulois*, the paper in which the novel was appearing. The circumstances probably led him to stress the innocence of his intentions more than he would otherwise have troubled to do, but we can see how very seriously Zola took his self-imposed functions of moral teacher at this period. Taking one allegedly licentious situation after another, he indicated the 'social lesson' which he expected to be drawn from each, and concluded categorically: 'Pas une page, pas une ligne de *Pot-Bouille* n'a été écrite par moi sans que ma volonté fût d'y mettre une intention morale. C'est sans doute une œuvre cruelle, mais c'est plus encore une œuvre morale, au sens vrai et philosophique du mot.'

Zola wrote these words in evident sincerity. His novel, towards the end, does broaden out on to a wider perspective, in which the corruption of his random sample of middle-class folk is shown to be symptomatic of a universal danger threatening that class. The danger can be exorcized, not, however, by political measures, still less by a return to religion, but by proceeding to a scientific examination of its causes and a scientific eradication of the evil. Characteristically, it is given to a doctor to suggest this solution. He is correcting a priest whose despairing verdict on his parishioners is that God must have forsaken them.

'Ne mettez donc pas Dieu là-dedans. Elles sont mal portantes ou mal élevées, voilà tout.'

Et, sans attendre, il . . . se lâchait sur les femmes, les unes qu'une éducation de poupée corrompait ou abêtissait, les autres dont une névrose héréditaire pervertissait les sentiments et les passions, toutes tombant salement, sottement, sans envie comme sans plaisir ; et d'ailleurs, il ne se montrait pas plus tendre pour les hommes, des gaillards qui achevaient de gâter l'existence, derrière l'hypocrisie de leur belle tenue ; et dans son emportement de jacobin sonnait le glas entêté d'une classe, la décomposition et l'écroulement de la bourgeoisie, dont les étais pourris craquaient d'eux-mêmes.

The attribution of sexual disorders to a poisoned ancestry or a warped upbringing is just what might be expected from a disciple of Taine. What is more personally revealing of Zola is that he should have thought that a society given to polygamy and polyandry was on that account alone heading for 'decomposition and collapse'. It is questionable whether the sexual practices of a class or society influence appreciably its chances of survival, except as they may affect its rate of reproduction. (In *Fécondité*, written seventeen years later, Zola concentrated on just this aspect, showing the connexion between promiscuity and small families: this was the only rational line of attack on sociological grounds.) The denunciation of moral looseness that runs through *Pot-Bouille* is a sign only of the uneasiness Zola felt when confronted with the sexual freedom that others permitted themselves but he recoiled from. *Pot-Bouille* and *Nana* are two differently angled exteriorizations of a still unresolved inner conflict.

Au Bonheur des Dames, in spite of its far sunnier treatment of the erotic theme, does not really represent any final abatement of this deep-seated disturbance. The story of the taming of Octave Mouret, now a millionaire, by the unambitious and instinctively virtuous

Denise Baudu, a story which ends with the ringing of wedding-bells off-stage, has the air of a prim mid-Victorian novel. Denise, who is made up of 'tout ce qu'on trouve de bon chez la femme, le courage, la gaieté, la simplicité', who remains chaste for reasons of 'logic' and pride, 'pour satisfaire son besoin d'une vie tranquille, et non pour obéir à l'idée de la vertu'—Denise is almost too good to be true. Louis Desprez, a young follower whose admiration of Zola never interfered with his critical detachment, informed the novelist that his new heroine was 'the product of logic more than of observation; she is the incarnation of an idea rather than a type taken off the streets; in consequence, she does not so much live as appear to live'.[1] Be that as it may, Denise does at least serve to remind us that Zola was never a misogynist. He quailed before the erotic frenzy which is depersonalized and anonymous; but he had only compassion for the flesh by which the scandal comes. His imagination saw the winds of passion laden with plague germs; now breathing softly with the perfumes of spring to suffocate Hélène Grandjean; now raging through the heavens, a pestilential blast blowing up from the iniquity of the Parisian underworld, toppling the ancient edifices of birth and the modern palaces of wealth; now circulating stilly and hotly round carpeted corridors and carefully curtained drawing-rooms. But for him woman, the vessel of desire, is always innocent; unwittingly she works evil, through frustration or perversion; and the evil invariably recoils on herself.

Au Bonheur des Dames was a transition novel, inaugurating the series of up-to-date economic or industrial studies which were to include *Germinal, La Terre, La Bête humaine, L'Argent*, and, beyond the *Rougon-Macquart* series, *Paris* and *Travail*. The war between the sexes, with their respective champions in Octave and Denise, pales before the death-struggle of a doomed commercial order. Nevertheless it was the 'omnipotence of woman' in the sense of her total engrossment of the vast mercantile enterprise that 'Le Bonheur des Dames' represents, which constituted what the novelist called 'le côté poème du livre'. Thus Zola's continuing preoccupation with the same issue can be certified; and it would be possible to trace it in all his books down to *La Bête humaine*, where Séverine, fundamentally innocent, is, by her maddening sexual attractions, the indirect cause of the deaths of two men, and perishes under the knife of her lover.

---

[1] *Lettres inédites de Louis Desprez à Émile Zola*, ed. G. Robert, p. 62.

At this point the answer to a question which exercised Zola's contemporaries and had a profound influence on his literary fortunes may be attempted with a certain degree of assurance.

Zola's presentation of the processes of sex is terribly simplified. He seems to have remained—at least over the period we have so far covered—profoundly unaware that love between man and woman could be considered from any aspect except as a matter of appetites to be satisfied or denied. Confronted with this immense and immemorial tree, lifting its huge cone of foliage and flowers into the sky, he confined himself to describing the roots. There is a story—whether authentic or apocryphal does not affect its usefulness as an illustration—that Zola once tried to secure Flaubert's adherence to his own view of love as a purely physical manifestation. 'Don't you agree', he asked, 'that, all said and done, that's all it comes to? (*N'est-ce pas, au total, qu'il n'y a que ça?*)' Flaubert, walking up and down the room in his voluminous Turkish trousers, answered genially: 'Why, yes, that comes into it (*Oui, il y a de ça*).' Zola insisted: 'Oui, oui, il n'y a que ça', and Flaubert once more introduced the all-important modification, from which he would not depart: 'Oui, oui, il y a de ça.'[1]

The question that arises is: what caused Zola to give so little consideration to the formidable extension of the erotic beyond the narrowly biological frontiers? This extension has by itself provided material for all poets who have sung of love, all dramatists who have portrayed it, all novelists who have analysed it—except the libertines: a reservation which explains why Zola acquired, in France, the reputation of being a descendant of Restif de la Bretonne, while in England the man who issued translations (even though bowdlerized) of *Nana*, *Pot-Bouille*, and *La Terre* was prosecuted, fined, and eventually imprisoned for publishing pornographic literature.

It is no full answer to say that Zola was simply being consistent with his professed materialism, his denial of spiritual values: for, in the first place, it is extremely rare for a creative artist to build his life-work on the basis of a metaphysical system, however strongly he may adhere to it; and in the second place, how many more rationalists, sceptics, and materialists—Stendhal, Flaubert himself, the Goncourt brothers—are there who were never deterred by their rationalism, their scepticism, their materialism from

[1] F. Frank, *Gustave Flaubert d'après des documents intimes et inédits*, quoted by A. Albalat, *Gustave Flaubert et ses amis* (1927), p. 121.

analysing the transcendent aspects of passion! Suggestions have also been made that this moral blindness in Zola was due to some organic infirmity. The first broad hint of a solution along these lines was contained in the 1887 'Manifeste contre *La Terre*' in which Zola was denounced by five young novelists who chose this method of making public their break with naturalism.[1] There have been more recent, post-Freudian interpretations deriving essentially from the same supposition. That of M. Charles Lalo may serve as an example.[1] This critic attempts to reconcile the contradiction between Zola's blameless private life and the sexual excesses he recounts in books like *Nana* and *Pot-Bouille*, by arguing that his literary work was the outlet for desires which he had relegated to the subconscious.[2]

The principal objection to this attractive thesis is that, for nearly the whole of his literary career, Zola was living what would surely be called a normal sexual life (abnormal only by the standards of Casanovas like Maupassant and Alexis). M. Lalo calls him 'ce bigame rangé' (referring to the liaison with Jeanne Rozerot which was posterior to the period we are surveying), but the consequences that follow from this assumption that monogamy, let alone bigamy, amounts to a dangerous measure of self-denial are, to say the least, disquieting.

Our own conclusion cannot be a simple one. There were a variety of factors, most of which have been touched on in the preceding pages: early sexual inhibitions possibly attributable to childhood experiences which will no doubt always remain obscure; a violent reaction set up by the first clash of youthful idealism with

---

[1] 'Le trouble d'équilibre qui résulte de sa maladie rénale contribue sans doute à l'inquiéter outre mesure de certaines fonctions, le pousse à grossir leur importance. Peut-être Charcot, Moreau (de Tours) et ces médecins de la Salpêtrière qui nous firent voir leurs caprolaliques pourraient-ils déterminer les symptômes de son mal. . . .' To this indelicate innuendo the writers added the insulting suggestion that Zola was also influenced by the practical consideration of the higher sales of reputedly indecent novels.

[2] Lalo, 'Le Complexe de Zola', *Revue des Cours et Conférences* (1937), pp. 508–21. According to Lanoux, it was the regularity of Zola's married life that accounted for 'ces explosions d'érotisme' in his works down to and including *La Terre*. They derive not from experience or observation but from his imagination, 'imagination fouaillée par la continence. Sa sexualité est dans l'encrier' (*Bonjour Monsieur Zola*, p. 110). A rather similar explanation is offered by Turnell: Zola's 'personal views on sexual morality were conservative' and his books provided him with the essential safety-valve, enabling him 'to preserve a highly precarious chastity' (*The Art of French Fiction*, p. 157).

the peculiarly sordid reality of the Rue Soufflot; later, a calm in the early period of married life, interrupted by a renewal of anxiety brought about, perhaps, by discussions with professional friends whose curiosity about the psychology of love had been lifelong; and finally, the revision of the whole question from the point of view of the moralist into which circumstances tended to turn Zola after the publication of *L'Assommoir*. The feature of his treatment of sexual problems which, however, needs to be chiefly emphasized is that it was not uniform; it passed through various phases, some of which we have still to explore. For Zola's attitude to relations between the sexes in the novels that follow *La Bête humaine* is noticeably different from his attitude up to that point; and here again we shall find that personal experiences determined both the change and the new viewpoint.

VIII

INTO BATTLE

NOTHING he ever wrote has damaged Zola's reputation more than the six volumes of critical theory and comment, published in a block between 1880 and 1882, and consisting of reprints of contributions, from 1875 onwards, to the St. Petersburg magazine *The European Herald* first of all, then successively to the Paris newspapers *Le Bien public*, *Le Voltaire*, and *Le Figaro*. Flaubert's cutting remark, 'Zola's overweening self-assurance in matters of criticism can be explained by his inconceivable ignorance',[1] has been echoed, in one form or another, by two or three generations of impatient intellectuals. It is right to say that their strictures tend to spare the judgements he passed on individual novel-writers and dramatists—these posterity has, on the whole, ratified—and are reserved for the reasoning by which he claimed to arrive at his judgements. It seems that as soon as Zola starts to rationalize his likes and dislikes and theorize about his generally sound instincts, he displays so absolute an incapacity to handle abstract ideas, such a marked inability even to think clearly, that his well-wishers usually agree to abandon this outpost of his production to his detractors, who are at liberty to train their guns on it and pulverize it if they wish.

It would be idle to attempt an apology for the first essay in *Le Roman expérimental*, which is no more than a curiosity in the history of literary ideas in France; or of the generalizations, dogmatic assertions, and sturdy *non sequiturs* which are plentifully strewn through the remaining pages of this 'grotesque, violent and narrow, but extremely able volume of destructive and constructive criticism',[2] and between the covers of *Les Romanciers naturalistes*, *Documents littéraires*, *Une Campagne*, and the two books of dramatic criticism. It had better be acknowledged at the outset that the concept of the 'experimental novel', with most of what this concept

---

[1] Made as early as 1878, in a letter to Mme Roger des Genettes.
[2] Gosse, *Questions at Issue*, p. 140.

involves, is infantile, and the manner of its presentation unbeliev-
ably naïve. But it would be a mistake to conclude from this that
Zola was insensitive to the conditions of his own art and blind to
the qualities of that of his rivals.

If it can be established that the critical works were not actually
intended by their author to be taken as a considered digest of his
views on the art of the novel, and if it appears more correct historically to describe them as just one more skirmish in Zola's impetuous
battle for recognition, then the seriousness of their implications is
halved. They remain as one of the more regrettable manifestations
of his itch to dominate; they are not a certificate of intellectual
shallowness. Blame attaches to Zola most, perhaps, for not having
left them to moulder in the newspaper files, as a less honest and
fearless writer might have done.

It is significant that he first sharpened his instrument of critical
judgement when he had to defend a specific artist or small group
of artists under heavy fire from the pundits. This was in 1866.[1]
A similar crusading zeal inspired him, at the period we have now
reached, to put the same edge on the blade of his literary theorizing.
Originally he had been moved to defend the painting of Manet and
the Batignolles school of artists; then, later, his own novels and those
of his friends and disciples. As time went on, Zola's criticism wore
an increasingly made-to-measure look and became more and more
aggressive and polemical, until finally he summed it all up, quite
candidly, in 1881: 'Je me sentais seul, je ne voyais aucun critique
qui acceptât ma cause, et j'étais décidé à me défendre moi-même;
tant que je demeurais sur la brèche, la victoire me semblait certaine.'

Ideas cannot be defended unless they first find some measure
of acceptance; and in consequence they need to be phrased in
such a way that they will impress themselves on as many minds as
they can reach. The minds of the many are unthinking; and in
addressing them, violent statement is notoriously more effective
than reasoned argument. Subtlety of thought only bewilders. 'En
critique, je crois qu'il faut des idées nettes', Zola remarked in his
essay on Stendhal in *Les Romanciers naturalistes*, and his cordial
acknowledgements of Bourget's *Essais de psychologie contemporaine*
(25 November 1883) were tempered by a doubt touching the
wisdom of the younger critic's method: 'Il faut un âge bien
troublé, pour en venir à ces complications du jugement, à ces

[1] See above, pp. 29–31.

nervosités de la compréhension.' He preferred concentration to dispersal, simplicity to the nuance. 'Mon sentiment est que le triomphe d'une idée unique demande la vie d'un homme', he declared at the end of his year's campaign in *Le Figaro*.

To popularize his one or two ideas, Zola neglected none of the devices practised by the professional advertiser and propagandist: the coining and putting into circulation of slogans and catchwords, the incessant repetition of a few striking phrases, the handling of the weapons of raillery and invective, even the affectation of modesty and self-depreciation. In his earlier days he had invented a formula to define the work of art: 'Une œuvre d'art est un coin de la création vu à travers un tempérament',[1] a saying which is perhaps most conveniently rendered into English by E. M. Forster's slightly amplified version: 'A novel is based on evidence plus or minus x, the unknown quantity being the temperament of the novelist, and the unknown quantity always modifies the effect of the evidence, and sometimes transforms it entirely.' If the accent was placed on the 'temperament', the formula could be used as an apt expression of the overriding importance Zola accorded in his earlier phase to originality in art. It jarred altogether with his advocacy of a depersonalized literature in the late seventies. Yet he continued to use it, although it no longer served his purpose, in his later critical works, changing it only to the extent of replacing the theological word *création* by the scientific one *nature*. Another slogan, which ruffled conservatives and baffled others, was: 'La République sera naturaliste ou elle ne sera pas.' It was actually an ironical twisting of a famous pronouncement made by Thiers in 1872: 'La République sera conservatrice ou elle ne sera pas.' What Zola seems to have meant by his formula was that he would prefer to see political and economic problems dealt with by a series of *ad hoc* measures, instead of being settled by an appeal to rigid, unvarying principles.[2] It must be admitted that Zola seems to be taking up here the same masterful attitude to words and their meanings as Humpty-Dumpty. However, the obscurity of the statement did not detract from his challenge. Its performance was double: it advertised naturalism, and it advertised Zola's republicanism.

[1] Zola first used the formula in his essay 'Proudhon et Courbet', *Le Salut public*, 26 July 1865.
[2] Zola came nearest to explaining what he meant in a review of É. Portalis, *Les Deux Républiques* (*Le Voltaire*, 20 July 1880).

'Naturalism' was the chief catchword used in Zola's later critical articles. The word was not employed in *Mes haines*; its first occurrence is commonly supposed to have been in the preface to the second edition of *Thérèse Raquin* (April 1868), where Zola wrote of 'le groupe d'écrivains naturalistes auquel j'ai l'honneur d'appartenir', but there are earlier instances of his use of the word from which one can see how Zola came to remove it from its original context, a purely biological one, and give it a literary connotation.[1]

The term 'naturalism' was preferred to 'realism' mainly because of the connexion immediately established with the natural sciences, but also because 'realism' had associations with an earlier school, that of Champfleury and Duranty, which Zola was anxious not to suggest. In any case, as he remarked superbly on one occasion, 'que ce mot soit bien ou mal choisi, peu importe. Il finira par avoir le sens que nous lui donnerons.'[2] He consistently denied having invented the word, claiming that Montaigne had used it 'avec le sens que nous lui donnons aujourd'hui', that it had been used by foreign critics, particularly in Russia, for thirty years previously, and by a score of French critics: all he had done was to repeat it indefinitely and indefatigably.[3] It was, of course, precisely the constant reiteration of the word, and its remorseless application to every branch of art and sphere of knowledge, that gave the word its propaganda force. It convinced nobody, for it was not an argument; it impressed thousands. Zola knew exactly what he was doing, and when Flaubert upbraided him in private for the abuse of 'naturalist professions of faith', he explained his design with remarkable frankness and force:

Je me moque comme vous de ce mot *naturalisme*, et cependant, je le répéterai, parce qu'il faut un baptême aux choses, pour que le public les croie neuves. . . . J'ai d'abord posé un clou, et d'un coup de marteau, je l'ai fait entrer d'un centimètre dans le cerveau du public, puis d'un

---

[1] Notably in a review of the second edition of Taine's *Essais de critique et d'histoire* (*L'Événement*, 25 July 1866). In a new preface written for this edition Taine had drawn a number of analogies between the work of naturalists (by which he meant natural scientists) and of social historians or historians of ideas. Zola's review harps on this theme.

[2] *Le Naturalisme au théâtre*, p. 147.

[3] See *Le Roman expérimental*, p. 91, and *Une Campagne*, p. 105. As a matter of strict fact, the word is not to be found in Montaigne, but was used by Belinsky, the Russian critic, in 1848. I have gone into this whole question in some detail in 'The Origin of the terms *naturalisme, naturaliste*', *French Studies*, vol. viii (1954), pp. 109–21.

second coup, je l'ai fait entrer de deux centimètres. Eh bien! mon marteau, c'est le journalisme que je fais moi-même autour de mes œuvres.[1]

This was not the only occasion on which Zola freely owned up to the large element of showmanship in his critical manifestos. To Jules Troubat, who had edited a collection of Sainte-Beuve's articles, he wrote (1 September 1879) expressing regret that he lacked the time to undertake a thorough study of Sainte-Beuve. 'Je ne suis qu'un critique de combat, qui déblaie sa route devant lui, puisqu'il n'y a personne pour la déblayer'; and he admitted 'l'insuffisance de mes articles, bâclés au milieu de la bataille, pour les besoins de la tactique et en vue de la victoire'. In an obituary of Littré, Zola deplored the limited influence that this great positivist had had on his age, and attributed it to his over-scrupulous intellectual honesty. 'Il lui a manqué un peu du cabotinage qui fait les grands acteurs de nos drames humains. . . . Quand on parle aux hommes, il faut toujours faire la part du mensonge, et il y a un besoin de mise en scène dans la foi la plus sincère.'[2] And Zola ended the preface of *Une Campagne* with a sentence which gave fair warning to the literal-minded: 'Le désir de la vérité ne suffit plus, dans nos temps troublés; il en faut la passion, qui exagère, mais qui impose.'

The avowed pragmaticism of the critical works complicates enormously the task of pronouncing on Zola's capability as a theoretician. Just how seriously ought the concept of the 'experimental novel' to be taken? Certainly the essay in which he works out the analogies between experimental medicine and the art, or science, of novel-writing is written with fire and, it seems, conviction. It is a coherent and exhaustive, but quite unacceptable, application to the craft of the novelist of the new view of therapeutics put forward by Claude Bernard in his *Introduction à la médecine expérimentale*. There is reason to believe that Zola had not read this book (which was published in 1865) when he started writing the *Rougon-Macquart* series: Henry Céard has taken credit

---

[1] *Journal des Goncourt*, entry for 19 Feb. 1877. Flaubert does not seem to have become any less sceptical as a result of this disclaimer. His comment to Maupassant, when Zola published the pamphlet *La République et la littérature* in 1879, was: 'C'est énorme! Quand il m'aura donné la définition du naturalisme, je serai peut-être un naturaliste. Mais d'ici là, moi pas comprendre.' Nevertheless, Flaubert had not scrupled himself to use the word, in the preface he wrote to Bouilhet's *Dernières Chansons* (1870).

[2] 'Hugo et Littré', *Le Figaro*, 13 June 1881 (*Une Campagne*, p. 251).

for having put it into Zola's hands, and the two men were not acquainted until 1876.[1] This means that Zola had already established his method of novel-composition independently of Claude Bernard, who can have taught him nothing. The evidence of dates perhaps also warrants the guess that the essay (first published in April 1879) was an unreflecting reaction to a first reading of the book: Zola plunged into print without giving himself time to consider where his audacious theorizing was taking him.

In fact, *Le Roman expérimental*, once the flourishes are stripped away, reduces itself to a simple rechristening, as 'experimentation', of the well-tried process of deduction from observation. Zola knew well enough that his audience, in the mass, never plumbed deeper than the name; but 'il faut un baptême aux choses, pour que le public les croie neuves'; and the 'experimental novel' smacked agreeably of the laboratory and the dissecting theatre. Perhaps the greatest dupes were the earnest critics who busied themselves refuting him; they provided Zola with gratuitous advertisement, the last thing they could have been minded to do.

The critical volumes of 1880-2 contain, however, much besides red herrings and shock headlines. It is possible to disentangle a set of literary criteria, many of them quite irreconcilable with those that guided Zola in 1866. There is little trace of his earlier eclecticism.

He seems in no doubt now about the superiority of realism as a literary formula over all others. The surviving romantics, and their etiolated descendants, the idealist novelists patronized by the *Revue des Deux Mondes*, are fiercely harried. True to his motto: 'Strike at the head', Zola assails Victor Hugo again and again with iconoclastic fury. His attacks were directed, it is true, not against Hugo the lyric poet but against his claim to the mantle of wisdom and prophecy. 'Si j'applaudis Victor Hugo comme poète, je le discute comme penseur, comme éducateur', he wrote in *Le Roman expérimental*, a sentence which might remind the irreverent of

[1] See M. Verne, 'Une Lettre de M. Henry Céard: Zola et le prêt du livre de Claude Bernard', *Information*, 22 July 1918. Céard's letter is quoted in full by R. Dumesnil, *La Publication des 'Soirées de Médan'*, pp. 46–48. But Zola had not needed to read Claude Bernard before inventing the term 'littérature expérimentale', which he used on several occasions in articles written for *L'Avenir national* in 1873 (25 Feb., 4 Mar., 15 Apr.) with a meaning close to, if not identical with, that given subsequently to the term 'naturaliste': 'La littérature expérimentale, la littérature d'un siècle de science'; 'la littérature expérimentale, l'étude du vrai ramenée à l'analyse des faits simples'.

Homais, who 'aurait voulu tout à la fois pouvoir couronner Racine de ses deux mains et discuter avec lui pendant un bon quart d'heure'. The contemptuous criticism of Hugo's poem *L'Âne* in *Une Campagne* is softened by a similar distinction drawn between the poet and the philosopher.

The longest and most serious study of Hugo is to be found in *Documents littéraires*. It appeared first, in Russian translation, in April 1877, and included an important digression in which Zola stated the view he had by then reached about literary evolution and the part the individual plays in it. He believes that there is such an evolution, which may be ascendant if the literary formulas that are invented are each better than the last; but there is not necessarily progress in literary works, since works are only partly determined by the formula; of equal importance is the personality of the artist.

Une formule n'est qu'un instrument donné par le milieu historique et social, et qui tire surtout sa beauté de la façon plus ou moins supérieure dont l'homme prédestiné sait en obtenir une musique. . . . De cette façon, on accepte toutes les grandes œuvres, les antiques et les modernes, les étrangères et les nationales, en les replaçant dans leurs milieux et en les regardant chacune comme la manifestation la plus haute d'un artiste à une époque donnée.

This passage seems to show that between 1866 and 1877 Zola lost little of his respect for the genius, 'l'homme prédestiné'; but the emphasis laid on the 'formula' is something new, and in the succeeding pages he stresses it more and more. The cardinal sins are to use an outmoded formula, as Victor Hugo does, and to attempt to exact respect for it from a new generation, which is what his devotees are guilty of doing.

In the essay entitled 'Le Roman expérimental', written two years after the study of Hugo, the importance attributed to the originality of the artist has noticeably dwindled and, if *Mes haines* is taken as the starting-point, it can be seen that Zola's attitude to this question has undergone a complete reversal. Instead of the 'temperament', that is the individuality, of the writer being alone considered worthy of the critic's attention, Zola now seems to be exclusively concerned with the accuracy of a novelist's observation and the strict determinism of his plot. The part of genius is merely to make an inspired choice of the experiment to be conducted, or in plain words, of the subject to be treated; genius is 'l'idée *a priori*, seulement il est contrôlé par l'expérience'. Zola, in this last stage of his critical development, seems anxious to sink the personality of the writer in a slough of anonymity. The kind of book that might be written in accordance with such recipes would probably approximate to the papers which in our own day incorporate the researches of social scientists. It might have great value; but this value would be properly non-literary.

It would certainly not be the kind of novel that Zola was writing at the time, or indeed ever wrote. His speculations in aesthetics ran flat against his own normal practice—a fact of which he was not unaware. In the preface to *Une Campagne*, he warned the reader not to confuse critic with novelist: the one was not there to plead the other's cause; Zola had 'cherché la vérité passionnément, à l'aide des méthodes scientifiques, *souvent contre ses propres œuvres*'. From Du Bellay to Jean-Paul Sartre, the case is perhaps unique of a treatise on the art of literature which was not an *apologia pro arte sua*. Zola's press campaigns were designed to advertise his productions, not to analyse them.

This being so, to anyone seeking to understand the nature of the man who, at the same time as he was engaged on the critical works, was also composing *L'Assommoir* and *Nana*, the fundamental impulse that gave rise to this furious theorizing is more important than the content and drift of the actual theories. This impulse was the very one which had led him in 1866 to defend a small group of disregarded painters against the shocked mistrust of almost the whole of Parisian society; it was the very one which was to cause him in 1898 to assert the innocence of Dreyfus in defiance of all the forces of respectability and settled authority in the country. It was the impulse to proclaim a 'truth' of which he was the sole repository, or which he alone dared to proclaim. A hankering after apostleship was one of Zola's most marked characteristics.

However, if we look for scriptural prototypes, then Samson may well seem more appropriate than St. Paul. Zola was a born fighter; his joy in the fray was almost proverbial among his friends. The very syllables of his name sounded in Maupassant's ear 'like two bugle-calls. . . . It seems to challenge fight, to threaten attack, to proclaim victory.' Goncourt observed that 'his great delight is to sense how he influences and dominates Paris from his modest room', and Daudet compared him to 'that storm-bird of which Mistral speaks in one of his poems, the seagull who wings his way through the hurricane, surrounded by lightning and spray, and "calmly fishes" the while'. Finally, Alexis, who was perhaps closest to him in these years, portrayed him as 'unshakable in his opinions . . . he will cling to his point of view, will never admit himself beaten, and will strive passionately to prove himself right. . . . He has the spirit of an intellectual dictator, forming a curious contrast with his easy-going affability, his lack of will-power in the daily concerns of life.'

His pugnacity bred enemies and sometimes lost him friends, but he remained unmoved in the growing storm of opposition which acted on him like a tonic. After the failure on the stage of his farce *Le Bouton de rose* in 1878, he commented defiantly: 'Cela me rajeunit, cela me donne vingt ans. . . . Le succès de *L'Assommoir* m'avait avachi. . . . Vraiment, quand je pense à l'enfilade de romans qui me reste à fabriquer, je sens qu'il n'y a qu'un état de lutte et de colère qui puisse me les faire faire!' The love of controversy was so much part of him that he used to read with a kind of eagerness every hostile review that appeared. On one occasion (a dinner party given by the Daudets in 1891), describing the pleasure he took in being pulled to pieces by an indignant critic, he started arguing the case of the group most bitterly opposed to his ideas (the symbolists) with such warmth that finally Coppée interjected sardonically: 'What! You don't mean to tell me, Zola, that you are developing an interest in the colour of vowels!'

This delight in punishment was not a form of spiritual masochism, but only another manifestation—paradoxical as it may seem —of the doubts that beset him. At least people were still taking notice of him, and the harder the blows rained the more assured he became. 'On m'attaque, donc je suis encore', he wrote six years before his death, at a time when *Lourdes* and *Rome* were rousing Catholics to a fury of indignation such as not even the most outspoken of the *Rougon-Macquart* novels had succeeded in provoking.

Since all he wanted from battle was the knocks, it is understandable that he should have been a lone warrior rather than a captain of men. Flaubert suspected him of wanting to lead a school, but he denied this repeatedly, in private and in public, insisting that naturalism was not a coterie but a movement or a phase of literary evolution. Such disclaimers did not prevent him from rallying support as occasion arose; but it was collaboration, not obedience, that he looked for, from 1867, when he invited Valabrègue to come to Paris in these terms: 'Je me disais que nous irions ensemble au combat et que nous nous soutiendrions au besoin', to the year of *L'Assommoir*, when he wrote to Edmond de Goncourt urging him not to slacken production: 'Il ne faut pas lâcher pied. Nous avons besoin d'achever la victoire. N'importe, nous avons porté cet hiver un rude coup.'

Most of his friends who were men of letters were regarded by Zola, whether they liked it or not, as 'naturalists'. In retrospect they seem a motley collection. They can be divided into two main groups. The first comprised his elders and contemporaries, in practice the men who, with Zola, attended the *dîners des Cinq* or the *dîners des auteurs sifflés*, so called because the main condition of participation was to have written an unsuccessful play. They were Flaubert, Edmond de Goncourt, Alphonse Daudet, and Turgenev (whose credentials were that he had been 'hissed in Russia'; he was taken at his word).[1] The second group consisted of his disciples, mostly younger men, five of whom, Maupassant, Huysmans, Alexis, Céard, and Hennique, were designated as the 'Médan group' after their joint publication, with Zola, of *Les Soirées de Médan* in 1880.

With the individual members of the first group Zola's relations passed through many vicissitudes. He remained on cordial terms with Flaubert and Turgenev for as long as they lived; but they died, Flaubert in 1880 and Turgenev in 1883, before the friendship had had to stand the test of time. Zola had occasional disagreements with Flaubert over some of the minutiae of the literary craft; but he never had any reservations to make about Flaubert's works save that there were too few of them, and the personal affection that each bore the other was strong. Turgenev acted as Zola's principal literary agent in Russia, advising him at what prices he could sell his articles to Stasyulevitch, giving him details about the translations of his novels as they appeared in Russia, suggesting what essay subjects were likely to appeal to the Petersburgers, informing him about the growth of his popularity among them. Turgenev's letters to Zola, which have been published,[2] are, apart from insignificant

---

[1] See A. Daudet, *Trente ans de Paris*, p. 335. The first of this celebrated run of dinners took place on 14 Apr. 1874. Edmond de Goncourt, in a passage of his diary deleted from the version published during his life, summarized the conversation as follows: 'On débute par une grande dissertation sur les aptitudes spéciales des constipés et des diarrhéiques en littérature; et de là, on passe au mécanisme de la langue française.'

[2] In É. Halpérine-Kaminsky, *Ivan Tourguéneff d'après sa correspondance avec ses amis français* (1901).

notes arranging meeting-times and -places, nearly all business letters, which show the care with which Turgenev looked after his friend's money interests, but give no indication what he thought of his writings. Judging from one or two hints in letters to other correspondents, Turgenev was not strongly attracted to Zola's more characteristic works, but he imparted these opinions in confidence,[1] and we may assume that he was sufficiently tactful not to let differences of this nature interfere with his friendship for a man whom he clearly admired greatly notwithstanding.

Zola, Daudet, and Edmond de Goncourt formed for many years a little knot which seemed tighter to the outsider than it actually was. One feeling at any rate united them—a deep respect for their art, too deep for them ever to debase it by insincerity; and they shared (in the early eighties) the same attitude to life, a 'ferocious pessimism'. The words were used by Henry James in 1884. His observation of this group may be taken as just that of the cosmopolitan onlooker, immensely struck by their intelligence but disagreeably surprised by their narrowness. After an evening with Daudet and Zola and a morning with Edmond de Goncourt, he wrote home: 'Seeing these people does me a world of good, and this intellectual vivacity and *raffinement* make an English mind seem like a kind of glue-pot. But their ignorance, corruption and complacency are strange, full strange.' The following day he wrote to Howells: 'There is nothing more interesting to me now than the effort and experiment of this little group, with its truly infernal intelligence of art, form, manner—its intense artistic life.'

But this scintillating triple star trembled perpetually under the stress of disruptive internal strains.

Zola and Daudet had known each other since the mid-sixties, when they were both pensioners of the redoubtable Villemessant (Daudet's *Lettres de mon moulin* were first published in *L'Événement*). *Les Romanciers naturalistes* contains a long monograph on Daudet, and, in addition, Zola wrote flattering reviews of *Les Rois en exil* and *Numa Roumestan* for the newspapers with which he was at the time collaborating.[2] He had given up reviewing when

---

[1] Thus, in a letter to Flaubert (Halpérine-Kaminsky, p. 97): 'J'ai mis le nez dans *l'Assommoir*. Je n'en suis pas enchanté. Ceci entre nous strictement. Il y a bien du talent, mais c'est lourd et on remue trop le pot de chambre.'

[2] *Le Voltaire*, 4 Nov. 1879; *Le Figaro*, 13 Sept. 1881.

Daudet's later books appeared; but the letters he wrote him, about *Sapho* and *L'Immortel*, contain extraordinarily generous and at the same time penetrating appraisals of these novels.[1]

Daudet, according to a young English lady-reporter who seems to have mixed freely in Paris literary circles at the time, was the only fellow writer who did not heartily dislike Zola.[2] But even Daudet, especially when chronic ill health started to sour his temper, found his invading personality and unfaltering productive capacity at times more than irritating. On such occasions his tart tongue exercised itself freely, as when a journalist asked him undiplomatically for an article to mark the completion of *Les Rougon-Macquart*. 'If I were to write that article', Daudet rapped out, 'it would be to advise Zola, now that the family tree of the Rougon-Macquarts is complete, to go and hang himself from the highest branch.'[3] When outbursts of this sort reached Zola's ears he pretended to discount them as leg-pulling on the part of the irrepressible creator of Tartarin. However, with all his skill in ignoring nuances, Zola must have recognized that he and Daudet were not birds of a feather. The southern temperament may produce sombre elegists like Leopardi, or wayward humorists like Cervantes. Zola and Daudet, both meridionals (the first by upbringing and ancestry if not by birth), belonged each to the opposite group. Their alliance was necessarily an uneasy one.

Apart from Duranty, the Goncourt brothers were the first of the earlier generation of realist writers with whom Zola made contact. An article praising *Germinie Lacerteux*[4] first brought him to their notice. Their gratitude was expressed in glowing terms, and they offered him there and then their friendship. In December 1865 he demonstrated his support vociferously at the first night of *Henriette Maréchal*; a few days later he posted an enthusiastic letter, in which he talked of this stormy performance as 'la bataille glorieuse du vrai contre la banalité et la routine', and enclosed a copy of *La Confession de Claude*. What they thought of this book we do not know; but *Thérèse Raquin* stirred them to the following solemn pronouncement: 'You and your book have our entire support. We

---

[1] These letters are not in the Bernouard edition of Zola's correspondence. They were published by G. Randal in *Quo Vadis*, vol. v (1952), pp. 23–42.

[2] Mrs. Belloc Lowndes, *Where Love and Friendship Dwelt* (1943), p. 182.

[3] L. de Robert, *De Loti à Proust*, p. 130.

[4] *Le Salut public*, 24 Feb. 1865; reprinted in *Mes haines*.

are with you in your ideas, your principles, and your affirmation of the rights of modern Art, of the Truth, and of Life.' (The capitals are the Goncourts' own.) Finally, yet another article by Zola on the work of the two novelists, published in *Le Gaulois* on 22 September 1868, was a civility which was repaid by an invitation to lunch. The long overdue meeting took place on 14 December.

It is probable that the Goncourts at this time regarded Zola chiefly in the light of a fighting critic, one of the very few who were not afraid to speak out in defence of their works. They shared his antipathy for the smugly sentimental novelists then in vogue, they were broadly united with him in demanding a sterner confrontation of the reader with the often ugly realities of society and the human soul. On the other hand they could not follow Zola in his ebullient enthusiasm for the impressionist painters: from Courbet onwards, the new trends of French art left these devotees of Hokusai quite unresponsive. But there is no reason to suppose that this topic necessarily came up for discussion, still less that the breach between Edmond and Zola can be attributed in part to the elder man's annoyance that a novice in connoisseurship should have shown a keener discernment than he and his brother.

The coolness that did set in, some years after the death of Jules, arose more probably from Edmond's jealousy at Zola's spectacularly successful exploitation (with *L'Assommoir*) of a vein, that of the working-class novel, which he believed he and his brother had been the first to work, and to which they had, therefore, a kind of prescriptive right. He noted sourly that Zola's book was already being called a masterpiece, this being a word rarely applied by critics to a work by a living writer, let alone 'un *jeune*'. Zola's eyes were opened to Goncourt's half-hostility by the preface to *Les Frères Zemganno* (1879). He refused to believe that Goncourt intended to split off from the group, but asked him to consider the 'misinterpretations' which the press would be bound to put on certain sentences. 'On va vouloir vous séparer de nous. Voilà ce qui m'a fait de la peine, sans que je vous accuse de rien.' In 1884 there came another crisis in their relations. Privately, as we know now that his diary has been published in an unexpurgated version, Edmond de Goncourt had for a long time suspected Zola of plagiarizing his novels. He had read him passages from *La Fille Élisa* when it was still on the stocks and at a time when Zola was busy with *L'Assommoir*. Since Zola worked faster than Goncourt, *L'Assommoir* came out before *La Fille Élisa*. When it did, the mortified author recognized, in the chapter describing Gervaise's attempts at soliciting in the streets, a couple of insignificant details which he was sure Zola must have remembered from these readings. At the time, he made no public complaint, but when *La Joie de vivre* was due to appear he became nervous, for it was known that Zola's new novel was to include a study of the onset of puberty in the heroine; and he, Goncourt, had chosen to deal with just this subject in the book he was then writing, *Chérie*. Again, he had given advance readings at which Zola had been present; and his annoyance, this time, was reported to Zola by Alphonse Daudet. Zola took up the matter frankly with the older writer, and forced him to admit that the chapter concerning Chérie's first menstruation was not among those that he had read aloud; but Goncourt remained resentful, for, once again, his rival's novel was due to be published before his, and he feared the public would conclude that it was he who was plagiarizing Zola.

In the years that followed Zola seems merely to have been careful to avoid open recriminations with this cantankerous survivor of a brilliant literary partnership. He was not always successful. Whatever he wrote, Goncourt told his friends that the new book was simply a re-edition of something someone else had written before. Zola was a mere literary cobbler, 'un ressemeleur en littérature'; *L'Œuvre* was a rehash of *Manette Salomon*, and he was sure that *La Terre* would turn out to be lifted from Balzac's *Les Paysans*. Zola who, 'when he argued some point of art with an adversary [was] vigorous yet nervous, truculent and on occasion insolent',[1] lost his temper at a dinner-party given by the Daudets on 10 April 1886. He tried to patch things up at another dinner-party (22 April) to which Edmond de Goncourt went in no very conciliatory mood and from which he came away unappeased. Then, on 26 April, Daudet wrote complaining of some harsh words Zola had used about a friend of his, a journalist (Drumont, the anti-semite). In his reply (27 April) Zola took Daudet mildly to task for being so susceptible, and added with pained dignity: 'Il y a . . . un malentendu qui va croissant, une impossibilité de nous dire ce que nous

---

[1] The description was given by an American who frequented him, Charles Henry Meltzer ('Personal Memories of Zola', *The Bookman*, vol. xvi (1902), p. 251).

pensons sans nous blesser, une divergence enfin dans les idées et dans les mots qui nous écartent de plus en plus. Votre lettre me fait une peine infinie, car elle est une preuve nouvelle du mal dont le "trio" est en train de mourir.'

The 'Manifeste des Cinq' the following year (1887), in the drafting of which Goncourt and Daudet may or may not have had a hand, might well have given the death-stroke to the friendship of the 'trio'; Zola applied artificial respiration by affecting to disbelieve completely the rumours of their complicity with the five young apostates. But the year after, an article in *Le Gaulois*, 'Zola jugé par Goncourt', reinforced Zola's doubts about Goncourt's good faith. This time he seems to have resigned himself to accepting the fact of the split, hoping only that it would never come to an open quarrel, and that they would always be able to shake hands when they met.

The history of the dissolution of this friendship has taken us beyond the period in which the 'battle for naturalism' was being fought; the encroachment on the years makes it possible to trace, however, some of the causes of the disintegration of the movement which were inherent from the start. Zola's bright ambitions to form a compact battalion of like-minded men of letters took too little account of the pettinesses against which literary talent is no preservative and which, indeed, it often seems to foster.

He reaped almost as much disappointment from the hopes he had placed on the band of young admirers who gathered round him in the late seventies. Alexis alone remained unswervingly devoted, even after the Dreyfus Affair which engulfed many of the loyalties that Zola still counted. 'Vous êtes, comme disait Flaubert, "un vieux solide" ', Zola wrote to him towards the end of his days, 'le plus fidèle entre les amis fidèles'. It had been a lifetime's connexion. At school in Aix, Alexis used to hear about Zola from Valabrègue; together, they read the *Contes à Ninon* behind a propped-up dictionary. In 1869 Alexis came to Paris and was introduced by Valabrègue to Zola. Already he owed his start in the world of letters to Zola's rather unscrupulous connivance at a literary hoax in which Alexis played, it seems, a fairly innocent part. He had sent Zola a poem he had written, inspired by Baudelaire; Zola, who was penning an obituary article on the poet for *Le Gaulois*, included with it this poem and succeeded, for a brief period, in passing it off as an unpublished work of the dead master. The protests of Baudelaire's executors were an opportunity quickly seized to reveal Alexis's name.[1]

Maupassant was introduced to Zola by Flaubert, Hennique by Alexis. The two remaining members of the Médan group, Céard and Huysmans, presented themselves humbly as admirers, and were accepted on those terms, some time in 1876. The custom was adopted of meeting at Zola's house every Thursday. Édouard Rod and Octave Mirbeau were two other constant attendants at these gatherings.

The project of forming, with his closest friends, a kind of mutual aid society was a very old one with Zola. He had expressed it as early as 1860, in a letter to Baille; the purpose would have been 'de former un puissant faisceau pour l'avenir, de nous soutenir mutuellement, quelle que soit la position qui nous attende'. The original objective of the Médan group was rather more limited, if we go by the statement made a good deal later by Alexis. Zola's first disciples, 'very different in temperament, origins, and character, but at any rate having common ties, analogous tendencies, and similar ambitions, reckoned on giving each other a push, at least over the first difficult hurdles, so that a start could be made in style. As for the future—well, it could take care of itself.'[2]

In France literary movements, like ships in other countries, are not infrequently launched with a bottle or more of champagne. The founding of the naturalist school was no exception. It dates, for practical purposes, from a dinner given by the younger writers (the five future authors of the *Soirées de Médan*, together with Octave Mirbeau) in honour of their elders, Flaubert, Goncourt, and Zola, at the Restaurant Trapp on 16 April 1877. One can imagine the occasion was convivial rather than business-like. Due publicity was assured, both by a humorous advance notice in *La République des lettres*, which printed the menu ('Potage purée Bovary — Truite saumonée à la Fille Élisa', etc.), and by an article, 'La Demi-douzaine', inserted under a pseudonym by Alexis in *Les Cloches de Paris*, in which he feigned high indignation that a handful of literary nobodies should have succeeded in raising so much dust.[3]

---

[1] See *Le Gaulois*, 10 and 19 Jan. 1869; also Alexis, *Émile Zola, notes d'un ami*, p. 49 and Dufay, 'Baudelaire, Zola et *les Vieilles Plaies*', *Mercure de France*, vol. cclxxxv (1938), pp. 251, 509–10.

[2] Alexis, 'Les Soirées de Médan', *Le Journal*, 30 Nov. 1893. Quoted by Dumesnil, *La Publication de 'Soirées de Médan'*, pp. 194–5.

[3] See Dumesnil, *L'Époque réaliste et naturaliste*, pp. 95–96.

These birthday junketings over, the school set about the business of collective survival, using the same methods as many before them and since. Members of the group wrote keenly appreciative monographs on each other's works. Both Huysmans and Rod published essays on *L'Assommoir*, the type-novel of naturalism;[1] a little later Maupassant, in a highly imaginative account of how *Les Soirées de Médan* came to be written, detailed the artistic aims of the school.[2] Zola reciprocated by compelling *Le Figaro*, with some difficulty, to accept a favourable review of *La Maison Tellier*: it appeared as part of a joint study of Alexis and Maupassant on 11 July 1881. He had already published a similar double article in the same paper on Huysmans and Céard.

There was even, about 1880, some talk of starting a newspaper entirely devoted to upholding the naturalist cause. This was a direct result of friction between Zola and Laffitte, of *Le Voltaire*, who was one of the few newspaper editors prepared to publish the writings of the group; Laffitte, however, was not to be relied on to print articles without tampering with them, and finally withdrew his support in September 1880, after a sensational squabble with Zola. The projected new periodical was to be called *La Comédie humaine*, and Huysmans was to edit it. Even Flaubert was enthusiastically in favour; but matters got no further than tentative negotiations with printers. 'Décès intra-utérin', Céard commented drily to Zola on 16 November.[3]

However, as Zola saw from the start, advertisements are wasted if the goods advertised are not being produced. An unflagging worker himself, he looked for the same cascading output from his colleagues. Céard told him that Huysmans had put aside *Les Sœurs Vatard* half-finished; Zola wrote back anxiously (16 July 1877):

Mais il faut qu'il travaille, dites-le-lui bien. Il est notre espoir, il n'a pas le droit de lâcher son roman, quand tout le groupe a besoin d'œuvres. Et vous, que faites-vous? Je vois bien que vous lancez d'anciennes

[1] Huysmans, 'Émile Zola et *l'Assommoir*', *L'Actualité*, 11 Mar.–1 Apr. 1877; reprinted as a 10-page pamphlet in 1880. Rod, *A propos de 'l'Assommoir'*, Paris, 1879.

[2] *Le Gaulois*, 17 Apr. 1880.

[3] See Xau, *Émile Zola*, p. 35, for Zola's account of his 'programme'; and also L. Deffoux, 'Huysmans fondateur de journal' and 'Un Projet d'hebdomadaire naturaliste: *La Comédie humaine*', *Mercure de France*, vol. cxxxvi (1919), p. 572 and vol. ccxxvii (1931), pp. 508–10. Huysmans had undertaken the brunt of the preparatory work; his letters to Zola in September, October, and November 1880 constitute a running commentary on his tribulations.

pièces; cela ne suffit pas, il faut en écrire de nouvelles, et des drames, et des comédies, et des romans. Nous devons d'ici à quelques années écraser le public sous notre fécondité.

The advice made little impression on Céard. In 1881 he published his first novel, *Une Belle Journée*, and after that he relapsed into a lethargy (as far as the writing of fiction was concerned) until after Zola had died and the battle for naturalism had become a memory. Huysmans, on the other hand, was, as Zola's letter suggests, the brightest star, after himself, in this new pleiad. He had brought out his first novel, *Marthe*, before he knew Zola personally. It was a brief account of the career of a prostitute, antedating Goncourt's *La Fille Élisa* and Zola's *Nana*; the fact that the two masters each in his turn applied himself to the same theme proves at least that Huysmans could anticipate the fashion. *Les Sœurs Vatard* was finished in 1879. Two more naturalist novels followed in 1881 and 1882 (*En ménage* and *A vau l'eau*), but *A rebours* (1884) broke with the tradition. Huysmans felt vaguely that naturalism was a cul-de-sac and that the blank wall at the end was already in sight. It was in the same year that the first translations of Dostoevsky appeared, and their success testified to a weariness with Zola's 'physio-logical' formulas which infected not only writers but the general public as well.

Zola did not reconcile himself calmly to the desertion of his most promising disciple. In the preface to the 1903 re-edition of *A rebours* Huysmans recounted how, as they were walking together in the neighbourhood of Médan, Zola 'stopped suddenly and, his eyes darkening, reproached me for writing the book, telling me I was striking a terrible blow against naturalism and causing the school to run off its course . . .'. His only answer to Huysmans's apologetic explanations was: 'Je n'admets pas que l'on change de manière et d'avis; je n'admets pas que l'on brûle ce que l'on a adoré.'

Maupassant's repudiation of the naturalists came earlier and hurt Zola less, since Maupassant, thanks to his training under Flaubert, had always been on the 'aesthetic' wing of the party, and in consequence was never much trusted. Privately he echoed Flaubert's horror of Zola's publicity methods: he reported how sandwich-men had been hired by *Le Voltaire* and were parading the boulevards to advertise *Nana*, then being serialized in that paper. 'I find this insane boosting so humiliating for everyone', he went on, 'that if anyone asked me if I was a man of letters, I should answer: No sir, I sell fishing-rods.'[1] 'Boule de suif', Maupassant's contribution to *Les Soirées de Médan*, secured him immediate fame, and after that he preferred to stand on his own feet. There was nothing sensational in the break; Maupassant simply withdrew, hat blandly doffed, into different circles of society and different spheres of art. The dedication of the *Contes de la Bécasse* (1883) to the four other disciples should be read as a polite leave-taking.

These desertions and disappointments made a melancholy impression on Zola which perhaps never faded. Years later, when Saint-Georges de Bouhélier came to him full of exultant talk about the 'naturist' school he was founding, Zola warned him not to pitch his expectations too high. 'Vous avez des amis; ils ont vingt ans, et vont comme vous à la bataille. C'est très bien. Mais ne vous illusionnez pas sur leur constance à vous suivre. Au moindre succès, vous vous séparerez.'[2] Experience had taught Zola that the early dissolution of such groupings was in the nature of things; this instability was not a vice peculiar to the Médan school, and, in fact, was proof of the vitality of its component members. The one or two brilliant writers in Zola's circle were bound, by the fact of their brilliance, to walk alone, each in his own path. The others had little to offer except sterile loyalty. It is hardly necessary to lay the blame at Zola's door, as did the signatories of the 'Manifeste des Cinq', because of his 'emigration' to Médan after the publication of *L'Assommoir*, his 'desertion', and his investment of his huge earnings in real property instead of a naturalist review. Nor need we join Anatole France in reproaching Zola with an arrogance and intolerance which estranged his followers,[3] since on more than one occasion he declared that, provided they did not shirk the truth, he did not mind how they presented it. Far from trying to equate the differing talents of his protégés with his own, he was always at pains to stress their individuality. He ended his essay on the 'Trois débuts' of Hennique, Huysmans, and Alexis by blaming the critics for giving the impression that all had been said when these three young

[1] Letter quoted by Albalat, *Gustave Flaubert et ses amis*, p. 227, along with other letters of Maupassant to Flaubert which well illustrate his latent hostility to Zola.

[2] Bouhélier, 'La Mort de Zola', *Le Figaro*, 1 Oct. 1927.

[3] France, *La Vie littéraire*, 3e série, pp. 372–3. The suggestion is made in an article on Octave Feuillet, in the course of which France is ironical about 'la terreur naturaliste'.

authors were classified under one heading as naturalists. The *Figaro* article on Alexis and Maupassant concluded with the words: 'Il n'y a ni chefs ni disciples, il n'y a que des camarades, qu'une différence d'âge sépare à peine.'

Perhaps the strongest single reason for the break-up of the school so soon after its notable collective production, *Les Soirées de Médan*, was that Zola himself lost heart in the struggle.

By refusing to go on writing for the papers after 1881, he claimed to be deliberately freeing himself for his more important work. 'Un dégoût violent me prend de mes articles au *Figaro*' he wrote to Céard on 6 May 1881. 'Je rêve, quand j'aurai lâché ça, un plongeon dans de longs travaux où je pourrai disparaître pendant des mois.' His contract with *Le Figaro* ran out on 22 September; on 5 November he told another correspondent (Jules Troubat): 'J'ai quitté la presse et j'espère n'y point rentrer. Dans les derniers temps, j'ai senti que je m'encanaillais. En somme, je me suis assez battu, que d'autres me remplacent. Moi, je vais tâcher de créer.' Such reflexions, however, might have occurred to him at any time in the previous three or four years—before that period journalism was an essential source of income. And they occurred at a moment when there was no sign that his ideas were likely to triumph, that his personal participation in the contest had ceased to be indispensable.

The primary motive for this retirement was none of those that Zola alleged, and for a good reason: it was a private one.

On 10 April 1880 he learned that Duranty had died the day before. Duranty had been, with Champfleury, the co-founder of the original realist movement in France in the sixties. In more recent years his fame had been largely eclipsed by new-comers, and he had gradually lost touch with the modern trend. To Zola he represented not only a venerable forerunner but one of his very oldest acquaintances among men of letters.[1] He had met Duranty first at Hachette's, when he was still an employee there; and outside working hours the two had a common meeting-ground in Guillemet's studio. Throughout the remainder of Duranty's life Zola persisted in a loyal though largely unavailing campaign to

---

[1] A very full account of the relations between Zola and Duranty has been provided by M. Parturier in *Le Bulletin du Bibliophile* (1948), pp. 49–73, 97–124. Nine of Duranty's letters to Zola were published by Auriant in *La Nef*, no. 20 (1946), pp. 43–58.

interest publishers and the public in his friend's work. Duranty's failure to win recognition was, characteristically, accounted by Zola the greatest tragedy in the man's life; in the brief obituary notice he inserted in *Le Voltaire*, he evoked compassionately the heart-ache of the artist whose works are received not even with scorn but with chilly indifference. He attended the funeral, a melancholy affair, for Duranty had no relatives and the men of letters who came to pay their respects were very few. If Zola did not feel his passing with great anguish, still, it must have caused him some distress of mind. To describe the funeral of Claude Lantier, the closing scene of *L'Œuvre*, he almost certainly used his memories of this occasion.

The real heart-break was when, on 8 May 1880, he received a telegram from Maupassant: *Flaubert mort*. The totally unexpected blow cracked the foundations of Zola's robust faith in life. 'Oh! mon ami', he wrote to Céard, 'il vaudrait mieux nous en aller tous. Ce serait plus vite fait. Décidément, il n'y a que tristesse, et rien ne vaut la peine qu'on vive.' And then, for the third time that year, on 17 October, the axe fell: Zola's mother died.

The sudden blast of mortality froze all the ardour that had, until then, carried him forward. Like all reformers and innovators, Zola had been living for the future. Bereavement robbed him of the future; it told him that even success, if it came, would astound a nameless generation; he himself might never see it or know of it, or savour his triumph and their incense. Flaubert had been less than nineteen years his senior and, in later years, no invalid; and Zola, who had already spent eleven years over his novel-cycle, had not written half of it yet.

What was there even to tell him that it was worth toiling over the remainder? *Rien ne vaut la peine qu'on vive.* In his obituary article on Flaubert there is an account—the passage is among the most moving Zola ever wrote—of how he and Daudet, on their way to Croisset, met the funeral procession coming along the road towards them. They joined it and walked back to Rouen, where Flaubert was to be buried. Apart from relatives and literary friends, no one accompanied them; his fellow townsmen were ignorant of Flaubert's passing, or indifferent. 'La vérité doit être', Zola concluded bitterly, 'que Flaubert, la veille de sa mort, était inconnu des quatre cinquièmes de Rouen et détesté de l'autre cinquième. Voilà la gloire!' What was then the use of cajoling and hectoring the public to give him and his friends their due as writers? The purest reputation is no charm against physical obliteration, and the so-called 'immortality' of genius is an empty word.

These are ancient truisms which, however, no one wholly believes until the moment arrives when they convince the heart as well as the mind. Théophile Gautier considered that his youth ended the morning he woke up, after a night spent sleeping in a *patio* of the Alhambra at Granada, stung by the thought: 'One day I shall be lying so and shall never again rise up.' He was twenty-nine. François Villon was thirty when he discovered that his youth

> Soudainement s'en est vollé
> Et ne m'a laissié quelque don.

For Zola the moment came at forty; and the knowledge that youth had passed was nothing to the rending certainty that his business was now to prepare to die. Charles Du Bos has named this experience *le réveil mortel*, since from that moment onward we are awakened to the fact that all things are uncertain but one, which is that we must die. In the next few years Zola's way was to take him down into the Valley of the Shadow, and was not to lead him up again until that strange variant of personal survival that is paternity gave him back hope, purpose, and zeal.

IX

THE VALLEY OF THE SHADOW

I F Zola's novels are read, as no one thinks of reading them today, straight through in the order in which he wrote them, a subtle change of texture will make itself felt somewhere half-way through the *Rougon-Macquart* cycle. Up to *Nana* the books are *gratuitous*, almost, it might be said, decorative; they reflect, record, not always flatly and seldom unemotionally; but whatever intentions they have (political intentions in *La Fortune des Rougon*, social ones in *L'Assommoir*) are rudimentary, perhaps accidental. In the later phase the works, while they never descend to pleading causes, are nevertheless *functional*; they serve to bring into prominence certain questions, certain problems: of a moral order in *Nana*, *Pot-Bouille*, and *Au Bonheur des Dames*; of an economic and social order in *Germinal*, *La Terre*, and *L'Argent*; of an aesthetic order in *L'Œuvre*, an international one in *La Débâcle*, a religious one in *Le Docteur Pascal*. This seems to be the characteristic quality and common denominator of the later books in the series, although it is not necessarily the quality most worth dwelling on.

This change of accent is consonant with the new preoccupations which descended on Zola when bereavement robbed him of his old assurance. Now that it had become agonizingly evident that existence is fashioned to the end of annihilation, that the most strenuous activity must peter out in a deathly stillness, he could no longer content himself with the raw material of existence or with activity merely for its own sake. The transcendent surged in on him. The rationalist channels of his intelligence were too deeply dug to permit complete surrender to mysticism, the fate that awaited his friend Huysmans. His disquiet remained human and terrestrial; but there were signs, over the period 1880 to 1884, that the strain was telling even on the intellectual dikes.

To attribute so radical a transformation to an accident of quite normal proportions—the loss of a cherished parent, following closely after the death of a deeply admired friend—may seem excessive. And, in fact, this double bereavement may have precipitated, but did not in itself bring about, the crisis. Zola's life had been for many years balanced between the sanguine and the melancholic; the events of 1880 threw a leaden weight into the second scale.

The vulnerable side of his character was fully known only to his most intimate friends; it formed no part of the popular myth about Zola which grew up with him and has not quite died yet, the myth which he himself termed *imbécile*, complaining that 'depuis trente ans[1] on fait de moi un malotru, un bœuf de labour, de cuir épais, de sens grossiers, accomplissant sa tâche lourdement, dans l'unique et vilain besoin du lucre'. Today refusal to see the duality of his nature can result only from prejudice.

His published correspondence and the observations of those in constant contact with him afford every now and then a glimpse of a Zola surprisingly tremulous, nerve-ridden, and excitable. In his twentieth year he had his periods of acute depression. 'Je suis presque continuellement indisposé', he wrote to Baille (21 September 1860). 'L'ennui me ronge; ma vie n'est pas assez active pour ma forte constitution, et mon système nerveux est tellement ébranlé et irrité que je suis dans un état perpétuel d'excitation morale et physique. Je suis incapable d'entreprendre quoi que ce soit. . . .' In this early period, too, we find the first signs of the hypochondria that plagued him for so many years: the disordered nerves affected the bodily organs, and the indispositions thus produced were magnified in turn by the imagination. In a further letter to Baille (10 June 1861) he complains of 'je ne sais quelle maladie physique, sur laquelle aucun médecin ne m'a répondu d'une manière satisfaisante. Mon système digestif est profondément troublé. J'éprouve des pesanteurs dans l'estomac et les entrailles; tantôt je mangerais un bœuf, tantôt la nourriture me dégoûte.' Undernourishment no doubt encouraged such queasiness: this was the time when Zola was subsisting on 'bread and coffee; or bread and a pennyworth of Italian cheese; or bread and a pennyworth of potatoes. Sometimes, nothing but bread! Sometimes, no bread at all!'[2]

[1] Zola was writing in 1896; the sentence occurs in a letter-preface written for Toulouse, *Enquête médico-psychologique sur la supériorité intellectuelle.*

[2] Alexis, *Émile Zola*, p. 52.

The *Journal des Goncourt* preserves numerous instances of Zola's proclivity to morbid fancies at a slightly later date. The Goncourts were, of course, fallible like all human observers; and in this subject particularly they were liable to attach a possibly exaggerated significance to what they saw and heard, being themselves hypersensitive and having a fixed idea of the artist as a man exclusively governed by his nerves. In entry after entry in which he is mentioned, Zola appears to be labouring under acute depression; in reality, probably the diarists did not concern themselves with noting the occasions on which he appeared hale and cheerful. The composite portrait of Zola that can be built up from the *Journal* is, therefore, likely to be more sombre than its original.

Their first impression of Zola was a mixed one: physically, he looked a thick-necked, strapping fellow, and yet his features were delicately, almost femininely modelled. Then the diary goes on to note 'the infirm, sickly, ultra-nervous side of him, which gives you at times the acute sensation of being in the company of a melancholy, impatient sufferer from heart-disease'. The Goncourts summed up their visitor as 'worried, anxious, deep, complex, evasive, difficult to decipher'.

After the disappearance of Jules, Zola, as we have seen, continued to see Edmond, who noted, one day in 1872 when they were lunching together: 'I watch him lift his glass of bordeaux with both hands, saying to me: "Look at all that trembling in my fingers!" And he tells me of his incipient heart-disease, of the early stages of a bladder-disease, of a threat of rheumatoid arthritis.'

These symptoms were purely imaginary, nothing but the fancies of a valetudinarian. The post-mortem which had to be performed on Zola because of the unusual circumstances of his death showed that his organs were practically all intact, as had, indeed, emerged from Dr. Toulouse's examination a few years before.[1] The doctor had attributed all these aches and pains to 'a certain want of nervous balance, an excessive emotivity, properly morbid. . . . It is correct to say that M. Zola is a true neuropath, seeing that his sufferings appear to occur independently of any detectable organic disorder.' Zola's heart was perfectly sound, in spite of the complaints he used to make of feeling his heart beating in his arm or his thigh. The trembling of his fingers was chronic, increased by any strain or emotion, and rendering him sometimes incapable of holding his

[1] Claretie, 'La Mort de Zola', *Revue de France*, vol. v (1922), p. 854.

papers when he was reading a speech in public. Finally, the 'bladder-disease' hints at another curious infirmity, again purely neurasthenic, that Toulouse describes somewhere in his treatise and which made train-journeys, in those days when carriages were not yet equipped with toilet facilities, an embarrassing ordeal for the author of *Les Rougon-Macquart*.

The irrational superstitions that Zola entertained for the greater part of his adult life[1] may be ascribed, in all likelihood, to the same neuropathic condition. They were of a perfectly harmless nature, but formed an odd contrast with the uncompromisingly rationalist philosophy that he professed. He believed particularly in the luck-bearing properties of certain numbers, and would add up the digits of the registration number to know whether it was safe to take a particular cab, or, if he was walking down a street, he would touch a fixed number of lamp-posts. He would confide these superstitions to his friends 'in a low voice, mysteriously, as if wary of a fearful ear listening to him from a dark corner of the room'. He had, further, an inexplicable terror of lightning, which he was so little able to control that, during a thunderstorm, he would have all the windows shuttered and the lamps lit, and sit even so with a hand-kerchief over his eyes.

If not quite what is called a 'pathological case', Zola exhibited at any rate, as these illustrations will have shown, some of the symptoms of the pathological condition of melancholia. There is accordingly little to wonder at in the black despair to which he gave way on the death of Flaubert and of his own mother in 1880. Towards the end of that year Edmond de Goncourt described a visit he received from Zola, who shambled in

with that gloomy, careworn air which is characteristic of his way of coming into a room. And really, I feel sorry for this man of forty who looks older than I do. He sits down heavily in an armchair, complaining grumblingly, rather like a child, of kidney trouble, of gravel, of palpitations, then he talks of the death of his mother, of the gap it has left in his home, speaking with intense pathos and at the same time a touch of dread for himself. And when he starts talking literature, talking about what he intends to do, he hints at his fear of not having the time to do it all.

[1] He seems to have cured himself of them towards the end of his life. When he came to England in 1898 Vizetelly watched for instances of this 'arithmo-mania' of which he had heard but noticed nothing more remarkable than a habit of counting, during his walks, the women's hairpins he saw lying in his path; and this was probably due to sheer wonder that there should be so many.

And Goncourt, whom fame never spoiled, is naïvely astonished that this man, 'with whose name the world rings', should be 'more unhappy, more dispirited, more sombre than the most abject of failures'.

The *dîners des Cinq* were not immediately abandoned on Flaubert's death. The after-dinner conversation of the diminished band used to turn ('curiously', thought Goncourt) on the twin subjects of love and death. One circumstance of his mother's death obsessed Zola long after her funeral. The staircase at Médan had been too narrow for the coffin, which had to be lowered through a window; and Zola could never look at the window without wondering whether his remains or his wife's would be the next to travel the same way. He described to his three friends how he and Alexandrine used to lie awake nightly—not in the dark, for they did not dare go to bed without a night-light—both unable to sleep for the thought of death, and too frightened or too ashamed to talk each other out of their fears. On some nights the strain became unbearable, and Zola would leap out of bed 'in a state of indescribable dread'. This particular confession was made in March 1882. There exists, however, fairly conclusive proof that these nightly terrors had been clawing at Zola and his wife for at least three years previously. Once again it is clear that the loss of his mother only precipitated an impending crisis.

In 1879 he sent Stasyulevitch a short story, 'La Mort d'Olivier Bécaille',[1] the plot of which might have been borrowed from Edgar Allan Poe. The hero, perpetually haunted by the fear of death, is, however, almost certainly a mouthpiece for Zola. This is how he describes his mental agony:

Le pis de ce tourment, c'est qu'on l'endure dans une honte secrète. On n'ose dire son mal à personne. Souvent le mari et la femme, couchés côte à côte, doivent frissonner du même frisson, quand la lumière est éteinte; et ni l'un ni l'autre ne parle, car on ne parle pas de la mort, pas plus qu'on ne prononce certains mots obscènes.

Death is feared by Olivier not for its physical pang, nor for its dark mystery, but for the irrevocable annihilation it implies,

la suppression totale de ce que j'étais; et cela pour toujours, pendant

---

[1] Published in *Vestnik Evropy*, Mar. 1879, and serialized in *Le Voltaire*, 30 Apr.–5 May 1879; subsequently reprinted in the collection *Naïs Micoulin*. On the connexions between this story and *La Joie de vivre* see R. J. Niess in *Modern Language Notes*, vol. lvii (1942), pp. 205–7.

des siècles et des siècles encore, sans que jamais mon existence pût recommencer. Je frissonnais parfois, lorsque je trouvais dans un journal une date future du siècle prochain : je ne vivrais certainement plus à cette date, et cette année d'un avenir que je ne verrais pas, où je ne serais pas, m'emplissait d'angoisse. N'étais-je pas le monde, et tout ne croulerait-il pas, lorsque je m'en irais ?

Never, perhaps, was Zola nearer to revoking the materialism which had contented him until then. In a conversation recorded by Edmond de Goncourt in March 1883, Zola reverted to the theme of his mother's death, and added that it had 'torn a hole in the nihilism of his religious convictions, the idea of an eternal separation being so frightful to him. And he tells me of his plan to put this obsession with death, and perhaps the twist given to a personal philosophy by the loss of a loved one—to put it all into a novel, with some such title as *La Douleur*.'

It had been Zola's original intention that this novel should be written immediately after *Nana*. Fernand Xau whose monograph (based on an interview with Zola) is dated 15 April 1880, quotes the novelist as denying a story that had been circulating to the effect that he was about to embark on a book about the struggles of the small shopkeeper undercut by the big modern store. 'Je ne me livrerai point à un travail aussi lourd, aussi épineux, aussi fatigant,' said Zola, 'après une étude qui, comme *Nana*, a remué soixante ou quatre-vingts personnages. Tout au contraire, je veux faire un roman intime. . . . Ce sera une sorte de réaction contre mes œuvres antérieures. Les deux idées de la douleur et de la bonté domineront cette étude. . . .' This statement tallies with Zola's declaration at the beginning of the first of the draft-plots he drew up, probably about Easter 1880, for the novel which was ultimately to be called *La Joie de vivre*: 'Voici le roman que je veux écrire. Des êtres bons et honnêtes, placés dans un drame qui développera l'idée de bonté et de douleur.'[1]

Zola never hesitated so much, never changed his mind so frequently, over the plot of any novel as over that of *La Joie de vivre*; it was, moreover, the only book of his which he started and then abandoned in sheer despair. In 1880 he made four attempts at producing a workable plan; then gave up. Another journalist who interviewed him a little later than Xau reported him as saying that 'he fears a work of this sort, in the state of mind in which he

[1] B.N. MS. *Nouv. acq. fr.* 10311, fol. 366.

finds himself at present, would stir his emotions too painfully'.[1]
Even when he returned to the book, in 1883, he drew up and discarded two more plots before he finally settled on a satisfactory
scenario.

It must be of significance that in all the earlier plans the heroine,
Pauline Quenu (to whose characteristic trait, 'la bonté', altruism,
self-sacrifice, he was committed in advance) was thought of as a
young married woman, placed between a husband and a passionate
admirer whom she was to reject in spite of being in love with him.
To heighten Pauline's moral stature Zola alternatively made her
husband unworthy of her, unfaithful to her, or unreasonably and
brutally jealous; while the lover was a man she had expected to
marry, who still attracts her strongly, who is 'la vie, la protestation
de la vie', and to whom she is drawn 'comme à la vie et à la santé'.
But in the final draft, the one ultimately adopted for *La Joie de
vivre*, Zola decided Pauline would be unmarried. Betrothed to a
young man she loves, she imagines he would be happier with
another girl, and releases him from his obligations.

It seems, then, that the novel only began to make headway when
Zola gave up the idea of making it a study of marriage. If we take
into account, further, that the work Zola actually embarked on,
when he temporarily shelved *La Joie de vivre*, was *Pot-Bouille*,
which is basically a study of the miseries of conjugal life, then we
are justified in asking the question whether the painful personal
preoccupation that inhibited progress with *La Joie de vivre* was
not so much his situation as bereaved son as his situation as a
mal marié.

In 1880 Alexandrine was forty-one. So long as Zola's mother
was alive it was possible for him to divide his affections in a normal
way between the two older women with whom he shared his childless home. Émilie Zola's death meant that henceforward the role of
mother, as well as that of wife, devolved on Alexandrine. This was
the kind of situation which both partners would eventually find an
intolerable strain. M. G. Conrad, Zola's earliest German disciple,
who was on visiting terms with him between 1878 and 1882, has
put on record certain pronouncements Zola made to him on the
subject of marriage, the disillusioned tone of which is quite striking.
'People have to learn to tolerate one another; living together is for
the most part unpleasant. Whichever way one turns there are the

[1] E. De Amicis, *Ritratti letterari* (1881), p. 68.

same annoyances, nothing can be gained by seeking complete bliss elsewhere.' (It should be said that Conrad had been asking Zola for his views on divorce, a burning topic at that time in France.) 'Imagine a sick man, tossing in bed from one side to another without managing to find a comfortable position. Well, that sick man is humanity in wedlock.'[1] Zola was speaking in general terms of course, but these are hardly the words that would be used by a happily married man; and it is reasonable to suppose that it was the risk of betraying his feelings too openly that deterred him from introducing the theme of conjugal maladjustment into his new novel.

The strains, unexpressed, persisted however under the surface. In October 1882 Zola had some sort of a breakdown: there were bouts of nausea, trembling fits, and he had to stay in bed. Injections of morphine restored him sufficiently to allow him at least to attend to his correspondence. On 25th he wrote to Céard:

Me voilà un peu remis. J'ai pu reprendre mon travail. N'importe, je ne suis guère solide. Je m'imagine que j'ai été effleuré par quelque chose de très grave qui m'a épargné, pour cette fois; car je reste tout bouleversé, comme après une grave maladie. La vérité est aussi que je suis abominablement fatigué. Quelle chose lourde qu'une plume!

Then on 2 November he told the same friend: 'Je suis toujours patraque, et le travail s'en ressent. Le pis est que ma femme va plus mal encore que moi, maintenant: elle a des étouffements nerveux qui me font passer des nuits pleines d'inquiétudes. J'ai beau aimer la vie, je retourne au pessimisme.'

However, *Au Bonheur des Dames* was completed on 25 January 1883 and exactly three months later Zola started writing *La Joie de vivre*.

The book represented, for its author, an attempt to rid himself of his neuroses by projecting them into a story. The hero, Lazare Chanteau, is a self-portrait to a limited degree.[2] By nature he is

[1] Conrad, *Émile Zola* (Berlin, 1906), pp. 76–77.

[2] For fuller details than there is room for here, see R. J. Niess, 'Autobiographical Elements in Zola's *La Joie de vivre*', *P.M.L.A.*, vol. lvi (1941), pp. 1133–49; M. Girard, 'Émile Zola ou la joie de vivre', *Æsculape*, vol. xxxiii (1952), pp. 198–203; and the section 'Lazare' in N. O. Franzén, *Zola et 'la Joie de vivre'* (Stockholm, 1958). The autobiographical aspect of this character was obvious to those who knew Zola well, to judge by Edmond de Goncourt's unfeeling comment: 'Rien de vraiment intéressant dans le livre, pour nous, que l'analyse que Zola a faite de lui-même, de sa peur de la mort, de son extraordinaire *coyonnade* morale sous le nom de Lazare' (*Journal des Goncourt*, vol. xiii, p. 88).

moping and pessimistic; his mother's death increases his sombre preoccupation with the brevity of life. Zola describes him 'listening to himself living', imagining he can follow the automatic functioning of his organs: stomach, kidneys, liver, and especially the heart,

qui sonnait des volées de cloche dans chacun de ses membres, jusqu'au bout de ses doigts. S'il posait le coude sur une table, son cœur battait dans son coude; s'il appuyait sa nuque à un dossier de fauteuil, son cœur battait dans sa nuque; s'il s'asseyait, s'il se couchait, son cœur battait dans ses cuisses, dans ses flancs, dans son ventre; et toujours, et toujours, ce bourdon ronflait, lui mesurait la vie avec le grincement d'une horloge qui se déroule. Alors, sous l'obsession de l'étude qu'il faisait sans cesse de son corps, il croyait à chaque instant que tout allait craquer, que les organes s'usaient et volaient en pièces, que le cœur, devenu monstrueux, cassait lui-même la machine, à grands coups de marteau. Ce n'était plus vivre que de s'entendre vivre ainsi, tremblant devant la fragilité du mécanisme, attendant le grain de sable qui devait le détruire.

Lazare hardly dare sleep at night for fear of never waking. He contracts the habit of touching certain objects when he leaves a room, lest he should never return. He invents private superstitions about numbers and the symmetrical arrangement of things.

Malgré sa vive intelligence, sa négation du surnaturel, il pratiquait avec une docilité de brute cette religion imbécile, qu'il dissimulait comme une maladie honteuse. C'était la revanche du détraquement nerveux, chez le pessimiste et le positiviste, qui déclarait croire uniquement au fait, à l'expérience.

Passages such as these, and others where Lazare is shown lying with his wife at night, both pursued by the spectre of annihilation and unable to find sleep, are undoubtedly fragments of a self-confession. But there is also much in Lazare's character that cannot be related to his creator.

He is more faithful than Zola to the logic of his neuroses. Since man's lease of life is so short, he sees no reason to devote himself to any ambitious task which he may have to leave uncompleted. He is tempted by large-scale undertakings—a project to extract chemicals from seaweed, another to stop erosion of the coast by the erection of breakwaters—but he embarks on them unmethodically and rapidly tires of them. He ends by choosing a rich wife and an idle life, consumed by an immense *ennui*. Zola's neuroticism was, for practical purposes, neutralized by his driving energy. Even temporary doubts about the permanence of his achievement, about his ability to carry through the task he had set himself, never seriously interfered with the rhythm of his production; indeed, creative work was the one barrier he could always raise against the threatening tide of nihilism.

Lazare was not intended to be simply a more deeply afflicted neuropath than his inventor. Part of the design was—the *ébauche* is explicit on this point—that he should represent the modern sceptic, in particular the man who refuses to subscribe to the faith in science that Zola himself embraced so whole-heartedly.

L'important, le fond même de Lazare est de faire de lui un pessimiste, un malade de nos sciences commençantes. Voilà qui est curieux à étudier: l'avortement continu dans une nature, et dans une nature intelligente, qui a connaissance des temps nouveaux, qui va avec la science, qui a touché à la méthode expérimentale, qui a lu notre littérature, mais qui nie tout par une sorte d'éblouissement, un peu d'étroitesse de vue et surtout beaucoup d'impuissance personnelle. Montrer en un mot un garçon très intelligent, en plein dans le mouvement actuel, et niant ce mouvement, se jetant dans le Schopenhauer. Pas de foi. — Variété de Werther et de René. Le romantisme a fait le désespéré mélancolique qui doute, — le naturalisme fait le sceptique qui croit au néant du monde, qui nie le progrès.[1]

Schopenhauer, who is named in these lines, was in the early 1880's the latest rage among the *avant-garde* intellectuals in France. Céard mentioned his name in a letter to Zola dated 13 January 1880: J. Bourdeau had just published a volume of extracts translated into French (*Pensées, maximes et fragments*) which Céard promises to lend him when he comes to Paris. Zola certainly read the book before writing *La Joie de vivre*[2] and may indeed have glanced at it before writing *Au Bonheur des Dames*; a minor character in this novel, Vallagnosc, is already a caricature of the new pessimist, his energy sapped by his conviction that nothing is worth the effort. Zola uses, to describe the set to which Vallagnosc belongs, the very formula employed in the passage from the *ébauche* of *La Joie de vivre* just quoted: 'les désespérés, les dégoûtés, les pessimistes, *tous ces malades de nos sciences commençantes*'. There were others, besides Céard, among Zola's friends and disciples, who were studying Schopenhauer appreciatively at this

[1] B.N. MS. *Nouv. acq. fr.* 10311, fols. 172–4.
[2] See Franzén, op. cit., pp. 74 ff.

time: notably Maupassant and Huysmans. Folantin, the hero of Huysmans's *A vau l'eau* (1882) quotes Schopenhauer with approval: 'man's life swings like a pendulum between suffering and tedium.' The phrase, taken from Bourdeau's anthology, was copied by Zola in the notes he took for *La Joie de vivre*.[1]

Knowing Schopenhauer only through the medium of a translation of extracts hastily perused, Zola can hardly be blamed for misunderstanding and misrepresenting the philosophy. In a sense it mattered very little: his Lazare was voicing, after all, the popular view of Schopenhauerism, which was inevitably distorted.[2] *La Joie de vivre* cannot be read as a serious critique of a metaphysical system. The novel does, nevertheless, dramatize a debate of unusual poignancy which in all probability was being conducted in Zola's mind over periods especially frequent during the years 1880 to 1883. The book is thus a true novel of ideas, of a kind Zola had not attempted up to then.

Albert Camus begins *Le Mythe de Sisyphe* by observing that there is only one really serious problem and fundamental question in philosophy, and that is, whether life is or is not worth living. This fundamental question is the one Zola meant to deal with in *La Joie de vivre*.

He told Van Santen Kolff, five years after the book was published, that his first idea for a title had been *Le Mal de vivre*, but that 'l'ironie de *la Joie de vivre* me fit préférer ce dernier'. Either title is, in fact, as apt as the other, the novel being as much concerned with the joy as with the ill of living. Pauline incarnates the first principle just as Lazare incarnates the second. The other characters revolve round these two, as mere subsidiaries.

Unfortunately, it must be admitted, Zola comes near to vitiating the philosophical argument from the start, for his two main characters hold their opposing views not out of intellectual conviction but out of innate, inherited propensity. Determinism often leads its adherents thus by a short cut to a brick wall. Pauline is the daughter of the pork butcher and his wife Lisa whom we met, brimming with good health and bursting with good living, in

---

[1] Ibid., p. 196.
[2] Cf. the letter Zola wrote to Édouard Rod (16 Mar. 1884), who had objected to Lazare's travesty of Schopenhauer's thought: 'Jamais de la vie je n'ai voulu en faire un métaphysicien, un parfait disciple de Schopenhauer, car cette espèce n'existe pas en France.'

Le Ventre de Paris. She has inherited sanity and steadiness (in her veins the Macquart depravity has been diluted below danger-point) and she cannot but accept life joyfully, delighting in all its products and processes, and peculiarly in the development of her own body as she begins to take on womanly form. She has also inherited a jealous possessiveness, of which she learns in time to rid herself in the interests of her own contentment.

Logically, the love of life makes her tenderly solicitous for every creature who fares ill in the struggle for life, beginning with the barnyard fowl, whose broken legs she sets in splints, and stray cats who find bowls of milk set down by her outside the house every night. Even as a child, she shows herself naturally gifted for nursing her uncle, a martyr to gout; and one of the last acts we see her engaged on is coaxing life into the weakly body of Lazare's new-born son. Less logically (for Zola viewed self-seeking as a more 'natural' instinct than self-sacrifice), she spends herself un-grudgingly for the greater happiness of those around her. It is nothing that she dissipates the thousands so laboriously amassed by her parents in financing Lazare and in acts of private charity; the real test comes when she has to subdue her own sexual cravings and release Lazare from his obligations to her so that he may marry Louise. She makes the sacrifice, experiencing the subtle joys of the truly altruistic; at this stage Pauline approaches the kind of im-molation of self which is the purest ideal of a Christian. Nowhere, and certainly not in the incense-steeped pages of *Le Rêve*, did Zola come nearer to creating a saint.

Yet *La Joie de vivre* is as anti-religious as *Le Docteur Pascal* or those counterblasts to Catholicism, *Lourdes*, *Rome*, and *Paris*. It is not thanks to Church teaching that Pauline discovers that 'it is more blessed to give than to receive', that 'he that loseth his life shall find it'. While Lazare secretly aspires to a lost faith which shall deliver him from the intolerable finality of death, Pauline is serenely agnostic. 'Il m'est impossible de croire des choses qui me semblent déraisonnables. Dès lors, à quoi bon mentir, en feignant de les accepter? D'ailleurs, l'inconnu ne m'inquiète pas, il ne peut être que logique, le mieux est d'attendre le plus sagement possible.' She undertakes welfare work among the debauched and feckless fisher-folk of the village, practising philanthropy with no hope of recognition or reward but, as it were, to maintain a healthy balance, to give herself some harmless occupation. If, incidentally, she contributes to lightening the burden of evil in the world, so much the better. Altruistic activity is Pauline's secret for the joy she finds in living. It is also Zola's first answer to the 'fundamental question' round which *La Joie de vivre* revolves. Life is worth living provided one devotes it to work which will benefit one's fellows; and most work, including the artist's, is aimed, even if indirectly, at increasing the sum of happiness of mankind. Life is evil only if, like Lazare, one yields to doubt and despair and fails to use one's talents to the full.

This humble and immemorial philosophy eludes the crux of man's helplessness in face of the infinite by a restatement of his condition. Considered as a unique and individual soul, he passes as fleetingly and ineffectually as a breath on a crystal; he is nothing more, in the words of a later poet, than

un défaut
Dans la pureté du Non-être.

Man must, however, look on himself not as a self-sufficient unit but as a unit in a society, in a race that has formed itself slowly in past aeons, has peopled the globe, and has a fertility which promises survival for millennia to come. *La Joie de vivre* ends symbolically, like that other 'novel of ideas', *Le Docteur Pascal*, with the birth of a male child. Lazare sees in his first-born only the person who will one day close his eyes. But Pauline has faith.

— Celui-là sera peut-être d'une génération moins bête, dit-elle tout à coup. Il n'accusera pas la chimie de lui gâter la vie, et il croira qu'on peut vivre, même avec la certitude de mourir un jour.

Lazare se mit à rire, embarrassé.

— Bah! murmura-t-il, il aura la goutte comme papa et ses nerfs seront plus détraqués que les miens. . . . Regarde donc comme il est faible! C'est la loi des dégénérescences.

— Veux-tu te taire, s'écria Pauline. Je l'élèverai, et tu verras si j'en fais un homme.

This is the long-term and human answer to the question. But there is an immediate, reflex response which is perhaps more convincing: it gives Zola the cue for the odd incident on which he closes his book, in the couple of pages that remain.

Véronique, the Chanteaus' housekeeper, is a curious, cross-grained old woman, taking little active part in the drama, though at different stages she sides violently with one or other of the chief actors. She begins by resenting Pauline's presence in the family which was happy enough without her. But when Mme Chanteau despoils the girl to humour her son she is scandalized, and switches her affections to Pauline. Then, finally, after Mme Chanteau's death, her former devotion to her mistress returns, and she becomes suspicious once more of Pauline. She ends by hanging herself on a pear-tree in the garden, and Chanteau's comment on this suicide winds up *La Joie de vivre*.

Ce misérable sans pieds ni mains, qu'il fallait coucher et faire manger comme un enfant, ce lamentable reste d'homme dont le peu de vie n'était plus qu'un hurlement de douleur, cria dans une indignation furieuse:
—Faut-il être bête pour se tuer!

When the intellect has had its say, the instincts cry the obvious answer: life is the only gift bestowed on man; at no price may he willingly relinquish it.

Thus, in the last resort, Zola reaffirms his belief in life and condemns nihilism. But *La Joie de vivre* is none the less a desperately sad book. Its message is reasonable and salutary, but scarcely heartening. In writing it, Zola had named his anxieties, but not yet dispelled them. They dropped back, temporarily innocuous, far beneath the surface of his mind, and in the depths took on magnified, distorted, and even more terrifying shapes. *La Joie de vivre* was published in February 1884. On 2 April he started writing *Germinal*.

X

CRY FROM THE PIT

ALMOST since its first appearance, *Germinal* has been considered by the bulk of critical opinion everywhere as probably the most important single contribution Zola made to literature. In his own country, it does not seem to have been the most sought after of his novels: Charpentier's catalogues in the year of Zola's death and twenty-five years later show that at both dates *Germinal* comes only sixth in order of popularity, after *Nana*, *La Terre*, *La Débâcle*, *L'Assommoir*, and *Lourdes*.[1] But Henry James, writing in 1903, suggested that the 'productions in which he must most survive' were *L'Assommoir*, *Germinal*, and *La Débâcle*, works in which 'the author's perceptions go straight, and the subject, grateful and responsive, gives itself wholly up', and in which he wrote out of 'a personal vision, the vision of genius, springing from an inward source'.[2] The splendours of *La Débâcle* have become tarnished with time, perhaps because the war this work chronicled, which when he was writing James could still see as cataclysmic, has now contracted to the status of a mere harbinger of the more awful struggles that the following century was to usher in. But *L'Assommoir* and *Germinal* remain rivals for the admiration of Zola's readers; they are his *Andromaque* and his *Phèdre*, the work in which he first asserted indisputable mastery of his medium, and that which he made the vessel for the darkest poetry of maturity.[3]

In the compositional technique adopted, *Germinal* differs altogether from *L'Assommoir* and, indeed, from all previous novels Zola had written. For the first time he employed a method of presentation which Balzac, notably, had favoured but which was not practised by Zola's other model, Flaubert. This method

[1] See L. Deffoux, 'Émile Zola et ses éditions depuis 1902', *Le Figaro*, 1 Oct. 1927.

[2] James, *The House of Fiction*, pp. 241–2.

[3] The differences between the two has perhaps never been better put than by Louis Desprez, who wrote to Zola immediately after reading *Germinal*: '*L'Assommoir* était plus *roman*; *Germinal* est plus *poème* . . .'. *Lettres inédites de Louis Desprez à Émile Zola* (ed. Guy Robert), p. 111.

involves the use of an extremely lengthy prologue, filling at least
a quarter of the novel, in order to develop the desired atmosphere
for the subsequent dramatic action. The most frequently quoted
instance, in Balzac, is *Eugénie Grandet*, a novel with probably no
other analogies with *Germinal*. The description of the miser's
house and family circle at Saumur, and the account of the disturbance set up by the arrival of Grandet's nephew from Paris, take up
rather more than half the entire book. This prologue covers the
events of little less than twenty-four hours; the story proper that
follows extends over some ten years or more.

The more traditional or conventional type of novel can be
represented as travelling steadily and without much resistance
down the stream of time. *Le Rouge et le Noir* or *Madame Bovary* or
War and Peace can be taken as examples of this method, which we
can regard as the normal one. *L'Assommoir* belongs to the same
class: along the course of Gervaise's life certain distinct points are
selected by the author, who focuses our attention on them for the
space of a chapter or less; but the impression of the unhurried and
uninterrupted progress of time never leaves us. In *Eugénie Grandet*,
on the other hand, and in certain other novels of *La Comédie
humaine*, interest is heaped up mountain-high at the beginning,
and thereafter the author needs merely to send his reader careering
down the slope he has artificially raised. Balzac, to change the metaphor, puts a brake on time at the outset, and we watch characters
who are new to us gesturing, speaking, and acting with preter-
natural slowness; then, suddenly, he releases the spring: the clock-
hands revolve at their ordinary speed, then, accelerating as though
they had accumulated momentum while he held them in check, the
days, the months, and the years start flitting past at an ever-
increasing rate.

This is not quite what Zola did in *Germinal*; *Eugénie Grandet*
remains the classic instance of this kind of artificial manipulation
of time. But one cannot fail to notice the immense industry with
which in his first eleven chapters (there are forty in all) Zola piles
up a huge pyramid of characters and atmosphere. These eleven
chapters cover the twenty-four hours between the arrival of Étienne
Lantier in the mining district and the end of his first day's work
underground. The first paragraph of the twelfth (chapter i of
part iii) opens with the words: 'Le lendemain, les jours suivants
Étienne reprit son travail à la fosse. . . .' The next paragraph begins:

'Et les jours succédaient aux jours, des semaines, des mois s'écoulèrent. . . .'

In adopting this form Zola did not have quite the same purpose in mind as Balzac. The earlier writer needed room in his exposition to paint the back-cloth against which his drama was to be enacted; without the rich and sombre colouring he uses the plot (in the case of *Eugénie Grandet* particularly) would seem petty, a domestic tussle of no special account. But in *Germinal* the drama needed no such setting off; it was moving enough in its own right. The function of the first eleven chapters is simply to accumulate the mass of impressions needed for the creation of a setting so far removed from the ordinary as to be almost otherworldly. Zola passes from one point to another in the grimy landscape and in the hot, damp galleries of the mines, registering wherever he goes brief visions of miners' cottages seen from outside and inside, introducing us into one where a family of nine is shown sleeping in one bedroom and on the landing outside, waking at four in the morning, dressing hastily and breakfasting meagrely; of other cottages emptying as men and girls, almost indistinguishable in their identical costume, tramp off to work; of the pithead in the half-light of dawn, a vast, dimly lit and shadowy hall, noisy with the rumble of trollies full of fresh-hewn coal; of cage-load after cage-load of workers dropping plumb into the depths of the earth under a constant patter of water oozing from an underground lake; of gangs of colliers toiling at the seam in semi-darkness, stripped almost naked because of the heat —'des formes spectrales' lit by an occasional lamp in the light of which glimpses are given of 'une rondeur de hanche, un bras noueux, une tête violente, barbouillée comme pour un crime'; of the soft hiss and cobwebby smell of fire-damp. Then, returning to the surface and to daylight, we are shown 'le ciel couleur de terre, les murs gluants d'une humidité verdâtre, les routes empoissées de boue, une boue spéciale au pays de charbon, noire comme de la suie délayée, épaisse et collante à y laisser ses sabots'; the straight roads linking up the towns, built up almost all the way, lined with little brick houses 'peinturlurées pour égayer le climat, les unes jaunes, les autres bleues, d'autres noires, celles-ci sans doute afin d'arriver tout de suite au noir final'; the occasional brick church, 'avec son clocher carré, sali déjà par les poussières volantes du charbon'; and, above all, taverns and beer-shops, at the rate of approximately one for every two dwelling-houses. And finally we are returned to the evening 'soup', the baths taken in the cottages, the miners gardening, chatting, or drinking, the children at play, the adolescents strolling in couples or mating in the waste ground round a disused mine.

When he has reached the end of this prologue, the reader has the impression of being completely enveloped by the atmosphere, of being himself a denizen of this narrow world. With a little imagination he finds himself breathing the air laden with coal-dust, feeling on his shins and shoulders the sore places rubbed by the jutting pieces of schist, experiencing the nausea of hard physical labour on inadequate rations. There is remarkably little plain description in all this: Zola has progressed since *Le Ventre de Paris* and *La Faute de l'abbé Mouret*. Everything is shown as seen and felt by one character or another; dozens are introduced, though it is principally through Étienne's observations that the mosaic is built up—since he is new to the mines, his impressions are more acute and more varied. Descriptive writing gives place to the technique of accumulating scores of minor incidents which merge into a general picture of 'a corner of nature'.

In the remaining parts of the book, the single dramatic conflict between strikers and management predominates. On two occasions it rises to a climax: the first is when a mob of starvelings spreads havoc over the countryside, smashing machinery and taking murderous vengeance on blacklegs and enemies like the grocer who had refused them credit; the second is when, several weeks later, they try to prevent a Belgian labour force from going down the pits, and clash bloodily with the military. There is one crowning catastrophe at the end, when an act of sabotage causes the pits to flood after the beaten strikers have resumed work. In the intervals between these three major incidents Zola shows the gradual sinking of the miners' hopes, their bickerings among themselves, the hunger and cold they endure, the whole siege of misery, in a succession of brief but significant episodes.

The question has more than once been asked: what moved Zola to choose a coal-mining area as the setting for his second, 'political' study of the working classes, rather than a steelworks, or a textile factory, in which strikes had been quite as bitter and disastrous ever since the days of Louis-Philippe at least?[1] An early list of

---

[1] J. Cain, 'La Genèse de *Germinal*', *Le Figaro littéraire*, 3 Oct. 1953; É. Tersen, 'Sources et sens de *Germinal*', *La Pensée*, no. 95 (1961), pp. 74-89.

projected novels includes mention of 'Un 2e roman ouvrier. —
Particulièrement politique, aboutissant à mai 71';[1] but the reference, by its date, to the Commune suggests he was thinking of a
Parisian setting. The statement he made to Xau in 1880 about his
future intentions includes the prediction: 'Je reprendrai le peuple.
Dans *l'Assommoir*, j'ai peint la vie du peuple. . . . J'étudierai l'idée
politique chez lui. J'assisterai aux réunions ouvrières et j'en ferai un
tableau; en un mot, je montrerai l'ouvrier dans son rôle social. Il y
aura dans ce volume une étude sur la presse et peut-être aussi sur
la magistrature.'[2] Here again, the terms Zola uses imply that he
had in mind some drama enacted in a big city; in fact, he came
nearest to realizing the aims set forth here in *Paris*, which belongs,
of course, not to *Les Rougon-Macquart* at all.

Everything points to the conclusion that the decision to write a
novel about a mining community was reached at a very late stage.
Edmond de Goncourt noted that on 16 January 1884 Zola was still
hesitating between starting a novel to be called *Les Paysans* (the
future *La Terre*), another novel about the railways, and 'something
relating to a strike in a mining area, which would begin with a man
of the middle classes having his throat cut on the first page . . . then
the verdict . . . men sentenced to death and others to prison . . . and
in the course of the trial, the introduction of a serious and far-
reaching study of the social question'. This synopsis fits *La Bête
humaine* as easily as *Germinal*. But Goncourt's conversation with Zola
antedated the start of work on the latter novel by only a few weeks.

Zola had never visited a coalfield, let alone gone down a mine or
talked with colliers. His imagination may have been stimulated by
one or two books: notably L.-L. Simonin's *La Vie souterraine, ou
les mines et les mineurs* (1867), a non-technical but informative and
readable work by a mining engineer; and possibly the odd novel,
like Malot's *Sans famille*, the young hero of which at one point
joins the pit-workers: Malot introduced the episode of the flooded
mine, with a group of colliers trapped in an air-bubble, which Zola
could not resist using in his turn.[3] But the bare notion of a world

---

[1] B.N. MS. *Nouv. acq. fr.* 10345, fol. 129. This list may have been drawn up
when Zola was still in the throes of planning *Les Rougon-Macquart*, but the lines
quoted, written in small characters at the bottom of the sheet, appear to have
been added at some subsequent date.

[2] F. Xau, *Émile Zola*, p. 50. He made a very similar prognostication to Alexis
a year or so later: see *Émile Zola, notes d'un ami*, p. 120.

[3] Cf. I.-M. Frandon, *Autour de 'Germinal'*, chaps. ii, iii. *Sans famille* appeared
in 1878.

underground, apart from any knowledge he may have gleaned of the conditions under which coal was mined, was sufficient to stir him painfully and to summon from the deepest reaches of imagination the grimmest of fantasies. More than anything else, it is this chain-reaction of private associations sparked off by the mere decision to situate his story in the bowels of the earth that gives to *Germinal* that powerful emotive shudder which makes a first reading of it so overwhelming an experience.

From time immemorial the underworld has struck speculative terror in the minds of men. Here Greek mythology consigned to eternal torment the great rebels and criminals: Ixion, Sisyphus, Tantalus. Traditionally, the Christian hell is situated below ground. 'Il faut le montrer [le houilleur] . . . au fond d'un véritable enfer', wrote Zola in the *ébauche*, and the phrase is to be understood in the most literal sense. One enthusiastic reviewer, after quoting a descriptive passage, declared: 'I know of no more fearfully dramatic pages in the *Inferno*, and if Dante had written them they would have long enjoyed classical status in our country.'[1] It is difficult not to agree with a modern student of the work who sees a deliberate intention behind Zola's choice of the name 'Le Tartaret' for the ignited seam that has been smouldering underground for years. Whether, however, he intended us to think of the defeated Titans chained in Tartarus who would one day burst forth to overthrow the Olympians is more doubtful.[2] It is none the less true that the miners of *Germinal* have fewer affinities with the irremediably damned wretches of a medieval hell than with the penned giants of Teutonic or pre-Hellenic cosmogony who, in some future cataclysm, will surge up from the depths and wreak revengeful havoc in the ultimate *Götterdämmerung*. The strike was to end in victory for the mining company, for capital, and defeat for the miners, for labour. But, wrote Zola in his notes: 'bien indiquer qu'ils plient devant la force des choses, mais qu'ils rêvent de vengeance. Les menaces de l'avenir, dernière page du livre. La secousse donnée à la société qui a craqué, et faire prévoir d'autres secousses, jusqu'à l'effondrement final.'[3]

The Mine was, then, the place of unjust torment, and the cosmic

---

[1] Philippe Gille, *La Bataille littéraire*, 3ᵉ série (1890), p. 76. Gille's review appeared in *Le Figaro*, 4 Mar. 1885.

[2] Philip Walker, 'Prophetic myths in Zola', *P.M.L.A.*, vol. lxxiv (1959), pp. 444–52 (see especially pp. 450–1).

[3] B.N. MS. *Nouv. acq. fr.* 10307, fol. 412.

injustice it represented boded cosmic vengeance. But, in addition, the dark, airless galleries below ground were the perfect symbol for the deep-buried corridors of the unconscious mind. One terrible episode in *Germinal* owes virtually nothing to Zola's reading of Simonin, and certainly nothing to what he may have witnessed at the Anzin colliery in the north-east which he visited in the course of collecting material for his novel. It reproduces a purely imaginary scene found in one of his earliest short stories, 'Le Sang', first published in 1863.[1] Four soldiers with Germanic names are warming themselves by a fire which they have lit on the battlefield. The corpses of the fallen lie all around. Night comes on, and each of the four dreams a dream. The first soldier, Gneuss, sees a trickle of blood springing from among the stones at his feet, then gushing more abundantly until it becomes a stream, and finally a broad river of blood washing the bodies of the slain along. Gneuss retreats before this apparition, but is stopped by a barrier of rock. The sea of blood, now filling the valley, rises slowly, covering his knees, his waist; and the gaping wounds of the corpses eddying round seem like so many grinning mouths mocking him in his terror. He struggles to gain a higher foothold on the rocks; slips down, and he is chin-deep in blood.

The last-but-one chapter of *Germinal* describes the flooding of the mine, a result of Souvarine's act of sabotage, and the ordeal of Étienne and Catherine, trapped below ground. Like Gneuss, they feel the flood lapping round their feet and creeping steadily up to waist-height. Like Gneuss, they flee, and like him they are stopped by a wall of rock.

Ils eurent d'abord l'eau aux chevilles, puis elle leur mouilla les genoux. La voie montait, ils se réfugièrent au fond, ce qui leur donna un répit de quelques heures. Mais le flot les rattrapa, ils baignèrent jusqu'à la ceinture. Debout, acculés, l'échine collée contre la roche, ils la regardaient croître, toujours, toujours. Quand elle atteindrait leur bouche, ce serait fini.

A little before, in an irresistible surge of jealous rage, Étienne had dashed out the brains of Catherine's lover, Chaval. And just as, in 'Le Sang', the river of blood had borne past Gneuss the bodies of those he had killed in battle, so, in *Germinal*, the current pitches the corpse of Chaval against Étienne's feet, repeatedly. Catherine,

---

[1] In the *Revue du mois*; reprinted in the *Contes à Ninon*.

reaching down to quench her thirst, feels the dead man's mous-
taches brush against her hand,[1] and spits out the mouthful of water:
'Elle croyait qu'elle venait de boire du sang, que toute cette eau
profonde, devant elle, était maintenant le sang de cet homme.'
Catherine's hallucination points to the connexion, which we might
otherwise have missed, between the story written by Zola at the
age of twenty-three and the episode inserted in the novel published
when he was forty-five. The central point of these two incidents is
the same: the relentlessly rising tide of blood (or water mistaken
for blood) which sweeps a dead body inexorably against a killer who
cannot escape. No better symbol could be invented to represent the
persistent fretting of an unresolved neurosis. It seems right to
conclude that this nightmare was Zola's own and that it recurred
over the years because it bodied forth the same deep psychological
disturbance that we have found necessary to postulate in order to
account for other features of his early works.[2]

Germinal has been called a 'post-impressionist' novel because in
it Zola distorted reality into hallucinatory shapes in order to objec-
tify 'inner experience', in much the same way as Van Gogh does in
his classical post-impressionist canvas *Café de nuit*.[3] This is obviously true, but just as the scene Van Gogh painted had its
starting-point in observed reality, so too Zola's work was constructed on a scaffolding of conscientious investigation and, like
all the other novels in the series, starts from the 'realistic' assumption that environment can explain everything. The mining community he depicted in *Germinal*, on the strength of a brief but busy
visit to one of the big collieries on the Flemish border[4] and of a

---

[1] This detail alone appears to have been borrowed from Simonin, who tells
the story of a miner drinking out of the floodwater and feeling there the corpse
of a drowned comrade (see Mitterand's notes to *Germinal* in the Pléiade edition).
But of course the man had not been murdered.

[2] The same incident in *Germinal* echoes in another detail *Thérèse Raquin*. It
will be recalled that Thérèse and Laurent, after their marriage, are kept apart
because they imagine that the corpse of Thérèse's murdered husband is perpetually between them: he is described several times as jealous, and they wonder
why they took the trouble to kill him since he has resuscitated in this way.
Étienne and Catherine are similarly troubled by the presence—the real presence,
however—of Catherine's murdered lover: 'Chaval ne voulait pas partir, voulait
être avec eux, contre eux. . . . Ce n'était pas la peine de lui casser la tête, pour
qu'il revînt entre lui et elle, entêté dans sa jalousie. Jusqu'au bout, il serait là,
même mort, pour les empêcher d'être ensemble.'

[3] Ph. Walker, 'Zola's art of characterization in *Germinal*', *L'Esprit créateur*,
vol. iv (1964), p. 66.

[4] He arrived at Valenciennes on 23 Feb. 1884. In a card to Céard he intimated

somewhat cursory perusal of a few technical works, was a race of men and women deformed in body and degraded in spirit by the controlling conditions of their lives. They inherit a debilitating physique from many generations of underground workers, all starved and stunted. Untaught, they are the natural prey of political firebrands; housed in one-bedroom cottages, made to work together in the mines without distinction of sex,[1] they are almost inevitably promiscuous in their habits; having no fate to fear worse than the life they habitually lead, they plunge into frenzied violence when their situation becomes intolerable. Deneulin, a small colliery owner brought to ruin by the rioting miners who wreck his machinery, finds he cannot, in his heart of hearts, blame the saboteurs: 'il sentait la complicité de tous, une faute générale, séculaire. Des brutes sans doute, mais des brutes qui ne savaient pas lire et qui crevaient de faim.'

It is a miracle that in such a fetid atmosphere some human virtues survive—that Maheu, for instance, on a rare occasion when his wife has been able to afford a piece of meat, scolds her for not giving the younger children their share, and sits them on his knees to feed them; that Chaval, brutal and tyrannical though he is, comes to Catherine's rescue when she swoons in an overheated gallery, and finds kind words of sympathy to encourage her when she recovers; that Zacharie, never greatly attached to his sister, works like a demon to deliver her when she is trapped in the flooded pit, and is killed by an explosion of fire-damp brought about by his reckless haste. Only Jeanlin, Catherine's younger brother, is utterly beyond redemption and emerges a moral monster, a teen-age thief and bully who ends by slily knifing an inoffensive Breton sentry one dark night just for the pleasure of committing murder. But Zola attenuated, in the final version, the portrait of this child-degenerate, whom he originally imagined as drinking himself into insensibility every evening, infecting a little girl with syphilis, and dragging the soldier he has stabbed but not killed outright to the mouth of a disused pit into which he tips him while the wretch is still alive.[2]

---

that he expected to be back by 4 Mar. See *Vingt messages inédits de Zola à Céard* (ed. A. J. Salvan), pp. 14–15.

[1] The employment of female labour in the mines had been made illegal in 1874, but *Germinal* is of course set in the pre-1870 period, when women still worked extensively below ground.

[2] B.N. MS. *Nouv. acq. fr.* 10307, fols. 442–3, 445–6; see also H. Psichari, *Anatomie d'un chef-d'œuvre: 'Germinal'*, pp. 127–30.

Though hardly heroic in any moral sense, the miner is undeniably the true hero in the literary acceptance of the word. He is depicted in representative types—four or five of them have just been named, and there are a dozen more in the book—but above all he is presented in the mass. This method was an innovation, and one which Zola found so suited to his genius that he brought it into regular use in subsequent novels—in *La Débâcle, Lourdes, Paris, Travail,* and *Vérité.* Towards the end of his life it became a recognized cliché that 'the crowd was often his unique, and always his favourite character', or even that 'the crowd was his hero, in whom he placed all the hope, all the warmth of enthusiasm that he refused to the individual'.[1] Both these observations overstate the case.

Crowd-scenes had been attempted in the earlier novels—notably in *Nana* and in *Au Bonheur des Dames*—and *L'Assommoir* had opened with a striking panoramic view of the army of workers descending into Paris in the early morning from the slums that ring the city. But not until he wrote *Germinal* did it occur to Zola what might be made out of a study of the behaviour of crowds; the book contains a series of instances of the type-phenomena of mass-psychology, as they have been catalogued since by trained investigators. There are crowds bent on amusement (the description of the *ducasse,* the miners' holiday, a scene of open-air jollity); crowds swayed by oratory (the strikers' forest meeting); crowds enraged and out of control (the march to Jean-Bart, Deneulin's colliery, with its sequel; the clash between the miners and the troops); crowds in a panic (the escape of the blackleg workers from Jean-Bart after the strikers cut the cables). Nearly all these scenes illustrate the truth that Zola intuitively grasped, that people in the aggregate are more ferocious, but also more cowardly, than each separate component of the group. Singly, his miners are on the whole as decent a lot of men as their circumstances and upbringing will allow them to be; but, like certain radioactive elements, once they are packed together in sufficient quantities a catastrophic qualitative change takes place. Négrel, who knows his workers well, is startled when he sees them pass, three thousand strong, on the road to Montsou, vengeful and furious,

---

[1] The first of these sentences occurred in Abel Hermant's oration over Zola's grave, which was published in *La Petite République,* 7 Oct. 1902; the second is taken from an obituary article by Gabriel Trarieux which appeared in *Pages libres,* 18 Oct. 1902.

une masse compacte qui roulait d'un seul bloc, serrée, confondue, au point qu'on ne distinguait ni les culottes déteintes, ni les tricots de laine en loques, effacés dans la même uniformité terreuse. Les yeux brûlaient, on voyait seulement les trous des bouches noires, chantant la *Marseillaise*, dont les strophes se perdaient en un mugissement confus, accompagné par le claquement des sabots sur la terre dure. Au-dessus des têtes, parmi le hérissement des barres de fer, une hache passa, portée toute droite; et cette hache unique, qui était comme l'étendard de la bande, avait, dans le ciel clair, le profil aigu d'un couperet de guillotine.

. . . Négrel se sentait blêmir . . . saisi là d'une épouvante supérieure à sa volonté, une de ces épouvantes qui soufflent de l'inconnu.

It is not only Négrel, the engineer, who recoils before a crowd that has got out of hand. Étienne Lantier, who realizes the strength the miners possess in their numbers and tries to fashion them into an instrument of political power, learns to his cost how treacherous and unmanageable such an instrument can become. He is an engine-man who has lost his job on the railways for an act of insubordination and who originally wandered into the mining area in search of employment. It was at a fairly late stage in planning his novel that Zola decided to make him the ringleader of the strike. Not he, but an unnamed 'Internationaliste' was cast, in the first part of the *ébauche*, for the part that ultimately devolved on Étienne: addressing the forest meeting, trying, for tactical reasons, to dissuade the infuriated strikers from committing wanton acts of destruction, and finally, agreeing to head the mob.[1] Étienne's role had been visualized as that of observer and rank-and-file participant merely. Having changed his conception of Étienne's importance in the events, as instigator, agent, and moderator, Zola was compelled to introduce a study of his political education and to confer on *Germinal* the extra dimension of a *Bildungsroman*. His hero's first lessons are received in the form of a kind of correspondence course in socialism provided by Pluchart, his foreman at Lille, now a propagandist for the (First) International. Encouraged by Pluchart's letters, Étienne begins to read: 'un fonds d'idées obscures, endormies en lui, s'agitait, s'élargissait.' Zola attributes his eagerness to devour pamphlets, newspapers, technical treatises, and whatever else comes his way, not so much to the desire to find solutions to the problems that puzzle him as to the humiliation of

---

[1] B.N. MS. *Nouv. acq. fr.* 10307, fols. 468–9; see also P. Aubery, 'Genèse et développement du personnage de Lantier', *French Studies*, vol. xvi (1962), pp. 142–53.

knowing himself to be uninstructed. 'Ainsi se prit-il pour l'étude du goût sans méthode des ignorants affolés de science.' He embraces socialism in precisely the same way (the resemblance is not pointed out by Zola and may not have occurred to him) as had his distant relative Silvère Mouret, whose fervour for the popular cause was narrated, with its tragical consequences, in *La Fortune des Rougon*.

The Maheu family provides him with an admiring and uncritical audience for his half-baked utopianism, and the next phase in his political evolution occurs when he realizes the power that his ideas, chaotic and contradictory though they still are, exert over his uneducated listeners. For Étienne discovers in himself an unsuspected talent for demagogic oratory.

As the days pass, the circle of his listeners widens; and the respect the colliers pay him swells his vanity and inflames his ambition. The decision to strike is taken largely on his initiative, though a cut in the miners' wages plays into his hands. The privations they endure do not at first weaken their will to resist, nor in any way curtail Étienne's popularity. His self-assurance steadily increases, and his pride is fed continually by the consciousness of power. At this point Zola drops the first hint of what will eventually deprive Étienne of the right to represent his own class: the success he enjoys among his fellows in itself causes him to lose sympathy with them—'il montait d'un échelon, il entrait dans cette bourgeoisie exécrée, avec des satisfactions d'intelligence et de bien-être, qu'il ne s'avouait pas'. It is true that his culminating triumph has still to come, when, in the forest meeting, he defeats the moderate Rasseneur, and has a resolution passed to make the strike general. For the first time he holds a crowd in the palm of his hand, and tastes power 'comme matérialisé dans ces trois mille poitrines dont il faisait d'un mot battre les cœurs'. But the following day's events destroy his illusions. He puts himself at the head of an army of strikers to ensure that the mines still open shall be closed; but the crowd slips out of his control, committing acts of sabotage and vengeance which he had never envisaged or intended. The pride of authority withers, and there remains only a sour distaste for the undisciplined horde which he had believed he could lead into the promised land. After the day's rioting he hides from the police in a disused pit, from which he is in no hurry to escape if it means returning to the village.

Quelle nausée, ces misérables en tas, vivant au baquet commun! Pas un avec qui causer politique sérieusement, une existence de bétail, toujours le même air empesté d'oignon où l'on étouffait! Il voulait leur élargir le ciel, les élever au bien-être et aux bonnes manières de la bourgeoisie, en faisant d'eux les maîtres; mais comme ce serait long! et il ne se sentait plus le courage d'attendre la victoire, dans ce bagne de la faim.

He decides that if he has the chance he will join Pluchart in Paris, 'lâcher le travail, travailler uniquement à la politique, mais seul, dans une chambre propre, sous le prétexte que les travaux de tête absorbent la vie entière et demandent beaucoup de calme'.

At the end of the book this is what he does, though not before he has experienced to the full the fickleness of the crowd, who turn on him and stone him when the strike is finally broken. His reflections after this incident show the bankruptcy of the demagogue and his fundamental impotence. He had never really been their leader; on the contrary it had always been the pressure of the mob behind that had guided his hand.

Il se sentait à bout de courage, il n'était même plus de cœur avec les camarades, il avait peur d'eux, de cette masse énorme, aveugle et irrésistible du peuple, passant comme une force de la nature, balayant tout, en dehors des règles et des théories. Une répugnance l'en avait détaché peu à peu, le malaise de ses goûts affinés, la montée lente de tout son être vers une classe supérieure.

Étienne Lantier, typifying the socialist who rises from the depressed classes, ends as a *déclassé*, detesting as much as ever the bourgeoisie but out of sympathy with the proletariat. Zola has traced the process clearly—too clearly perhaps: under the compulsion to acquire knowledge so as to fit himself to be the leader of his class, he becomes coated with a thin layer of culture which is sufficient to open his eyes to the brutishness of the starvelings he champions. His gorge rises against them, and though he will continue to fight their cause, this is only because he has identified it with his own personal aspirations. He might well become, in the future, a noted political figure,[1] but like them all, like Eugène Rougon before him, he will find his driving force mainly in the lust for power.

[1] In point of fact, as we learn in *Le Docteur Pascal*, Étienne takes part in the Commune, is arrested, condemned to death, then pardoned and exiled to New Caledonia.

In Souvarine, Zola introduced a second and very different example of the militant socialist. Instead of being, like Étienne, a worker in instinctive revolt, he is an intellectual of aristocratic origin. His presence in *Germinal* is puzzling, best accounted for, perhaps, by Zola's wish to stress the explosiveness of the industrial situation. That a Russian refugee should be found during the Second Empire working in a French coal-mine is for a start almost incredible. Russian political *émigrés* congregated for preference in London or Switzerland at this period, and came to Paris only after the establishment of the Third Republic; in Russia itself, moreover, the political terrorism of the Nihilists did not become widespread until well after 1870. The Russian critic M. K. Kleman, in a study of Zola which deserves translation into a language better known in Zola's own country, has brought to light a number of similarities between Souvarine's career in Russia, as related in *Germinal*, and various outrages committed by Russian terrorists between 1878 and 1881.[1] The presumption is that these details were communicated to Zola by Turgenev, possibly during the *dîners des Cinq*, before and after the death of Flaubert. In the west Turgenev enjoyed the reputation of being exceptionally well informed about the Russian revolutionary movement; his novel *Virgin Soil*, translated into French in 1877, was looked on as a source-book, especially when historical fact came to corroborate his fiction: the assassination, on 24 January 1878, of Trepov, the governor of St. Petersburg, by the woman terrorist Vera Zasulitch, appeared to have been prefigured in the history of Turgenev's heroine Marianne Sinetzkaya.

Turgenev's picture of what he himself had named 'the Nihilist' was adopted unquestioningly by Zola. But this picture was not copied from Turgenev's fictional heroes (Bazarov in *Fathers and Children*, Nezhdanov in *Virgin Soil*); it arose far more probably out of suggestions made by the Russian author in private conversations. During the last year of his life (he died in 1883) Turgenev was planning a fresh book on the Russian revolutionary movement, which he never had time even to start; his English translator Ralston has, however, left a record of the theme of the book, as Turgenev communicated it to him. Turgenev planned to call attention in his new work to the divergencies he detected between the development of socialism in Russia and in the west, divergencies which had come dramatically to a head in the quarrel between

[1] Kleman, *Emil' Zola, sbornik statey*, pp. 174–5.

the Russian, Bakunin, and the German, Marx, at the 1872 congress of the International, held at The Hague. It seems as though Zola, in *Germinal*, carried out to a small degree Turgenev's intention, by stressing the opposition between the view-points of Étienne and Souvarine and attributing this, by implication, to differences of race.

Souvarine is a follower of Bakunin, afire with all the fanatical mysticism which is traditionally credited to the Slav. He backs Étienne in his plans to enrol the miners in the International, believing that Bakunin will be able to make it an instrument of his policy. But this policy, and even more so the methods of implementing it which Souvarine, on occasion, expounds ('il faut qu'une série d'effroyables attentats épouvantent les puissants et réveillent le peuple'), horrify the French socialist.

— Non! non! murmura Étienne, avec un grand geste qui écartait ces abominables visions, nous n'en sommes pas encore là, chez nous. L'assassinat, l'incendie, jamais! C'est monstrueux, c'est injuste, tous les camarades se lèveraient pour étrangler le coupable!

Et puis, il ne comprenait toujours pas, sa race se refusait au rêve sombre de cette extermination du monde, fauché comme un champ de seigle, à ras de terre. Ensuite, que ferait-on, comment repousseraient les peuples?

It is due to Souvarine that the strike does not end altogether as it might have, with the strikers beaten and the Company in a stronger position than ever. At the risk of his life he descends the ladders and with a saw and a brace-and-bit—inadequate tools for the job, as a more technically-minded novelist has since pointed out[1] —weakens the lining of the main shaft so that on the following day (the day when the miners return to work) the water underground sweeps the tubbing away and floods the entire pit. The earth subsides, all the pithead machinery is engulfed, and a nearby canal breaks its banks and empties into the crater. From a neighbouring hillock Souvarine watches the destruction he has caused,

et il jeta sa dernière cigarette, il s'éloigna sans un regard en arrière, dans la nuit devenue noire. Au loin, son ombre diminua, se fondit avec l'ombre. C'était là-bas qu'il allait, à l'inconnu. Il allait, de son air tranquille, à l'extermination, partout où il y aurait de la dynamite, pour faire sauter les villes et les hommes. Ce sera lui, sans doute, quand la bourgeoisie agonisante entendra, sous elle, à chacun de ses pas, éclater le pavé des rues.

[1] Pierre Hamp, *Il faut que vous naissiez de nouveau* (1935), p. 46.

The bomb-throwing Russian terrorist is a figure which Turgenev may have elaborated for Zola, but which it is certain he did not implant in his mind. The Crimean War started when Zola was at the impressionable age of thirteen, and who knows what strange stories of the half-Asian Empire and its inhabitants, retailed in the press of the time or brought back by combatants, were still lurking in his memory from that period? As a schoolboy at Aix he had known a young Russian student at the Faculty of Law, and he never forgot finding in his room a grey-covered pamphlet written in Russian which the student translated for him. It was a treatise on the best way to blow up Paris, compiled by a Russian officer domiciled in France at the end of the eighteenth century. The plan was soberly devised: the catacombs were to be entered outside the city, filled with explosives, and the whole left bank would have been destroyed.[1] In the making of Souvarine, a distrust of the Russian character which reached down into Zola's subconscious merged with a more recent aversion from the Russians as the principal advocates of a theory of violent social change.[2]

Anarchist terrorism (of the 'propaganda by deed' type) did not start to manifest itself in France until after *Germinal* was published; when it did, the novel acquired an unexpected and sinister prestige. It was read by certain desperadoes who regarded Souvarine as a new Prometheus, and not by any means the criminal fanatic that Zola himself had meant to portray. Émile Henry, one of several anarchists arrested for bomb-outrages in 1893–4, quoted at his trial Souvarine's words in justification of his refusal to explain his motives: 'Tous les raisonnements sur l'avenir sont criminels, parce qu'ils empêchent la destruction pure et simple et entravent la marche de la révolution.'[3] Young Guillaume Apollinaire ended a letter to a school-friend, in 1898, with the remark: 'I shall leave you with a prayer for the arrival of Souvarine, the man who must come, the fair-haired man who will destroy towns and men.'[4] More con-servative readers reacted differently—though quite as violently—to

---

[1] Zola recalls this in one of his 'chroniques' in *L'Événement illustré* (9 May 1868).

[2] The trial (in 1882) of Prince Kropotkin, implicated in a bomb-throwing incident at Lyons—a trial which was given wide publicity—may have reinforced Zola's russophobia.

[3] See P. Aubery, 'Quelques sources du thème de l'action directe dans *Germinal*', *Symposium*, vol. xiii (1959), p. 70, and R. Ternois, *Zola et son temps*, p. 338.

[4] Quoted by Margaret Davies, *Apollinaire* (1964), p. 23.

the impact of Zola's alarming creation. It can hardly be doubted that Joseph Conrad modelled his 'Professor', the obsessional manufacturer of dynamite in *The Secret Agent* (1907), on Souvarine. Indeed, the concluding words of his novel will be found to be a recognizable echo of the passage from *Germinal* quoted above, describing Souvarine's departure in the dusk. Zola had added a notable demigod to the infernal mythology of the 'red peril'. Those who are old enough to remember the campaign waged in the popular press to discredit the Soviet state in the first decade of its existence will recognize, if they recall the figure of 'Popski' in a certain children's strip-cartoon, Souvarine's ultimate, puerile descendant.

To correspond to his three socialists, the Marxist Lantier, the trades-unionist Rasseneur, and the anarchist Souvarine, Zola chose three representatives of the threatened middle class: Deneulin, the small capitalist who has bought a concession and exploits his own mine with hired labour; Hennebeau, the salaried manager of a colliery administered by a joint-stock company; and Grégoire, a shareholder in this company.

The Grégoires, being avowedly comic characters, represent a new departure for Zola. Humour is scarcely observable in his earlier works. In *Germinal* it finds a first timid outlet, and we shall see it flowing much more exuberantly in *La Terre*. This humour has its source in irony, which Havelock Ellis called 'the soul of Zola's work', the thing that gives it 'distinction and poignant incisiveness'. It is an irony, however, which disturbs more than it amuses, being morose, tinged at moments with a sardonic savagery, in fact little different from Flaubert's *grotesque triste*, which, as its inventor declared, 'ne fait pas rire, mais rêver longuement'.

The appearance of the Grégoires almost anywhere in the book is a signal for this *grotesque triste*. We are introduced to them at the beginning of the second part: a Pickwickian couple, good-natured, well-nourished, fresh-complexioned, with crisp white hair. Their only child came to them late, and they treat her with boundless indulgence. 'Elle n'était pas jolie, trop saine, trop bien portante, mûre à dix-huit ans; mais elle avait une chair superbe, une fraîcheur de lait, avec ses cheveux châtains, sa face ronde au petit nez volontaire, noyé entre les joues.' They live quietly in a secluded, well-heated house, waited on by a few contented servants, eating well, sleeping well, without a care in the world.

Into this cosy atmosphere shuffles the miner's wife, La Maheude, with two of her younger children. She has tramped over through the March wind and mud in expectation of charity. The Grégoires are charitable—intelligently so, never giving cash, in accordance with the *idée reçue* that the poor spend every available penny on drink. La Maheude, who has not the money to buy her husband and elder children a meal when they come in from work, is sent away with a parcel of warm clothes for the children, while Cécile unconsciously acts on the legendary proposal of Marie-Antoinette and pushes a *brioche* into their hands. 'Les pauvres mioches, qui n'avaient pas de pain, s'en allèrent, en tenant cette brioche respectueusement, dans leurs menottes gourdes de froid.'

The Grégoires are neither insensitive nor hypocritical; they are a couple of amiable innocents. Léon Grégoire's great-grandfather had invested a portion of his life-savings, 10,000 francs, to buy a share in the Montsou colliery at the beginning of its history. Rather less than a century later, this initial investment is yielding annually five times the value of the principal. The share has thus been the family providence, enabling it through three generations to live in ease and idleness, and promising the same sybaritic existence to Cécile, her children, and her children's children, provided they are not numerous. The arrangement seems so natural to the Grégoires, they are so convinced of their right to their income, that when Négrel, Cécile's fiancé, amuses himself by proving them to be social parasites marked down for liquidation in the next revolution, the old man gasps with indignation.

— De l'argent volé, ma fortune! Est-ce que mon bisaïeul n'avait pas gagné, et durement, la somme placée autrefois? Est-ce que nous n'avons pas couru tous les risques de l'entreprise? Est-ce que je fais un mauvais usage des rentes, aujourd'hui? . . . Ah! je ne dis pas, il y a des action-naires qui abusent. Par exemple, on m'a conté que des ministres ont reçu des deniers de Montsou, en pot-de-vin, pour services rendus à la Compagnie. C'est comme ce grand seigneur que je ne nommerai pas, un duc, le plus fort de nos actionnaires, dont la vie est un scandale de prodigalité, des millions jetés à la rue en femmes, en bombances, en luxe inutile. . . . Mais nous, mais nous qui vivons sans fracas, comme de braves gens que nous sommes! nous qui ne spéculons pas, qui nous contentons de vivre sainement avec ce que nous avons, en faisant la part des pauvres! . . . Allons donc! il faudrait que vos ouvriers fussent de fameux brigands pour voler chez nous une épingle.

Grégoire's hints of millions wasted in lavish living and political jobbery take us back to *La Curée*, to *Son Excellence Eugène Rougon*, and to Nana, one of whose lovers, the financier Steiner, 's'était associé avec un maître de forges, en Alsace; il y avait là-bas, dans un coin de province, des ouvriers noirs de charbon, trempés de sueur, qui, nuit et jour, raidissaient leurs muscles et entendaient craquer leurs os, pour suffire aux plaisirs de Nana'. The evidence of the earlier books is enough to show that Zola was perfectly aware of the extent to which social injustice was liable to flourish under a system of uncontrolled capitalism. If, in *Germinal*, he was content to make no more than a passing reference to the more disgraceful of these abuses, this was for reasons of art: in order to preserve the illusion of impartiality his *rentiers* had to be made as humanly sympathetic as was consistent with truth. Their *naïveté* acquits them of deliberate villainy.

This *naïveté* occasionally touches the upper registers of comedy. Thus the incident in which, at the height of the rioting in Montsou, the Grégoires placidly walk up the main street and are allowed to pass unharmed by the disconcerted rabble, provides an unexpectedly ludicrous scene in an act of bestial violence. M. Grégoire's subsequent comment on the bloodthirsty yells: 'Bread! Bread! Death to the bourgeois!' is worthy of being coupled with the historic remark of a queen of France already recalled: 'Why, of course [he says], they don't mean any harm really. When they have shouted themselves hoarse, they will go home and eat their supper with all the more appetite.'

Zola miscalculated in punishing the Grégoires so heavily at the end. When the strike is all over and the miners beaten into submission, Cécile is strangled by Bonnemort, now in his dotage, one day when she is making a round of charity visits. Originally, Zola had envisaged for the girl a humdrum marriage to Négrel.[1] By choosing, instead, this melodramatic extinction of the line of the *rentiers* at the hands of Bonnemort, the ancient industrial serf, he may have had in mind to introduce a piece of prophetic symbolism; but if so, the symbolism, it has to be admitted, starts uncomfortably out of the picture, and weakens the caricatural unity of the Grégoires. More probably Zola felt under compulsion to leave none of his characters unscarred by suffering.

[1] See E. M. Grant, 'Marriage or Murder: Zola's hesitations concerning Cécile Grégoire', *French Studies*, vol. xv (1961), pp. 41–46.

Deneulin's end, on the other hand, is both apt and typical. An owner-manager, he is a survival from an earlier phase of the growth of capitalism. When the strike, spreading to his own employees, ruins him, he is forced to sell out to the big joint-stock company and become one of its paid servants.

Zola gave Deneulin many virtues: an excellent manager of men, courageous, hard-working, and far-sighted, he bears little resemblance to the blood-sucking exploiter of convention and legend. His mine is better equipped than those belonging to the Montsou syndicate, and his workers are attached to him. Between socialism itself, believed unattainable, and monopolistic capitalism, condemned as inhuman, this middle term of paternally administered private enterprise appears to have commended itself most to Zola; but it was already under sentence of strangulation, and in showing his small *entrepreneur* devoured by a cartel, Zola was accurately reflecting the trend of economic development in his day.

Hennebeau, finally, unlike Grégoire and Deneulin, enjoys no inherited wealth, and has worked his way up from very humble beginnings by sheer industry and intelligence. He has, it is true, made a rich marriage, but his personal income is fixed by the directors he serves. 'Je suis un salarié comme vous', he tells the deputation of strikers; 'je n'ai pas plus de volonté ici que le dernier de vos galibots. On me donne des ordres, et mon seul rôle est de veiller à leur bonne exécution.'

He may be typical of the managerial class of his time, but Zola did his best to present him as a human being, not simply as the representative of a particular social grouping. Through Hennebeau more than through any other character, the drama is lifted out of the political and economic context and raised to the plane of universal truth. The intention was, as Zola wrote to Édouard Rod, 'de mettre au-dessus de l'éternelle injustice des classes l'éternelle douleur des passions'; and he asked his captious disciple: 'Comment n'avez-vous pas compris que cet adultère banal n'est là que pour me donner la scène où M. Hennebeau râle sa souffrance humaine en face de la souffrance sociale qui hurle?' The scene in question is situated in one of the most celebrated chapters in *Germinal*, that in which the maddened strikers scour the countryside smashing machinery and punctuating a discordant rendering of the 'Marseillaise' with the cry for food. The responsibility for calling up troops to quell the riot rests on Hennebeau; and Zola,

with his usual instinct for dramatic suspense, chooses that moment
to deprive him of the power to act. His wife has left the house with
Négrel to fetch Cécile and Deneulin's daughters who have been
invited to lunch; and an accident discovers to him the intrigue that
has been going on under his roof. His jealousy is that of the man
still passionately in love with his wife, but repulsed by her, and
tolerating her perverse infatuations for a succession of temporary
lovers. But Négrel is his own nephew, and this time his fury and
despair pass all bounds. Zola achieves impressive drama of quite a
new kind by stationing the frenzied mob outside his window,
shouting insults up at him and threatening to storm his house,
while he watches them from behind a shutter, envious of their
freedom from spiritual torment and moral inhibitions.

Il leur en aurait fait cadeau volontiers, de ses gros appointements,
pour avoir, comme eux, le cuir dur, l'accouplement facile et sans regret.
Que ne pouvait-il les asseoir à sa table, les empâter de son faisan, tandis
qu'il s'en irait forniquer derrière les haies, culbuter des filles, en se mo-
quant de ceux qui les avaient culbutées avant lui! Il aurait tout donné,
son éducation, son bien-être, son luxe, sa puissance de directeur, s'il
avait pu être, une journée, le dernier des misérables qui lui obéissaient,
libre de sa chair, assez goujat pour gifler sa femme et prendre du plaisir
sur les voisines. Et il souhaitait aussi de crever la faim, d'avoir le ventre
vide, l'estomac tordu de crampes ébranlant le cerveau d'un vertige :
peut-être cela aurait-il tué l'éternelle douleur. Ah! vivre en brute, ne
rien posséder à soi, battre les blés avec la herscheuse la plus laide, la plus
sale, et être capable de s'en contenter!
— Du pain! du pain! du pain!
Alors, il se fâcha, il cria furieusement dans le vacarme :
— Du pain! est-ce que ça suffit, imbéciles?
Il mangeait, lui, et il n'en râlait pas moins de souffrance. Son ménage
ravagé, sa vie entière endolorie, lui remontaient à la gorge, en un hoquet
de mort. Tout n'allait pas pour le mieux parce qu'on avait du pain. Quel
était l'idiot qui mettait le bonheur de ce monde dans le partage de la
richesse? Ces songe-creux de révolutionnaires pouvaient bien démolir la
société et en rebâtir une autre, ils n'ajouteraient pas une joie à l'humanité,
ils ne lui retireraient pas une peine, en coupant à chacun sa tartine.
Même ils élargiraient le malheur de la terre, ils feraient un jour hurler
jusqu'aux chiens de désespoir, lorsqu'ils les auraient sortis de la tranquille satisfaction des instincts, pour les hausser à la souffrance inassouvie des passions. Non, le seul bien était de ne pas être, et, si l'on
était, d'être l'arbre, d'être la pierre, moins encore, le grain de sable, qui
ne peut saigner sous le talon des passants.

The problem here so strikingly dramatized is an old one. Zola may have learnt at school how La Bruyère stated it, with the important rider which is not to be found in *Germinal*:

One wonders whether, in comparing the different conditions of men, their hardships and advantages, one might not observe a mixture or a sort of compensation of good and evil which would establish equality between them, or which would at least bring it about that the one condition should be hardly more desirable than the other. He who is powerful, rich, and lacks nothing, may frame this question; but it must needs be left to a poor man to decide it.[1]

Zola, acquainted equally with extremes of poverty and wealth, should have been as qualified as a man might be both to put and decide the question; but he preferred to end his chapter with Hennebeau still in tears at the window and the famished rioters still roaring below.

His answer to the question must be looked for elsewhere than in the novel. In a letter to the editor of *Le Figaro* Zola defended himself against the reproach made by his reviewer of having 'insulted the lower classes' in *Germinal*: 'Pourquoi veut-on que je calomnie les misérables? Je n'ai eu qu'un désir, les montrer tels que notre société les fait, et soulever une telle pitié, un tel cri de justice, que la France cesse enfin de se laisser dévorer par l'ambition d'une poignée de politiciens, pour s'occuper de la santé et de la richesse de ses enfants.' Writing to the editor of a provincial newspaper in which *Germinal* was to be serialized, he was even more explicit:

Germinal est une œuvre de pitié, et non une œuvre de révolution. Ce que j'ai voulu, c'est crier aux heureux de ce monde, à ceux qui sont les maîtres: 'Prenez garde, regardez sous terre, voyez ces misérables qui travaillent et qui souffrent. Il est peut-être temps encore d'éviter les catastrophes finales. Mais hâtez-vous d'être justes, autrement, voilà le péril: la terre s'ouvrira et les nations s'engloutiront dans un des plus effroyables bouleversements de l'Histoire.'

Marxist critics rightly refuse to regard *Germinal* as constituting evidence that Zola contemplated an ultimate dictatorship of the proletariat with eagerness, with equanimity, or indeed with anything but dread and despair.[2] It is true that he affirmed, in the

---

[1] *Les Caractères.* Des Grands, 5.

[2] J. Fréville (*Zola, semeur d'orages*, pp. 114–15) points out that Zola's views were founded not on Marx's theory of the class struggle but on an application to human history of Darwin's theory of natural selection.

opening lines of the *ébauche*, that his subject was 'la lutte du capital
et du travail . . . la question qui sera la question la plus importante
du XXe siècle'. But the class struggle, as he saw it, could end in
one of only two ways: by a general collapse into anarchy and
barbarism, or by a reconciliation of conflicting interests. *Germinal*
was intended to warn the bourgeois reader against the first possibility, and to urge him to make the necessary concessions to secure
the second, desirable consummation. *Germinal*, in short, is neither
a revolutionary nor a reactionary work; remaining carefully and
intentionally neutral, Zola left unexamined the full political significance of the social issues that he raised, while he made their
existence, and gravity, blindingly clear. It is arguable, however,
that in 1885 the mere exposure and graphic portrayal of social
injustice constituted in itself a revolutionary act. *Germinal*, as
Henri Barbusse wrote, 'made the ghosts of the damned of the earth
walk the streets of the capitals. It revealed to every passer-by their
physical shapes with eerie frightfulness, and their existence—if not
their destiny—to the marrow. And thus it spread an uneasiness
that is the nightmare of revolutionary truth.'[1] In publishing this
novel Zola was surely fulfilling what Sartre has defined as 'the
writer's function': 'to ensure that no one may remain in ignorance
of the world and that no one may call himself guiltless of what
goes on in it.'[2]

[1] H. Barbusse, *Zola*, trans. Mary B. and F. C. Green (1932), pp. 172–3.
[2] J.-P. Sartre, *Situations II*, p. 74.

XI

THE ARTIST'S LIFE

I T is not easy to decide exactly at what point Zola became consecrated as one of the leading writers of the age. Abroad—in
Russia and in Germany particularly—he did not need to wait
so long for celebrity as in his own country. In France *L'Assommoir*
certainly made him the centre of attention, and by the time *La
Débâcle* was published, in 1892, his reputation was secure. Somewhere within these fifteen years greatness became his acknowledged
due, and there is much to be said for fixing on 1885 as the turning-
point. It was in that year that Victor Hugo died, and the last bar to
primacy fell. 'This has taken a great weight off me', Zola declared
to Alphonse Daudet as they were refreshing themselves in a café
after the national obsequies given to Hugo. 'That old man down
there, in his little house at the end of his avenue, has been an inconvenience to me since his eightieth birthday celebrations. Now he
won't inconvenience me any more.'[1] And indeed, whatever his
enemies might say, Zola seemed the only possible successor to the
title of Prince of Letters, especially since, at the same moment,
Germinal was being acclaimed almost unanimously by the critics.

Hugo and Zola had perhaps more in common than either of them
would have been happy to recognize. A contemporary, Robert de
Bonnières, pointed out at the time some of the ways in which they
resembled each other: both tireless workers, both serenely indifferent to the work of others.[2] He might have added: both anti-
clericals, both men of the left, both interested in social causes.
Germinal might have been called *Les Misérables* if Hugo had not
used the title first. As he grew older, Zola came to resemble the
departed poet more and more. Jeanne Rozerot was his Juliette
Drouet; 'J'accuse' proved a more effective *Napoléon le Petit* and,

---

[1] Léon Daudet, *Fantômes et vivants* (1914), pp. 156–7. All the anecdotes told
about Zola by this writer, who was excessively biased, are open to suspicion;
but this one is to some extent corroborated by a similar story related by Edmond
de Goncourt in his diary (under the date: 24 May 1885).

[2] R. de Bonnières, *Mémoires d'aujourd'hui*, 2ᵉ série (1885), p. 276.

like Hugo before him, Zola, to avoid the consequences of his audacity in publishing it, was obliged to resign himself to exile among the subjects of Queen Victoria. And in two quite basic respects their artistic genius ran in similar channels: both were visionaries; and both had a penchant for the epic. Zola would have appreciated the sweeping conception of *La Légende des siècles*, though he would also have noted how it petered out, after the first two series, in pretentious banality. The phrase 'une épopée pessimiste de l'animalité humaine' was coined by Jules Lemaître, in his review of *Germinal*, to describe *Les Rougon-Macquart*; and indeed, a quarter of a century earlier, Zola had been fired by the ambition to become the modern counterpart of Homer. When, in 1860, he was still fumbling his way towards some 'unexplored path' which might lead him away from 'the common herd of scribblers of our age', he felt, as he told Baille, that: 'Le poème épique — j'entends un poème épique à moi et non une sotte imitation des anciens — me paraît une voie assez peu commune.' When he had still to publish the first volume of *Les Rougon-Macquart* he described the coming series to the Goncourts as 'une épopée en dix volumes'; and before it was far advanced, he announced his ambition to 'prendre la terre, la posséder dans une étreinte, tout voir, tout savoir, tout dire. Je voudrais coucher l'humanité sur une page blanche, tous les êtres, toutes les choses; une œuvre qui serait l'arche immense.'[1] If 'the earth and all humanity' are here an almost Hugolian flourish, Zola may well have hoped, after Balzac, that his work would be large enough to contain the modern City, *urbs et orbis*.

C'est lui qui me parle de l'art nouveau [he wrote of Paris a bare eighteen months after Paris had emerged from the horrors of the Commune and its bloody repression], avec ses rues vivantes, ses horizons tachés d'enseignes et d'affiches, ses maisons terribles et douces où l'on aime et où l'on meurt. C'est son immense drame qui m'attache au drame moderne, à l'existence de ses bourgeois et de ses ouvriers, à toute sa cohue flottante dont je voudrais noter chaque douleur et chaque joie. . . . et si j'avais quelque orgueil suprême, je rêverais de le jeter tout chaud et tout plein de son travail géant, dans quelque œuvre gigantesque.[2]

The tragic hero of Zola's *L'Œuvre*, Claude Lantier, shares Zola's ambition to gather up the City in one all-embracing vision and project it into a 'gigantic work'. Claude is the same painter, a little

---

[1] Preface (dated 1 Oct. 1874) of *Nouveaux Contes à Ninon*.
[2] *Le Corsaire*, 3 Dec. 1872.

older and gruffer, much less talkative and whimsical, that we met in *Le Ventre de Paris*: as fascinated in the later novel as in the earlier by the streets, the buildings, and the denizens of the modern metropolis.

Quand il traversait Paris, il découvrait des tableaux partout; la ville entière, avec ses rues, ses carrefours, ses ponts, ses horizons vivants, se déroulait en fresques immenses, qu'il jugeait toujours trop petites, pris de l'ivresse des besognes colossales. Et il rentrait frémissant, le crâne bouillonnant de projets, jetant des croquis sur des bouts de papier, le soir, à la lampe, sans pouvoir décider par où il entamerait la série des grandes pages qu'il rêvait.

When finally he fixes on the subject for the vast composition he plans shall be his masterpiece (a view of the Seine from one of its bridges, looking downstream towards the Île de la Cité), he has reached the foot of his Calvary. The canvas is painted, scraped, repainted, a hundred times; the struggle goes on for years, with the picture never completed, a perpetual, obsessional torment afflicting the unfortunate artist.

Ah! cet effort de création dans l'œuvre d'art, cet effort de sang et de larmes dont il agonisait, pour créer de la chair, souffler de la vie! Toujours en bataille avec le réel, et toujours vaincu, la lutte contre l'Ange! Il se brisait à cette besogne impossible de faire tenir toute la nature sur une toile, épuisé à la longue dans les perpétuelles douleurs qui tendaient ses muscles, sans qu'il pût jamais accoucher de son génie.

This passage (from chapter ix) repeats—textually in places—the opening lines of the *ébauche* of *L'Œuvre* which, however, provide the additional hint that Zola was attributing to Claude no more and no less than his own agonies in the incessant creative labour:

Avec Claude Lantier, je veux peindre la lutte de l'artiste contre la nature, l'effort de la création dans l'œuvre d'art, effort de sang et de larmes pour donner sa chair, faire de la vie: toujours en bataille avec le vrai, et toujours vaincu, la lutte contre l'ange. *En un mot, j'y raconterai ma vie intime de production*, ce perpétuel accouchement douloureux; mais je grandirai le sujet par le drame, par Claude qui ne se contente jamais, qui s'exaspère de ne pouvoir accoucher de son génie, et qui se tue à la fin devant son œuvre irréalisée.[1]

L'Œuvre is a work of self-confession as much as *La Confession de Claude* had been, but the autobiographical method used is less

[1] B.N. MS. *Nouv. acq. fr.* 10316, fol. 262. My italics.

straightforward than it had been in the maiden novel: Zola, instead
of projecting himself into one figure, distributes himself between
two or perhaps three. From Claude Lantier we may turn to Pierre
Sandoz, the writer, Claude's closest friend. Whereas Claude
refuses to compromise an inaccessible ideal in the interests of production, and so produces little or nothing, Sandoz is resigned to
compromises, having realized that sterility is the worse evil:

produisant quand même, sans la logique de Claude qui se tue. Sachant
que l'œuvre est imparfaite, et s'y soumettant, avec une grande tristesse.
Allant toujours devant lui, courtes joies, continuelles angoisses. Jetant
les œuvres, allant au bout, sans vouloir s'arrêter, sans regarder en
arrière, ne pouvant se relire. Toute ma confession. *Un écho pratique et
résigné de Claude.*[1]

Sandoz does, indeed, echo Claude's yearning to fix all nature in
a work of art: 'Ah, que ce serait beau, si l'on donnait son existence
entière à une œuvre, où l'on tâcherait de mettre les choses, les
bêtes, les hommes, l'arche immense!' And just as Claude is dissatisfied with his painting, because he can detect in it traces of
Delacroix's romanticism and Courbet's realism, so too 'Sandoz
haussa désespérément les épaules: lui aussi se lamentait d'être né
au confluent d'Hugo et de Balzac'. Zola gave Sandoz his own
curriculum vitae: his father a foreigner, an inventor, dying in his
prime, leaving his widow in a difficult financial situation; the boyhood spent in Provence, then the minor clerkship in Paris enabling
him to support his ailing mother; the publication of his first book,
'une suite d'esquisses aimables, rapportées de Plassans, parmi
lesquelles quelques notes plus rudes indiquaient seules le révolté,
le passionné de vérité et de puissance'. Like Zola, Sandoz loves to
gather his friends round him of an evening, at first in his bachelor
chambers, later, having married and grown more prosperous, in
more spacious apartments where Henriette, his wife, a figure lightly
but affectionately sketched in, cooks them delicious *bouillabaisses*.
L'Œuvre was, according to an Italian friend who got to know her in
later life, of all her husband's novels Mme Zola's favourite, which
she could never refer to without emotion. She would take it from
the shelf and press it to her heart, exclaiming sentimentally that
this book was her cross of honour, her reward.[2]

[1] Ibid., fols. 287–8. Italics represent Zola's underlining.
[2] L. D'Ambra, *Trent'anni di vita letteraria. Il viaggio a furia di remi* (Milan,
1928), p. 213.

Sandoz turns to journalism which he views, as Zola viewed it, as a temporary expedient, though a useful vehicle for propagating his views. 'Cette gueuse de presse, malgré les dégoûts du métier, est une sacrée puissance, une arme invincible aux mains d'un gaillard convaincu. . . . Mais, si je suis forcé de m'en servir, je n'y vieillirai pas, ah! non!' He launches his novel-series, a shadow *Rougon-Macquart*, written likewise under the aegis of positivism: 'étudier l'homme tel qu'il est, non plus leur pantin métaphysique, mais l'homme physiologique, déterminé par le milieu, agissant sous le jeu de tous ses organes.' The series is to revolve round the fortunes of the members of a single family, and is planned to run to fifteen or twenty volumes, 'une suite de romans à me bâtir une maison pour mes vieux jours, s'ils ne m'écrasent pas'. The first volumes are violently attacked by the critics, but the wind of favour turns, his books become popular, his sales shoot up, and, living comfortably before, Sandoz can now afford to live luxuriously.

Sandoz is the public image Zola wanted to give of himself: hard-working, honest, a kindly husband, a stalwart friend, a genial host, and a much misunderstood writer. He is also, fundamentally, the successful author in his beginnings, not the 'prince of letters' that Zola had become by the time he wrote *L'Œuvre*. So he invented a third character, Bongrand, named simply 'le vieux' in the *ébauche*. 'Je l'appelle le vieux,' he wrote, 'mais il ne faut pas qu'il ait plus de cinquante ans. Un Manet très chic, un Flaubert plutôt.' But also, undoubtedly, a Zola nearing his fifties. 'La bataille est plus âpre encore, plus douloureuse, pour l'artiste qui veut se maintenir, que pour l'artiste qui veut arriver. Ce dernier a l'espoir en avant, le rêve de ce qu'il sera; tandis que l'autre se voit décliner et roule dans le désespoir de ce qu'il a été.'[1] Bongrand is a painter, but an epic painter: the picture that made his name, many years earlier, and determined a new movement in the history of art, was of a village wedding, 'une noce débandée à travers les blés, des paysans étudiés de près, et très vrais, qui avaient une allure épique de héros d'Homère'. Since then he has been struggling not to fall below this achievement; with each new picture he starts he feels all the nervousness of a tiro, his heart beating, his mouth dry. He implores words of encouragement from younger artists, not daring to trust his own judgement. 'Mon malheur doit être que j'ai à la fois trop et pas assez de sens critique.'

[1] B.N. MS. *Nouv. acq. fr.* 10316, fols. 289, 274.

This was undoubtedly Zola's 'misfortune' too: a greater degree of 'critical sense' would perhaps have served to warn him away from certain subjects and would have saved him from certain errors of taste; with a lesser degree he would have achieved a modicum of serenity which might have added little to his art but would have given him more contentment in his work. For contentment was hard for him to come by, either in the process of writing a book or when the book was written. Bongrand's despair at the thought that he would never repeat the masterpiece of his earlier days merely echoes Zola's melancholy outburst to Goncourt: 'Au fond, je ne referai plus jamais un roman qui remuera comme *l'Assommoir*, un roman qui se vendra comme *Nana*.' And Bongrand's confession: 'Oui, à chacun de mes tableaux, j'ai encore une grosse émotion de débutant', had been made by Zola to Alexis years before: 'Il me semble que je suis toujours un débutant. J'oublie les vingt volumes que j'ai derrière moi, et je tremble, en me demandant ce que vaudra mon prochain roman.' Alexis went on to observe that, in spite of fame and fortune, Zola was a profoundly unhappy man. 'Though acknowledged as a master, he perpetually feels himself a mere beginner. A celebrity he may be, but he sits down at his desk every morning terrified he will find himself incapable of writing two lines.'[1] He had his 'bad days', as he confessed in a remarkable outburst to the Italian reporter, Edmondo De Amicis, who visited him shortly after the appearance of *Nana*,

days in which I seem to be done for, not for that day only but for good and all; days in which I might as well be dead. I sit down at my desk bright and early in the morning, not realizing the condition I am in, and the moment I pick up the thread of my novel, I feel a frightening emptiness and silence inside my head. Characters, localities, scenes, episodes, everything is as it were frozen inside a black fog which I feel I shall never be able to pierce with a single ray of sunlight. And so I sit here for hours, with my hand in my chin, staring at the window like one who has lost his memory.[2]

But, Zola added, all artists are subject to such fits of black depression. There were only two in the whole of the century who never doubted their powers: Hugo, who could not imagine it possible that he should write a bad line, and Courbet, who was convinced it was not in him to paint a bad picture. One of the episodic

---

[1] *Émile Zola, notes d'un ami* (1882), pp. 206, 209.
[2] De Amicis, *Ritratti letterari* (Milan, 1881), p. 69.

characters in *L'Œuvre*, the sculptor Champbouvard, was designed to set off Bongrand, being an obese, self-idolizing celebrity, who 'poussait le manque de sens critique jusqu'à ne pas faire distinction, entre les fils les plus glorieux de ses mains, et les détestables magots qu'il lui arrivait de bâcler parfois'. In the *ébauche* Champbouvard is designated 'le monstre enflé de sa personnalité, sans critique, et qui est devenu dieu: Courbet, Hugo'.[1]

It is true that these confessions of self-doubt were all made at a time (1881–2) when, as we have seen, Zola was hovering on the brink of a nervous breakdown. But years later the same despair, the same distrust of his own abilities, the same doubts as to the value of his achievement, are periodically expressed in his correspondence. When he was nearing the end of *Germinal* he wrote to Edmond de Goncourt, who had read the early instalments in *Le Gil Blas*: 'Je suis ici . . . dans le doute de ce sacré bouquin qui me donne tant de peine. . . . Tant mieux si le commencement vous plaît, ça prouve que je ne suis pas un imbécile, comme j'en ai peur parfois.' Five years later, starting on the second chapter of *La Bête humaine*: 'Quel terrible métier,' he wrote to Alexis, 'où l'on recommence toujours, et où, chaque fois, on débute, avec les mêmes difficultés et les mêmes angoisses!' Later still, when he was in the thick of writing *La Débâcle*, Van Santen Kolff inquired whether he was pleased with the way the new novel was going. Zola's answer was characteristically morose: 'Ne vous ai-je pas déjà dit que je n'étais jamais content d'un livre pendant que je l'écrivais? Je veux tout mettre, je suis toujours désespéré du champ limité de la réalisation. L'enfantement d'un livre est pour moi une abominable torture, parce qu'il ne saurait contenter mon besoin impérieux d'universalité et de totalité.' Age did not calm this fever. When he was turned sixty, in 1901, a German visitor asked him whether he felt satisfaction during the writing of a book, or only after it was completed. 'After, only afterwards,' Zola burst out hurriedly, with the look of a man who is reminded of the torture-chamber. A book may be conceived in joy, he explained; but until one is delivered of it, one is sick. 'Out of ten days, there are not two when one is at peace. My condition is like that of a pregnant woman.'[2]

The figure of speech by which Zola equated the labour of writing with that of giving birth to a child was more than a cliché: it was

[1] B.N. MS. *Nouv. acq. fr.* 10316, fol. 286.
[2] Alfred Kerr, 'La Maison de Zola', *Nouvelles littéraires*, 8 Oct. 1932.

for him a hallucinatory and self-evident truth. Of the fifty or sixty possible titles he had noted down, before fixing on *L'Œuvre*, half a dozen at least express this metaphor. *Faire un enfant* heads the list; one finds too *Enfantement, Accouchement, Le Siècle en couche, Les Couches du siècle,* and the arresting *Les Couches saignantes.*[1] But there was one vital difference between parturition and creation: the artist has no joy in what he brings into being. 'Moi', says Sandoz, 'je m'accouche avec les fers, et l'enfant, quand même, me semble une horreur.' Is there any reward that the artist may look for, then? He is certain to be slighted and reviled during his lifetime: but has he at least the consolation of knowing that posterity will honour him for his labour? Not even that perhaps.

On est comme le fidèle qui supporte l'abomination de cette terre, dans la ferme croyance à une autre vie, où chacun sera traité selon ses mérites. Et s'il n'y avait pas plus de paradis pour l'artiste que pour le catholique, si les générations futures se trompaient comme les contemporains, continuaient le malentendu, préféraient aux œuvres fortes les petites bêtises aimables! . . . Ah! quelle duperie, hein? quelle existence de forçat, cloué au travail, pour une chimère!

Sandoz cannot endure the thought. But Claude, more sombre, acquiesces in the futility of artistic as of all other activity. 'Nous sommes plus fous encore que les imbéciles qui se tuent pour une femme. Quand la terre claquera dans l'espace comme une noix sèche, nos œuvres n'ajouteront pas un atome à sa poussière.' The artist's life is then consumed in the exhausting and pointless pursuit of a shadow. Significantly, it is Sandoz, most closely modelled on Zola's likeness, who utters the long lamentation about his thraldom to a monstrous monomania.

Dès que je saute du lit, le matin, le travail m'empoigne, me cloue à ma table, sans me laisser respirer une bouffée de grand air; puis, il me suit au déjeuner, je remâche sourdement mes phrases avec mon pain; puis, il m'accompagne quand je sors, rentre dîner dans mon assiette, se couche le soir sur mon oreiller, si impitoyable, que jamais je n'ai le pouvoir d'arrêter l'œuvre en train, dont la végétation continue, jusqu'au fond de mon sommeil . . . Ma pauvre femme n'a pas de mari, je ne suis plus avec elle, même lorsque nos mains se touchent . . .; mais est-ce que je puis m'échapper des pattes du monstre! . . . Plus rien n'est à moi, j'ai rêvé des repos à la campagne, des voyages lointains, dans mes jours de misère; et aujourd'hui que je pourrais me contenter, l'œuvre commencée est là

[1] B.N. MS. *Nouv. acq. fr.* 10316, fols. 317–18.

qui me cloître: pas une sortie au soleil matinal, pas une escapade chez un ami, pas une folie de paresse! Jusqu'à ma volonté qui y passe, l'habitude est prise, j'ai fermé la porte du monde derrière moi, et j'ai jeté la clef par la fenêtre ... Plus rien, plus rien dans mon trou que le travail et moi, et il me mangera, et il n'y aura plus rien, plus rien!

And Sandoz ends on a cry of revolt: 'Ah! une vie, une seconde vie, qui me la donnera ... !'; a cry which, if one accepts him—as one is bound to—as Zola's mouthpiece, has a prophetic ring. It was two years only after the publication of *L'Œuvre* that Jeanne Rozerot was to grant him this 'second life'.

In the novel it is Claude who is offered it, who accepts it for a while, then thrusts it aside and returns to his damnation. The dramatic field of force in *L'Œuvre* is generated by the dipolarity of the erotic and the aesthetic; flesh and canvas are at odds throughout. Claude Lantier is presented at the start as shy of women, almost ignorant of the emotions, all his virility going into his painting. Zola invented a brilliant and audacious scene to display this in an initial chapter as spell-binding in its quieter way as the openings of *Nana, Germinal,* and *La Bête humaine.* Returning to his lodgings in the Île Saint-Louis one wet and stormy night, Claude finds a girl sheltering in the porch of the house where he has his studio. She stammers an improbable story of a derailment, a late arrival in Paris, a drunken cabby, an address at Passy where she is expected. 'Une farceuse', decides the painter, 'quelque gueuse flanquée à la rue et qui cherche un homme.' He cannot refuse her shelter but, not to give her an excuse for spending more than the night there, lets her sleep on her own in his bed and makes do himself with the sofa. In fact, he has misjudged her. Christine's story is true; she had travelled up that day from the provinces, there had been a long delay on the line, the servant who was to meet her at the station had gone away. She has come to take up a post as lady's companion in an establishment at Passy.

He is the first to wake up in the morning, and sees that sheet and shift have slipped off the girl as she sleeps, leaving her torso uncovered. He picks up his pencil and starts sketching. 'Tout son trouble, sa curiosité charnelle, son désir combattu, aboutissaient à cet émerveillement d'artiste, à cet enthousiasme pour les beaux tons et les muscles bien emmanchés. Déjà, il avait oublié la jeune fille, il était dans le ravissement de la neige des seins, éclairant l'ambre délicat des épaules.' The artist's abnegation of sex, as Zola denotes it in these lines, is almost more strikingly illustrated by a curious muddle in the sentence of the *ébauche* where he first jotted down the scene. He probably meant to write: 'et le matin, quand elle s'éveille, elle le trouve dessinant une partie de son corps', but what is actually there in the manuscript is: 'quand il s'éveille, il la trouve dessinant une partie de son corps', Claude's somnambulistic absorption in his work being unconsciously reproduced in Zola's confusion of the genders.

He characterized Christine as 'une sensuelle pudique'. A long time passes before she becomes Claude's mistress; she yields to him finally in a rush of compassion, trying to soothe the rawness of his disappointment when the first picture he exhibits meets with loud derision. They bury themselves at Bennecourt, a little village on the Seine a few miles outside Paris, and Claude almost gives up painting. 'Désormais, toute sa tendresse de la chair de la femme, cette tendresse dont il épuisait autrefois le désir dans ses œuvres, ne le brûlait plus que pour ce corps vivant, souple et tiède, qui était son bien.' The honeymoon lasts three years, until the siren-song of Paris and his earlier artistic ambitions proves irresistible. He has not yet grown indifferent to Christine; but she knows she has a rival—one to whom he will give his whole life and who will never satisfy him. In time her enemy takes on visible shape, as the nude bather Claude tries to put in the centre of his last, unfinished river scene.

The earlier picture, on which he had been engaged when Christine first took refuge with him, had involved a nude in the foreground too, and for months he had been unable to complete it, dissatisfied with professional models. Finally one afternoon she had understood what he had not dared to ask of her, and had undressed and posed for this figure. This was at a time when their relations were still innocent; and after the three-hour pose is over and the sketch taken in utter silence, she puts on her clothes again, but they can still say nothing to one another. Zola is content merely to observe that the girl and the man are alike overwhelmed by a great sadness, 'une tristesse infinie, inconsciente et innommée ... leurs paupières se gonflèrent de larmes, comme s'ils venaient de gâter leur existence, de toucher le fond de la misère humaine.' One wonders whether he himself saw the explanation of this: that Claude had already betrayed Christine, using the beauty of her body for another purpose than for the act of love, the only legitimate one. The scene in chapter iv is paralleled in chapter ix when, to economize the expense of a model, Christine once more poses for him in the nude. They are married now, but Claude's desire for her is dead, though he still appreciates the perfection of her parts; as he works he dilates on them with enthusiasm, but using a painter's vocabulary. She realizes she cannot win him back; he sees her as an object to be rendered in pigments, not as a woman, his wife and mistress. In another extraordinary burst of psychological insight Zola shows Christine's weird and intense jealousy of her own portrait that Claude is painting.

> Elle ne se trompait pas, elle sentait bien qu'il préférait sa copie à elle-même, que cette copie était l'adorée, la préoccupation unique, la tendresse de toutes les heures. . . . Quelle souffrance de prêter sa chair, pour que l'autre naquît, pour que le cauchemar de cette rivale les hantât, fût toujours entre eux, plus puissant que le réel, dans l'atelier, à table, au lit, partout! Une poussière, un rien, de la couleur sur de la toile, une simple apparence qui rompait tout leur bonheur, lui, silencieux, indifférent, brutal parfois, elle, torturée de son abandon, désespérée de ne pouvoir chasser de son ménage cette concubine, si envahissante et si terrible dans son immobilité d'image!

This is the cruel reality underlying Sandoz's almost apologetic words quoted earlier: 'ma pauvre femme n'a pas de mari . . .': the frigidity of the artist of whom his latest biographer has written that 'sa sexualité est dans l'encrier'.[1] It may be plausibly surmised that Alexandrine felt many a secret twinge of jealousy in respect of half a dozen of her husband's lovingly elaborated heroines—of Renée, of Albine, of Nana herself, and perhaps even of Christine Hallegrain—long before she had occasion to be openly jealous of Jeanne Rozerot.

In the last chapter of *L'Œuvre*, Christine's desperate fight with the still uncreated phantom of paint reaches its melodramatic climax. She discovers that in his obsession with this last picture which years of work have left still in the state of formless intentions, Claude has started sleep-walking, and painting at night with unseeing eyes. Coming on him thus, she startles him awake and, her frenzied desire communicating itself to him at last, she reawakens also the lover. It is the apparent victory of life over art, but is immediately followed by a crushing reversal when Christine, waking in the early hours after a deep sleep, finds Claude no longer

[1] A. Lanoux, *Bonjour Monsieur Zola*, p. 110.

beside her and, running into the studio, sees his hanged body gently swinging in front of his unfinished masterpiece.

Back in 1866, just before he launched in *L'Événement* the series of studies of the current art-exhibition which was to win him such notoriety, Zola published a short piece in the same paper under the heading 'Un Suicide'. A painter by the name of Jules Holtzapfel had, a few days earlier, blown out his brains in his studio; a note was found explaining that he had been reduced to despair by the committee's rejection of his submissions that year. It has been suggested that the ending of *L'Œuvre* derives from this incident.[1] But Zola may well have heard from Manet the story of his young assistant or apprentice named Alexandre, a moody lad who hanged himself one day in the artist's studio. Manet, who had made the boy the subject of the picture known as *L'Enfant aux cerises*, was so deeply affected by the occurrence that he had to move to another studio.[2] One of Baudelaire's prose poems, 'La Corde', is founded on the incident, as its dedication 'à Édouard Manet' shows.

Modern criticism of *L'Œuvre* has tended to concentrate on such niceties. But nothing is more deceptive and dangerous than the elucidation of a *roman à clefs*. On which of the many artists he knew did Zola base the career and character of Claude Lantier? Cézanne is the obvious candidate. The reminiscences that Sandoz and Lantier exchange (in chapter ii) about their school-days in Provence are exactly what one can imagine Zola and Cézanne evoking after dinner at Médan any time up to the publication of *L'Œuvre*. Cézanne may not have spent several years, as Claude did, living at Bennecourt, but he certainly spent most of one summer there, occasionally visited by Zola in the company of Alexandrine Meley.[3] Hortense Fiquet, whom he married as late as April 1886 (after *L'Œuvre* was published) had borne him one child out of wedlock, a son; and correspondingly, in the novel, Claude fathers a son

---

[1] J. Rewald, *Cézanne et Zola* (1936), p. 132, and R. J. Niess, 'Émile Zola: from fact to fiction', *Modern Language Notes*, vol. lxiii (1948), pp. 407–8. The full text of 'Un Suicide' may be read in P. Brady's valuable study, 'Claude Lantier', *Cahiers naturalistes*, no. 17 (1961), pp. 10–18.

[2] The story was related in Antonin Proust's reminiscences on Manet, *Revue blanche*, vol. xii (1897), p. 168. A. Tabarant (*Manet et ses œuvres*, 1947, p. 25) quotes a confirmatory note on *L'Enfant aux cerises* by Berthe Morisot, to whose husband the picture originally belonged.

[3] See R. Walter, 'Zola et ses amis à Bennecourt (1866)', *Cahiers naturalistes*, no. 17 (1961), pp. 19–35.

before he marries Christine.[1] Hortense Fiquet, again, regularly posed for Cézanne in the studio. Cézanne was, of course, ignored by the critics throughout this period; he submitted frequently for the official *salons*, but only once, in 1882, was a work of his accepted, and then only thanks to the patronage of Guillemet, just as Claude's *Enfant mort* is hung only because Fagerolles, a member of the jury and for long an admirer of Claude's work, exercises his right to a 'charity'. In short, there were enough similarities between the external circumstances of Cézanne's life and the career of the painter-hero of *L'Œuvre* for Cézanne, at least, to imagine his old friend had put him into his book and given him a sorry part to play. As soon as he read the new novel he sent the author a cool and curt acknowledgement, and never wrote to him again or consented to see him. Was he offended? or is it not more probable that he was terrified, seeing in Claude Lantier's decline into near-madness and self-destruction one of the possible roads that he himself might take? For Cézanne was morbidly subject to self-doubt.

There remains much in Zola's portrait of Claude that reminds us of quite different painters. Cézanne did not exhibit in the famous 'salon des refusés' of 1863, as Claude did. The picture, *Plein Air*, that Claude sends in on this occasion, has a certain compositional similarity with *Le Déjeuner sur l'herbe*, one of the two canvases of Manet's that were hung at the 'salon des refusés'. The merriment that Manet's pictures provoked among the visitors was recalled by Zola, in tones of high indignation, in his 1867 *plaquette* on Manet; he seems to be recalling it again in the fifth chapter of *L'Œuvre*. Claude Lantier is regarded by many of his fellow artists as the leader of the new school of painting; Cézanne never had, nor wanted, this distinction, but Claude Monet was widely regarded in the seventies as heading the impressionist group. Most of the pictures Zola describes his hero as painting (apart from *Plein Air* and the last, unfinished work) can be identified as verbal transcriptions of various canvases by Monet.[2] Cézanne had no imitators at this time; Zola shows Lantier as having several, including the adroit Fagerolles who is able to adapt, soften, and sweeten the unpopular

[1] The description of Claude's civil wedding, a scamped and drab affair (chap. viii) is likely to have been based on Zola's memories of his own, in 1870. Manet, too, it should be noted, married his mistress (in 1863) after the birth of a son nine years before.

[2] See R. Walter, 'Émile Zola et Claude Monet', *Cahiers naturalistes*, no. 26 (1964), pp. 51–61.

artist's style, to make of it something the public will accept and like. Here he was thinking of certain fashionable painters of his day like Bastien-Lepage and particularly Gervex of whom he had written in 1879: 'je ne dis pas que Gervex copie les peintres impressionnistes; mais . . . il me paraît évident qu'il réalise ce que ces peintres ont voulu exprimer, en se servant des procédés techniques qu'il doit à sa fréquentation de l'atelier de Cabanel.'[1] And apart from such well-known figures as Manet and Monet there may have been others, forgotten today, who contributed their quota. When E. A. Vizetelly brought out his translation of *L'Œuvre*[2] he wrote an interesting preface in which he made a number of acute suggestions most of which subsequent research in Zola's private papers has confirmed.[3] Besides mentioning Cézanne and Manet as originals of Claude, he asserted that Zola had also used his memories of 'a certain rather dissolute engraver, who sat for [Manet's] famous picture *Le Bon Bock*'; while 'the original of [Christine] was the poor woman who for many years shared the life of the engraver'. The rubicund beer-drinker who posed for *Le Bon Bock* was in fact an engraver, called Émile Bellot. The success of Manet's portrait of him gave him a celebrity he had never enjoyed in the practice of his own art; but of his earlier life, and in particular of his relations with the 'poor woman' who was his life's companion, it seems impossible to discover anything.

L'Œuvre is a book that holds perhaps a greater fascination for art-historians than for any other class of reader. No other novel evokes so fully and effectively the artistic life of the period when the Impressionists were gradually coming to the fore. Exhibitions aroused the same kind of eager interest then as film festivals today; even the popular press, at certain times of the year, was full of reports and rumours about the work of artists who were in the public eye. We learn from the pages of Zola's novel what these annual exhibitions in the Palais de l'Industrie were like, how the crowds behaved—and what huge, motley, avid crowds they were.

[1] *Salons*, ed. Hemmings and Niess, p. 229. Fagerolles is referred to regularly in the *ébauche* of *L'Œuvre* as 'le Gervex'.

[2] *His Masterpiece*, London, Chatto & Windus, 1902.

[3] e.g. that Mahoudeau was based on Solari, Fagerolles on Gervex, Champbouvard on Courbet, and (as far as his sculpture is concerned) on Clésinger. Vizetelly is almost certainly reproducing here information furnished by Zola, with whom he is known to have been in correspondence from 1892 until his death. A batch of 60 letters from Zola to Vizetelly was auctioned at Sotheby's in 1924, but the present whereabouts of these letters is unknown.

We are conducted round the studios, the cafés which were the haunts of painters, writers . . . and reporters. The theorizing that went on, the jealousies and admirations that found utterance, the incessant talk that surrounded the emergence of these august and now fabulously expensive works of art—talk that has long since evaporated as the drops of sea-water from the sheen of priceless pearls—all this is preserved in the pages of *L'Œuvre* more vividly than in a score of books of memoirs.

But for this reason too, the novel has very much the air of a period piece. Its assumptions are not those of our age. The artist still labours, no doubt, in anguish of spirit, still sometimes fails to achieve what he can conceive; but his tribulations have lost the power to touch us deeply. The theme of the suffering creator is, in fact, a relic of the romantic era: *L'Œuvre* of which the hero is, ironically, alleged to be a naturalist, a militant anti-romantic, is recognizable today as being, more than any other volume in *Les Rougon-Macquart* series, a work of pure romanticism, hewn from the same vein as produced Musset's 'Nuit de mai', Vigny's 'Stello', and Baudelaire's 'Mort des artistes':

> Il en est qui jamais n'ont connu leur Idole,
> Et ces sculpteurs damnés et marqués d'un affront,
> Qui vont se martelant la poitrine et le front,
> N'ont qu'un espoir, étrange et sombre Capitole!
> C'est que la Mort, planant comme un soleil nouveau,
> Fera s'épanouir les fleurs de leur cerveau!

XII

EARTH, HEAVEN, AND HELL

B Y upbringing, as we have seen, Émile Zola had been a 'country
boy', disconcerted and made unhappy by his first contacts
with city life. But the idea of using his knowledge of the ways
of the countryside as the staple of one of his novels occurred to him
only after the labour of writing *Les Rougon-Macquart* was well
advanced: the first hint to the public that such a book would
eventually take its place in the series was not made till 1880. Guy
Robert, whose monograph on *La Terre* is certainly the most
exhaustive study ever made of any single work of Zola's, connects
the decision, plausibly enough, with the novelist's move to Médan
in 1878.[1] Here, by his own admission, he paid careful heed to the
titbits of village scandal that reached his ears and got himself
elected to the local council largely with the idea of acquiring
insight into parish politics. His impressions accumulated slowly,
overlaying earlier experience gained in boyhood rambles around
Aix and during the summer months spent at Bennecourt in early
manhood. When he did begin on the novel of which he had predicted that it would be his 'œuvre de prédilection', it was with the
same frenzied haste as had possessed him when he started *L'Assommoir*. On 23 February 1886 he announced to Céard that he had
completed *L'Œuvre* that morning, and 'me voilà déjà mordu par
mon roman sur les paysans. Il me travaille, je vais me mettre tout
de suite à la chasse aux notes et au plan. Je veux m'y donner tout
entier.' On 6 May he wrote from Châteaudun: he had found the
setting he was looking for. Three weeks later, in a letter to Van
Santen Kolff, he confessed himself 'frightened' by the undertaking,
for the novel would be

un des plus chargés de matière, dans sa simplicité. J'y veux faire tenir
tous nos paysans, avec leur histoire, leurs mœurs, leur rôle; j'y veux
poser la question sociale de la propriété; j'y veux montrer où nous allons,
dans cette crise de l'agriculture, si grave en ce moment. . . . Ajoutez que

---

[1] *'La Terre' d'Émile Zola, étude historique et critique*, chap. x.

j'entends rester artiste, écrivain, écrire le poème vivant de la terre, les saisons, les travaux, les champs, les gens, les bêtes, la campagne entière.

Let it be said at once that Zola remained above all an artist, and for this reason, although no item in his programme was forgone, all except the last were relegated to subordinate positions. The peasants' history is, in practice, confined to the last chapter of the first part, where it is presented by the device of having Jean Macquart read a Bonapartist pamphlet to the farm-workers one winter evening; the pamphlet, designed to win the peasants over to the Imperial régime, traces their bitter history from the days of feudal serfdom down to the revolution. The 'social question of property' links up with the question of the agricultural crisis in that the wastefulness of a smallholder economy puts French agriculture at a cruel disadvantage in competing with the produce of the spacious ranches of North America. But the arguments for and against free trade, for and against collective farms, amount to little more than an occasional interlude, a means of emphasizing the narrowness of the countryman's outlook and of procuring a menacing finale to the novel, with the schoolmaster's predictions of ruin and a flight from the land. Although Zola understood them well enough for his purpose, he gave rather less place to economic questions in *La Terre* than he had in *Germinal*, where they are fundamental.

He had a more accurate impression of the book when he had completed it. The real subject, as he wrote to Lepelletier, then emerged as threefold: 'la terre, l'amour, l'argent'; but since possession of land is desired as a means of making money, and since money is reinvested in land or cattle or agricultural tools, in fact *La Terre* is found to revolve round two themes only: love and the earth. The two are intimately connected.

La Terre was not the first novel of Zola's to deal with peasant life: there had been a forerunner, *La Faute de l'abbé Mouret*. It is true that peasants play only a subsidiary part in this earlier book; but the little that is said of them is enough to show that Zola's conception of country life had hardly changed in the thirteen years' interval. In both books the villagers' behaviour knows no moral restraints; rarely is a bride brought to church unless she is pregnant or perhaps already a mother. Their profligacy, however, is simply the brutish satisfaction of periodic appetites, their emotions being reserved for the earth. They farm their land with the passionate tenderness of a lover cherishing his first mistress, or, as Archangias puts it baldly, 'ils forniqueraient avec leurs pièces de terre, tant ils les aiment'. They are godless, but retain a certain respect for ministers of religion and a deep reserve of superstition. This picture needed only to be extended and deepened for the Artaud family in *La Faute de l'abbé Mouret* to become the Fouan family in *La Terre*. Godard, the parish priest in the latter book, is as contemptuous of his flock as Archangias in the former; in rebuking Fouan for not marrying his son Buteau to Lise, who is with child by him, Godard is in exactly the same situation as Serge Mouret, who tried to persuade Bambousse to allow his daughter to marry her lover Fortuné; in both books the argument used to the priest is the same: 'Mais il y a un enfant! — Bien sûr . . . Seulement, il n'est pas encore fait, cet enfant. Est-ce qu'on sait? . . .'

The passionate cleaving to the earth, amounting to an erotic frenzy—something that was only hinted at in *La Faute*—is of primary importance in *La Terre* and gives the book its overpowering odour of sweat and manure. In different degrees, the lust for land runs in the veins of most of the main characters in *La Terre*.

It is an appetite which does not lessen with the years. The tragic patriarch Fouan is described as 'desséché et rapetissé dans un travail si dur, dans une passion de la terre si âpre que son corps se courbait, comme pour retourner à cette terre, violemment désirée et possédée' (*désirée et possédée*: Zola's vocabulary is deliberately ambiguous, here and elsewhere). The opening chapters tell how Fouan, too old now to till the soil, makes over his fields to his sons and daughter, in three lots, like Lear (the work-sheets of *La Terre* show that Zola was thinking of *King Lear* not only at this point but later in the book, when Fouan, who has no Cordelia among his children and no Edgar to keep him company, wanders homeless and hungry through a stormy night). To abandon his land is no small matter, though Fouan lacks the gift to express in words

la tristesse infinie, la rancune sourde, le déchirement de tout son corps, à se séparer de ces biens si chaudement convoités avant la mort de son père, cultivés plus tard avec un *acharnement de rut*, augmentés ensuite lopin à lopin, au prix de la plus sordide avarice. . . . *Il avait aimé la terre en femme qui tue et pour qui on assassine.* Ni épouse, ni enfants, ni personne, rien d'humain: la terre! Et voilà qu'il avait vieilli, qu'il devait *céder cette maîtresse* à ses fils, comme son père la lui avait cédée à lui-même, *enragé de son impuissance.*

Towards the end of his life, ill-treated by his children, friendless,

sinking slowly into idiocy, Fouan's last occupation, before his legs
fail him, is to revisit the fields that were once his, 'dans cette manie
des vieux passionnés que hantent leurs maîtresses d'autrefois'.
Zola derives this quasi-sexual obsession with the soil from the
peasant's historical origins. After the long era of serfdom 'la terre,
fécondée de son effort, passionnément aimée et désirée pendant
cette intimité chaude de chaque heure, comme la femme d'un autre
que l'on soigne, que l'on étreint et que l'on ne peut posséder; la
terre, après des siècles de ce tourment de concupiscence', had at
last, at the Revolution, become his own, 'sa chose, sa jouissance,
l'unique source de sa vie. Et ce désir séculaire, cette possession
sans cesse reculée, expliquait son amour pour son champ, sa
passion de la terre, du plus de terre possible, de la motte grasse,
qu'on touche, qu'on pèse au creux de la main.'

His love is a true infatuation, for the earth is insatiable yet never
contents her lovers. Not only Fouan but all the farmers know the
capriciousness of their paramour. A sudden hailstorm, lasting only
ten minutes, may strip the fruit-trees and the vines, and the peasant
can make only the futile gesture of throwing stones at the sky and
reviling the Deity in whom he has ceased to believe. The earth has
its martyrs: Palmyre, for instance, who after gathering hay in the
heat of noon is struck dead with sunstroke in the middle of a field
—'elle était allongée, la face au ciel, les bras en croix, comme
crucifiée sur cette terre, qui l'avait usée si vite à son dur labeur,
et qui la tuait'.

Palmyre is the most wretched of the bondservants of the earth.
Hourdequin, the gentleman-farmer, is the richest and most intelligent landowner in the district, yet the earth ruins and kills him
just as surely, if more gradually. His love of the earth is of a different
quality from Fouan's, for it has not been bequeathed to him by a
venerable line of *adscripti glebae*; rather, it was 'une passion sentimentale, intellectuelle presque, car il la sentait la mère commune,
qui lui avait donné sa vie, sa substance, et où il retournerait'. When
he inherited, as a young man, his father's estate (his father, a
townsman, had bought it during the Revolution, when the possessions of the nobles were being auctioned),

il l'avait aimée en amoureux, son amour s'était mûri, comme s'il l'eût
prise dès lors en légitime mariage, pour la féconder. Et cette tendresse ne
faisait que grandir, à mesure qu'il donnait son temps, son argent, sa vie
entière, ainsi qu'à une femme bonne et fertile, dont il excusait les ca-

prices, même les trahisons. Il s'emportait bien des fois, lorsqu'elle se montrait mauvaise, lorsque, trop sèche ou trop humide, elle mangeait les semences, sans rendre des moissons; puis, il doutait, il en arrivait à s'accuser de mâle impuissant ou maladroit: la faute en devait être à lui, s'il ne lui avait pas fait un enfant.

Always the same erotic imagery, elaborate, baroque, crowds to Zola's mind and flows from under his pen.

If there is one character in *La Terre* transported to the point of madness by this lust for the soil, for which 'land-hunger' is all too weak a term, it is Fouan's younger son Buteau. 'C'est chez lui surtout que j'étudie la passion de la terre', Zola noted before he started writing. 'Son amour n'est que le rut du mâle grisé par la terre.'[1] He has the characteristic sensual gesture of scooping up a handful of loam and holding it to his face, sniffing it and letting it trickle through his fingers. It is he who, at the carving up of his father's property, insists that every single field should be divided into three, rather than take his chance on the luck of the draw. Even so, exasperation at being given what he considers to be the worst share causes Buteau to refuse the land for a long while. When finally he accepts (some of the plots having increased in value because of the construction of a new road), his pride of ownership is ecstatic.

A aucune époque, quand il s'était loué chez les autres, il n'avait fouillé la terre d'un labeur si profond: elle était à lui, il voulait la pénétrer, la féconder jusqu'au ventre.[2] Le soir, il rentrait épuisé, avec sa charrue dont le soc luisait comme de l'argent. En mars, il hersa ses blés, en avril, ses avoines, multipliant les soins, se donnant tout entier. Lorsque les pièces ne demandaient plus de travail, il y retournait pour les voir, en amoureux.

Buteau's baffled fury at being compelled to surrender part of his holding to his sister-in-law Françoise when she marries is the wrath of a pasha compelled to surrender a favourite concubine to his overlord.

One character stands outside this circle of grimly covetous husbandmen: Jean Macquart. Of all the twenty novels, none is so perfunctorily linked as *La Terre* to the Second-Empire family

[1] B.N. MS. *Nouv. acq. fr.* 10328, fols. 484–5.
[2] Popular identification of plough with phallus and furrow with vulva reaches back into the depths of time—probably to the earliest agrarian civilizations; one word serves in several languages of South Asia to designate both phallus and spade. The primitivism of *La Terre* was attained quite effortlessly by Zola, who needed no special documentation to inspire him here.

chronicle which Zola had set out to write. Jean has a certain part to play in the story, but it could have been played by anyone else: the fact that he is the brother of Lisa Quenu and even, incredibly, Nana's uncle has no relevance to anything in *La Terre*. He is the man from outside, with his army service behind him, and his carpenter's trade. He takes his place in village life in much the same way as Étienne Lantier, another intruder, settles down with the miners; like Étienne again, he falls in love with a girl belonging to this endogamous community. Zola noticed the similarity, and was a little troubled by it. 'Ne pas le faire ressembler à Étienne', he wrote early in the *ébauche*, 'ne pas sans doute lui faire quitter son métier et en faire un paysan'; and again, thinking of Jean's love-affair with Françoise: 'cela ressemble un peu trop à Étienne et à Catherine.'[1] In the end he waived his scruples and let the similarities stand.

The gain was that, as in *Germinal*, he had a character to whom everything that is routine to the others is new and strange. Jean, while fully participating in the seasonal toil and in the loves and quarrels of the villagers, yet remains aware of the experiences he is undergoing, having known a different life; and Jean's awareness becomes ours. He had come to the land in a spirit of vague romantic anticipation. 'Il fut ravi d'abord, il goûta la campagne *que les paysans ne voient pas*, il la goûta à travers des restes de lectures sentimentales, des idées de simplicité, de vertu, de bonheur parfait. telles qu'on les trouve dans les petits contes moraux pour les enfants.' Ten years pass, he has married Françoise, the most country of country girls, but he still remains different from the other farm-workers if only in the pleasure that he takes in his work. 'Jamais il ne devait devenir un vrai paysan. Il n'était pas né dans ce sol, il restait l'ancien ouvrier des villes, le troupier qui avait fait la campagne d'Italie; et ce que les paysans ne voient pas, ne sentent pas, lui le voyait, le sentait, la grande paix triste de la plaine, le souffle puissant de la terre, sous le soleil et sous la pluie.' His love of the land is a poet's—Zola's, in fact—while theirs is visceral if not venereal; and this is why over these ten years he has gradually come to detest the peasantry among whom he had expected to make his home. 'Si la terre était calme, bonne à ceux qui l'aiment, les villages collés sur elle comme des nids de vermine, les insectes humains vivant de sa chair, suffisaient à la déshonorer et à en empoisonner l'approche.' Françoise, with his child in her

[1] B.N. MS. *Nouv. acq. fr.* 10328, fols. 405, 411.

womb, is killed in what passes as an accident. Later he discovers
the truth: that she had been raped by her brother-in-law, that her
own sister, in the ensuing fight, had thrown her on to the point of
a scythe. But Jean decides not to denounce his wife's murderers.
'De vrais loups, lâchés au travers de la plaine, si grande, si calme!
Non, non! c'était assez, ces bêtes dévorantes lui gâtaient la campagne! Pourquoi en faire traquer un couple, la femelle et le mâle,
lorsqu'on aurait dû détruire la bande entière. Il préférait partir.'
He leaves, then, not as Étienne did at the end of *Germinal*, hopefully, to continue the struggle in a new arena, but in despair and in
revulsion against the abominations practised by those who work on
the land he still loves as dearly as ever.

On the purely human plane, *La Terre* must be judged a tragedy
or even a double tragedy: for the fate of old Fouan is a good deal
more terrible than Jean's. But the total impression the work leaves
is quite different and, it may be, less depressing than, for instance,
Far from the Madding Crowd, even though Hardy's picture of rural
life is infinitely less harsh. Huysmans was not the only reader who
found that 'in spite of the placid cruelty of the book, . . . it is suf-
fused—the book, I mean—by an enormous gaiety'. Certain characters have a purely comic function, like M. and Mme Charles, who
have accumulated a tidy fortune running a brothel in Chartres, and
have retired to live in a comfortable house in the village where
everyone knows how they made their money and no one is so rude
as to refer to it. 'Un bon vieux grand-père à tabatière,' Zola wrote
in his preliminary notes, 'une grand'mère digne, à cornettes, une
fille blonde idéale, et les dessous, la matière dont on a fait la fortune. Raillerie terrible, et bon enfant.'[1] He did not notice, apparently, that he was repeating himself once again: in *Germinal*
too there had been an elderly, highly respectable couple, living in
retirement with a charming, fair-haired daughter. The parallel is
instructive: the Grégoires saw no harm in the fact that the dividends
that keep them in idleness are drawn from the bodily labour of the
miners, any more than the Charleses see any wrong in having
derived a handsome income all their lives from the bodily prostitution of the brothel inmates. It could hardly be more delicately
suggested that free-enterprise capitalism is a disorderly house.
But Zola's irony, as exercised in *Germinal*, was savage compared
with the indulgent mockery he permits himself in *La Terre*. The

[1] Ibid., fol. 469.

two grandparents, whose married daughter has taken over the establishment at Chartres, bring up their granddaughter with the greatest solicitude, and old M. Charles in particular flies into fearful rages whenever the crudity of the villagers' manners threatens to sully her innocence. But Élodie can evidently use her head, and has a fair measure of native cynicism. Her parents having died, she herself proposes she should 'take over the business', and the Charleses, surprised but delighted, agree, shedding a few sentimental tears: 'ils reconnaissaient le cri de la vocation.'

The other vehicle of comedy in the book is Buteau's elder brother Hyacinthe, a wastrel and a drunkard, who is highly contemptuous of the slow old ways of the countryside, having been unsettled, perhaps, by his army service in Algeria. Spoken of usually by an ironical sobriquet as 'Jésus-Christ' (one of the villagers in Médan bore this nickname, bestowed for a fancied resemblance to the figure in conventional pious representations), he prefers to sell his land rather than cultivate it, spending the proceeds on wild sprees; and he is capable, when in his cups, of defending this course with a mock-seriousness that leaves his brother gasping.

As the story proceeds, 'Jésus-Christ' gains in importance until he finally emerges as a comic creation not entirely unworthy of being placed beside Falstaff or Pantagruel. But the humour is not, in this case, ironical; it is, rather, as primitive as the very subject of *La Terre*. A taste for earthy ribaldry was something Zola shared with his master Flaubert, though Flaubert preferred for the most part to indulge it privately. There is, however, a short passage in *La Tentation de Saint Antoine* which foreshadows, and may have suggested, the comedy of Hyacinthe's phenomenal flatulence. It will be remembered that the vision of past gods vouchsafed to St. Antony culminates in the appearance of Jehovah. Immediately before, with deliberate irreverence, Flaubert introduces the god Crepitus, whose account of the honours he used to receive in pagan days is a burlesque parody of the vaunts of the other deities. 'I used to go my way, in company with the other necessities of life, causing no scandal . . . I was joyous, I made men laugh. And, contentedly expansive by reason of me, the guest exhaled all his mirth through the apertures of his body.' The whole passage is intentionally grotesque, but these lines, in which Flaubert insists on the innocently comic aspect of the act which Crepitus personifies, are enough to show the filiation of ideas between *La Tentation* and *La Terre*.

To quote many of the illustrations that Zola gives of the powers of his incorrigible Hyacinthe would be to risk conveying an incorrectly balanced impression of *La Terre*. One thing must be said, however: his feats are all quite legendary; and, as Rabelais knew when he made Pantagruel drown an army in his own water ('et y eut déluge particulier dix lieues à la ronde'), and Molière who, when an enema has to be administered to Pourceaugnac, has him pursued by a whole band of apothecaries armed with syringes, the only way to turn nastiness into art is by monumental exaggeration. Hyacinthe's crowning triumph is to drive off a bailiff's man by imitation rifle-fire, the valley re-echoing to his 'cannonade'. The scene, as Zola records it, is effective as comedy and offensive only to bailiff's men and our latter-day Leavisites. Whether it squares with the realist aesthetic is another question.

It became almost a dogma of nineteenth-century literary criticism that Zola, by such scenes as these, had irrevocably forsworn the realism of which he had made himself the prophet. Proust, in *Le Côté de Guermantes*, catches echoes of this *idée reçue* as it circulated in Parisian drawing-rooms in the nineties. 'But Zola is not a realist, madame', the Duchess of Guermantes informs the Princess of Parma. 'Your Highness should notice how he enlarges everything he touches. You will say that he touches only what . . . brings good luck! But he turns it into something immense; his dunghill is epic! He is the Homer of the cesspit! *Il n'a pas assez de majuscules pour écrire le mot de Cambronne.*' The Duchess had probably not reflected that this unprintable word (or its equivalents and near relations) are acceptable in Zola precisely because they are, as it were, 'written in capitals'.

The exaggeration of reality for comic effect is met with in several of Zola's works before *La Terre*. The tremendous goose, which is the *pièce de résistance* of the banquet Gervaise gives on her name-day, is of dimensions which recall the monster turkey with which the Cratchits regale themselves at the end of *A Christmas Carol*; here, if nowhere else in *L'Assommoir*, Zola succeeded in catching something of Dickens's genial good humour. The same exaggeration is the source of a comic episode in *Pot-Bouille* which, however, is far removed from anything the English novelist would have attempted. A working woman, a tenant of one of the upper rooms of the house, is evicted by the concierge who is scandalized by her advanced pregnancy. Zola makes great play with this swollen belly

which 'semblait jeter son ombre sur la propreté froide de la cour,
et jusque sur les faux marbres et les zincs dorés du vestibule . . .
emplissait l'immeuble d'une chose déshonnête, dont les murs
gardaient un malaise'. In *Germinal* there is a similar use of comic
enlargement in La Mouquette's enormous and frequently dis-
played backside, and in the vast silhouette of the widow Désir,
'une forte mère de cinquante ans, d'une rotondité de tonneau, mais
d'une telle verdeur, qu'elle avait encore six amoureux, un pour
chaque jour de la semaine, disait-elle, et les six à la fois le dimanche.'
But these flights of fancy, in *L'Assommoir*, *Pot-Bouille*, and *Germinal*, are episodic. In *La Terre* Zola appears to have made no
attempt to check the urge to magnify reality.

By its subject, the book lent itself much more than preceding
novels to this kind of excess. It is not a dark, obstructed work: the
confined spaces of apartment-house and mine give way to a broad
plateau, swept by the wind and cleansed by the rain. The descriptive passages are one of the beauties of *La Terre*: the snow-covered
landscape at the end of the first part of the book, when the Beauce
stretches out under the stars 'toute blanche, plate et immobile
comme une mer de glace'; the hay-making scenes and the grape-
picking scenes, and the corn-harvest in August, when the plain is
'une mer blonde, incendiée, qui semblait refléter le flamboiement
de l'air, une mer roulant sa houle de feu, au moindre souffle'; then,
after the harvest, the yellowness of the parched, stripped soil.
Although the Beauce is situated well inland, Zola habitually uses
sea images in these descriptions, as though the immensity of the
plain needed to be further expanded by a comparison with the still
vaster ocean. He notes in Françoise 'ce coup d'œil de matelot,
cette vue longue des gens de plaine, exercée aux détails, capable de
reconnaître un homme ou une bête, dans la petite tache remuante
de leur silhouette'; and Fouan, his sons and son-in-law 'avaient la
face rêveuse et figée, la songerie des matelots, qui vivent seuls, par
les grands espaces'. In bad weather Buteau looks out on his farm
'de même que le pêcheur regarde de sa falaise la mer démontée, où
la tempête lui vole son pain'. It is hard to resist quoting, at least in
part, the magnificent piece of prose-poetry which goes before these
words, at the beginning of part III of *La Terre*. It is still sometimes
said that Zola was no stylist;[1] a fragment such as this, isolated

---

[1] 'He was certainly not a "stylist" in the accepted sense. I can think of many
passages in the *Rougon-Macquart* that I have read with pleasure and interest,

though it is, suggests that the judgement may have been too hastily arrived at:

C'était l'époque où la Beauce est belle de sa jeunesse, ainsi vêtue de printemps, unie et fraîche à l'œil, en sa monotonie. Les tiges grandirent encore, et ce fut la mer, la mer des céréales, roulante, profonde, sans bornes. Le matin, par les beaux temps, un brouillard rose s'envolait. A mesure que montait le soleil, dans l'air limpide, une brise soufflait par grandes haleines régulières, creusant les champs d'une houle, qui partait de l'horizon, se prolongeait, allait mourir à l'autre bout. Un vacillement pâlissait les teintes, des moires de vieil or couraient le long des blés, les avoines bleuissaient, tandis que les seigles frémissants avaient des reflets violâtres. Continuellement, une ondulation succédait à une autre, l'éternel flux battait sous le vent du large. Quand le soir tombait, des façades lointaines, vivement éclairées, étaient comme des voiles blanches, des clochers émergeant plantaient des mâts, derrière des plis de terrain. Il faisait froid, les ténèbres élargissaient cette sensation humide et murmurante de pleine mer, un bois lointain s'évanouissait, pareil à la tache perdue d'un continent.

Horrifying and yet strangely peaceful, ribald and grave in turns, *La Terre* is a kind of *summa* of all that is characteristic of Zola. For this alone, perhaps, it has a better claim to be styled epic than any other of his works. In contrast with *L'Assommoir* and particularly with *Pot-Bouille*, nearly all the action of *La Terre* takes place out of doors. The freshness of the air blows away much of what would otherwise be sordid in Zola's invention. The apposite note is given at the outset, in the account of the covering of Françoise's cow. Françoise, aged fourteen, assists the bull, and Jean, who has been watching her, 'ne songeait pas à lâcher une de ces gaillardises, dont les garçons de la ferme s'égayaient avec les filles qui amenaient ainsi leurs vaches. Cette gamine semblait trouver ça tellement simple et nécessaire, qu'il n'y avait vraiment pas de quoi rire, honnêtement. C'était la nature.'

It is no mere play of words to say that the leader of the naturalists was almost bound to make a masterpiece out of the subject of Nature herself. He may have missed something, and distorted much, in the picture he presented of the countryman and countrywoman; but he grasped, and conveys inimitably, what distinguishes the lives of those who plough and plant from the lives of all other

but I cannot recall a single instance in which pleasure was derived from the formal beauty of the style. Zola's prose is almost devoid of rhythm or music; it has no magic and no grace.' M. Turnell, *The Art of French Fiction*, p. 180.

men—a certain patterning of experience, according to which everything repeats itself after a given cycle of events. The first chapter
of the book opens with a description of Jean sowing the grain, and
returns to the same description at the close of the chapter. The
regular, circular sweep of the sower's right arm is also the last image
that the book evokes, on the very last page. Thus, the structure
itself and the fabric of the novel are fashioned according to the
great circle of Nietzsche's eternal return.[1] Each year wanes, but
the springtime will always come and Nature will renew herself.
Each man ages and dies, but his own seed has engendered successors, and his body, committed to the earth, nourishes the green
plants which ensure bread for his posterity. Man dies not.

L'homme, mon enfant, a été créé à l'image de la terre. Et, comme la
mère commune, nous sommes éternels : les feuilles vertes renaissent
chaque année des feuilles sèches ; moi, je renais en toi, et toi, tu renaîtras
dans tes enfants. Je te dis cela pour que la vieillesse ne t'effraye pas,
pour que tu saches mourir en paix, comme meurt cette verdure, qui
repoussera de ses propres germes au printemps prochain.

This passage comes not from *La Terre* but from a story published as early as 1866:[2] the vision which gives unity and colouring
to the later masterpiece had been vouchsafed to Zola over twenty
years before. The germs of life are indestructible: the body does
not die but dissolves to give the soil new vigour. The idea is implicit
in the last chapter of *La Terre*, which records, among other things,
the burial of old Fouan. In front of Jean stretches the broad plain
with the sowers in the fields, and at his feet is the open grave with
the coffin at the bottom, 'le cercueil, diminué encore, avec son
étroit couvercle de sapin, de la couleur blonde du blé; et des
mottes grasses coulaient, le recouvraient à moitié, il ne voyait plus
qu'une tache pâle, comme une poignée de ce blé que les camarades,
là-bas, jetaient aux sillons'.

For a materialist there is no other kind of survival: heaven is but
a touching dream. It is here, no doubt, that one should seek the
link between *La Terre* and the next novel in the series, *Le Rêve*.
The leap from the earthiness of the one to the exalted transcen-
dentalism of the other disconcerted his critics. His admirers re-

---

[1] Cf. L. E. Harvey, 'The cycle myth in *La Terre* of Zola', *Philological Quarterly*, vol. xxxviii (1959), pp. 89–95.
[2] 'Les Quatre Journées de Jean Gourdon', serialized in *L'Illustration*, 15 Dec.
1866–16 Feb. 1867 and reprinted in *Nouveaux Contes à Ninon*.

garded it as evidence of the magnificent versatility of a powerful artist;[1] his detractors grumbled, with Anatole France, that they preferred Zola on all fours to Zola with wings.[2] But Zola, who believed in surprising his public, had foreseen and intended this bafflement. 'Je voudrais faire un livre qu'on n'attende pas de moi': these are the opening words of the *ébauche* of *Le Rêve*.

The dream referred to in the title is not, however, the dream of life eternal, or any such specifically religious vision, even though the novel, set in a cathedral city, with a pious heroine surrounded exclusively by godly elders and devout companions, exudes the odour of sanctity as powerfully as its predecessor had the effluvium of animal manure. Angélique's dream is 'ce que rêvent les jeunes filles', the dream of Cinderella and the Sleeping Beauty and the beggar-maid who became King Cophetua's consort.

> Oh! ce que je voudrais, ce que je voudrais, ce serait d'épouser un prince.... Un prince que je n'aurais jamais vu, qui viendrait un soir, au jour tombant, me prendre par la main et m'emmener dans un palais.... Et ce que je voudrais, ce serait qu'il fût très beau, très riche, oh! le plus beau, le plus riche que la terre eût jamais porté! Des chevaux que j'entendrais hennir sous mes fenêtres, des pierreries dont le flot ruissellerait sur mes genoux, de l'or, une pluie, un déluge d'or, qui tomberait de mes deux mains, dès que je les ouvrirais....

An unaccountably ambitious and immodest dream, one might think, to haunt the imagination of a fifteen-year-old foundling brought up in cloistered quiet by an ageing couple of God-fearing embroiderers, who have 'done their duty' by her, teaching her gently but firmly the virtues of obedience and humility. But Angélique is the disowned daughter of Sidonie Rougon; her 'dream' is but a girlish version of the lust for wealth that fills her uncle Saccard the financier and the lust for power that drives her other uncle Eugène Rougon the politician. Discussing the book before its publication, Zola foretold that it would concern 'un rejet sauvage des Rougon-Macquart transplanté dans un milieu mystique et soumis à une culture spéciale qui le modifiera. Là est l'expérience scientifique. . . .'[3] But, as in all Zola's 'experiments', the outcome depends on the whim of the experimenter. In this case he decided that heaven (the Catholic environment) should triumph

---

[1] Cf. P. Ginisty, *L'Année littéraire 1888*, p. 369.

[2] France, *La Vie littéraire*, 2ᵉ série, p. 285.

[3] Letter to Van Santen Kolff, 22 Jan. 1888.

over what he calls, in his fourth chapter, 'le démon du mal héréditaire'. Had he so willed it, Angélique might equally well have rebelled against her environment and demonstrated, in her avid yearning for the pleasures of this world, a contrary proposition—as did another foundling, 'fille du diable', brought up similarly by another church-going, childless couple, who was to make her appearance the year after the publication of *Le Rêve*, in Stryienski's transcription of Stendhal's posthumous novel *Lamiel*.

For Zola Christianity meant one thing above all: a belief in the miraculous. Short of hypocrisy, only the sick, the mentally debilitated, and the over-imaginative could adhere to a religious faith. The invalids of *Lourdes* will belong to the first category; Marthe Mouret and her son Serge had illustrated the second (in *La Conquête de Plassans* and *La Faute de l'abbé Mouret*); Angélique is the example he found of the third group. Her favourite reading in childhood had been *The Golden Legend*; she has grown up in close familiarity with the miraculous, 'et elle le créait elle-même, à son insu: il naissait de son imagination échauffée de fables, des désirs inconscients de sa puberté; il s'élargissait de tout ce qu'elle ignorait, s'évoquait de l'inconnu qui était en elle et dans les choses. Tout venait d'elle pour retourner à elle, l'homme créait Dieu pour sauver l'homme, il n'y avait que le rêve.' Zola's respect for the gift of imagination, rather than any respect for religion, saves the novel from cynicism—except in so far as it may be cynical to suggest that the Christian ideals of purity of heart and humility have no place outside fairy-tales. For *Le Rêve* is describable only as a fairy-tale. Angélique's dream-prince arrives, handsome and rich as she had wished, respectful, adoring, and nobly born; and she marries him, but not before a 'miracle' is performed in her favour, the double miracle of her own recovery from almost mortal illness, and of the change of heart in the bishop, Félicien's stern and haughty father, converted from absolute prohibition of the match to acquiescence in it. Zola rejected only the traditional ending of fairy-stories: the 'poor girl' does not 'live happily ever after' with her prince; instead, Angélique dies suddenly, immediately after the marriage ceremony, with the first kiss she exchanges with her husband.

Le Rêve was the sixteenth novel of the cycle. The two last volumes had been earmarked for special purposes a long time back: the one as the war-novel, the other as a 'scientific' epilogue to the entire series. Nearing the end of his undertaking, Zola realized that he was going to be hard put to it to find room for all the themes he hoped to introduce. As he admitted to the Dutch journalist Van Santen Kolff, who in these years was the recipient of so many interesting confidences, 'je vais être obligé de tasser un peu les uns sur les autres les mondes qu'il me reste à étudier. C'est pourquoi, dans le cadre d'une étude sur les chemins de fer, je viens de réunir et le monde judiciaire et le monde du crime.' *La Bête humaine*, half finished when these words were written, has, as he implies here, three themes; but crime and the law are complementary, while neither has any obvious connexion with railways. Zola had in effect fused two separate novels. The earliest programmes, dating back to the late sixties, include a murder-mystery, 'un roman de cours d'assise [*sic*], comme je comprends ce genre abandonné aux fournisseurs brevetés de feuilletons, et dont on pourrait tirer une œuvre hautement littéraire et profondément émouvante';[1] defined elsewhere, more succinctly, as 'un roman judiciaire (Province)'.[2] Nowhere is there any mention of a novel about railways. In the schedule of projected works he gave to Xau in 1880 the 'étude sur les chemins de fer' has its place, but is listed quite separately from the 'roman judiciaire'; the one is to have Étienne Lantier as hero, the other 'l'un des fils de Lantier'. A statement to Goncourt on 16 January 1884 implies again that the railway novel was not to be the murder novel; rather, the crime theme was apparently then regarded as due for incorporation in the novel about 'une grève dans un pays de mine', i.e. *Germinal*.[3]

The railway no doubt imposed itself as an indispensable 'monde à étudier' when Zola began to develop his characteristic vein, the novel dealing with some specific aspect of the industrial age. The steam-engine was not merely the critical invention of the century, as the flying-machine was to be of the next; it was also, as Dickens discovered years before Zola, a colourful and occasionally horrific entity in its own right. The train sweeping through the countryside, plunging into tunnels, shrieking, rattling, and snorting, gave

---

[1] B.N. MS. *Nouv. acq. fr.* 10303, fol. 63.
[2] Ibid., 10345, fol. 23. On fol. 129 there is another list of novels to be written, which includes 'le roman judiciaire. — Etienne Lantier'. Underneath, Zola wrote in smaller characters: 'chemin de fer'. This seems to have been a later addition; the list bears other signs of having been periodically revised and kept up to date but it is, of course, impossible to say when the various additions were made.
[3] Cf. above, p. 191.

an impression, when it first came on the scene, of truly diabolic power. What is now rapidly becoming a glamorous anachronism was then a portentous innovation, the violent impact of which is nicely conveyed in Verlaine's lines:

> Une odeur de charbon qui brûle et d'eau qui bout,
> Tout le bruit que feraient mille chaînes au bout
> Desquelles hurleraient mille géants qu'on fouette;
> Et tout à coup des cris prolongés de chouette.[1]

It is clear, then, that the railway theme, with its overtones of infernal ferocity, was less inappropriate than might seem to a novel about crime. The first decision Zola made was to solder environment to action by having a murder take place in a railway compartment. There had been a number of precedents. Two incidents in particular came to his mind: one which occurred under the Second Empire, when a judge called Poinsot was found murdered on the Basle–Paris express; and one which took place much more recently when Barrême, prefect of the department of Eure, was killed in a railway carriage and thrown out of the window. In neither instance were the murderers brought to book.[2]

The two themes connected also on a more symbolic level. Of the two murders in La Bête humaine that are investigated by the judicial authorities, the first is a crime passionnel. Roubaud, discovering that Grandmorin had had relations with his wife before their marriage, forces her to be his accomplice in murdering the older man in the express from Paris to Le Havre; with luck favouring them, Roubaud and Séverine, though suspected, are not charged. Later, Séverine becomes the mistress of Jacques Lantier, an engine-driver who happened to be the only witness of the crime, imperfectly glimpsed from a field as the train thundered by at speed. Unknown to anyone, Jacques is a homicidal maniac, and eventually murders Séverine. The two crimes are thus committed, the first in obedience to the most primitive of passions, jealousy, and the second in response to an almost bestial, uncontrollable impulse to kill. The two criminals are employees of the railway (Roubaud is assistant stationmaster at Le Havre) and the scene of their crimes is the train itself, and an abandoned house situated a

---

[1] La Bonne Chanson (1870).
[2] See M. Kanes, Zola's 'La Bête humaine', pp. 22–23, and E. M. Grant, 'L'Affaire Poinsot-Jud, Mérimée et Zola', Cahiers naturalistes, no. 23 (1963), pp. 313–15.

few yards away from the line. The juxtaposition and mingling of the ultra-modern with the atavistic was deliberate, as the *ébauche* shows:

Montrer toujours le flot de voyageurs circulant, . . . le commerce accru, . . . l'échange des idées, la transformation des nations, le mélange des races, la marche vers une unification universelle. Les idées qui se répandent, se pénètrent et s'unifient. Et sur ce fond, sur ce roulement mécanique des trains, sur ce résultat social et intellectuel, montrer le statu quo du sentiment, la sauvagerie qui est au fond de l'homme, par mon drame mystérieux et poignant. Voilà l'hérédité de la bête, le mari qui se rue sur l'amant, Étienne qui tue par atavisme : le lointain homme primitif. . . .[1]

Had his design been effectively carried out, *La Bête humaine* would have been the modern tragedy *par excellence*, for Zola seems to have had a premonition here of what would prove the greatest problem facing the coming century: the survival, in a race superbly equipped technically, of instincts and impulses which a new pattern of living has rendered obsolete and inappropriate. But his main theme became overgrown by a tangle of collateral ones, some of which derived from new and temporary preoccupations, while others expressed dormant anxieties which a very recent personal experience had reawakened in all their old intensity.

Jacques Lantier, the homicidal maniac, is an almost attractive character, intelligent, capable, with principles of decency. After he and Séverine have become lovers, the idea that they should rid themselves of Roubaud occurs to both of them simultaneously, by a kind of thought-transmission.[2] But Jacques discovers that he cannot commit murder out of a rational consideration of where the balance of his interests lies. Séverine arms him with the very knife with which Grandmorin had been stabbed to death, and they ambush Roubaud one evening in the marshalling yards, lurking together in the pool of black shadow cast by a heap of coal. Roubaud, who is doing his nightly tour of inspection, walks straight towards Jacques.

[1] B.N. MS. *Nouv. acq. fr.* 10274, fols. 399–400. The hero of *La Bête humaine* is here called Étienne, Zola's original intention having been that the book should be a pendant to *Germinal*, with the same character cast for the leading role in both novels. This proved inconvenient; see Kanes's discussion of the circumstances, op. cit., pp. 19–21, 31–34.

[2] End of chap. viii. There is a striking similarity here between the dialogue of Jacques and Séverine and the conversation (*Thérèse Raquin*, chap. ix) in which the idea of murdering Camille is first mooted between Laurent and Thérèse.

Trente mètres à peine les séparaient, chaque pas diminuait la distance, régulièrement, rythmé comme par le balancier inexorable du destin. Encore vingt pas, encore dix pas : il l'aurait devant lui, il lèverait le bras de cette façon, lui planterait le couteau dans la gorge, en tirant de droite à gauche, pour étouffer le cri. Les secondes lui semblaient interminables, un tel flot de pensées traversait le vide de son crâne, que la mesure du temps en était abolie. Toutes les raisons qui le déterminaient défilèrent une fois de plus, il revit nettement le meurtre, les causes et les conséquences. Encore cinq pas. Sa résolution, tendue à se rompre, restait inébranlable. Il voulait tuer, il savait pourquoi il tuerait.

Mais, à deux pas, à un pas, ce fut une débâcle. Tout croula en lui, d'un coup. Non, non! il ne tuerait pas, il ne pouvait tuer ainsi cet homme sans défense. Le raisonnement ne ferait jamais le meurtre, il fallait l'instinct de mordre, le saut qui jette sur la proie, la faim ou la passion qui la déchire. Qu'importait si la conscience n'était faite que des idées transmises par une lente hérédité de justice! Il ne se sentait pas le droit de tuer, et il avait beau faire, il n'arrivait pas à se persuader qu'il pouvait le prendre.

Roubaud, tranquillement, passa. . . .

Jacques is capable of only one sort of murder, at the prompting not of his reason and will but of the atavistic blood-lust, and his victim must be a woman. Séverine plans another attempt on her husband's life; this time it is to take place in the isolated house by the railway line which she has inherited from Grandmorin. Roubaud will be decoyed here, and Jacques will have an unshakeable alibi. In the event, just before Roubaud arrives, Jacques is overwhelmed by the desire to plunge the knife into Séverine. The temptation had visited him on two previous occasions, but he had resisted it; this time the impulse is too strong.

Originally Zola had intended that Jacques should confess to this murder in open court, 'une scène grande pour finir. . . . Étienne se levant, faisant l'aveu de son crime, pourquoi il a tué, comment.' Between these lines in the *ébauche*, Zola wrote the words: 'réponse au roman russe.'[1] The question of the 'right to murder' was, in fact, a topical one at the time *La Bête humaine* was being written, since it had been raised in a number of Dostoevsky's novels, *Crime and Punishment*, *The Possessed*, *The Brothers Karamazov*, all of which had been translated into French for the first time between 1884 and 1888.[2] Ivan Karamazov, representing the modern irre-

---

[1] B.N. MS. *Nouv. acq. fr.* 10274, fol. 411.

[2] Kanes (op. cit., pp. 32–33) discusses *Crime and Punishment* in relation to

ligious intellectual, is faced with the dilemma that if moral com-
mandments have no divine sanction, then 'everything is permitted',
and the right to murder established. Zola was bound to question
the logic of this. The doctrine that atheism leads to crime revolted
his good sense. *La Bête humaine* was in a measure designed to
illustrate a more acceptable explanation of the psychology of the
murderer, by invoking a theory of pathological alienation brought
about either through the pressure of a violent emotion (Roubaud)
or through psychological degeneration due to vitiated heredity
(Jacques).

Reports in the French press of the nauseating exploits of 'Jack
the Ripper' in the East End of London in 1888 may have influenced Zola's invention, to a minor degree in providing him with the
name of his central character, and to a major degree in suggesting
that it should be invariably young women that Jacques is tempted
to murder, and that he always wants to use a knife on them.[1] At the
same time one cannot overlook the recurrence in *La Bête humaine*
of the obsessive associational complex between sexual love and
death, never far below the surface in Zola's writing, but never so
strongly marked since *Thérèse Raquin*, written over twenty years
earlier. One of the most haunting scenes he ever composed occurs
in chapter viii, where Séverine first admits to Jacques that Roubaud
and she had murdered Grandmorin, describes how it was done,
and recalls how she had felt during the act. Séverine and Jacques
are spending their first night together, in the very room in which
Roubaud had forced her to confess that she had, as a girl, submitted to Grandmorin's senile embraces, and, after beating her
with his fists and dragging her across the room by the hair, had
frightened her into writing the note to Grandmorin which was to
make him catch the train to Le Havre that they were due to travel
on. The associations the room has for Séverine act on her irresis-
tibly.[2] 'Une excitation croissante se dégageait des choses, les
souvenirs la débordaient, jamais encore elle n'avait éprouvé un si

---

La Bête humaine but does not mention *The Brothers Karamazov*, the memory
of which would have been fresher in Zola's mind (the translation was published
in 1888).

   [1] In addition, just as no one suspects Jacques of the murder of Séverine, so
similarly the 'harlot killer of Whitechapel' escaped detection in spite of the most
strenuous efforts of the police.

   [2] As do the furnishings of the hotel room in Mantes on Madeleine Férat, when
she spends a night there with her husband, having slept in it earlier with her
lover (*Madeleine Férat*, chaps. ix, x).

cuisant besoin de tout dire à son amant, de se livrer toute. Elle en avait comme le désir physique, qu'elle ne distinguait plus de son désir sensuel.... Comme cela serait bon, de ne plus rien cacher, de se fondre en lui tout entière!' And just as Thérèse had satisfied the longing to make confession, by pouring the details of her crime into Mme Raquin's unwilling ear, so Séverine whispers her story to Jacques as they lie in bed together, with the snow muffling all sounds outside, and no light in the room save what is afforded by the red reflection of the stove on the ceiling, 'une tache ronde et sanglante' which in Séverine's imagination 's'élargissait, semblait s'étendre comme une tache de sang'. After the first wave of sexual desire has been satisfied, she starts:

— Oui, nous l'avons tué.

Le frisson du désir se perdait dans un autre frisson de mort, revenu en elle. C'était, comme au fond de toute volupté, une agonie qui recommençait.

Jacques listens avidly. This temptation that he has been fighting off all his life, she has yielded to it, she has broken the taboo, she is initiated. When she has told him the whole story, he still presses her for more details. The last question he asks is: what did she feel when she was holding the victim's feet and the knife was driven in? was it . . . pleasure? Séverine cannot answer. 'C'est affreux, ça vous emporte, oh! si loin, si loin! J'ai plus vécu dans cette minute-là que dans toute ma vie passée.' This is precisely the reply she might have given if her lover had asked her to describe her sensations during a sexual orgasm. Jacques is indulging in the very voyeurism of homicide; and now, his curiosity as satisfied as it can be, having finished with the orgiastic contemplation of a reconstructed killing, he makes love to her again. 'Ils se possédèrent, *retrouvant l'amour au fond de la mort*, dans la même volupté douloureuse des bêtes qui s'éventrent pendant le rut.'

When one is interpreting Zola's novels one may safely assume that the more excessive the scene, the more likely it is to figure a private drama. The essential element in the passage just summarized stands out clearly: a tormenting guilt-feeling drowned in a tide of sensual pleasure. It is necessary now to turn to Zola's biography, for the gloomy, overheated mood in which he composed *La Bête humaine* has its explanation in the turn his life was taking in the autumn of 1888 and the winter of 1889.

XIII

NEW LIFE, NEW HOPE

IT happens, rarely enough, that a few lines in one or other of the *ébauches* of Zola's novels provide unexceptionable evidence of the state of mind he was in at the time, about which his biographers would otherwise have no knowledge. When he sat down at his desk one morning in early November 1887, to work out the plot of the novel subsequently entitled *Le Rêve*, he sketched out first of all a scenario, discarded in the event, which bears, however, a striking resemblance to the plot of *Le Docteur Pascal* written some years later. It was to turn on the love of a man of forty for his ward, aged sixteen. The girl would not at first have been unresponsive, but later would turn to a lover nearer her own age, with whom the elder man would suffer her to depart.

The dramatic interest of the story was to arise from the guardian's struggles to dominate the inclination he felt for his young ward. He was to be what we should now probably call a psychical research worker, 'spirite ou alchimiste moderne, ou s'occupant de suggestion'. As he writes, Zola warms to the idea. 'Cela serait bon, symbolique, le montrerait d'abord acharné à l'inconnu, laissant passer la jeunesse, n'aimant pas, à la recherche d'une chimère.' Then, in the manuscript, comes the revealing parenthesis: 'Moi, le travail, la littérature qui a mangé ma vie, et le bouleversement, la crise, le besoin d'être aimé. . . .' The final jottings, before he pushed the papers away and fell into an idle daydream, are hardly less significant: 'Cette enfant bouleversant tout l'inconnu, étant la revanche de la réalité, de l'amour. Après toutes les recherches, il n'y a que la femme, c'est l'aveu. Des sanglots, une vie manquée. La vieillesse qui arrive, plus d'amour possible, le corps qui s'en va.'[1]

This is a repetition of Sandoz's outburst: 'une seconde vie, qui me la donnera!', but with a specificity Zola had not dared risk in *L'Œuvre*. At forty-seven he saw that he must hurry if he was ever to know the reality that he had imagined and so passionately evoked

---

[1] B.N. MS. *Nouv. acq. fr.* 10323, fols. 221–2.

in *La Fortune des Rougon*, in *La Faute de l'abbé Mouret*, in *La Joie de vivre*, and in *L'Œuvre*, and that he was to picture once more in *Le Rêve*: the ineffable tenderness of a young girl's love.

At the big, childless house at Médan there was a suitable establishment of domestics, which the following spring was reinforced by a young seamstress, the child of a miller who had remarried after the girl's mother had died in her infancy. Jeanne Rozerot was at this time just turned twenty. Photographs show her as having an attractive, but not a strikingly handsome face, with large, surprised eyes and a pouting mouth; she possessed, too, that 'heavy crown of black hair' which Zola had given to Miette Chantegreil in the first novel of the *Rougon-Macquart* series, and which had been worn, as one or two surviving portraits show, by his mother when she was young. These early photographs of Jeanne were taken not at Médan but at Royan, near Bordeaux, where the Zolas joined the Charpentiers for their summer holidays that year. Mme Zola, unwell again, stayed mostly indoors, while the novelist, who had finished *Le Rêve*, went for walks, sometimes in Jeanne's company. She left their employment when they moved back to Paris; but, submissive, uncounselled, breathlessly uplifted, perhaps, by the homage of one of the leading citizens of France, Jeanne allowed him to instal her in a flat. By the end of the year they were lovers.[1]

Secrecy was essential, but Zola, who had early adopted the motto: 'Je viens vivre tout haut', accommodated himself with difficulty to the necessity. Within the first six weeks of the liaison he made a half-confession to Edmond de Goncourt; the diarist, interested but uncomprehending, noted the conversation.

At one point I talk to Zola about how our lives have been dedicated to the written word to a degree of self-abnegation perhaps unequalled by anyone, at any period; and we admit to one another that we have been real martyrs to literature, perhaps a couple of infernal dupes. And Zola confesses to me that this year, when he is verging on his fifties, he has been experiencing a recrudescence of life, a desire for physical enjoyment; and, breaking off suddenly, he bursts out with the words: 'My wife isn't by—let me tell you, I can't see a young girl walking past like

---

[1] Armand Lanoux has deduced the date on which the liaison began from the message on a greetings card, dated 11 Dec. 1898, which Zola sent to Jeanne from England on what was presumably the tenth anniversary. See 'Un amour d'Émile Zola', *Le Figaro littéraire*, 24 Apr. 1954.

that one over there without asking myself: Isn't that perhaps more worth while than a book?'

A couple of letters he wrote six weeks after this exchange with Goncourt show something of the mingled restlessness, exultation, and remorse that the clandestine adventure was causing him. Van Santen Kolff had been surprised that his letters were not being answered, and Zola apologized: 'je traverse une crise, la crise de la cinquantaine sans doute. . . . Il est des semaines, des mois, où il y a tempête dans mon être, tempête de désirs et de regrets. Le mieux alors serait de dormir.' On the same day (6 March 1889) he wrote to Huysmans: 'Moi, je continue de flâner. Toute ma paresse refoulée s'épanouit. Je n'aurais qu'un tout petit effort à faire pour ne plus toucher une plume. C'est une crise d'indifférence, un sentiment de l'à quoi bon, que je suis curieusement en moi. Je vais pourtant me remettre à mon roman, sans enthousiasme, je vous assure, mais parce qu'il le faut.'

The novel referred to here is of course La Bête humaine, on which in all likelihood some preliminary work had been done before Jeanne became his mistress. By chance or by design, he had lodged Jeanne in the rue Saint-Lazare, very close to the terminal which was to be the setting for some of the scenes in the new novel; others were to take place in Le Havre, and he visited the town in mid-March, accompanied by Mlle Rozerot. On 5 May, his documentation completed, his plans all drawn up, he began writing the book.

The confined and airless atmosphere of La Bête humaine is one of its most striking features: almost every scene of importance takes place behind closed doors, some in the room overlooking the Gare Saint-Lazare which is used by Roubaud and Séverine and later by Séverine and Jacques; some in the cottage of the level-crossing keeper or in the close-curtained house where Séverine is finally done to death; others again in the chambers in which Denizet, the investigating magistrate, conducts his inquiries.[1] Equally noteworthy is the secrecy cloaking every movement. Not one character but has something to hide from the others: Roubaud and Séverine their murder of Grandmorin; Phasie, the whereabouts of her secret hoard; Misard, that he is stealthily poisoning

---

[1] This aspect of La Bête humaine has been excellently analysed by Antoinette Jagmetti in the chapter entitled 'l'Espace' of her monograph 'La Bête humaine' d'Émile Zola, étude de stylistique critique (1955).

Phasie so as to lay his hands on it; Jacques, that he is a congenital murderer; even the Minister of Justice withholds from the investigating magistrate a vital piece of evidence which would pin the responsibility for Grandmorin's murder on the real culprits. And, of course, with secrecy goes guilt: consciousness of guilt imposes secrecy and secrecy fosters the sense of guilt.

This is the sense in which *La Bête humaine* transposes the emotional and moral 'crisis' through which the author, by his own admission, was passing at the time. Séverine's longing to confess was Zola's too, though Zola had no murder to confess to, unless it were the murder of his principles—principles founded, however, on the imaginary fear of parental reprobation of which, having nerved himself to defy it, he had at last ridded himself, though it took him time to realize this. Eventually he took his closest friends into his confidence; these friends told others, and so the story circulated. His wife remained in ignorance until November 1891, when she came across Jeanne's letters which he had unwisely been preserving. Alexandrine's reactions were predictably impetuous to a degree that frightened Zola, who wired Céard to call at Jeanne's flat and remove her and the children to a place of safety. In the long run this violence was less damaging than cold resentment might have been. With Alexandrine nothing was driven below ground, her fury spent itself painfully at the time, but was followed by calmer acquiescence.

Meanwhile the birth of his two children had helped to dispel the uneasiness that Zola had felt in contracting an extra-marital tie. Perhaps he persuaded himself in the long run, and especially when he saw what charming, intelligent, and good-looking children they were, that what he had really desired was not a young mistress but the joys of paternity. Most of his biographers have adopted uncritically the convenient thesis that Zola had been for many years dissatisfied and disappointed that no children had been born of his marriage.[1] There is no sound evidence in support of the suggestion, but equally, it is difficult to disprove it. An avowal of Mme Zola's, put on record by Louis de Robert shortly after her death in 1925,

[1] M. Batilliat, *Émile Zola* (1931), p. 49; A. Zévaès, *Zola* (1945), p. 283; J. Castelnau, *Zola* (1946), p. 91; etc. E. Lepelletier, who appears to have put the story into circulation, went so far as to argue (*Émile Zola, sa vie, son œuvre* (1904), p. 414) that Zola began to long for a family when he became converted to social optimism and in consequence of this conversion; but this is putting the paternal cart before the political horse.

seems to take us as near to the truth as we can get. 'Why,' she ex-
claimed, 'did he not want children by me when it was still possible
for me to give him children?'[1] The implication of this remark
would be that at no period of his life was Zola anxious for an heir;
but that, so long as his financial resources remained straitened (and
Mme Zola was close on forty before a steady and adequate income
became assured), for motives of prudence he preferred not to found
a family. Had his wife been ten years younger than he, instead of a
year older, Zola might have become the father of legitimate children; but it is possible that even so he would have made Jeanne
his mistress.

At all events, the prospect of becoming a father effectively
banished the uneasiness he had felt at an earlier stage in the association. His private correspondence, during the eighth month of
Jeanne's first pregnancy, reflects a mood of joyous optimism and
vitality. 'Je traverse une période très saine de travail, je me porte
admirablement bien, et je me retrouve comme à vingt ans, lorsque
je voulais manger les montagnes', he wrote to his publisher (27
August 1889). The novel that followed La Bête humaine, which
was L'Argent, was not put in train until after the birth of Denise.
The subject—high finance, bulls and bears, booms and crashes—
would not appear to lend itself to gaiety; nevertheless Zola laid it
down, on the first page of the ébauche, that the keynote of the new
work would be optimism. 'Je voudrais, dans ce roman, ne pas conclure au dégoût de la vie (pessimisme). La vie telle qu'elle est, mais
acceptée, malgré tout, pour l'amour d'elle-même, dans sa force.
Ce que je voudrais, en somme, [ce serait] qu'il sortît de toute ma
série des Rougon-Macquart.' The book would be about money, but
would not corroborate the dismal proverb that money is the root of
all evil. 'Montrer que l'argent est devenu pour beaucoup la dignité
de la vie; il rend libre, et est l'hygiène, la propreté, la santé,
presque l'intelligence.'[2]

L'Argent can be grouped, in Zola's series, with Germinal and
Au Bonheur des Dames and may even be regarded as their essential
complement: the book in which he demonstrated and justified the
mechanism thanks to which productive enterprise and the distri-
butive trades function under laissez-faire capitalism. This mechanism was inhuman but ultimately beneficent; adopting the concepts

[1] L. de Robert, De Loti à Proust, souvenirs et confidences (1928), p. 140.
[2] B.N. MS. Nouv. acq. fr. 10268, fols. 378, 379.

of Ricardian economics, Zola argued that the play of the free market was the only valid way of increasing efficiency and so, in the long run, wealth. Hennebeau had faced the workers' delegates, who had come to protest against a cut in wages, with an adaptation of Ricardo's theory of the 'iron law': the mining company, he said, 'n'est pas la maîtresse du salaire, elle obéit à la concurrence, sous peine de ruine. Prenez-vous-en aux faits, et non à elle.' Octave Mouret, the creator of the emporium which had stolen their trade from all the small shopkeepers in the neighbourhood, uses the same argument to Denise, after he has reduced her uncle Baudu, the haberdasher, to bankruptcy: Baudu was doomed from the start and he, Mouret, was only an agent of the power—the power of economic progress—which has crushed him. Mouret needed to ruin Baudu in order to make the profits which permitted him to enlarge and brighten his premises, satisfy the shoppers with a wider and cheaper range of goods, and house his employees more comfortably. The greater well-being of the many is secured at the cost of pauperizing a few: 'il fallait ce fumier de misère à la santé du Paris de demain. . . . Toute révolution voulait des martyrs, on ne marchait en avant que sur des morts.' In *L'Argent*, the same convenient theory is invoked, this time to justify the havoc periodically caused by violent fluctuations of the money-market.

L'Argent was also, to a limited extent, a sequel to *La Curée*, since the central character was Saccard, reappearing in a somewhat different guise,[1] this time with the object of wresting control of the stock-market from Gundermann, the Jewish millionaire. The imagery of warfare is freely used to dramatize this rather unfamiliar type of conflict; Saccard had his 'Marengo', his 'Austerlitz', and at the end his 'Waterloo'. The shadow of Balzac falls over these pages, but unlike Balzac, Zola had to rely on his imagination to picture the workings of a speculator's mind. There is something strained and artificial in his insistence on the Napoleonic parallel. His ponderously inert material refused to come to life, as he seems to have realized when the book was two-thirds written. Goncourt, with a sardonic smile on his lips, heard him grumbling to Charpentier that 'money's all right as a motive, but when you have

[1] The difficulties that Zola experienced in attaching the new Saccard to the old are discussed in R. B. Grant, 'The problem of Zola's character-creation in *L'Argent*', *Kentucky Foreign Language Quarterly*, vol. viii (1961), pp. 58–65.

Money taken as a study in itself . . . there's altogether too much money.'

Considered, however, purely as a reflection of the change in the author's attitude to life in his fiftieth year, *L'Argent* is a work of some interest. His new optimism gave him the figure of Mme Caroline, who is extraneous to the action but provides a vital commentary on it. The character-sketch he made of her in his preliminary notes includes a sentence which betrays the subjective source of this creation.

Elle *est l'espoir*. Elle aime vivre, pourquoi? elle n'en sait rien. Elle est comme l'humanité qui vit dans la misère affreuse, ragaillardie par la jeunesse de chaque génération. Dès qu'elle est dans la rue, au soleil, elle se reprend à aimer, à espérer, à être heureuse. L'âge qui vient n'a même pas de prise sur elle. *Me mettre tout entier là-dedans*.[1]

Mme Caroline is a woman of thirty-six. She has been married to a millionaire brewer whose brutalities drove her to leave him. She is well read and widely travelled. Her past has brought her experience without embittering her. She becomes first Saccard's housekeeper, and later his mistress, without feeling any love for him, or anything but an unwilling admiration for his energy and boldness. She discovers him to be foolhardy, faithless, and utterly lacking in moral principles. When the collapse comes she sees with her own eyes some of the domestic calamities that Saccard's bankruptcy causes: a shareholder who had invested his daughter's dowry sees the girl take to the streets; a young stockbroker, with a wife and children, is driven to suicide; a noblewoman and her daughter are reduced to beggary. Yet when she visits Saccard in his cell she is won over once more by the indomitable spirit of the man whose strength and audacity she finds unimpaired. Saccard is a force of nature; like life itself, he is vulgar, ruthless, even criminal, but at least he is dynamic, and this is why Caroline finds it impossible to withhold her confidence in him.

Saccard is the high priest of the religion of gambling which he expounds to Caroline one day when he has to overcome her scruples about illegal speculative operations.

—Oui, la spéculation. Pourquoi ce mot vous fait-il peur? . . . Mais la spéculation, c'est l'appât même de la vie, c'est l'éternel désir qui force à

---

[1] B.N. MS. *Nouv. acq. fr.* 10268, fols. 405–6. The last sentence in italics is not underlined in the original.

lutter et à vivre.... Voyons, pensez-vous que sans ... comment dirai-je ?
sans la luxure, on ferait beaucoup d'enfants ? ... Sur cent enfants qu'on
manque de faire, il arrive qu'on en fabrique un à peine. C'est l'excès qui
amène le nécessaire, n'est-cepas ?
—Certes, répondit-elle, gênée.
—Eh bien! sans la spéculation, on ne ferait pas d'affaires, ma chère
amie.

A hundred enterprises founder, but one succeeds; a hundred ships
set sail, and one returns with a cargo of gold. 'Ah! dame!' concludes
Saccard, 'il y a beaucoup de saletés inutiles, mais certainement le
monde finirait sans elles.'

This baroque apology for commercial adventure is not a mean-
ingless conceit on Saccard's lips. Several times in *L'Argent* Zola
harks back to the analogy between the conception of a child and
the fruition of financial schemes; he uses it for the last time in the
very last paragraph of the book:

Et Mme Caroline était gaie malgré tout avec son visage toujours
jeune, sous sa couronne de cheveux blancs, comme si elle se fût rajeunie
à chaque avril, dans la vieillesse de la terre. Et, au souvenir de honte que
lui causait sa liaison avec Saccard, elle songeait à l'effroyable ordure
dont on a également sali l'amour. Pourquoi donc faire porter à l'argent
la peine des saletés et des crimes dont il est la cause ? L'amour est-il
moins souillé, lui qui crée la vie ?

It is still the puritanical author of *Pot-Bouille* who writes these
words, the ascetic for whom love had been a disgraceful carnal
appetite; but now a new dignity ennobles the physical spasm. Love
is no longer just the copulative instinct, it is seen also to be the
genetic, the indispensable creative urge. Zola's attitude to sex has
switched abruptly away from the moody abhorrence that had
characterized it from *La Confession de Claude* down to *La Terre*
and *La Bête humaine*; although he has still a long way to go before
emerging into the serene paganism of *Fécondité* and *Travail*, he is
clearly orientated in that direction.

If *L'Argent* was intended to stand apart from the other novels
of the series by reason of its new-found optimism, *La Débâcle* was
to be distinguished just as much by its unprecedented didacticism.
Didacticism, however, is often a drawback only in the eyes of
posterity, and *La Débâcle* proved to be the best-seller of Zola's
lifetime. It was translated on the day of publication into every
language reckoned to be civilized—even English, being the first

Zola novel that a British firm dared to bring out after Henry Vizetelly had been dragged through the Central Criminal Court for his issue of *The Soil* in 1888. A powerful reason for the acceptability of *La Débâcle* among the Victorians was that, by way of an exception, Zola had forborne to 'Paint the mortal shame of nature with the living hues of art' as Alfred Lord Tennyson had so prettily chided him with doing everywhere else.[1] Zola's soldiers, even the Prussians, are sometimes brutal but oddly never licentious.

On the Continent, however, *La Débâcle* appealed chiefly as the fullest and most vivid account of the Franco-Prussian War that any novelist had till then produced.[2] The events Zola recounted were recent enough to be still topical and had, in one way or another, affected almost all his readers, at any rate in France. These are, of course, the factors which as a general rule tend to make war-novels popular twenty or thirty years after any war. But there were particular reasons for the attention given to *La Débâcle*. Defeat had stimulated public interest in the army and in army life, while in the late eighties the activities of the Boulangist group had whipped it up to fever pitch. Between 1887 and 1889 barrack-room novels like Henry Fèvre's *Au port d'armes*, Lucien Descaves's *Misères du sabre* and *Sous-offs*, and Abel Hermant's *Cavalier Miserey* testified by their successes (often scandalous) to the country-wide preoccupation with the state of the armed forces. *La Débâcle* did not merely provide ex-soldiers and civilians in the fighting zones with the opportunity to relive their experiences; its pages were conned by patriots of all political hues eager to trace the causes of the national humiliation. Zola obliged them out of all measure: he not only explained why the war was lost, but showed them how the next one could be won.

It was his first real *roman à thèse*. In several other works he had indicated what he supposed were the causes of the particular social disorder or calamity that formed his theme. Never before had he so

[1] *Locksley Hall, Sixty Years After* (1886).

[2] Its most notable predecessor was perhaps Hector Malot's *Souvenirs d'un blessé* (1872) of which Zola had written, in his review in *La Cloche*, 23 May 1872: 'l'écrivain fait passer sur nous un vent de mort, l'effarement de la défaite, l'écroulement de tout un monde, la débandade du troupeau humain.' But Zola had rightly criticized Malot for his occasional 'bavardage': 'Le romancier s'est trop pressé, et je crains bien que, comme tant d'autres, il n'ait fourni des documents au lieu d'arrêter en traits précis et voulus la triste épopée de nos désastres.'

unequivocally pointed, within the text of a novel, to the cure for the ill. The treatment he advised was deduced directly from his diagnosis of the malady. France had fallen behind the times; Prussia had applied the lessons of modern science in organizing her national life, and in order to rise from her shame, France would have to follow suit. 'Malheur à qui s'arrête dans l'effort continu des nations', proclaims one of the characters in *La Débâcle*. 'La victoire est à ceux qui marchent à l'avant-garde, aux plus savants, aux plus sains, aux plus forts!' The message was a variation on the old battle-cry: 'La République sera naturaliste ou elle ne sera pas', where 'naturalist' is to be understood as meaning 'imbued with the scientific spirit'. Through the Alsatian Weiss, who here and elsewhere speaks for him, Zola lists among the fatal weaknesses of the French defence 'l'armée, certes d'une admirable bravoure de race, toute chargée des lauriers de Crimée et d'Italie, seulement gâtée par le remplacement à prix d'argent, laissée dans sa routine de l'école d'Afrique, trop certaine de la victoire pour tenter le grand effort de la science nouvelle'. Zola was not far from accusing the Imperial army of *romanticism*. He personifies this army, with its good and bad qualities, in the quixotic lieutenant Rochas, whose one answer to all Weiss's warnings is to recall the splendid victories of the past, when it needed but 'one corporal and four men, and immense armies bit the dust'. Zola granted Rochas an honourable death on the field of battle, a death which was intended to symbolize the smashing of the legend that the lieutenant incorporated.

Rochas is not the only character in *La Débâcle* who simply personifies an attitude of mind: they all do. This simple, allegorical univalence is symptomatic of Zola's decreasing interest in the novel as a form of art reflecting human complexity. He informed Robert Sherard (who reported the statement in his preface to the English translation, *The Downfall*) that 'each character represents one *état d'âme psychologique* of the France of the day'.[1] Jean Macquart, according to the *ébauche*, was to epitomize 'l'âme même de la France, équilibrée et brave, bien qu'attachée au sol', while his companion and fellow soldier, Maurice Levasseur, was to stand for the brilliant and decadent element in the nation, responsible for the catastrophe. 'Dans le symbole, il serait l'autre partie de la France: les fautes, la tête en l'air, l'égoïsme vaniteux.'[2] For Maurice,

---

[1] Quoted in Helen Rufener, *Biography of a War-Novel: Zola's 'La Débâcle'* p. 26. [2] B.N. MS. *Nouv. acq. fr.* 10286, fols. 11, 12.

Sedan is the stroke of Nemesis, and he can see no future into which he will be able to fit. Jean, however, takes a more level view of the defeat.

On avait reçu une sacrée roulée, ça c'était certain! Mais on n'était pas tous morts peut-être, il en restait, et ceux-là suffiraient bien à rebâtir la maison, s'ils étaient de bons bougres, travaillant dur, ne buvant pas ce qu'ils gagnaient. Dans une famille, lorsqu'on prend de la peine et qu'on met de côté, on parvient toujours à se tirer d'affaire, au milieu des pires malchances. Même il n'est pas mauvais, parfois, de recevoir une bonne gifle: ça fait réfléchir. Et, mon Dieu! si c'était vrai qu'on avait quelque part de la pourriture, des membres gâtés, eh bien! ça valait mieux de les voir par terre, abattus d'un coup de hache, que d'en crever comme d'un choléra.

Readers of *War and Peace* will remember the conversations that Pierre Bezukhov—another slightly deranged intellectual—has with the peasant Platon Karataev when both are prisoners of war. Whether Zola was imitating Tolstoy here or not is hard to say: it is known that Turgenev sent him a copy of *War and Peace* when a French translation was made in 1879, but positive evidence that he read it is lacking.[1]

After the battle the two friends are separated, Maurice returning to Paris while Jean remains in the north, recovering from a wound. When he can get up again he rejoins the regular army; Maurice, meanwhile, has taken up arms with the Communards. By an unlucky chance Jean shoots his friend across a barricade during the street-fighting of 21–28 May 1871. As he lies dying, Maurice realizes that he is one of the 'membres gâtés' of whom Jean had spoken, and which Jean has now struck off. 'C'était la partie saine de la France, la raisonnable, la pondérée, la paysanne, celle qui était restée le plus près de la terre, qui supprimait la partie folle, exaspérée, gâtée par l'Empire, détraquée de rêveries et de jouissances.' The burning of Paris during the struggle is seen as a sacrificial fire, 'la nation crucifiée expiait ses fautes et allait renaître'. In spite of the death of Maurice, the vision of a nation about to be reborn gives Zola a hopeful note on which to end his novel, and it becomes clear that his whole purpose has been to lead up to this climax. On the last page he gives Jean's reflections as he looks out over the smoking city.

Il lui sembla, dans cette lente tombée du jour, au-dessus de cette cité

[1] See my *Russian Novel in France*, p. 20.

en flammes, qu'une aurore déjà se levait. Par delà la fournaise, hurlante encore, la vivace espérance renaissait, au fond du grand ciel calme, d'une limpidité souveraine. C'était le rajeunissement certain de l'éternelle nature, de l'éternelle humanité, le renouveau promis à qui espère et travaille, l'arbre qui jette une nouvelle tige puissante, quand on en a coupé la branche pourrie, dont la sève empoisonnée jaunissait les feuilles.

One may hazard the guess that the themes of rebirth, rejuvenation, and renewal would not have been worked into the story of the events of 1870 and 1871 but for the heightened sense of the value and joy of life that Zola owed to Jeanne Rozerot. It might not perhaps be altogether wrong, either, to see in Zola's recent parenthood the source of the unprecedented didacticism of *La Débâcle*. The status of father is commonly felt to carry with it that of educator; and besides, having children gave him a concern for the future of France such as had never filled him to the same extent before. It went on growing as his children grew. One wonders whether the history of the Dreyfus Affair would have been quite the same if Jeanne had not borne him Denise and Jacques.

In the spring of 1892 only one more book remained to be written for the twenty-volume cycle to be complete. For years Zola had been looking forward to the moment when he would set his hand to this final novel, not only because it would mark the completion of the whole crushing undertaking, but because of the intrinsic interest he hoped it would have for those who had followed the fortunes of the Rougon-Macquarts from the beginning. Shortly after finishing *La Bête humaine*, he told Goncourt about his plans for *L'Argent* and *La Débâcle*, and added: 'Au fond le livre qui me parle, qui a un charme pour moi, c'est le dernier . . .'; and later, having started on it, he spoke of it to the diarist as the book which would give to the whole series the effect of 'l'anneau du serpent qui se mord la queue'. An English journalist extracted in an interview some more concrete reasons for his contentment. *Le Docteur Pascal* was to be above all, Zola told him, an apology for the rest of the series.

It amuses me . . . because in it I am able to defend myself against all the accusations that have been brought against me. . . . People, especially abroad, have accused me of being a pornographer. This I shall refute through Pascal. It has been said that all my characters are rascals—people of bad lives. Pascal will explain that this is not so. Zola has been charged with a lack of tender-heartedness. Pascal will show that this is not so.[1]

It would be difficult to state more unequivocally that Pascal's words and thoughts were to be understood as Zola's words and thoughts. The pseudonym 'M. Pascal' which Zola adopted in 1898 when he was hiding from French government agents at the Grosvenor Hotel, London, was transparent to anyone acquainted with his writings: Vizetelly persuaded him to change it at his next move.[2] With the exception of Sandoz in *L'Œuvre*, he never created a character more specifically charged with the function of expressing his own ideas. Sandoz gives us Zola's philosophy of art; Pascal his philosophy of life. For Pascal is the naturalist pure and unalloyed: *l'homme-nature*, his creator defined him. 'Le docteur Pascal n'avait qu'une croyance, la croyance à la vie. La vie était l'unique manifestation divine. La vie, c'était Dieu, le grand moteur, l'âme de l'univers.' In passage after passage like this one, Zola's own optimistic pantheism is glowingly expressed by his hero. After her uncle's death Clotilde mentally recapitulates the 'message' of his life's work.

Tout se résumait dans la foi ardente en la vie. Comme il le disait, il fallait marcher avec la vie qui marchait toujours. Aucune halte n'était à espérer, aucune paix dans l'immobilité de l'ignorance, aucun soulagement dans les retours en arrière. Il fallait avoir l'esprit ferme, la modestie de se dire que la seule récompense de la vie est de l'avoir vécue bravement, en accomplissant la tâche qu'elle impose. Alors, le mal n'était plus qu'un accident encore inexpliqué, l'humanité apparaissait, de très haut, comme un immense mécanisme en fonction, travaillant au perpétuel devenir. Pourquoi l'ouvrier qui disparaissait, ayant terminé sa journée, aurait-il maudit l'œuvre, parce qu'il ne pouvait en voir ni en juger la fin? Même, s'il ne devait pas y avoir de fin, pourquoi ne pas goûter la joie de l'action, l'air vif de la marche, la douceur du sommeil après une longue fatigue? Les enfants continueront la besogne des pères, ils ne naissent et on ne les aime que pour cela, pour cette tâche de la vie qu'on leur transmet, qu'ils transmettront à leur tour. Et il n'y avait plus, dès ce moment, que la résignation vaillante au grand labeur commun, sans la révolte du moi qui exige un bonheur à lui, absolu.

---

[1] Sherard, *Émile Zola*, pp. 251–2.
[2] It is possible, however, that Zola was remembering Jules Vallès, who had written several letters to him from London in 1876–7 using the cover-name M. Pascal: see A. Zévaès, 'Une correspondance Zola–Vallès', *Commune*, no. 53 (1938), pp. 553–63.

The essence of this morality is abnegation: the renunciation of personal happiness, personal achievement, even personal knowledge and understanding, in favour of social betterment and the pursuit of scientific truth which can only be a communal enterprise. An austere doctrine and not to everyone's tastes. The 'philosophy' is only one aspect of the novel. Equally prominent is the sentimental side. In *Le Docteur Pascal* Zola dramatized his last love as he had dramatized his first in *La Confession de Claude*. The book carried two dedications. The first was printed on the front page: the public might read that 'this novel which is the summary and conclusion of my whole work' was written for his wife and in memory of his mother. The copy he sent to Jeanne Rozerot was inscribed on the title-page: 'To my darling Jeanne— to my Clotilde who has given me the royal banquet of her youth', etc.[1] The equation Clotilde=Jeanne is thus as valid as the equation Pascal=Zola.

In particular, the history of Pascal's love for Clotilde can be easily taken to be a transcription of Zola's for Jeanne. It was for a long time thought that the *ébauche* of *Le Docteur Pascal* would afford final proof of this reasonable surmise. But the document was not among the manuscripts Mme Zola donated to the Bibliothèque Nationale. Instead, she either gave it away or sold it, and it passed through various hands before being finally acquired by the Swiss collector, M. Martin Bodmer. Now that it is available for consultation, it proves to contain no revelations, and only a single direct reference, brief but poignant, to Zola's personal drama, at the bottom of the 17th folio, from which Mme Zola could easily have snipped it off had she been so minded. The interest of the manuscript lies elsewhere. It is evident that the novelist was by no means sure whether he should allow his hero to consummate his passion for the girl he was to fall in love with (who was originally not to be his niece Clotilde, but a friend of hers), and that he was even more doubtful about whether a child should be born of this liaison: 'Ça m'a l'air petit de finir la série sur cet enfant à naître.' He decided finally in favour of such an ending: 'Une série sur l'hérédité ne peut finir que sur une naissance.' But these very hesitations, and the way in which they were resolved simply in order to give greater symbolic point to the story, suggest that *Le*

[1] A photographic reproduction of this page is given in Zévaès's biography of Zola.

Docteur Pascal was at any rate not envisaged as being a public confession of his idyll with Jeanne and its fruitful culmination.

At the same time, the autobiographical element is unmistakably there, emerging particularly, perhaps, in certain passages where Zola appears to have been remembering, to attribute it to Pascal, the stormy nostalgia for youth that had filled him a little before he met Jeanne.

... la jeunesse chez la femme, une jeune fille qui passait, le troublait, le jetait à un attendrissement profond. C'était même souvent en dehors de la personne, l'image seule de la jeunesse, l'odeur pure et l'éclat qui sortait d'elle, des yeux clairs, des lèvres saines, des joues fraîches, un cou délicat surtout, satiné et rond, ombré de cheveux follets sur la nuque; et la jeunesse lui apparaissait toujours fine et grande, divinement élancée en sa nudité tranquille. Ses regards suivaient l'apparition, son cœur se noyait d'un désir infini. Il n'y avait que la jeunesse de bonne et de désirable, elle était la fleur du monde, la seule beauté, la seule joie, le seul vrai bien, avec la santé, que la nature pouvait donner à l'être.

To compare such a passage as this, which is by no means the only one of its kind in *Le Docteur Pascal*, with certain descriptions in *Nana* of 'the golden beast', 'the libidinous monster of the Scriptures', is to realize the completeness of the revolution in Zola's attitude to sexual questions which an intervening personal experience had brought about.

Such a comparison will also help to measure the literary decline which this new idyllic strain precipitated. The heavy-footed satyr lusting after complaisant nymphs is a theme which might inspire a Mallarméan ode but is ruinous in a realist novel, at least when treated as Zola treated it. In *Le Docteur Pascal* all the tried principles by the application of which Zola had achieved integrated and lofty works of art are rejected: objectivity, irony, the adherence to logical determinism, the refusal to philosophize and to read a sermon into the study of human nature. The last novel of *Les Rougon-Macquart* makes a regrettably discordant coda.

It is not too much to say that it ends not only the 'Natural and Social History of a Family under the Second Empire' but also the period of Zola's specifically artistic production. If one reads on through the *Lourdes–Rome–Paris* trilogy, and if one still has the courage to trek through the 'deep desert sand' (the words are Henry James's) of the *Évangiles*, it can only be to mark the melancholy spectacle of an artist in gradual disintegration. In 'Madame

Sourdis', a short story published in 1880, Zola unwittingly predicted the whole history of the latter part of his career, with its steady loss of virility and vitality; and Gourmont epitomized it when he wrote, on Zola's death, that the ending of this life spelt no great loss to literature. 'M. Zola, for a long time, for more than ten years, had "given up writing"; he was engaged in mixing humanitarian mortar. Having given proof at least of powers of hard work and determination, he outlived himself in order, perhaps, to demonstrate that in art hard work and determination are nothing, and that the finished work is everything.'[1]

[1] *Epilogues, réflexions sur la vie*, 3ᵉ séric (1905), p. 97.

XIV

THE THREE CITIES

WHEN, in the year of *Nana*, Paul Alexis was collecting information for his biography of Zola, one of the questions he asked his friend was what he planned to do when the twenty volumes of his novel-cycle were all completed. Zola gave him a perplexed look through his pince-nez. 'Après? mon ami, après? je ferai peut-être autre chose, quelque chose de tout différent. . . . De l'histoire par exemple; oui, quelque chose comme une Histoire générale de la Littérature française. . . . Ou des contes pour les petits enfants. . . . Ou peut-être rien. . . . Je serai si vieux! je me reposerai.'

The *History of French Literature*, which in the event was never even started, might have been no less informative a book than Taine's *History of English Literature*, and would probably have had the same limitations. He spoke about the project again a year or two later, in conversation with Edmond de Goncourt, and this time his purpose becomes plainer: the History was to be a hobby to occupy him during his years of retirement, when, the Rougon-Macquart books finished, his life of active production had ended: 'ce serait pour moi un prétexte de cesser d'être en communication avec le public, de me retirer de la littérature sans le dire . . . je voudrais être tranquille . . . oui, je voudrais être tranquille.' However, it must be remembered that, at the time he expressed these longings, Zola was traversing the phase of discouragement that followed the collapse of his hopes of a rapid and overwhelming victory for naturalism, and coincided with the cessation of his active campaign for the new school. It was probably about the same time that he confided to M. G. Conrad his longing to leave France altogether, once his history of the Rougon-Macquart family was completed, and seek out some 'lovely island in the blue sea; and there, sit quiet and bask in the warm sun and enjoy the spectacle of nature until my eyes close. Never to say another word or write another line, but sit quite still in contemplation.' But Zola did not belong to the select group of writers who, like Racine, had the wisdom to end their lives in studious meditation. In 1890 he was agreeing with Goncourt that to give up writing altogether would perhaps require more strength of mind than he possessed, and at the beginning of 1893, busy with the first chapters of *Le Docteur Pascal*, he told Van Santen Kolff that his one desire was to finish the book quickly and press on with *Lourdes*, for which he had already started accumulating material.

Lourdes had been on his itinerary when, in the summer of 1891, he undertook a tour of the south of France, accompanied by his wife. The little town was full of pilgrims, all the best rooms in the hotel where he had intended to stay were taken, and, moreover, it was pouring with rain. He made up his mind to leave the following morning.

Mais je suis un moment sorti . . . et la vue de ces malades, de ces marmiteux, de ces enfants mourants apportés devant la statue, de ces gens aplatis à terre dans le prosternement de la prière . . . la vue de cette ville de foi, née de l'hallucination de cette petite fille de quatorze ans . . . la vue de cette cité mystique en ce siècle de scepticisme . . . la vue de cette grotte, de ces défilés dans le paysage, de ces nuées de pèlerins de la Bretagne et de l'Anjou. . . .

Edmond de Goncourt, who was listening to this cataract of impressions (at dinner with the Zolas and the Charpentiers), remembered that at this point Mme Zola broke in to remark that the sight was indeed—colourful. Her husband took her up gruffly. 'Il ne s'agit pas de couleur . . . ici, c'est un remuement des âmes qu'il faut peindre. . . . Eh bien, oui, ce spectacle m'a empoigné de telle sorte que, parti pour Tarbes, j'ai passé deux nuits entières à écrire sur Lourdes.'

He may have been exaggerating or the diarist may have misunderstood him: he appears to have written no more than nine pages at Tarbes.[1] Headed 'Un roman sur Lourdes', they give no hint of a plot for a novel, but at least indicate a theme: 'montrer le besoin de surnaturel persistant chez l'homme . . . étudier et peindre ce duel incessant entre la science et le besoin du surnaturel.' His notes were not intended for immediate exploitation: Zola was still tied to completing *Les Rougon-Macquart* of which

[1] Bibliothèque d'Aix-en-Provence, MS. 1456, fols. 208–16. An analysis of the contents, with extracts, will be found in René Ternois, *Zola et son temps*, pp. 149–51.

the last two volumes were at the time unwritten. He kept very quiet about what was, after all, only a half-formed intention. The first visit to Lourdes had taken place ten months ago when Goncourt listened to Zola's account of it in July 1892. Shortly afterwards reporters got hold of the story and Zola's next visit to Lourdes, during the 'national pilgrimage' of 1892, was widely publicized. Press interviews that he gave while staying in the Pyrenean town aroused the curiosity of believers and freethinkers alike: Zola was thought to be on the verge of conversion.

He may well have been. The stresses of his private life at this juncture were violent enough to have cracked the hard shell of his rationalism as had, temporarily, the bereavements he had suffered in 1880. His second child Jacques was born while he was actually in the south with his wife; knowing he would be unable to be at Jeanne's side when her time came, he had arranged that Céard should insert a code message in the personal column of *Le Figaro* to give him the news. Alexandrine's discovery of her husband's infidelity occurred in November of the same year. Thereafter, for some weeks if not for months, Zola lived in perpetual dread not simply of a scandal but of some atrocious revenge his wife might take on her rival and her rival's infant children.[1] But in the interval between his second visit to Lourdes and the actual composition of the work, Zola had time to recover his grip on his former scepticism, and when *Lourdes* was published, it became immediately clear that one miracle the Grotto had not been able to bring about was the reclamation of this obdurate infidel.

As he phrased it in a letter to Van Santen Kolff, the argument of the new novel was that the cult of Our Lady of Lourdes amounted to a blasphemy against the scientific spirit, an attempt to 'turn back the clock'.

Mon point de départ est l'examen de cette tentative de foi aveugle, dans la lassitude de notre fin de siècle. Il y a réaction contre la science, et l'on essaye un retour à la croyance du dixième siècle, à cette croyance des petits enfants qui s'agenouillent et qui prient, sans examen. Imaginez

[1] 'Il a eu à craindre de se voir éclaboussé du sang de ses enfants, du sang de sa maîtresse, assassinés par sa femme, à craindre de se voir lui-même défiguré par cette furie, cette furie dont les hurlements le forçaient à se calfeutrer la nuit dans sa chambre, pour qu'on ne l'entendît pas' (*Journal des Goncourt*, vol. xx, pp. 225-6). Goncourt is reporting here Daudet's account of certain confidences Zola made him in 1895; obviously there may have been embroidering on the part of Zola himself, of Daudet, of Goncourt, or by all three.

les misérables malades que les médecins ont abandonnés: ils ne se résignent pas, ils en appellent à une puissance divine, ils l'implorent pour qu'elle les guérisse, contre les lois mêmes de la nature. Tel est l'appel au miracle. Et, en élargissant la chose, mon symbole est que l'humanité est une malade, aujourd'hui, que la science semble condamner et qui se jette dans la foi au miracle, par besoin de consolation.

The problem had already been raised in *Le Docteur Pascal,* where the distress of humanity robbed of its old faith by scientific scepticism had been poignantly expressed by Clotilde.

The conflict between new rationalism and old religion was growing exceptionally acute in France in the last ten or fifteen years of the century. Zola's old enemy Brunetière had led off the attack against the materialist agnosticism of the naturalists; it was he who invented the phrase that stung Zola like a hornet: 'la banqueroute de la science.' Brunetière's campaign had received invaluable support from Vogüé and his revelation (in 1886) of the *Christian* novelists of Russia, Tolstoy and Dostoevsky. The movement gathered strength, dividing as it went into independent groups of thinkers, some closely, some very loosely, attached to the Church, but all in full reaction against positivism. The most progressive school of thought was that headed by Paul Desjardins, whose pamphlet *Le Devoir présent* attracted much attention when it was published in 1891. Desjardins denounced the apologists of science (Zola was named here along with Taine, Renan, Darwin, and Leconte de Lisle) and preached a return to a Christianity purified of dogma. His 'Union pour l'Action morale', founded the following year, was the centre of the movement known as 'neo-Christianity' or 'lay religion'. At the other extreme were the modern mystics, the dabblers in occult sciences, whose influence on the symbolist movement in poetry is well known. Zola saw two of his disciples, Hennique with *Un Caractère* (1889) and Huysmans with *Là-bas* (1891), sacrifice to this new fashion.

In the political no less than in the literary and philosophical fields the positivists and anti-clericals were on the defensive. The young French Republic was being persistently and successfully wooed during those years by a most astute statesman, Leo XIII. Sovereign Pontiff since 1878, he worked steadily for a reconciliation between the Vatican and France, mainly in order to gain French support for his claims against the new Italian monarchy which had shorn the papacy of temporal power. In a series of encyclicals, culminating in *Rerum novarum* (1891), Leo XIII made his wishes gradually clear; and it was with his full approval that Cardinal Lavigerie, Archbishop of Algiers, made the startling gesture of toasting the Third Republic at an official dinner attended by the (anti-republican) officers of a French naval unit. French Catholics were invited to desert the monarchical cause and rally to the new régime; hence the name, *le ralliement*, given to the new policy the effect of which was to lessen the previous anti-clerical bias of domestic policy and to encourage the parties of the Right to forget their dissensions and unite to form a common front against the rising menace of socialism and free-thought.

Lourdes requires to be interpreted against the background of this thoroughpaced religious revival of the early nineties. The tone is far from being belligerently anti-clerical. Clearly, Zola gives no credit to tales of miraculous cures at Lourdes; but he does not suppose, as he did when he was writing on the same subject for *La Cloche* in 1872, that such tales were invariably invented by the unscrupulous to impose on the unthinking.[1] At the same time he felt under no obligation to dissemble the gross superstition of some of the pilgrims, or to draw a veil over the more disgraceful aspects of the thaumaturgical industry that had sprung up at Lourdes, the immense profits made by the Fathers of the Grotto from the sale of holy water, wax tapers, etc., the intrigues to prevent the pilgrims being diverted from the Grotto to other places like Bernadette's cottage, the whole business side of this renascence of faith.

The new novel was as expertly organized as any that Zola had written. His craftsmanship had appeared to be wavering in the last two books of the previous series, *La Débâcle* which is ill joined, *Le Docteur Pascal* which sags and straggles. For *Lourdes* he used that quinary construction which we have met once before in *Une Page d'amour*: the five-part division, with five chapters in each part.[2] The several parts correspond to successive days in a five-day

---

[1] See *La Cloche*, 6 June, 16 July, 29 Sept. 1872. Zola's usual weapon in these anti-religious pieces was light-hearted raillery. 'Vos miracles n'ont jamais servi à rien. C'est de la physique amusante. . . . Toujours des figures de saints qui pleurent le sang, toujours des jeunes filles soulevées de terre, des dames en robe bleue qui se promènent en l'air, des os qui ont des caprices de guérison, c'est vraiment banal à la longue, c'est fade.'

[2] Zola's liking for the fivefold division shows itself too in a type of writing he favoured, in which a particular subject or character was illustrated by five successive sketches. Examples may be found in *Le Capitaine Burle* ('Comment on meurt'), in *Madame Sourdis* ('Comment on se marie'), in *Une Campagne*

sojourn at Lourdes made by Pierre Froment, the hero of all three novels in the trilogy, and the father-to-be of the four sons whose life-stories were to occupy the later tetralogy, *Les Quatre Évangiles*.

The plan was well conceived if Zola's purpose was to give a picture of Lourdes as seen by a sceptical but passionately interested spectator at the time when the influx of pilgrims was at its height. The faithful whose cases he describes range from the humblest of working women to millionaires, and their presence at Lourdes is due to every kind of motive, from the purest to the most self-interested. Zola hit on the least artificial way of introducing them: they are all travelling on the same train as Pierre, most of them in the same compartment. But those who come to the shrine to be healed in body—the consumptives, the paralytics, the hysterics—engage the reader's attention less, perhaps, than the others who are neither diseased nor crippled, and who gather at Lourdes for more or less inadmissible reasons. On the whole they are less often disappointed than the real invalids. Mme Maze hopes that her piety will be rewarded by the return of her husband, who deserted her in the first year of their marriage; coincidence (or the Virgin) wills it that he tires of his mistress about the same time, and does in fact rejoin his wife. Mme Désagneaux is barren, and returns to Paris confident that she will not be childless much longer. Mme de Jonquière is a lady of rank who hopes that her daughter, who is travelling with her, will find at Lourdes a suitable husband; and the Virgin arranges the match. The mysteriously beautiful Mme Volmar makes a practice of spending three days at Lourdes every year, though each time she remains shut up in her hotel room, overcome, so she says, by fatigue. Pierre discovers her secret in the course of his stay. Her husband is brutal and jealous, her mother-in-law a tyrannous bigot. Once a year she escapes from their control, using this pilgrimage as a pretext, and is enabled to spend three nights with her lover. And finally there is the grotesque Vigneron family. M. Vigneron is a civil servant. He and his wife have one son, scrofulous, with an abscess on one leg and a necrosed backbone, who has not long to live. A fourth member of the family party is the boy's aunt, a rich woman with a weak heart; should she die first, their son will inherit her estate. The devout couple harbour two secret wishes: the first is that Vigneron's superior should

('Femmes honnêtes'), and in *Le Bien public*, 6 Aug. 1877, where he gives five sketches of typical priests in various social settings.

in some way be removed so that Vigneron may be promoted to his position; the second is that God may think fit to recall the aunt before the nephew. Both these desires are granted. When he opens the telegram announcing the death of his departmental head, Vigneron naïvely exclaims to his wife: 'Ah, ma bonne amie, la sainte Vierge est décidément avec moi.... Ce matin encore, je lui ai demandé mon avancement, et elle m'exauce!' The sudden death of the aunt from heart-failure leaves them trembling with exultation and gratitude to Our Lady of Lourdes.

Morte, mon Dieu! est-ce que c'était leur faute? est-ce qu'ils avaient réellement demandé cela à la sainte Vierge?... Ils n'avaient jamais voulu la mort de personne, ils étaient de braves gens, incapables d'une action mauvaise, aimant bien leur famille, pratiquant, se confessant, communiant comme tout le monde, sans ostentation.... La sainte Vierge n'était-elle pas la suprême sagesse, ne savait-elle pas mieux que nous-mêmes ce qu'elle devait faire pour le bonheur des vivants et des morts?

It must be admitted that Zola was occasionally a little heavy-handed in his use of irony.

This medley of characters makes the book interesting but is not sufficient to give it artistic cohesion. There is certainly less variety in the character range of a masterpiece like *L'Assommoir*, but *L'Assommoir* is a masterpiece and *Lourdes* is not. It is not difficult to see why. Lourdes, the city, is the only unifying point in the book; it is the vast torch round which these moths of a score of different species circle and in which some of them are consumed. Now a novel may have—and usually does have—one or several specific geographical settings; but if the author relies on this setting to give him his subject, the novel will fail to satisfy, for a novel is bound to have movement of some kind, be it only the ponderous and almost imperceptible drift of *War and Peace* or *L'Éducation sentimentale* or *A la recherche du temps perdu*. *Lourdes* is a static, stagnant work; what action it has is clogged and paralysed by the proliferating descriptions and disputations that envelop it. This is why one closes the book with the odd impression of having listened to a single brief anecdote told by the hour.

The action is really played inside the mind of Pierre Froment. The presence in the novel of a doubting priest had not been envisaged in the first *ébauche*, composed in September 1892. Only when Zola returned to his planning, in July 1893, did he decide to include a character whose attitude to Lourdes would undergo the same gradual transformation from hostility and incredulity to understanding and indulgence as had his.

Il faudrait un homme qui représentât la libre pensée, le libre examen, la foi au seul progrès par la science, qui fût contre la superstition... qui jugeât que l'expérience du christianisme croule et qu'il faut autre chose, mais il ne sait pas quoi. Il irait à Lourdes pour voir, pour se renseigner. ... Il y va, monté contre ces momeries, presque avec colère. Il faudrait, pour qu'il évoluât, qu'il fût touché d'abord, puis qu'à la fin il sentît le besoin d'autre chose.[1]

When he eventually decided to make the hero of *Lourdes* a priest, he obviously could not keep in all respects this character of a susceptible free-thinker. He made Pierre Froment a young man originally ordained in compliance with his mother's wish. A sincerely devout woman, she had brought him up to regard his father, killed shortly after his birth by an explosion in his laboratory, as a victim of divine wrath. Pierre realized the truth about him only when his mother died and he went through his papers; then he was illuminated by the intuition of his father's noble thirst for knowledge, his integrity, and his humanity. This revelation causes Pierre to wonder whether the pursuit of scientific truth may not be a worthier aim in life than the meditation of religious mysteries to which he has committed himself perhaps too hastily. His purpose in coming to Lourdes is to discover the truth about Bernadette Soubirous, the shepherdess whose visions in 1858 led to the discovery of the wonder-working spring in the grotto, and to arrive at a conclusion about the authenticity of the supernatural cures that are allegedly performed there. The part of his being that has been bequeathed to him by his mother yearns to find at Lourdes evidence to shore up his tottering faith; while the rational clear-sightedness inherited from his father makes his ultimate disbelief a foregone conclusion.

Most of the book, when Zola is not engaged in following the fortunes of his numerous minor characters, is taken up with this conflict between reason and faith in Pierre's mind, and with the scenes he witnesses that sway him one way or another. Huysmans succeeded brilliantly in using such an abstract altercation as the subject of a number of his later novels; but this was because Huysmans had experienced it in himself. Zola could use only what

[1] Bibliothèque d'Aix, MS. 1455, fols. 72–73. Quoted by Ternois, op. cit., p. 287.

intuition he possessed and what sympathy he could muster; but neither his intuitions nor his sympathies were strong enough to infuse real drama into Pierre's struggle with his intellectual doubts. It is too obvious that Zola preferred to have him a doubter, and was planning from the very start to lead him away from the superstitious practices with which Christianity had become contaminated, to a new religion—one which would promise its adherents an earthly, not merely a heavenly, paradise: socialism, in other words.

Lourdes was not, in the first instance, intended to have a sequel, but by the time he settled down to write it Zola had decided that it would be only the first novel in a trilogy to be called *Les Trois Villes*. The second, *Rome*, shows Pierre still unwilling to abandon spiritual solutions in favour of political ones. In the interval of time between the action of the two books he has devised his own 'new religion', a variant on Desjardins's 'neo-Christianity' considered particularly in its social implications. He writes a book, *La Rome nouvelle*, for which he draws on his experiences in the Paris slums, and in which he calls on the Pope to put himself at the head of the new socialist movements in Europe. To defend his book against the charges of impiety and the threat of condemnation by the Congregation of the Index, Pierre journeys to Rome, and the second novel of the trilogy is primarily concerned with his efforts to persuade influential Italian prelates, up to the Holy Father himself, that he conserves a filial respect for the Church and that his book is merely a bold interpretation of the Pope's own policy.

There is a genuine historical background to *Rome*. Leo XIII's concern over the condition of the working classes under unrestricted capitalism had been voiced notably in *Rerum novarum*, and there were, no doubt, many Catholics in France who believed that the Vatican did intend to support the more moderate demands of the workers. In this encyclical, the Pope showed that his eyes were open to the inadequacy of wage-levels, the excessive hours of work exacted, the herding of the sexes together in workshops and factories, and the disintegration of family bonds resulting from this promiscuity. He did not commit himself to specifying what measures should be taken, beyond an appeal to the conscience of employers to remedy these evils; but his attitude undoubtedly encouraged the formation about this time of Catholic trade unions, in France as elsewhere. *Rome* thus deals with questions widely discussed at the time it was written and published; but, for that very reason, the novel has lost much of its interest now that the questions have lost their topicality.

Fortunately, *Rome* has other themes which are of more lasting importance. The only novel that Zola ever wrote with a non-French setting, it represents his one attempt to judge the character of a foreign nation—one with which he was ill acquainted in spite of his Italian ancestry. He had paid a first, unpremeditated visit to the Peninsula just after his second and longer excursion to Lourdes. Acting on an impulse he had crossed from Monte Carlo to Genoa on 27 September 1892. He was back in Monte Carlo two days later, but the Genoese had given him a flattering welcome, improvising a banquet in his honour and, as he said on his return, inspiring him with the desire to travel more widely in the land of his forefathers. He had, as a matter of fact, been planning a holiday in Italy ever since 1880.

When he took it, in 1894, it was in all respects a 'working holiday'. According to his normal procedure (abandoned, exceptionally and in a way fortuitously, when he wrote *Lourdes*), he had sketched out the main lines of his novel before acquainting himself with the environmental setting he proposed to give it. He had acquired at most a few second-hand notions of Italy and the Italian national character from such works as *La Chartreuse de Parme*, Taine's *Voyage en Italie*, the Goncourts' *Madame Gervaisais*, and Bourget's latest novel *Cosmopolis*. He arrived in Rome on 1 November and, Baedeker in hand, went about his business like a supremely conscientious tourist, setting down his impressions and reflections in a diary running to 400 manuscript pages[1] on which he drew heavily later when composing the long descriptive passages that abound in *Rome*. Some of these are vivid pen-pictures: that of the sunset behind St. Peter's, which closes the fourth chapter, or of the Tiber, flowing as it had flowed for centuries, but with its turbid waters bearing now no vessels save a rotting house-boat, moored by one of its shores, where never a living soul seems to come. But when one turns from what needed only observant eyes to what demanded understanding, Zola's limitations begin to show themselves. His Romans are a collection of dummies galvanized into sporadic life, when they are not merely

---

[1] Published by Ternois: Zola, *Mes Voyages*, 1958. (The volume also contains Zola's account of his second visit to Lourdes.)

French types with Italian names (Cardinal Boccanera, for instance, simply repeats the Bishop of Beaumont in *Le Rêve*). It could hardly have been otherwise. Zola questioned all those who could give him information, but the six weeks he spent in Rome were not long enough for him to verify from personal observation the accuracy of what was told him; he accepted everything on trust, noted each detail in his diary, and worked it into his novel. He had planned to give considerable space to a typical specimen of Italian womanhood. He watched the ladies he met at a few aristocratic and middle-class social gatherings to which he was invited, and paid careful attention to a few obliging Italian informants—male for the most part. A conversation he had with a Roman nobleman, Prince Odescalchi, is summarized in the diary; part of it has an obvious bearing on the character of Benedetta, which Zola had partially elaborated before he came to Rome. 'Selon lui, la femme très ignorante. Capable d'une longue fidélité et de passions. Ma femme possible: mal mariée, aimant un petit cousin et se réservant pour lui (vierge), avec une sorte de superstition dévote.' On the basis of this, Zola felt himself free to introduce the melodramatic and highly irrelevant tale of Benedetta's arranged marriage to a man with whom she refused to have connubial relations, preferring expensive and hazardous divorce proceedings which would leave her at liberty to wed the man of her choice, her cousin Dario. It is possible, as René Ternois has suggested, that this part of the plot is founded on a few lines in Stendhal's *Promenades dans Rome* concerning the dissolution of the marriage of a young Roman woman on the grounds of her husband's impotence, notwithstanding that he was known to have had three illegitimate children by his mistress.[1] But the climax of the story is unlikely to have been anything but Zola's own invention. Before Benedetta's second marriage can be celebrated, Dario is accidentally poisoned. There follows the extraordinary scene in which Benedetta, violating at last her vow to the Madonna to remain chaste until she is Dario's wedded wife, strips off her clothing in front of her woman and a priest (Pierre) and lies down beside the dying man. The two lovers expire together and are buried in the same coffin. No doubt Zola intended the incident to symbolize the victory of natural instinct over religious scruples, but in his choice of illustration he was clearly not concerned with what would be typically Italian or

[1] *Zola et son temps*, p. 411.

typically Roman. The choice was highly personal and can be traced right the way back to certain fantasies embodied in the *Contes à Ninon.*[1]

Much space is given to social and economic questions in *Rome*, but here again, apart from what he could see with his own eyes during visits to the city's slums, Zola was forced to rely on French or Belgian newspapermen stationed in Rome, or on articles he chanced to read in the *Revue des Deux Mondes* or the *Revue de Paris* before he set off for Italy. Some of the conclusions he reached in *Rome* are, however, if not penetrating, at least solid. He observed that destitution was not attended with the same horrors under every climate: in Italy the relative warmth of the winters made it possible for paupers and the unemployed to survive them more easily than they could in the more northerly latitude of Paris. He noticed the patriotic pride and the ingrained fecklessness and fatalism of the southern Italians, which explained why so few of them adhered to international socialist movements. A sense of family honour was far more deeply implanted in the Italian lower classes than in the French; they were less disrespectful of the Church and correspondingly more ignorant. As for the other classes, the aristocracy was impoverished and condemned to idleness, and the middle class, of recent formation, had no traditions, no honesty, no education. Zola's judgement on the Italian nation was devastating: that nation had not yet been properly called into being. Little wonder that the critical reception given to *Rome* in Italy was frigid.[2]

Among Catholics the book was, of course, damned from the start. *Lourdes* had been placed on the Index within a month of its appearance; the same interdiction fell on *Rome* almost automatically. The Roman Catholic Church is much more vigorously assailed in this second novel; some of the accusations that Zola makes or implies are lurid in the extreme. Don Vigilio's morbid terror of the Jesuits, whom he sees as the insidious and all-powerful enemy, are substantiated rather than contradicted by subsequent happenings. The lower ranks of the Italian priesthood are judged to be ill instructed, ill paid, and time-serving. They are typified, in *Rome*,

---

[1] See above, p. 16.

[2] It appeared in instalments in *La Tribuna*, 24 Dec. 1895–15 May 1896, more or less concurrently with its publication in France, in *Le Journal*, 21 Dec. 1895–8 May 1896.

by the timorous Vigilio, who is a secretary in the service of Cardinal Boccanera, by his colleague Papirelli, a flagellant schemer, and by the ferocious country priest Santobono, a creature of Cardinal Sanguinetti, who brings the basket of poisoned figs that are intended to remove Sanguinetti's rival Boccanera and instead kill Boccanera's nephew. The cardinals are chiefly represented by these two; Boccanera is a figure of some majesty, narrow-minded but vehement and splendidly stoical under the stroke of fate that robs him of both nephew and niece and destroys all hope of the continuance of his ancient line; Sanguinetti is ambitious, an intriguer waiting with disguised impatience for the death of Leo XIII which may give him his opportunity to mount the papal throne.

Zola's treatment of the figure of the Pope is one of the few clear merits of the novel. He had hoped, before he left France, that he might be granted a private audience. The French ambassador to the Vatican, Count de Béhaine, happened to be a cousin of Edmond de Goncourt, who gave Zola a letter of recommendation. But Béhaine's efforts could not overcome the effect of *Lourdes*, while certain tactless remarks made by one of the speakers at an Italian Press Association banquet given in Zola's honour finally made his audience a diplomatic impossibility.[1] The hero of *Rome* was more successful: right at the end of his stay Pierre Froment is, after many disappointments, informed that the Pope will receive him privately. The mystery and solemnity of this nocturnal interview are rendered in one of the best chapters in the novel. Pierre's nerves, and the reader's too, have been prepared for the occasion by the harrowing details of the poisoning scene and Benedetta's death in Dario's arms. Zola succeeds in the difficult task of making the Pope appear anachronistic and yet not absurd, and the French priest humbled and yet not humiliated.

The faults of *Rome*—its interminable digressions, its reiterated hammerings on the same dull themes, its implausible melodrama— are glaring; yet it does possess a certain plunging power which makes it possible to read the book once, though one would hardly read it a second time for pleasure. Pierre came to Rome to save his

[1] The text of the petition Zola addressed to the Sovereign Pontiff has been published (G. De Luca, 'Ah, quell'udienza!—Emilio Zola e Leone XIII', *Nuova Antologia*, vol. cdxxxiii (1945), pp. 57–61). He had the consolation of being received by the King of Italy but this interview was of little use to the author of *Rome*.

book from interdiction. He has little idea, when he arrives, whose protection he ought to solicit; and he is guided through the labyrinthine ways of the ecclesiastical world by a man who, as he finally realizes, is his most implacable enemy: the infinitely subtle, urbane, and intelligent Assessor of the Holy Office, Monsignor Nani. Nani has decoyed him to Rome to show him the vanity of his dream of the papacy voluntarily renouncing its claims to temporal power; and all the ceremonies he tells him to attend, all the visits he advises him to make to high-placed clerics, all the obstacles that he secretly raises are part of a deep-laid design to baffle and discourage Pierre. But Nani's purpose is not at first apparent; and Pierre's frustrated search for a man with influence whom he can convince of the rightness of his cause, the unvarying answer he receives after every interview ('I have no power in the matter; have you seen so-and-so?'), the revelations of seemingly infinite concentric circles of authority seem at times to anticipate the involute perplexities of a Kafka novel.

When he was still writing the concluding chapters of *Rome*, Zola accepted an invitation from the editor of *Le Figaro* to contribute a series of articles.[1] In 1881 he had ended his 'campaign' in *Le Figaro* by pledging himself solemnly never to write for the daily press again; and for fourteen years he had kept his word. At most he had inserted an occasional letter, always bearing on some literary matter: an indignant protest against the manner of Desprez's death, on 9 December 1885;[2] a reply to Sarcey's criticism of Busnach's dramatization of *Le Ventre de Paris*, on 3 March 1887; and the long statement, 'Retour de vacances', on 11 October 1892, in which he dealt with objections to *La Débâcle* made by the Bavarian officer Captain Tanera. The 'new campaign' of 1895–6 broke this almost complete silence.

Significantly, only a minority of the articles in the new series touched, even remotely, on literature. There were a couple concerning Verlaine and his followers, one refuting a charge of plagiarism in *Rome*, two or three more about the financial side of publication, copyright, and the efforts of the Société des Gens de Lettres to safeguard authors' interests. In one article he discusses

---

[1] Subsequently collected in *Nouvelle Campagne* (1897).
[2] Louis Desprez had been tried for publishing the supposedly pornographic *Autour d'un clocher* and sent to prison in 1884. He was in delicate health and died shortly after his release.

the evolution of painting since the days when he broke a lance for Manet; there are a couple more about cruelty to animals and its prevention. But for the most part he used his column in *Le Figaro* to air his opinions about current political or social topics. There can be no clearer indication of his growing unwillingness to consider himself solely or even principally a novelist. During his first 'campaign' Zola had not been afraid to make such a categorical statement as: 'The less a writer is committed, the greater he is (l'écrivain est d'autant plus grand qu'il est dégagé davantage).'[1] *Lourdes* had initiated the era of committed literature; and from then until his death Zola's literary greatness went on shrinking the more he allowed himself to be *engagé*. Whether there is any necessary and natural interrelation between commitment and uninspired writing is a question which, of course, the isolated study of this one writer cannot be expected to decide.

Most of the stages by which Zola travelled from detachment to commitment can be confidently indicated. He had never been blind to the existence of social injustice; it provided the theme of several of the stories included in the *Nouveaux Contes à Ninon*, all of which were written before 1874. 'Le Chômage' is a lavishly pathetic account of the miseries of a working-class family when unemployment reduces them to famine. 'Les Épaules de la marquise' is an unsubtle satire on the selfishness of the rich. A young lady of rank wakes one January morning and asks her maid if it is thawing outside. The maid answers that, on the contrary, it is freezing harder than ever.

—On vient de trouver un homme mort de froid sur un omnibus.

La marquise est prise d'une joie d'enfant; elle tape ses mains l'une contre l'autre, en criant:

—Ah! tant mieux! j'irai patiner cette après-midi.

There is obviously a difference, however, between sterile indignation of this sort and the curiosity that was later to lead Zola to investigate socialist remedies for economic injustice.

Adverse criticisms of *L'Assommoir* by left-wing writers were probably responsible for first orientating Zola towards socially committed literature. In addition, the example of a man like Jules Vallès may have exerted a certain gravitational pull on Zola. He had admired the strength and originality of Vallès's work. In a review

[1] 'Émile de Girardin', *Le Figaro*, 8 May 1881; *Une Campagne*, p. 223.

of *La Rue* in 1866 he wrote that the author's talent 'me paraît surtout fait de verve et d'énergie', and thirteen years later he recommended the *Jacques Vingtras* tetralogy even more warmly. 'Je désire qu'on lise ce livre. Si j'ai quelque autorité, je demande qu'on le lise, par amour du talent et de la vérité. Les œuvres de cette puissance sont rares. Quand il en paraît une, il faut qu'elle soit mise dans toutes les mains.'[1] But, having paid this tribute, Zola allowed himself a regret that Vallès should be wasting his time and energy on political agitation; and he made the same lament in a *Figaro* article ('Souveraineté des lettres') on 30 May 1881.

Vallès did not let these reproaches pass unanswered. He took up the question in two articles in *Le Réveil* (24 July and 1 August 1882). In the first he argued that the naturalists, Flaubert, the Goncourts, Zola, even Alexandre Dumas fils, were socialists in spite of themselves, for their pictures of the distress of the lower orders and the corruption of the bourgeoisie necessarily enforced the same lessons as those openly taught by active socialists. They talk socialism without knowing it, as Molière's Monsieur Jourdain, in his innocence, found he had been talking prose all his life. Vallès's second article was provoked by an intervention of Alexis in defence of Zola. This time Vallès hit back much harder. The attitude adopted by Zola and Alexis was sheer cowardice. Only monks and eunuchs disdained public life; whoever affected neutrality was willy-nilly on the side of the oppressors. The argument between Alexis and Vallès did not end there, but Zola was careful not to be drawn into it.[2]

Circumstances were slowly swinging him over to Vallès's point of view. Although, as we have seen, *Germinal* was a strictly 'neutral' work, its preparation inevitably involved Zola in a study —admittedly cursory—of the different socialist systems jockeying for supremacy at the time. Some of his information was derived from his own reading, some from Alexis, who was in touch with the most prominent of French socialists, Jules Guesde. A little later *La Terre* obliged Zola to acquaint himself with socialist thinking about land tenure. 'Toutes les fois maintenant que j'entreprends une étude', he commented to a correspondent in 1886, 'je me heurte au socialisme.' This time he secured a personal interview with Guesde, taking notes which he filed with the rest of his documentary

---

[1] *L'Événement*, 26 June 1866; *Le Voltaire*, 24 June 1879.
[2] See Gaston Gille, *Jules Vallès* (1941), pp. 353-60.

material for *La Terre*. Two aspects of Guesde's thought seem to
have particularly impressed Zola: the Marxist's conviction that the
developments he predicted were historically inevitable because
they were controlled by scientifically verifiable laws; and the
entrancing vision he conjured up of a society in which mechaniza-
tion would all but eliminate the need for human labour. 'L'âge d'or
que Guesde m'a dépeint avec des yeux flamboyants: tout le monde
travaillant peu et jouissant davantage, profitant des arts, flânant,
mangeant, et baisant, pendant que les machines travailleront.'[1]
This dream was to be the inspiration of *Travail*, written fifteen
years later.

One of the characters in *L'Argent* is a theoretical socialist and
allegedly a disciple of Karl Marx. This character, Sigismond
Busch, is given no active part to play in the novel, but Zola was
evidently anxious that the socialist point of view should not go by
default. However, Sigismond is a sadly deviationary Marxist;
Zola may not have intended this, but he found himself briskly taken
to task by Marx's French son-in-law, Paul Lafargue, for confusing
dialectical materialism with humanitarian utopianism.[2]

It is clear, then, that by the time he came to write *Paris*, Zola
had for a number of years been thinking, however confusedly,
about social injustice and how it could be eliminated. He took very
little interest, however, in the programmes of the left-wing political
parties of his day, and he had the haziest ideas about the aims of
the trade-union movement. In reality he believed in socialism far
less than he did in the revolutionary power of technology. Bertheroy, his principal spokesman in *Paris*, observes in the concluding
chapter: 'la science seule est révolutionnaire, la seule qui, par-
dessus les pauvres événements politiques, l'agitation vaine des
sectaires et des ambitieux, travaille à l'humanité de demain, en
prépare la vérité, la justice, la paix!' It was not a message calculated to commend *Paris* to progressive men at the time. Blum's
measured comments on this conclusion can scarcely be bettered:

> There is a great deal of self-deception and a sort of fetishism in wait-
> ing docilely for science to renovate society. Assuredly, I am far from
> wanting to argue a case against science; we must love and respect science,

---

[1] Quoted by A. Zévaès, *Zola*, p. 137. Cf. id., 'Émile Zola et Jules Guesde',
Commune, no. 42 (1937), pp. 689–95.
[2] Lafargue, *Critiques littéraires*, pp. 209–10. Lafargue's review of *L'Argent*
first appeared in *Die Neue Zeit*, 1891–2.

and look to it for everything, but *not to it alone*. Science is the essential instrument, but it has to be handled properly, for it has power to work good or evil. Every day it increases our wealth; it extends its dominion over the world; but if we do not refashion the traditional order of society, the very advance of science will serve to promote injustice and propagate iniquity.[1]

Paris has few literary merits. Although Zola avoided the mistake he had made in *Lourdes*, of relying on a static account of the city and its affairs to carry him through, this final novel of the trilogy is a good deal more untidily put together than the first, and, worse, it confirms disastrously the impression one was beginning to receive from *Rome* that some of Zola's most precious gifts, imagination and inventiveness, had started to leak away. One can accept the constant echoes of current and recent political events (the Panama scandal, the 'opportunist' policy of Leo XIII, the bomb outrages which were worrying the French authorities from 1892 onwards), for all this is explainable as conscientious 'documentation'; but there are unmistakable signs of the growing difficulty Zola was encountering in the creation of fresh fictional characters, and this is more disquieting. For the first time, he made recognizable copies of public figures and incorporated them in his novel just as he found them in real life. A 'key' was easily constructed by contemporaries. The chemist Bertheroy, with his belief in the power of science to usher in an age of plenty, justice, and happiness for all, is quite obviously, in all points, Berthelot, Pasteur's successor as secretary of the Academy of Sciences and, by a more recent appointment, Minister of Public Instruction. The anarchist Salvat, who is executed for exploding an infernal machine in the doorway of a financier's house, was clearly intended to recall Vaillant, put to death in 1893 for throwing a bomb from a gallery in the Chamber of Deputies. The two newspaper editors, Fonsègue and Sagnier, are created in the image of Hébrard, of *Le Temps*, and Édouard Drumont, in charge of the muck-raking anti-Semitic *Libre Parole*. Mège, the socialist deputy in *Paris*, can be confidently identified with Guesde, who had been returned to Parliament in 1893; Mège's personal appearance is Guesde's, and he is given Guesde's notorious unpopularity with his fellow socialists. The dividing-line between reality and fiction is indistinguishable in many places, and parts of *Paris* are no more than efficient *reportage*.

[1] Blum, 'Les livres: Émile Zola, *Paris*', *Revue blanche*, vol. xv (1898), p. 553.

The exhaustion of his literary powers shows even more strongly in the way Zola frequently, in *Paris*, appears to be copying himself. Characters, situations, even descriptive passages are embarrassingly reminiscent of his earlier books. Hyacinthe, the effete son of the millionaire Baron Duvillard, is a reincarnation of Saccard's degenerate son Maxime: 'androgyne avorté, incapable même des grands attentats et des grandes débauches'—the words might have come from *La Curée* or *L'Argent*. Duvillard has a mistress, Silviane d'Aulnay, who exploits him exactly as Nana did her wealthy lovers, and for the same unconscious reasons: 'Elle était . . . le commencement de la justice et du châtiment, reprenant à mains pleines l'or ramassé, vengeant par ses cruautés ceux qui avaient froid et faim.' Just as Nana obliged Muffat to prevail on an unwilling theatre manager to give her a certain part she coveted, so Silviane insists that Duvillard use his influence with the Minister of Fine Arts to have her cast as Pauline in a Comédie-Française production of *Polyeucte*. One of the most effective scenes in *Germinal* had been that in which Hennebeau cries out to a mutinous and starving mob, who cannot hear him, that moral suffering can sometimes hurt more than an empty belly. Zola staged the same scene in *Paris* with only a superficial variation. He shows a prosperous manufacturer whose dearly loved wife has run mad and who, when Pierre tries to stir his feelings on behalf of his starving work-people, breaks out with the same protestations as Hennebeau: 'Mais je sais des tristesses aussi grandes, des abominations qui empoisonnent l'existence davantage encore. . . . Ah! le pain, croire que le bonheur régnera quand tout le monde aura le pain, quel imbécile espoir!' The description, in *Paris*, of the army of workers tumbling out at dawn from their dwellings in the north of the city and pouring along the streets to start a new day of toil has rightly been regarded as an anthology-piece; but it should not be forgotten that Zola had depicted the scene once before, and with greater technical skill, in the first chapter of *L'Assommoir*. Those so minded will not miss the irony of circumstance that willed it that this book, which ends in an eloquent glorification of the principle of fertility, should have been the one in which the onset of artistic sterility in the author was for the first time clearly perceptible.

In one respect, however, the old breath of epic grandeur persists. *Paris* succeeds at least in living up to its title. The great metropolis in which Zola had been born and in which he had spent nearly all his life has passed into this novel as fully, perhaps, as it could without shattering the framework altogether. Zola did for the modern city what Hugo, in *Notre-Dame de Paris*, had tried to do for the medieval one; and Hugo's task was simplicity itself compared with Zola's. In preceding novels, in *Le Ventre de Paris*, in *L'Assommoir*, in *Au Bonheur des Dames*, or in *L'Argent*, he had confined his theatre of action to a single district in the city; in *Pot-Bouille* or in *Une Page d'amour*, to one or two houses only; here, the whole capital is the setting, the very protagonist. For in the last resort it was not in socialism, science, justice, or any such chilly abstraction, but in the numberless roofs and the network of streets, the solid tentaculated agglomeration massed round the huge hump of the Seine, that Zola saw the promised regeneration of mankind.

Paris, c'était la cuve énorme, où toute une humanité bouillait, la meilleure et la pire, l'effroyable mixture des sorcières, des poudres précieuses mêlées à des excréments, d'où devait sortir le philtre d'amour et d'éternelle jeunesse. . . . La lie humaine tombait au fond de la cuve, et il ne fallait pas vouloir que, visiblement, chaque jour, le bien triomphât; car souvent des années étaient nécessaires pour que, de la fermentation louche, se dégageât un espoir réalisé, dans cette opération de l'éternelle matière remise au creuset, demain refait meilleur. Et, si, au fond des usines empestées, le salariat restait une forme de l'antique esclavage, . . . la liberté n'en était pas moins sortie de la cuve immense, en un jour de tempête, pour prendre son vol par le monde. Et pourquoi la justice ne sortirait-elle pas à son tour, faite de tant d'éléments troubles, se dégageant des scories, d'une limpidité enfin éclatante, et régénérant les peuples?

By justice, Zola was referring in this passage to social justice, clearly a thing of the future. Legal justice, the right of every Frenchman accused of a crime to a fair trial, he did not imagine in jeopardy; it had been secured at the beginning of the century, and he believed that nothing short of a cataclysm could remove it. Even before *Paris* was published (in March 1898) he had learned that, amazingly, this belief was founded on a fond illusion.

XV

THE LAST ACT

THE impact of the Dreyfus Affair on Zola was several times more powerful than the impact he made on the Affair. The most recent account in English of the whole business devotes fourteen pages to Zola out of a total of 400;[1] this is a handy and reasonably accurate measure of the extent of his influence over the course of events that started on the evening of 26 September 1894 when Major Henry, an officer in the so-called Statistical (counter-espionage) Section of the French War Office, pieced together a torn-up sheet of flimsy paper, part of the contents of the German military attaché's waste-paper basket which were regularly delivered to Henry by a charwoman in the German Embassy who was on the pay-roll of the Statistical Section. The piece of paper in question (called, in the ensuing inquiry, the *bordereau*) listed five different military secrets which the writer was proposing to pass on to the German attaché. Henry and his colleagues made some rapid and shaky deductions, passed over the real culprit, Major Walsin-Esterhazy, and concluded, on the basis of a roughly approximate similarity in handwriting, that the traitor was Alfred Dreyfus, an intelligent but personally unattractive young officer of considerable private means, a member of a Jewish family settled for some generations in Alsace.

Dreyfus was arrested on a charge of high treason on 15 October. Although the evidence of his guilt was flimsy and the presumption of his innocence strong, the charge was held proved after trial by court martial held *in camera* (19–21 December 1894); Dreyfus was awarded the maximum sentence, life-imprisonment. Too many highly-placed officers in the secret service had staked their reputations on his guilt; most of them had no marked prejudice against Dreyfus because of his race, but undoubtedly there was a traffic in military information and having committed themselves imprudently to the proposition that the spy could only be Dreyfus, they

[1] Guy Chapman, *The Dreyfus Case: a reassessment* (1955).

disliked having to admit themselves mistaken. They might have been better disposed to allow reasonable doubts to weigh with them, had it not been that a vociferous section of public opinion was clamouring for the punishment of the traitor. One of the unhappier by-products of the defeat of 1871 was a disposition in the country to look askance at all supposedly untrustworthy elements of the population: the Jews were, in this situation as in similar situations at other times in other countries, the obvious targets for suspicion. Dislike of the Jews had been exacerbated by certain financial scandals in the 1880's: the crash of the Union Générale, a Lyonnais banking organization, for which the house of Rothschild bore some blame (Zola had founded *L'Argent* on this episode); and the affair of the Panama Company in which two Jewish financiers were found to have been bribing members of the Chamber of Deputies. The most virulent Jew-baiter of the time was Édouard Drumont. We have seen how, in 1886, Zola nearly quarrelled with Alphonse Daudet by uttering some disparaging remarks about Drumont, regardless of the esteem in which Daudet held him. On this occasion Drumont's name had come up in conversation almost certainly in connexion with the polemical work he had just published, *La France juive*. This book caused a considerable stir, and Drumont was encouraged to go on and found an anti-Semitic newspaper, *La Libre Parole*. It was in the columns of *La Libre Parole* that the news of the arrest of Dreyfus was first leaked. The line the newspaper took was that there existed a danger that Dreyfus's co-religionaries would rally round and purchase his acquittal. Other organs of the gutter-press took up the hue-and-cry, and Dreyfus's judges were therefore, from the start, under considerable pressure to bring in a verdict against their prisoner.

Zola does not appear to have paid any particular attention to the events of the end of 1894, although he did listen with passionate interest to an account of the public degradation of Dreyfus which took place in the École militaire on 5 January 1895 in front of an abusive crowd of journalists. Having been stripped of his badges of office, and forced to watch his sabre symbolically broken, the unfortunate man was paraded round the courtyard, still loudly proclaiming his innocence, while the bystanders booed and hissed. Léon Daudet, who had been an eyewitness, told the story at a dinner-party to which the Zolas had been invited. The author of *Les Rougon-Macquart* was deeply moved by the drama of the situation, and thought of bringing the scene into a novel. Then Dreyfus's name dropped out of the front page, and Zola, never suspecting a miscarriage of justice, forgot about it, as did most other people.

If the matter did not rest there, this was largely thanks to the devotion of Mathieu Dreyfus, Alfred's brother, who gradually found—or enlisted—a nucleus of sympathizers; in 1897 two of them, Arthur Ranc, an opponent of Zola since the days of *L'Assommoir*, and Joseph Reinach, nephew of the Reinach who had committed suicide at the time of the Panama scandal, broached the question with a highly-respected Alsatian senator, Auguste Scheurer-Kestner. Zola was tackled from another side: he was visited by Bernard Lazare, the author of a pamphlet called *La Vérité sur l'affaire Dreyfus*, published abroad in 1896, and by a lawyer, Louis Leblois. On 13 November 1897 he accepted an invitation to lunch with Scheurer-Kestner who ran through all the evidence pointing to Esterhazy as the man responsible for the treasonous activity for which Dreyfus was suffering in a lonely cell on Devil's Island. The evidence was overwhelming, for Esterhazy was an audacious rascal, convinced that the military chiefs would cover him whatever happened; he had continued his efforts to make money by selling military information and had done nothing to cover up his tracks. Scheurer-Kestner's notes of Zola's reactions have been published.[1] He was tremendously excited ('C'est passionnant, c'est horrible! C'est un drame épouvantable! Mais que c'est donc grand en même temps!'), but he was far from imagining he ought to intervene personally to press for rectification of the judicial error; the drama remained for him a drama, none of his concern really, but promising literary material. He recalled his own state of mind in the notes he later jotted down under the heading 'Impressions d'audience', raw material for an eventual book of memoirs:[2]

> Ce que j'avais vu, pour les lettres, dans l'affaire: une trilogie de types: le condamné innocent, là-bas, avec la tempête dans son crâne; le coupable libre ici, avec ce qui se passait en lui, tandis qu'un autre expiait son crime; et le faiseur de vérité Scheurer-Kestner, silencieux et agissant . . .

---

[1] A. Zévaès, *Le Cinquantenaire de 'J'accuse'*, pp. 20–21.

[2] Extracts from this forty-one-page manuscript have been published by J. Kayser in *La Nef*, no. 39 (1948), pp. 55–66. See also, by the same author, 'J'accuse!', *Europe*, vol. xxvi (1948), pp. ˙1–21.

[J'avais] l'arrière-pensée d'un drame peut-être, d'une œuvre où je dresserais ces trois types.

He saw Rodays, the editor of *Le Figaro*, and it was agreed that he should publish a few articles to prepare the public for the action Scheurer-Kestner was to take. The first of these articles (25 November) was devoted to the elder statesman whom Zola had cast in the role of 'faiseur de vérité'; it terminated with the ringing prediction, 'la vérité est en marche et rien ne l'arrêtera'. Nevertheless, the opening words of the article show that Zola was still viewing the affair as a passionately interested onlooker; the situation was simply one that made an obvious appeal to the man of letters and student of human nature that he was:

Quel drame poignant, et quels personnages superbes! Devant ces documents, d'une beauté si tragique, que la vie nous apporte, mon cœur de romancier bondit d'une admiration passionnée. Je ne connais rien d'une psychologie plus haute.

This detachment melted away in the course of the succeeding six weeks as Zola gradually realized that more was at issue here than the righting of a blunder committed by a few stupid generals. The anti-revisionist press grew more violent and scurrilous than ever, anti-Semitic agitation was increasing in virulence, the Cabinet —with an eye on the elections six months off—was supine or evasive. Zola's naïve optimism was shaken. He published two pamphlets, a *Lettre à la jeunesse* (14 December 1897) and a *Lettre à la France* (6 January 1898), in the second of which he issued a grave warning about the dangers confronting the nation. A dictatorship of the right was a real possibility, the army and the church combining to reverse the trend towards enlightenment, freedom, and justice which the Revolution had initiated, and to bring back medieval intolerance and inquisitorial fires.

The decision to throw himself wholeheartedly into the fight for revision of the 1894 judgement was arrived at only when, on 11 January, Esterhazy was acquitted by court martial of the charge of holding treasonous communication with the representatives of foreign powers. The suspicious resemblance between his handwriting and the lines on the *bordereau* was explained away on the hypothesis that Esterhazy's hand had been imitated. In the eyes of the law Dreyfus remained, as before, the only possible author of the *bordereau*. By this time no unprejudiced person, even if he believed Dreyfus guilty, could reasonably regard Esterhazy as a maligned patriot. A packet of letters he had written several years earlier to a woman-friend had been passed on to Scheurer-Kestner: Esterhazy had written, notably, that nothing would make him happier than to die sabring Frenchmen in the uniform of a captain of uhlans. These letters had been published in *Le Figaro* on 29 November; one of them was set in facsimile alongside a facsimile of the *bordereau*. If, after that, a French court martial concluded that there was no case against Esterhazy, then there seemed little hope that justice would ever be obtained for Dreyfus; republican institutions, democracy itself, were in the gravest peril.

The stupefaction with which the news was received among the partisans of revision, their disarray and sudden despondency after high hopes, are movingly recalled in Léon Blum's memoirs.[1] Not for a moment had the possibility that Esterhazy would go free been seriously considered; his acquittal seemed to leave no hope for any future manœuvre to secure a reversal of the earlier verdict against Dreyfus. 'It was one of those moments when all faith ebbs away, leaving one feeling lost and alone in an eternally hostile world.' Two days later, the publication of *J'accuse*, as Blum put it, 'smashed the windows of this padlocked room in which the revisionist cause was condemned to die of asphyxia'.

Composed as an open letter to the President of the Republic, *J'accuse* was, as is clear from the title (chosen by the editor of *L'Aurore* who printed it on 13 January), much more than an indignant protest against Esterhazy's acquittal. It was an audacious, uncompromising arraignment of those who had presided and given evidence at the trial of Esterhazy; an arraignment, too, of Dreyfus's judges, who were accused of having allowed irregularities in the conduct of the earlier trial. Most of those he pilloried were staff-officers, many of high rank: it was truly 'the pen against the sword', and Zola knew the risks he ran; he had taken legal advice as to the penalty he would incur if he were taken to court. On the other hand, his trial would have to be held in public (the two courts martial, Dreyfus's and Esterhazy's, had been conducted behind closed doors); and, however carefully the prosecution and the presiding magistrate handled matters, it would be difficult or impossible for them to silence all reference to the growing mass of evidence pointing to the innocence of Dreyfus.

[1] *Souvenirs sur l'affaire* (1935), pp. 124–9.

J'accuse was only incidentally intended to bring to public notice the fact that the course of justice had been twice perverted in the military courts; it was, as Zola wrote towards the end of his 'open letter', primarily designed to bring about a revision of the verdict brought in against Dreyfus in 1894, 'un moyen révolutionnaire pour hâter l'explosion de la vérité et de la justice'. The mood of exasperated indignation in which it was composed is understandable when one considers the atmosphere of feverish unrest at the time and the shocked horror which the news of Esterhazy's whitewashing spread among Dreyfus's sympathizers. Beyond that, Zola's boldness and the decisiveness of his reaction were in character. He was not a timid man, even though often diffident in public. Twice before, when he was still a relatively unknown and unbefriended young author, he had not hesitated to risk prosecution and loss of livelihood by publishing newspaper articles calculated to cause embarrassment and anger in the governing circles of the time.[1] In 1898 he was the most prominent literary figure in France, and in the world at large only Tolstoy was more revered. He knew this, knew it would not buy him impunity, but knew also that his name would give weight to what he wrote and to what he said in court. It was for this reason, and not through any desire to pose as the lone champion of Dreyfus against the dark forces of tyranny and obscurantism, that Zola used the first person instead of drawing up some manifesto for multiple signatures. 'Nous accusons' would have been a formula relatively lacking in bite, and a mass-trial would not have magnetized public attention in the same way.

The case came up in the second week of February. The outcome could scarcely be in doubt; witnesses for the prosecution, when pressed by the defence, pretended that the interests of national security required them to keep their lips sealed; the jury could not have refused to bring in a verdict against Zola without by implication declaring lack of confidence in the General Staff. It was Zola's word against the army's: an abstract principle against an entrenched

[1] For publishing an article entitled 'Vive la France!' in *La Cloche*, 5 Aug. 1870, Zola received a summons to appear in court to answer a charge of sedition; however, the disastrous turn the war took over the next few days led to the indefinite deferment of the hearing. On 22 Dec. 1872 an article he wrote called 'Le lendemain de la crise' caused such fury among right-wing deputies that the government was obliged to placate them by ordering the suppression of the newspaper, *Le Corsaire*, in which it had appeared. On this occasion Zola was not threatened with prosecution but, of course, his income from journalism was cut at a time when he could ill afford to forgo these earnings.

institution. 'I bequeath to posterity', declared the defendant, 'the name of General Pellieux [who had conducted the inquiry into the charges against Esterhazy] and the name of Émile Zola. Posterity will make its choice.' Posterity has done so, but was not present at the trial.

In spite of the efforts made by the presiding magistrate to prevent the hearing of evidence that did not directly concern the court martial of Esterhazy, the revisionists succeeded at least in establishing beyond reasonable doubt that Esterhazy had written the *bordereau* which had been considered, in 1894, to have been in Dreyfus's handwriting. This was done by subpoenaing palaeographers from the École des Chartes whose testimony was unanimous and damning. But confronted with the obstinate refusal of the staff-officers in the box to answer certain questions, the two defending barristers (Labori and Clemenceau) were unable to prove that Esterhazy's judges had acquitted him by order, as Zola had alleged. When the jury pronounced him guilty of the charge of defamation, pandemonium broke out in the court-room. There were shouts of 'A bas Zola! Mort aux juifs! Vive l'armée!', and Clemenceau later declared that if the verdict had been different, Zola and his defenders would have been lynched on the spot.

An appeal was allowed on a technicality and a new trial was held at Versailles. Once again, the outcome was a foregone conclusion, but Zola's legal advisers urged him to leave the country before the sentence (twelve months' imprisonment) was pronounced. This was a tactical manœuvre, designed to ensure that the case was 'kept open'; it is difficult to see how the revisionists thought they would gain more by Zola's disappearance than they would have by his submitting to the penalty of the law. His stand had evoked more sympathy within the country than he may have realized, as he watched the howling mob of right-wing rowdies who had to be dispersed by the police at the end of each session of the court before he could return home.[1] To have served his prison sentence would certainly not have diminished his prestige or his usefulness as the Dreyfusards' principal standard-bearer. But the decision had

---

[1] Of the 1,900-odd letters, telegrams, and postcards addressed to Zola from places in France in 1898, only 350 expressed disapproval of his action. He received over 6,000 missives from abroad, mostly from Germany, Italy, and the territories of the Austro-Hungarian Empire; of these, 50 at the most were hostile. See J. Kayser, 'Émile Zola et l'opinion publique', *La Nef*, no. 49 (1948), pp. 47–58, and no. 50 (1949), pp. 23–37.

to be made in a hurry and he accepted the advice he was given. On 18 July he left France for an unknown destination (actually London) and went into hiding in Surrey for fear a process-server from the Versailles court might run him to earth. His angry resentment at the necessity for concealment is obvious not only in the letters he wrote at the time but also in the diary he kept during the first few weeks of his stay in England.[1] Perhaps, had he been able to foresee the time that would be needed before the Affair could take a more favourable turn, he might have insisted on staying in France, braving the discomforts of a prison cell. He originally counted on a triumphal repatriation in a matter of weeks. On 21 August, only a month after his arrival in Great Britain, he talked in a letter to Alfred Bruneau, the opera composer for whom he had begun writing librettos in these years, about his probable return in the autumn in time to hear the first rehearsals of their latest joint work. In October he wrote that he was preparing for his stay to prolong itself till January. In November he betrayed his impatience in a letter to Alexis: 'J'en ai assez, il faut que cela cesse. L'exil n'est plus possible, avec l'hiver qui commence. Aussi, me voilà à compter les jours, dans l'attente heureusement certaine de la victoire.' But the Dreyfus Affair went its cumbersome way, taking no account of the rigours of an English winter. In December Zola pleaded with Charpentier: 'Je n'en puis plus d'impatience et de détresse, à me sentir aussi loin de la bataille et de tous ceux que j'aime. Je suis donc prêt à risquer même un peu de ma victoire pour aller vous retrouver tous, si cela n'est pas jugé trop imprudent.' Ten days before Christmas, his bitterness and restlessness found expression in a long, plaintive letter to the wife of his admirer Octave Mirbeau:

L'homme nerveux et passionné que je suis n'est pas fait pour l'exil, pour la résignation et le silence. Vous avez parfaitement deviné que ma torture est d'être ici à l'abri, dans trop de paix et de sécurité, pendant que les autres se battent. Il y a des jours où j'en arrive à me mépriser un peu, où il me semble que je ne fais pas mon devoir. ... On n'imagine pas tout ce que je souffre ici, moralement, intellectuellement, dans l'impuissance d'agir où je me trouve. Et je ne parle pas de mon pauvre cœur, arraché à tout ce que j'aime.

[1] This diary ('Pages d'exil') is properly a collection of memoranda for a book Zola intended to write about his experiences in England. It has been published with an introduction by C. A. Burns (*Nottingham French Studies*, vol. iii (1964), pp. 2–62).

His intervention in the Affair brought Zola nothing but tribulation. On the material plane the legal expenses were heavy, while the unpopularity he incurred reduced his income from royalties to a fraction of what it had been before.[1] His steadfast refusal to make any financial profit from his part in the Affair did not help mend his fortunes; in 1899 he refused, for instance, an offer of £1,000 from the London *Graphic* for an article giving his impressions of the Rennes trial. He even abstained from recovering the 30,000 francs awarded in a libel suit to the handwriting experts whose competence and good faith he had challenged in *J'accuse*. On the moral plane the Affair brought about the rupture of several old friendships (such as that with François Coppée), but, on the other hand, it earned him the admiration of others who had formerly disregarded or disparaged him (notably Anatole France and Jean Jaurès) and the devotion of many young men he never knew—among them Marcel Proust and Charles Péguy. Perhaps the greatest disappointment Zola had to endure was the unsatisfactory conclusion of the Affair. The 'explosion of truth and justice' to which he had looked forward in *J'accuse* never came; instead, when at last Dreyfus was brought back to France for a second trial which should have ended in a triumphant rehabilitation, he was for the second time found guilty. Zola protested in terms the very extravagance of which shows the degree of nervous exasperation he had by now reached.

Quand on aura publié le compte rendu *in extenso* du procès de Rennes, il n'existera pas un monument plus exécrable de l'infamie humaine. Cela dépasse tout, jamais document plus scélérat n'aura encore été fourni à l'histoire. L'ignorance, la sottise, la folie, la cruauté, le mensonge, le crime, s'y étalent avec une impudence telle, que les générations de demain en frémiront de honte.[2]

Mournfully he confided to Bruneau, two days after this article appeared: 'Entre nous, j'ai la conviction que la lutte est finie. Ce sera la grâce, puis une amnistie louche et bâtarde, les honnêtes gens et les coquins dans le même sac.' This is precisely what happened. Dreyfus was pardoned on 18 September 1899; the amnesty was passed by the Senate on 2 June 1900, and became law

---

[1] Certain figures are given by Vizetelly, *Émile Zola*, pp. 414, 460, 489–90. Vizetelly estimates that in 1898 Zola's income was a third of what it had been in 1897. *Rome*, published in 1896, sold 100,000 copies in the first two years, but only another 6,000 between 1898 and Zola's death in 1902.

[2] 'Le Cinquième Acte', *L'Aurore*, 12 Sept. 1899: *La Vérité en marche*, p. 111.

on 24 December. At each of these measures Zola raised a clamorous protest;[1] their effect was, indeed, to encourage the belief that Dreyfus had been correctly found guilty in 1894, that his partisans had been either bribed or hoodwinked, and that the Government was simply seeking to put an end to a disgraceful agitation which might otherwise drag on indefinitely. The truth was still stifled. Zola had been in his grave four years before the Rennes verdict was reversed and the miscarriage of justice righted.

Zola's participation in the Affair did not interfere noticeably with the pace of his literary production. At the time of the Versailles trial, he had completed all the preliminary work for the first volume of his last novel-series, *Les Quatre Évangiles*; and when he crossed the Channel he was ready to begin the first chapter. The day after his arrival in London he asked his friend Fernand Desmoulin, who was returning to Paris, to bring him back some linen (he found that English shirts were uncomfortably cut) and the material he had collected for *Fécondité*. A fortnight later he began writing the book, finishing it on 27 May 1899, nine days before his return to France. His letters from England make frequent allusions to the work which alone saved him from giving way to melancholy, he said; it is true that his exile was also brightened by alternating visits both from his legal wife and from Jeanne Rozerot and the two children.

It would be difficult to find in *Fécondité* the slightest evidence that it was written in England, or that its author was labouring under any spiritual distress at the time of its composition. It was the most lyrically optimistic of any of Zola's books since *Le Docteur Pascal*. One reason why the mood of the novel does not reflect the circumstances in which it was written was that the idea that underlay it had taken root in Zola's mind some years before it began to flower. The genesis of *Fécondité* must be looked for in one of the essays in *Nouvelle Campagne*, entitled 'Dépopulation', which was originally published in *Le Figaro* on 23 May 1896. The opening words are: 'Voici une dizaine d'années que je suis hanté par l'idée d'un roman, dont je n'écrirai sans doute jamais la première page.' This novel would be concerned with the growing practice of limiting the size of families, the various means adopted to that end,

---

[1] 'Lettre à Madame Alfred Dreyfus', *L'Aurore*, 29 Sept. 1899; 'Lettre au Sénat', ibid., 29 May 1900; 'Lettre à M. Émile Loubet, Président de la République', ibid., 22 Dec. 1900.

from contraception to infanticide, and the various reasons why married couples were disinclined to rear large numbers of children; reasons not only of an economic order, for Zola assigned much importance to the influence of literature and the arts, the nihilism of Schopenhauer, Wagner's exaltation of virginity. 'L'enfant a cessé d'être littéraire', he wrote; the writer who could restore the child to a place of honour in literature would be performing a salutary task. Zola's projected novel would be called *Le Déchet*, for he held that all attempts to control the birth-rate were acts of criminal waste.[1]

The special interest of this article is that it demonstrates the strictly personal origin of Zola's concern with the question round which *Fécondité* was to revolve. Allowing for slight exaggeration, the phrase 'une dizaine d'années' takes us back to the beginning of his liaison with Jeanne Rozerot. We have already seen that there is much to be said for the suggestion that Zola felt himself largely absolved of wrongdoing when he knew that Jeanne was pregnant. There is not a line in any of his novels or articles before *Le Docteur Pascal* to suggest that sexual relations that do not result in procreation are disgraceful; but in *Le Docteur Pascal*, and increasingly in *Fécondité*, this idea is strenuously insisted on. It has its place too in the *Figaro* article: 'Tout amour qui n'a pas l'enfant pour but n'est au fond qu'une débauche.'

However, although *Fécondité* has a subjective basis and may be interpreted as a kind of elaborate sublimation of the author's own sexual guilt-feeling, the book would doubtless never have taken the form it did had it not been for the dwindling of the birth-rate which was provoking much serious and anxious discussion in France in the nineties; *Fécondité* was in every respect a tract for the times. Zola could hardly have missed reading an article, 'Le Triomphe de Malthus', which appeared in *Le Figaro* on 6 March 1896, at a time when he himself was contributing to that paper. The author, Hugues Le Roux, put forward two main explanations why fewer and fewer French children were being born each year, and why France was not founding young oversea nations as England was. His first point (which, understandably, Zola did not incorporate in *Fécondité*) was that the French mother was too attached to

[1] A book with this title had originally been planned to follow his novel on the Lourdes miracles. The decision to give *Lourdes* two sequels obliged Zola to postpone carrying out the project until 1898-9.

her children; she could not imitate her Anglo-Saxon sister who bore son after son and was content to see them, as soon as they reached man's estate, emigrate and perhaps never return. In the second place, Le Roux found that the French middle classes preferred one-child families so as to be able to pass on their possessions undivided to a single heir. Zola did not forget this reading of the situation: his family of *entrepreneurs*, the Beauchênes, are careful only to have one son, who will be the sole inheritor of the business. Neither did he overlook the two injunctions to youth with which Le Roux ended his article: Marry young, for love and not for the bride's dowry; and betake yourselves to the colonies. The hero of *Fécondité* is twenty when he marries his seventeen-year-old sweetheart; one of his sons leaves France for French Equatorial Africa and helps populate the empty lands of Senegal with an energy of which his father has full reason to feel proud.

If Zola's novel holds any interest for us today, this can lie only in the faithful reflection it transmits of one of the major preoccupations of good Frenchmen at the time it was written. Criticism centring on the ideas Zola propounded in *Fécondité* is misdirected unless these ideas are put back into their context: the context makes many of them excusable. Even so, one feels one would have had Zola write on almost any subject rather than this. Nothing could surely have been more dangerous than to suggest that the greatness of France depended on the rate of expansion of its population. H. G. Wells, in his *Anticipations*, written in the same year as *Fécondité*, appraised the situation much more lucidly when he prophesied that the French language (and with it the products of the French mind) stood a better chance of diffusion in the coming century than German; and did so in spite of 'a disposition in the world, which the French share, to grossly undervalue the prospects of all things French, derived, so far as I can gather, from the facts that the French were beaten by the Germans in 1870, and that they do not breed with the *abandon* of rabbits and negroes. These are considerations that affect the dissemination of French very little.'

Whether or not Zola's thesis is forgivable or even arguable, his method of presenting it is completely indefensible. Judged purely as a work of art, *Fécondité* is an excellent example of the aberrations into which 'committed literature' is apt to tempt the unwary.

One of the characters in the book is a society novelist exploiting the current fashion for disillusioned and decadent literature. Zola gives a synopsis of one of his works, *L'Impérissable Beauté*, which reads oddly like an inverted parody of *Fécondité* itself.[1] It is

l'histoire subtile d'une comtesse, Anne-Marie, qui, pour fuir un mari grossier, un mâle faiseur d'enfants, se réfugiait, en Bretagne, près d'un jeune artiste d'inspiration divine, Norbert, lequel s'était chargé de décorer de ses visions la chapelle d'un couvent de filles cloîtrées. Pendant trente ans, son travail de peintre évocateur durait, tel un colloque avec les anges, et le roman n'était que l'histoire des trente années, de ses amours pendant trente ans, aux bras d'Anne-Marie, dans une communion de caresses stériles, sans que sa beauté de femme fût altérée d'une ride, aussi jeune, aussi fraîche, après ces trente ans d'infécondité, que le premier jour où ils s'étaient aimés. Pour accentuer la leçon, quelques personnages secondaires, des bourgeoises, des épouses et des mères de la petite ville voisine, finissaient dans une déchéance physique et morale, une décrépitude de monstres.

Fécondité may have been less anti-socially inspired, but it was certainly poured into exactly the same mould as this imaginary novel that Zola held up to ridicule. It concerns a couple, Mathieu Froment and his wife Marthe, who escape together into the country and breed a family of twelve lusty children, both of them remaining healthy and handsome and living to see 158 direct descendants (not counting those who have left to colonize the French oversea empire) gather round them for their diamond wedding. The lesson is driven home by the lamentable histories of some half-dozen other couples, whose attempts at birth-control are, without exception, direly punished. There are the Beauchênes, already mentioned; their one son is a sickly child, who dies of galloping consumption as a young man, when his mother is too old to produce another heir. After this disaster, Beauchêne's business begins to go to pieces and is bought up by one of Mathieu's sons. Beauchêne has a sister, Séraphine, who is a nymphomaniac; the desire to indulge her passions without the risk of maternity leads her to submit to sterilization. As a result of the operation she loses her beauty and her capacity for pleasure, runs mad, murders and

---

[1] There can be little doubt that Zola had in mind Maupassant's story *L'Inutile Beauté*, published in 1890. Although its plot is not in every way identical with that of *L'Impérissable Beauté*, Maupassant's thesis is the exact opposite of Zola's in *Fécondité*, which can be regarded as a counterblast to it and to similar works, like Tolstoy's *Kreutzer Sonata* (published in French translation also in 1890).

mutilates the surgeon who had operated on her. There is a couple representative of the lower middle class, the Moranges, who are ambitious and fear the encumbrance of a large family. They want no more children after their first, Reine, and when Mme Morange conceives a second time she goes to an abortionist in whose hands she dies. Morange's punishment does not end there: later, his daughter Reine, on whom his affections have centred, is killed by another abortionist. Morange goes slowly mad with grief and ends by dashing his brains out. A third family is composed of Séguin, who is Mathieu's landlord, his wife, and their two children. When Séguin learns he is to be a father for the third time he flatly accuses his wife of having conceived the new child outside wedlock. This brutal insult does eventually drive Valentine to adultery; her three children are badly trained, being left in the charge of the servants; the eldest, revolted by her mother's conduct, takes the veil. Then there are a few minor characters, a miller, one of Mathieu's country neighbours, with an only son, who, of course, goes to the bad, and a pathetic couple, deeply in love, who postpone the moment of starting a family in order not to interrupt their happiness; when they want a child they are too old, the husband goes blind, and the wife is murdered by a gang of ruffians in Paris. It would seem that some vengeful divinity broods over the world of *Fécondité*, to strike, with an armoury of appropriate or inappropriate visitations, at all who refuse to be fruitful. *Fécondité* is the Niobe myth turned inside out.

It is true that Mathieu does not entirely escape misfortune: a favourite daughter is carried off by a chill caught in a rainstorm on the eve of her betrothal; one son is murdered; a serious quarrel breaks out between two of the brothers. But the Froments are so numerous and so united a family that a gap made by the death of one of their members is soon filled by the birth of another, and dissensions are short-lived. This was, of course, the moral Zola wanted to point.

A moral story needs, however, to have a certain plausibility if it is to teach its lesson; and *Fécondité*, especially towards the end, moves steadily into the zone of folklore and fairy-tale. The very style becomes rhapsodic, the descriptions nebulous, the characters cease to converse, but vaticinate windily. There are passages written in deliberate imitation of Biblical language. In the *Évangiles* Zola openly posed as the Messiah of the twentieth century, even to the point of giving to the heroes of each of the four books the names of the authors of the Christian Gospels.

He admitted freely to Octave Mirbeau, who had reviewed the new novel in *La Plume*, 'les défauts de mon livre, les invraisemblances, les symétries trop volontaires, les vérités banales de morale en action'. The excuse he offered to those of his readers who reproached him with these excruciating lapses into didacticism was that the situation in France was too serious for him to continue to cultivate art for art's sake. Vizetelly quotes from a letter Zola wrote to him after the appearance of the second volume of the series, *Travail*:

I am writing these books with a certain purpose before me, a purpose in which the question of form is of secondary importance. I have no intention of trying to amuse people or thrill them with excitement. I am merely placing certain problems before them, and suggesting in some respects certain solutions, showing what I hold to be wrong and what I think would be right. When I have finished these *Évangiles*, when *Vérité* and *Justice* are written, it is quite possible that I shall write shorter and livelier books. Personally I should have everything to gain by doing so, but for the present I am fulfilling a duty which the state of my country imposes on me.[1]

As it happened, *Travail* was a book superior in many ways to *Fécondité*. The opening chapter constitutes a beginning as full of 'atmosphere' as any Zola wrote, vying with that of *Le Ventre de Paris* or *Nana*. It is a description of the town of Beauclair, which has sprung up round a big steel-works. The workers are on strike at the time, there are threats of violence in the air, the streets are patrolled by the police, the shopkeepers are on the watch for pilferers. We are left with a vivid impression of a grimy industrial town one wet evening, with its hideous factories, its dingy houses, its surly or suspicious inhabitants. The next two or three chapters, which are also introductory, give further proof of the sureness of Zola's touch and the keenness of his eye surviving unimpaired into this period of decline. Luc Froment has come to Beauclair at the invitation of Jordan, a friend of his, who owns a blast-furnace there but is considering selling it to the steel-manufacturers; Jordan is a scientist, and wants only to be left in peace to carry on his researches without the cares of running a business enterprise. Luc, as a result of what he sees during his visit, decides to stay and

[1] Vizetelly, op. cit., p. 499.

found a new factory near Jordan's furnace, organized on a collectivist basis. He reaches this decision after meeting and listening to dozens of people of every class—workers, managers, capitalists, officials, farmers, a priest, a schoolmaster, a magistrate—representative types whom Zola draws with all his old skill at succinct but telling characterization. A few of these characters are stereotyped repetitions from earlier books: the priest, for instance, resembles rather too closely the Abbé Mauduit in *Pot-Bouille*, and the *rentier* class are represented in *Travail* by a smug couple copied exactly from the Grégoires of *Germinal*; they are as devoted to their one daughter, Louise, as the Grégoires had been to Cécile, the only difference being that Louise is turbulent and disobedient while Cécile had been placid and docile. But otherwise all these characters in *Travail* seem freshly minted.

Luc founds not merely a new factory in competition with the old one at Beauclair, but a new city, with its own laws and religion, which will swallow up and supplant its rival. What he does is to put into practice the ideas of Fourier, one of the early-nineteenth-century socialists whose works he chances on in Jordan's library. The new city, the Crècherie, is simply a Fourierist phalanstery.

Fourier still had some followers in France at the time *Travail* was written—sufficient of them, at any rate, to organize a banquet to express their appreciation to Zola for rallying to their cause. Nevertheless, Fourierism was a system without any hope of ever being implemented. It was already evident that the immediate future of French socialism lay with Marxism, and Jaurès, who reproached Zola with minimizing the importance of the class struggle, a necessary prologue to the establishment of the socialist state, was undoubtedly speaking for the majority of progressive thinkers.[1] His adherence to an out-of-date and unfashionable form of socialism is a reminder of how undisciplined and self-centred Zola remained even in commitment. *Les Quatre Évangiles* are as subjective in inspiration as *La Confession de Claude*. It was for personal reasons that Zola had glorified maternity in *Fécondité*, and for personal reasons similarly that he preached Fourierism in *Travail*. Fourier and the disciples who elaborated his doctrine looked for the rise of a brotherhood of workers not through any violent revolution but through the experimental discovery that

[1] Jaurès, 'Conférence sur *Travail* d'Émile Zola', *Revue socialiste*, vol. xxxii (1901), pp. 641–53.

co-operation yields greater general prosperity than strife or competition, and that the happiness of the individual is inseparably linked to the welfare of the whole community. Another article of their belief was that it was wiser to utilize the passions of the individual for the general good than to suppress them; for no passion is evil, the seven deadly sins are an invention of theologians. As Zola wrote in *Travail*:

Il n'y a pas de concupiscents, il n'y a que des cœurs de flamme qui rêvent d'infini dans la joie d'amour. Il n'y a pas d'homme colère, d'homme avare, d'homme menteur, gourmand, paresseux, envieux, orgueilleux, il n'y a que des hommes dont on n'a pas su diriger les forces intérieures, les énergies déréglées, les besoins d'action, de lutte et de victoire. Avec un avare, on fait un prudent, un économe. Avec un emporté, un envieux, un orgueilleux, on fait un héros, se donnant tout entier pour un peu de gloire.

The attraction of this system for Zola was twofold. It traced a path to universal harmony which by-passed revolutionary violence; and Zola was bourgeois enough to abhor the wastefulness and injustice of terrors, red or white: he had condemned anarchist excesses implicitly in *Germinal*, explicitly in *Paris*, and now, in *Travail*, he has an anarchist who, at Luc's instance, turns over from manufacturing home-made bombs to fashioning exquisite pottery. And secondly, the theory of the free development of human passions, the doctrine that all inhibition is conducive to evil, chimed with Zola's anti-Catholicism.

Le coup de génie était d'utiliser les passions de l'homme comme les forces mêmes de la vie. La longue et désastreuse erreur du catholicisme venait d'avoir voulu les mater, de s'être efforcé de détruire l'homme dans l'homme, pour le jeter en esclave à son Dieu de tyrannie et de néant. Les passions, dans la libre société future, devaient produire autant de bien qu'elles avaient produit de mal, dans la société enchaînée, terrorisée, des siècles morts.

The sanctification of passion provided Zola in addition with further justification of his own conduct with Jeanne Rozerot: his hero Luc is surrounded by three affectionate women, and in the social paradise of the Crècherie free love is the rule; the very church in which weddings used to be celebrated in the bad old days is razed by lightning and left in ruins.

The first part of *Travail* may be said to incorporate the new Gospel according to Fourier; the second part relates the Acts of the Apostles Luc and Jordan, and includes the destruction by fire of Old Babylon, the evil capitalist factory, which is replaced by the New Jerusalem, Luc's Crècherie. The third and last part is pure prophecy: it is Zola's 'Book of Revelations'. The classes fuse into a single society, as the younger generations grow up and inter-marry. Other communities are founded on the model of the original phalanstery, collective farms spring up all around, new schools apply improved educational methods, hours of work in the factory are reduced to two a day, the machines are sparkling, silent, electric-ally driven. On holidays they are decked with flowers, and in the evenings the workers join in open-air feasting; and such is the spirit of fraternity in the city that even the birds lose their shyness and hop about among the tables pecking at crumbs.

This earthly elysium was timed to come to pass during the second half of the twentieth century. Predictions have a way of provoking melancholy consternation among those who live in the period that was being anticipated. The principal miscalculation made by Zola was to assume that spiritual progress would keep pace with technical advance. Applied science has made even more rapid strides than Zola foresaw (the scientist Jordan, as he lies dying, *circa* 1950, is still at the stage of predicting the conquest of the air and the invention of wireless); but the moral nature of man has remained what it was, if it has not retrogressed. Consequently the utopia of *Travail* seems as distant today as it did in 1901. Only some of the grimmer events which he expected in the transitional period have taken place in striking conformity with Zola's fore-casts. To have presaged the frightful carnage of the coming world war, as he does in the last chapter of *Travail*, needed, perhaps, no remarkable powers of divination when the armaments race was starting and international 'incidents' were becoming increasingly ominous. More noteworthy is the description of a 'collectivist revolution' brought about by a *coup* in a 'Great Republic':

Dès le lendemain, ils ont appliqué leur programme entièrement, à coups de lois et de décrets. L'expropriation en masse a commencé, toute la richesse privée est devenue la richesse de la nation, tous les instruments de travail ont fait retour aux travailleurs. Il n'y a plus eu ni propriétaires, ni capitalistes, ni patrons, l'État seul a régné, maître de tout, à la fois propriétaire, capitaliste et patron, régulateur et distri-buteur de la vie sociale.

The state encountered furious resistance from the dispossessed;

a costly civil war ensued; and when the revolutionaries had won, the running of the system necessitated the creation of a new bureaucracy, 'une organisation compliquée semblait repousser peu à peu, encombrer les rouages de la société naissante. On retombait à l'enrégimentement de la caserne, jamais cadres plus durs n'avaient parqué les hommes en des cases plus étroites.' But in the end the collectivist state was humanized and pacified, and learned to coexist in fraternal solidarity with other nations.

For the plot of *Vérité*, the third novel of *Les Quatre Évangiles*, Zola quite simply transposed the dramatic events of the Dreyfus Affair, adding at the end a scene of rehabilitation and restitution which he did not live to see enacted in reality. All the prominent figures in the Affair have their counterparts in the novel. The Jewish officer Dreyfus becomes the Jewish school-teacher Simon. The crime of which he is accused and for which he is wrongfully sentenced is the violation and murder of a schoolboy, his nephew. The real culprit (the Esterhazy of the case) is a monk, Gorgias, one of the teachers at the church school that the dead boy attended. The evidence that swayed the jury (*Vérité* is the nearest approach to a detective novel that Zola ever wrote) is a forgery, like the forgeries of Henry that helped keep Dreyfus on Devil's Island; when Simon's brother, with Marc Froment's help, discovers absolute proof of the prisoner's innocence, there is a second trial, and a second mockery of justice, obviously recalling the fiasco at Rennes. P arallels, down to the minutest details, could be multiplied.

The significant aspects of the transposition are that the crime committed is of an altogether more bestial nature, and that the guilty man is a servant of the Church. In the Dreyfus Affair of history it is true that a number of Catholics were anti-revisionists and that a number of Dreyfusards were anti-Catholics. In *Vérité* the split between believers and free-thinkers, the former on Gorgias's side and the latter on Simon's, is made much more absolute. The suggestion Zola makes is that religion blunts a man's sense of justice.

Actually, *Vérité* goes far beyond that in its criticism of the Church. The book aims to discredit Catholicism by every means, and recoils from no imputation, however monstrous. Moreover, it is not merely anti-Catholic, it is anti-Christian. In *Les Trois Villes* the objection to Christianity had been that it was inadequate for the modern era; in *Vérité* it is condemned outright as iniquitous from its very origins.

The burden of the accusation that Zola, through the medium of his hero Marc, brings against Christianity is that it makes servility its highest ideal. *Vérité*, as he noted in the *ébauche*, was to illustrate 'la thèse contraire à celle de l'Évangile: "Heureux les pauvres d'esprit", etc. Avec les pauvres d'esprit on ne fait que des bêtes, des esclaves. La duperie du royaume du ciel. La misère des siècles perpétuelle par l'ignorance sainte du catholicisme.'[1] These jottings are expanded in various parts of the book, notably on the very last page:

Une parole exécrable avait osé dire: 'Heureux les pauvres d'esprit!' et la misère de deux mille ans était née de cette mortelle erreur. La légende des bienfaits de l'ignorance apparaissait maintenant comme un long crime social. Pauvreté, saleté, iniquité, superstition, mensonge, tyrannie, la femme exploitée et méprisée, l'homme hébété et dompté, tous les maux physiques et moraux étaient les fruits de cette ignorance voulue, érigée en système de politique gouvernementale et de police divine. La connaissance seule devait tuer les dogmes menteurs, disperser ceux qui en vivaient, être la source des grandes richesses, aussi bien des moissons débordantes de la terre que de la floraison générale des esprits. Non! le bonheur n'avait jamais été dans l'ignorance, il était dans la connaissance, qui allait changer l'affreux champ de la misère matérielle et morale en une vaste terre féconde, dont la culture, d'année en année, décuplerait les richesses.

This tirade can be left without comment as far as its substance goes; and one can only marvel at the juvenile brio of this impiety in a sexagenarian as capable, evidently, of passionate conviction and confidence in the future as the most idealistic reformer of twenty.

The negative thesis of *Vérité*, represented by this fierce indictment of religion, is balanced by its positive side, the advocacy of improved or intensified primary education. The two things were complementary, for Zola held that the quickest way to detach France from Catholicism was to turn each little French boy and girl into a sound Cartesian. This, at any rate, seems to be the guiding principle adopted by Marc in his classroom and recommended by the more sensible of his superiors, like Salvan, the director of the École Normale from which Marc graduated, who speaks with enthusiasm about 'le bataillon sacré des instituteurs

---

[1] B.N. MS. *Nouv. acq. fr.* 10343, fol. 309.

primaires qui devaient instruire tout le peuple de France, à la seule clarté des certitudes scientifiquement établies, pour le délivrer des ténèbres séculaires et le rendre enfin capable de vérité, de liberté et de justice'. The fact that Denise and Jacques were now of school age largely accounts for this preoccupation with educational aims and methods, which is visible too in *Travail* but hardly at all in any previous works. But it must be remembered too that Zola had, in 1898, been forcibly reminded how easily an ill-educated citizenry could be turned into a mindless rabble by unscrupulous propagandists; and furthermore, that the book was composed at a time when anticlerical feeling was running strongly: the law forbidding members of 'unauthorized' religious congregations to teach was passed, under Waldeck-Rousseau's ministry, on 1 July 1901.

The fourth of the *Évangiles* was to be called *Justice*. Though the title would hardly suggest this, it was to deal with the problem of disarmament, which the Hague Conference of 1899 and the outbreak of the Boer War in the same year had, in different ways, made topical. Zola's intentions in this unwritten novel can be deduced from a few notes to be found in the papers relating to *Fécondité*:

La justice qui réunit l'humanité, la rassemble, la ramène à la famille unique (?), qui assure la paix et fait le bonheur final. . . . La justice, où je fais rentrer 'l'humanité', les peuples se fédérant, revenant à la famille unique, la question des races étudiée et résolue, la paix universelle à la fin.[1]

The programme Zola suggested should be implemented during the twentieth century had thus four points, each made in one of the novels of his tetralogy: the expansion of the population, the reorganization of the economy, the improvement of education, and the abolition of war. The first of these aims has been only too successfully achieved, and some progress has been made with the second and third. The last remains dangerously unfulfilled, of course, but as early as 1898, in the thick of the *affaire*, Zola saw how it might come about, and included in his 'Impressions d'audience' a remarkable forecast of what we have come to call hopefully the 'nuclear stalemate': 'Est-ce que la guerre ne va pas être tuée par ces armements excessifs, par ces nouveaux engins de

---

[1] B.N. MS. *Nouv. acq. fr.* 10301, fols. 1, 10. Cf. also M. Le Blond, 'Les Projets littéraires d'Émile Zola au moment de sa mort', *Mercure de France*, vol. cxcix (1927), pp. 5–25.

mort qui doivent raser des cent mille hommes, par ces nations en armes, qui n'oseront plus s'attaquer, sans craindre de s'entre-détruire en huit jours?'

On 2 July 1902 Zola wrote to Alfred Bruneau from Médan: 'Je passe de délicieuses après-midi dans mon jardin, à regarder tout vivre autour de moi. Avec l'âge, je sens tout s'en aller et j'aime tout plus passionnément.' Zola had then less than three months to live. No one who knew him could have suspected it: his robust good health would normally have carried him over another twenty years at least; his wife, frailer than he, survived until 1925.

Instead he met death as his master Flaubert had met it, annihilation bursting over him in a thunderclap. 'Belle mort,' Zola had written on that occasion, 'coup de massue enviable, et qui m'a fait souhaiter pour moi et pour tous ceux que j'aime cet anéantissement d'insecte écrasé sous un doigt géant.'

He finished *Vérité* on 8 August, but remained in the country idling for a few weeks until on 28 September he decided to return to town rather earlier in the year than usual. The weather was still warm at Médan, so much so that Mme Zola wanted to stay on,[1] but a rainstorm over Paris made it wet and chilly on their arrival; instructions were accordingly given to light a fire in the bedroom that evening. The following morning neither Zola nor his wife were heard to get up at the usual hour, but it was supposed they were resting after the fatigues of the move. Later in the morning the alarm was raised. Force had to be used to enter the room, since Zola had bolted the door on the inside according to his usual custom—he had an irrational dread of sleeping in a room where any stranger might walk in. The novelist was found dead, his wife unconscious but still living.

An inquest was, of course, necessary. Zola's death was due to carbon monoxide poisoning; his body had been found on the floor, while his wife was still lying on the bed, a few feet higher up, where the dense toxic gas was in a weaker concentration. Mme Zola said in evidence that she had woken in the night feeling sick; her husband, hearing her groan, told her he was ill too and could do nothing for her. She urged him to call the servants, but he demurred, not wanting to rouse the household in the middle of the night, and assured her that they would have got over their indis-

---

[1] See Saint-Georges de Bouhélier, 'La Fatalité dans la mort d'Émile Zola', *Revue bleue*, 5e série, vol. ix (1908), pp. 412–15.

position by the morning. These were, apparently, Zola's last words: 'Demain nous serons guéris.'

The carbon monoxide could have come only from the burning ovoids in the grate, which, however, would have produced fumes only if the chimney was not drawing. Accordingly, on the coroner's instructions, similar fires were laid and lit on 8 and 11 October. Samples of air taken on the two succeeding mornings were analysed, but found to contain carbon monoxide only in minute and harmless proportions; guinea-pigs who had been left in the room overnight were alive in the room the following day. Inspection of the flue revealed some soot, but not in sufficient quantities to block the passage. It was noted that the chimney issued on to the roof of the neighbouring house, where some repairs had recently been undertaken.

Although the presence of a toxic concentration of carbon monoxide in the atmosphere of the room during the night of 28–29 September remained unexplained, the coroner did not bring in an open verdict, but ruled that Zola's death was due to accidental causes; and since the experts' reports remained confidential, the public—and Zola's later biographers—accepted this version of the fatality. In the tense political atmosphere of 1902 a different verdict, particularly in respect of the death of so prominent a champion of Dreyfus, might have created a disturbing situation.

The question of the circumstances in which Zola met his end was reopened in 1953, when a communication was made to the newspaper *La Libération* by a 68-year-old correspondent who chose this way of unburdening himself of certain confidences which he alleged had been made to him in 1927 by a friend who had died shortly afterwards. This friend, by trade a fitter of heating appliances, and a nationalist by political persuasion, had sworn him to secrecy and then revealed that back in 1902, while doing some work on the roof of a certain building, he and his mates decided to stop up the chimney coming from the adjoining house, the proprietor of which they knew to be Zola. This was done on the day on which the novelist returned to Paris; they cleared the chimney the following morning, to avert suspicion.[1]

This hearsay evidence, coming to light half a century after the event, constitutes of course no proof that Zola was murdered in the way described. On the other hand the newspaper's informant

[1] J. Bedel, 'Zola a-t-il été assassiné?', *La Libération*, 29 Sept.–2 Oct. 1953.

could not have known that the evidence presented at the coroner's court was insufficient to explain how the supposed accident had occurred; this fact came to light only after an investigation of the court records undertaken by the newspaper in consequence of receiving this information. The negative results of the analysis of the air, and the survival of the guinea-pigs, are entirely explicable if one accepts the hypothesis that the chimney was blocked at its outlet and subsequently cleared. Further, as Zola's son, Dr. Jacques Émile-Zola, disclosed in a later interview with a reporter from *La Libération*,[1] his father had received in the last four years of his life hundreds of letters threatening him with death. The crime, if crime it was, could not have been calculated: whatever happened, chance must have played a large part in the fatality. It could have been known that the chimney came from the Zolas' apartment but it could not have been known that it came from their bedroom. Nor could it have been known that a smokeless fuel was to be used; a wood or coal fire burning in a blocked chimney would merely have filled the room with smoke. On balance, it seems prudent to conclude that Zola might have had to pay with his life for his audacity in publishing *J'accuse*; but we shall probably never be able to say with certainty that he did die a political martyr.

The military funeral that Zola was given, the remarkable grave-side oration of Anatole France, the translation of the novelist's ashes to the Panthéon in 1908 are events which do not touch Zola any longer, but only the fixed, official, canonized abstraction into which death turned him:

Maigre immortalité noire et dorée.

Let us rather leave him with, in our ears, that reiterated lament of Mme Charpentier which has about it all the fretful, impotent inanity of life: 'C'est trop bête! . . . Et il meurt comme ça! Est-ce bête? . . . Concevez-vous ça? Ils n'avaient qu'à ouvrir les fenêtres! Et ils ne l'ont pas fait! Enfin, non, c'est trop bête! . . .'

---

[1] Published in that paper 6 Oct. 1953. Dr. Émile-Zola was also interviewed by a reporter from *Le Monde* to whom he expressed his belief that it was entirely possible that his father had been murdered: see G. Reuillard, 'Zola assassiné?', *Le Monde*, 1 June 1954.

EPILOGUE

WHEN Zola was still alive, Havelock Ellis once tried to put himself into posterity's shoes and cast a backward look on the novelist's work from some such vantage-point as we enjoy today. Referring chiefly to *Les Rougon-Macquart*, Ellis foretold that

for a vivid, impartial picture—on the whole a faithful picture—of certain of the most characteristic aspects of the period, seen indeed from the outside, but drawn by a contemporary in all its intimate and even repulsive details, the readers of a future age can best go to Zola. What would we not give for a thirteenth-century Zola! . . . But our children's children, with the same passions alive in their hearts under incalculably different circumstances, will in the pages of the *Rougon-Macquart* series find themselves back again among all the strange, remote details of a vanished world.

Havelock Ellis's 'children's children' are the generation which is now coming to Zola with fresh minds and eyes. Is it true that the description of society they find in the novels has no application to the world in which they live? Is the novelist no more than the careful chronicler of a buried past, of the era of horse-cabs, gas-lighting, billycock hats, and large-hearted optimism, the era bounded at one end by Charles Dickens and at the other by H. G. Wells? Or has this pictured universe some more comprehensive validity which embraces the present as well as the past? For unless it has, Zola will be found to have written no more than period pieces, on which the dust will grow steadily thicker from year to year.

He runs little risk of such a fate. His work has a living interest which it owes to the one significant innovation that his vision of the universe contained. Zola was the first writer to show a society in which the aggregate was greater than the separate unit. All through the novels of his maturity and decline runs this one fruitful and fundamental idea. It manifests itself artistically in his characteristic descriptions of crowds in which the individual founders and is lost to view; in the way his imagination was time and time again captivated by huge impersonal entities, factories and bazaars and mines and markets, battlefields and railways, cities; in his evident incapacity to isolate, explore, and expound the self-sufficient character. It declares itself too in his thought, in the glorification of human fertility and productive labour, in the rapt fascination with which he brooded over ancestry and progeny; there is always the same idea, that the individual is negligible, that what matters is the whole, and the contribution the individual makes to the whole. Among the last lines Zola wrote was a quotation he copied from Alfred Fouillée: 'Quoi qu'en puisse dire Ibsen, "l'homme fort" n'est pas "l'homme seul", mais l'homme uni par la pensée et par le cœur à tous les autres hommes, l'individualité en qui vit l'humanité entière.' Zola added the comment: 'Là est le sujet de mon roman.' The novel he referred to was the unwritten fourth Gospel, *Justice*; but in one book after another, from *La Confession de Claude* onwards, can be found illustrations of this dictum. Here we have the distinguishing feature of Zola's work—this refusal to treat the unit as anything but a component of the mass, to see the individual as anything more than a representative splinter of its caste, class, nation, or ultimately of mankind. The outsider, the unassimilated stranger, has no place in Zola's novels; every character is a function, none is an unrelated integer. It is in this that Zola most truly broke with the past and initiated a new and durable phase in the European novel, all unawares dealing Romanticism the blow from which it has not recovered; for the Romantic idea was enshrined in forceful, sometimes splendid, sometimes criminal individuals, in a René, a Julien Sorel, a Vautrin, an Indiana; and the Romantic writers, even Balzac, painted society only as a sombre backcloth against which the floodlit hero could be more brilliantly picked out. Zola was the first of those who raised sociology to the dignity of art; he was the prophet of a new age of mass-psychology, mass-education, and mass-entertainment, an age in which the part is never greater than the whole. An age without fineness, almost certainly; without fire and without colour, perhaps: but an age, it may be, of greater strength and broader justice; on that no one can speak yet with finality, for this age that Zola wrote of is, without the least doubt, our own age.

BIBLIOGRAPHY

I. WORKS PUBLISHED DURING ZOLA'S LIFETIME

A. THE EARLY NOVELS

1. *La Confession de Claude.* 1865.
2. *Le Vœu d'une morte.* 1866.
3. *Les Mystères de Marseille.* 1867.
4. *Thérèse Raquin.* 1867.
5. *Madeleine Férat.* 1868.

B. LES ROUGON-MACQUART

(Dates given are those of newspaper publication. The novel was normally issued in book form in the month during which serialization was completed, or in the succeeding month. Exceptions to this rule are noted.)

1. *La Fortune des Rougon.* Serialized in *Le Siècle*, 28 June–10 August 1870 and, after a hiatus due to the war, 18–21 March 1871. Published October 1871.
2. *La Curée.* Opening chapters only serialized in *La Cloche*, 29 September–5 November 1871. Published January 1872.
3. *Le Ventre de Paris.* Serialized in *L'État*, 12 January–17 March 1873.
4. *La Conquête de Plassans.* Serialized in *Le Siècle*, 24 February–25 April 1874.
5. *La Faute de l'abbé Mouret.* Serialized in *Vestnik Evropy*, January–March 1875.
6. *Son Excellence Eugène Rougon.* Serialized in *Le Siècle*, 25 January–11 March 1876.
7. *L'Assommoir.* Serialized in *Le Bien public*, 13 April–7 June 1876, then (*Le Bien public* having refused to continue publication) in *La République des Lettres*, 9 July 1876–7 January 1877.
8. *Une Page d'amour.* Serialized in *Le Bien public*, 11 December 1877–4 April 1878.
9. *Nana.* Serialized in *Le Voltaire*, 16 October 1879–5 February 1880.
10. *Pot-Bouille.* Serialized in *Le Gaulois*, 23 January–14 April 1882.
11. *Au Bonheur des Dames.* Serialized in *Le Gil Blas*, 17 December 1882–1 March 1883.
12. *La Joie de vivre.* Serialized in *Le Gil Blas*, 29 November 1883–3 February 1884.
13. *Germinal.* Serialized in *Le Gil Blas*, 26 November 1884–25 February 1885.
14. *L'Œuvre.* Serialized in *Le Gil Blas*, 23 December 1885–27 March 1886.
15. *La Terre.* Serialized in *Le Gil Blas*, 29 May–16 September 1887.
16. *Le Rêve.* Serialized in *La Revue illustrée*, 1 April–15 October 1888.
17. *La Bête humaine.* Serialized in *La Vie populaire*, 14 November 1889–2 March 1890.

18. *L'Argent*. Serialized in *Le Gil Blas*, 30 November 1890–3 March 1891.
19. *La Débâcle*. Serialized in *La Vie populaire*, 21 February–21 July 1892.
20. *Le Docteur Pascal*. Serialized in *La Revue hebdomadaire*, 18 March–17 June 1893.

C. LES TROIS VILLES
1. *Lourdes*. Serialized in *Le Gil Blas*, 15 April–15 August 1894.
2. *Rome*. Serialized in *Le Journal*, 21 December 1895–8 May 1896.
3. *Paris*. Serialized in *Le Journal*, 23 October 1897–9 February 1898.

D. LES QUATRE ÉVANGILES
1. *Fécondité*. Serialized in *L'Aurore*, 15 May–4 October 1899.
2. *Travail*. Serialized in *L'Aurore*, 3 December 1900–11 March 1901.
3. *Vérité*. Serialized in *L'Aurore*, 10 September 1902–15 February 1903.

E. SHORT STORIES AND PLAYS
1. *Contes à Ninon*. 1864.
2. *Nouveaux Contes à Ninon*. 1874.
3. *Théâtre*. 1878.
4. *Le Capitaine Burle*. 1882.
5. *Naïs Micoulin*. 1884.

F. CRITICAL AND POLEMICAL WORKS
1. *Mes haines*. 1866.
2. *Le Roman expérimental*. 1880.
3. *Les Romanciers naturalistes*. 1881.
4. *Documents littéraires*. 1881.
5. *Le Naturalisme au théâtre*. 1881.
6. *Nos auteurs dramatiques*. 1881.
7. *Une Campagne*. 1882.
8. *Nouvelle Campagne*. 1897.
9. *La Vérité en marche*. 1901.

II. COLLECTIONS PUBLISHED POSTHUMOUSLY

1. *Poèmes lyriques*. 1921. (The librettos of six operas written for Alfred Bruneau.)
2. *Madame Sourdis*. 1929. (Short stories.)
3. *La République en marche, chroniques parlementaires*, ed. J. Kayser. 1956. (Reports of the sittings of the Assembly at Bordeaux and Versailles, 1871–2.)
4. *Salons*, ed. F. W. J. Hemmings and R. J. Niess. 1959. (The art criticism.)
5. *L'Atelier de Zola*, ed. M. Kanes. 1963. (A selection of newspaper articles from the period 1865–70.)
6. *Lettres de Paris*, ed. P. A. Duncan and Vera Erdely. 1963. (Extracts from articles published in *Vestnik Evropy*, 1875–80.)

III. CRITICAL EDITIONS

The most complete is that edited by Maurice Le Blond and issued by the Bernouard Press, 1928–9. An excellent edition of *Les Rougon-Macquart*, with a full and authoritative critical apparatus by Henri Mitterand, is being issued currently in the Bibliothèque de la Pléiade series; the set, when completed, will run to five volumes.

IV. LETTERS

The basic collection is that of the Bernouard edition (*Correspondance*). Other letters have been published as follows:

M. K. LEMKE, *M. M. Stasyulevitch i ego sovremenniki v ikh perepiske*, vol. iii, St. Petersburg, 1912. (44 letters from Zola to Stasyulevitch over the years 1875–89.)

A. ZÉVAÈS, 'Une Correspondance Zola–Vallès', *Commune*, no. 53 (1938), pp. 553–63.

R. J. NIESS, *Émile Zola's Letters to J. Van Santen Kolff*. St. Louis: Washington University Press, 1940.

——'Nine letters from Émile Zola to Frans Netscher', *P.M.L.A.*, vol. lvi (1941), pp. 261–5.

G. ROBERT, 'Lettres inédites à Henry Fèvre', *Revue d'Histoire littéraire de la France*, vol. l (1950), pp. 64–82.

G. RANDAL, 'Sept lettres inédites d'Émile Zola à Alphonse Daudet', *Quo Vadis*, vol. v (1952), pp. 23–42.

J. C. LAPP, 'Zola et Maurice de Fleury', *Revue des Sciences humaines*, fasc. 73 (1954), pp. 67–75.

A. J. GEORGE, 'Some unpublished correspondence of Émile Zola', *Symposium*, vol. x (1956), pp. 271–6.

M. GIRARD, 'Deux lettres inédites de Zola à Huysmans', *Revue d'Histoire littéraire de la France*, vol. lviii (1958), pp. 372–3.

A. J. SALVAN, *Émile Zola. Lettres inédites à Henry Céard*. Providence, R.I.: Brown University Press. 1959.

—— *Vingt messages inédits de Zola à Céard*. Providence, R.I.: Brown University Press. 1961.

J. CHRISTIE, 'Zola, Labori and *La Grande Revue* (1900); an unpublished correspondence', *Renaissance and Modern Studies*, vol. iv (1960), pp. 44–58.

—— 'Zola, Labori, and Frédéric Passy, an unpublished correspondence concerning Zola's *Travail* (1901)', *Nottingham French Studies*, vol. i (1962), pp. 26–38.

C. BELLANGER, 'Une correspondance inédite . . .', *Les Cahiers naturalistes*, no. 26 (1964), pp. 5–44. (Exchange of letters between Zola and Géry-Legrand, 1863–5.)

J. C. LAPP, 'Émile Zola et Ludovic Halévy: notes sur une correspondance', *Les Cahiers naturalistes*, no. 27 (1964), pp. 91–100.

V. MANUSCRIPT MATERIAL

There are two main collections of Zola's manuscripts: one at the Bibliothèque Nationale, Paris (B.N. MS. *Nouvelles acquisitions françaises* 10268–345), and one at the Bibliothèque d'Aix-en-Provence (MS. 1590–1606). The first of these collections contains material concerning *Les Rougon-Macquart* and *Les Quatre Évangiles*, the second that concerning

Les Trois Villes. Part of the *dossier* of *Le Docteur Pascal* is in the Bodmer Library, Geneva; the manuscript of *Nana* is in the Pierpont Morgan collection, New York.

VI. JOURNALISM

A small proportion of the articles written by Zola for the press was published in collections during his lifetime (see above, I (F), 'Critical and Polemical Works'). Certain others have appeared more recently (II, 3–6). But for the most part it is still necessary for the student to consult the original newspaper files. The following list comprises the principal series:

Le Petit Journal, 21 January–1 June 1865.
Le Salut public (Lyons), 23 January 1865–1 January 1867.
L'Événement, 2 February–15 November 1866.
Le Figaro, 30 November 1866–15 April 1867.
L'Événement illustré, 23 April–1 September 1868.
La Tribune, 14 June 1868–9 January 1870.
Le Gaulois, 22 September 1868–30 September 1869.
Le Rappel, 15 May 1869–13 May 1870.
La Cloche, 2 February 1870–20 December 1872.
Le Sémaphore (Marseilles), 14 February 1871–20 May 1877.
Le Corsaire, 3–22 December 1872.
L'Avenir national, 25 February–10 June 1873.
Vestnik Evropy (St. Petersburg), March 1875–December 1880.
Le Bien public, 10 April 1876–24 June 1878.
Le Voltaire, 9 July 1878–31 August 1880.
Le Figaro, 20 September 1880–22 September 1881.
Le Figaro, 1 December 1895–13 June 1896.
L'Aurore, 13 January 1898–22 December 1900.

VII. STUDIES OF ZOLA'S LIFE AND WORK

The following list includes the principal documentary sources of our knowledge of Zola's life, together with a selection of the more useful books and articles that have been written about his work.

ADHÉMAR, Hélène et Jean. 'Zola et la peinture', *Arts,* 12–18 December 1952.

ALBALAT, Antoine. *Gustave Flaubert et ses amis.* Paris, Plon, 1927. ('Relations de Zola avec Flaubert', pp. 233–40.)

ALEXIS, Paul. *Émile Zola, notes d'un ami.* Paris, Charpentier, 1882. 338 pp.

ALMÉRAS, Henri d'. *Avant la gloire: leurs débuts. Première série.* Paris, Société française d'Imprimerie et de Librairie, 1902. ('Émile Zola', pp. 188–96.)

ANTOINE, André. *Mes souvenirs sur le Théâtre-Libre.* Paris, Fayard, 1921. 324 pp.

—— *Mes souvenirs sur le Théâtre Antoine et sur l'Odéon.* Paris, Grasset, 1928. 297 pp.

ARAGON, Louis. *La Lumière de Stendhal.* Paris, Denoël, 1954. ('Actualité d'Émile Zola', pp. 245–57.)

ARRIGHI, Paul. 'Zola à Rome', *Revue de Littérature comparée*, vol. viii (1928), pp. 488–99.
—— 'Zola en Italie. Zola et De Sanctis', *Revue de Littérature comparée*, vol. xxvii (1953), pp. 438–46.
ARTINIAN, Artine, et MAYNIAL, Édouard. 'Lettres inédites de Guy de Maupassant à Émile Zola', *Bulletin du Bibliophile* (1950), pp. 131–58.
ATKINS, Stuart. 'A possible Dickens influence in Zola', *Modern Language Quarterly*, vol. viii (1947), pp. 302–8. (*Thérèse Raquin.*)
AUBERY, Pierre. 'Quelques sources du thème de l'action directe dans *Germinal*', *Symposium*, vol. xiii (1959), pp. 63–72.
—— 'Genèse et développement du personnage de Lantier', *French Studies*, vol. xvi (1962), pp. 142–53.
AUERBACH, Erich. *Mimesis. Dargestellte Wirklichkeit in der abendländischen Literatur*. Berne, Francke, 1946. (Zola, pp. 451–7.)
AURIANT, L. 'Les dessous de *Nana*', *L'Esprit français*, no. 72 (1932), pp. 147–51.
—— 'Quelques sources ignorées de *Nana*', *Mercure de France*, vol. cclii (1934), pp. 180–8.
—— 'Une autre source ignorée de *Nana*', *Mercure de France*, vol. ccliv (1934), pp. 223–4.
—— '*Venise sauvée* ou les débiteurs découverts', *Mercure de France*, vol. cclviii (1935), pp. 297–308. (Concerns the borrowing from Otway in *Nana*.)
—— 'Balzac et Zola', *La France active*, no. 159 (1937), pp. 100–8.
—— 'Émile Zola et les deux Houssaye', *Mercure de France*, vol. ccxcvii (1940), pp. 555–69.
—— *La Véritable Histoire de Nana*. Paris, Mercure de France, 1942. 146 pp.
—— 'Duranty et Zola', *La Nef*, no. 20 (1946), pp. 43–58.

BAILLOT, Alexandre. *Émile Zola, l'homme, le penseur, le critique*. Paris, Société française d'Imprimerie et de Librairie, 1924. 190 pp.
BANDY, W. T. 'Zola imitateur de Baudelaire', *Revue d'Histoire littéraire de la France*, vol. liii (1953), pp. 210–12.
—— 'Quelques pages retrouvées de Zola', *Mercure de France*, vol. cccxxii (1954), pp. 359–63.
BARBUSSE, Henri. *Zola*. Paris, Gallimard, 1932. 296 pp.
BARJON, Louis. *Mondes d'écrivains, destinées d'hommes*. Tournai, Casterman, 1960. ('Le monde du réalisme: Zola', pp. 13–30.)
BATILLIAT, MARCEL. *Émile Zola*. Paris, Rieder, 1931. 83+xl pp.
BEDEL, Jean. 'Zola a-t-il été assassiné?', *Libération*, 29 September–2 October 1953.
BELLOC LOWNDES, Mrs. Marie Adelaide. *Where Love and Friendship dwelt*. London, Macmillan, 1943. (Zola, pp. 180–6.)
BERGERAT, Émile. *Souvenirs d'un enfant de Paris. Les années de bohème*. Paris, Fasquelle, 1911. ('Émile Zola chez Théophile Gautier', pp. 398–403.)
BILLY, André. 'Les amours de Zola', *Le Figaro littéraire*, 1 May 1954.

BILLY, André. 'Sur Mme Alexandrine Zola', *Le Figaro littéraire*, 12 June 1954.

BRADY, Patrick. 'Claude Lantier', *Les Cahiers naturalistes*, no. 17 (1961), pp. 10–18.

—— 'Les clefs de *l'Œuvre* de Zola', *Australian Journal of French Studies*, vol. i (1964), pp. 257–71.

BRAIBANT, Charles. *Le Secret d'Anatole France*. Paris, Denoël et Steele, 1935. ('Anatole France et Zola', pp. 285–302.)

BRANDES, Georg. *Émile Zola*. Berlin, Eckstein, 1889. 30 pp.

BRISSON, Adolphe. *L'Envers de la gloire. Enquêtes et documents inédits*. Paris, Flammarion, 1904. ('Émile Zola: l'aube de la gloire', pp. 70–89; 'Le caractère d'Émile Zola', pp. 90–105.)

BROMBERT, Victor. *The Intellectual Hero. Studies in the French Novel, 1880–1955*. Philadelphia and New York, Lippincott, 1961. ('The apostolate of Marc Froment', pp. 68–79.)

BROWN, Calvin S. *Repetition in Zola's Novels*. Athens, Georgia, University of Georgia Press, 1952. 124 pp.

—— 'Music in Zola's fiction, especially Wagner's music', *P.M.L.A.*, vol. lxxi (1956), pp. 84–96.

—— and NIESS, Robert J. 'Wagner and Zola again', *P.M.L.A.*, vol. lxxiii (1958), pp. 448–52.

BROWN, Sydney Barlow. *La Peinture des métiers et des mœurs professionnelles dans les romans de Zola*. Montpellier, Impr. de la Charité, 1928. 219 pp.

BRUNEAU, Alfred. *A l'ombre d'un grand cœur. Souvenirs d'une collaboration*. Paris, Fasquelle, 1932. 235 pp.

BURNS, Colin A. 'Émile Zola et Henry Céard', *Les Cahiers naturalistes*, no. 2 (1955), pp. 81–87.

—— 'Documentation et imagination chez Émile Zola', *Les Cahiers naturalistes*, nos. 24–25 (1963), pp. 69–78.

—— 'Zola in exile. Notes on an unpublished diary of 1898', *French Studies*, vol. xvii (1963), pp. 14–26.

—— 'Émile Zola: *Pages d'exil*, publiées et annotées par Colin Burns', *Nottingham French Studies*, vol. iii (1964), pp. 2–46, 48–62.

CAIN, Julien, 'La genèse de *Germinal*', *Le Figaro littéraire*, 3 October 1953.

CARIAS, Léon. 'France et Zola avant l'Affaire', *La Grande Revue*, vol. cxxiv (1927), pp. 402–38.

CAROL-BÉRARD. 'L'intelligence musicale de Zola', *Revue mondiale*, vol. clv (1923), pp. 187–92.

CARTER, Lawson A. *Zola and the Theater*. New Haven, Yale University Press, 1963. viii+231 pp.

CASTELNAU, Jacques. *Zola*. Paris, Tallandier, 1946. 253 pp.

CÉARD, Henry. 'Zola intime', *Revue illustrée*, vol. iii (1887), pp. 141–8.

—— *Lettres inédites à Émile Zola*, publiées et annotées par C. A. Burns. Paris, Nizet, 1958. 428 pp.

CÉZANNE, Paul. *Correspondance* recueillie, annotée et préfacée par John Rewald. Paris, Grasset, 1937. 319 pp.

CHABAUD, Alfred. 'Un épisode inconnu de l'enfance d'Émile Zola', *Mercure de France*, vol. ccx (1929), p. 508.

CHAMBRON, Jacqueline. 'Réalisme et épopée chez Zola. De *l'Assommoir* à *Germinal*', *La Pensée*, no. 44 (1952), pp. 122–34.

CHAMPSAUR, Félicien. *Les Hommes d'aujourd'hui, no. 4. Émile Zola*. Paris, Cinqualbre, 1878. 3 pp. (unpaginated).

CHEMEL, Henri. 'Zola collaborateur du *Sémaphore* de Marseille', *Les Cahiers naturalistes*, no. 14 (1960), pp. 555–67 and no. 18 (1961), pp. 71–79.

CHENNEVIÈRE, Georges. 'Émile Zola', *Europe*, vol. xv (1927), pp. 504–23, and vol. xvi (1928), pp. 85–102.

CIM, Albert. *Le Dîner des Gens de Lettres. Souvenirs littéraires*. Paris, Flammarion, 1903. 347 pp.

CLARETIE, Jules. 'La mort de Zola', *Revue de France*, vol. v (1922), pp. 853–6.

COGNY, Pierre. 'Émile Zola devant le problème de Jésus-Christ, d'après des documents inédits', *Studi Francesi*, no. 23 (1964), pp. 255–64.

CONRAD, Michael Georg. *Émile Zola*. Berlin, Marquardt, 1906. 100 pp.

CRESSOT, Marcel. 'Zola et Michelet. Essai sur la genèse de deux romans de jeunesse, *La Confession de Claude, Madeleine Férat*', *Revue d'Histoire littéraire de France*, vol. xxxv (1928), pp. 382–9.

—— 'La langue de *l'Assommoir*', *Le Français moderne*, vol. viii (1940), pp. 207–18.

CROCE, Benedetto. *Poesia e non poesia. Note sulla letteratura europea del secolo decimonono*. Bari, Laterza, 1923. ('Zola e Daudet', pp. 279–90.)

D'AMBRA, Lucio. *Trent'anni di vita letteraria. I. La partenza a gonfie vele.* Milan, Corbaccio, 1928. ('Incontro con Emilio Zola', pp. 169–89.)

—— *Trent'anni di vita letteraria. II. Il viaggio a furia di remi.* Milan, Corbaccio, 1928. ('La vedova di Emilio Zola', pp. 211–18.)

DANGELZER, Joan-Yvonne. *La Description du milieu dans le roman français de Balzac à Zola*. Paris, Presses modernes, 1938. ('Le milieu chez Zola', pp. 193–248.)

DAUDET, Alphonse. *Trente Ans de Paris. A travers ma vie et mes livres.* Paris, Marpon et Flammarion, 1888. 344 pp.

DAUDET, Mme Alphonse. *Souvenirs autour d'un groupe littéraire*. Paris, Charpentier, 1910. 257 pp.

DE AMICIS, Edmondo. *Ricordi di Parigi*. Milan, Treves, 1879. ('Emilio Zola', pp. 213–90.)

—— *Ritratti letterari*. Milan, Treves, 1881. ('Emilio Zola polemista', pp. 51–106.)

DECKER, Clarence Raymond. 'Zola's literary reputation in England', *P.M.L.A.*, vol. xlix (1934), pp. 1140–53.

DEFFOUX, Léon. 'Émile Zola pendant la Commune', *Mercure de France*, vol. clxxiii (1924), pp. 853–4.

—— 'Émile Zola et la sous-préfecture de Castelsarrasin en 1871', *Mercure de France*, vol. cxci (1926), pp. 336–46.

—— 'Émile Zola et ses éditions depuis 1902', *Le Figaro*, 1 October 1927.

DEFFOUX, Léon. *La Publication de 'l'Assommoir'.* Paris, Malfère, 1931. 152 pp.

—— and ZAVIE, Émile. *Le Groupe de Médan.* Paris, Payot, 1920. 316 pp.

DELHORBE, Cécile. *L'Affaire Dreyfus et les écrivains français.* Paris, Attinger, 1932. ('Émile Zola', pp. 45–80.)

DE LUCA, Giuseppe. 'Ah, quell'udienza!—Emilio Zola e Leone XIII', *Nuova Antologia*, vol. cdxxxiii (1945), pp. 57–61.

DE SANCTIS, Francesco. *Saggi critici* a cura di Luigi Russo. Bari, Laterza, 1952. ('Studio sopra Emilio Zola', vol. iii, pp. 235–76.)

DESPREZ, Louis. *Lettres inédites de Louis Desprez à Émile Zola.* Paris, Les Belles Lettres, 1952. 130 pp.

DESSIGNOLE, Émile. *La Question sociale dans Émile Zola.* Paris, Clavreuil, 1905. 415 pp.

DOUCET, Fernand. *L'Esthétique d'Émile Zola et son application à la critique.* The Hague, De Nederlandsche Boek- en Steendrukkerij, 1923. 360 pp.

DREYFOUS, Maurice. *Ce qu'il me reste à dire. Un demi-siècle de choses vues et entendues.* Paris, Ollendorff, 1912.

—— 'Théophile Gautier et Émile Zola', *Bulletin de l'Association Émile Zola*, no. 7 (1912), pp. 251–3.

DUBOIS, Jacques. '*Madame Gervaisais* et *la Conquête de Plassans'*, *Les Cahiers naturalistes*, nos. 24–25 (1963), pp. 83–89.

DUBUC, André. 'Une amitié littéraire: Gustave Flaubert et Émile Zola', *Les Cahiers naturalistes*, no. 28 (1964), pp. 129–36.

DUFAY, Pierre. '*Nana* et Blanche d'Antigny', *Intermédiaire des Chercheurs et des Curieux*, vol. xcvi (1933), pp. 502–4.

DUMESNIL, René. *La Publication des 'Soirées de Médan'.* Paris, Malfère, 1933. 207 pp.

DUNCAN, Phillip A. 'Genesis of the Longchamp scene in Zola's *Nana'*, *Modern Language Notes*, vol. lxxv (1960), pp. 684–9.

—— 'Zola's "An Election at Villebranche" ', *Symposium*, vol. xv (1961), pp. 286–96.

DUPUY, Aimé. 'Hommes politiques, fonctionnaires et magistrats dans *les Rougon-Macquart'*, *Revue socialiste*, no. 64 (1953), pp. 173–91.

—— *1870-1871. La Guerre, la Commune et la presse.* Paris, Armand Colin, 1959. ('Émile Zola, chroniqueur parlementaire à Bordeaux et à Versailles', pp. 151–66.)

EBIN, Ima N. 'Manet et Zola', *Gazette des Beaux-Arts*, vol. xxvii (1945), pp. 357–78.

EDWARDS, Herbert. 'Zola and the American critics', *American Literature*, vol. iv (1932), pp. 114–29.

EICHENHOLZ, M. 'Romany *Lurd, Rim, Parizh* E. Zolya i ikh sud'ba v Rossii', *Literaturnoe nasledstvo*, nos. 33–34 (Moscow, 1939), pp. 457–590.

ELLIS, Havelock. *Affirmations.* London, Constable, 1898. ('Zola', pp. 131–57.)

ERNST, Fritz. *Aus Goethes Freundeskreis und andere Essays.* Berlin and

Frankfurt am Main, Suhrkamp Verlag, 1955. ('Der Dichter der *Rougon-Macquart'*, pp. 189–209.)

Europe. Numéro spécial. 30ᵉ année (1952), nos. 83–84. 252 pp.

FAURE, Gabriel. *Pèlerinages passionnés, 2ᵉ série.* Paris, Fasquelle, 1922. ('Au Paradou', pp. 183–210.)

FLAUBERT, Gustave. *Correspondance, nouvelle édition augmentée.* Paris, Conard, 1926–33. 9 vols.

FRANCE, Anatole. *La Vie littéraire.* Paris, Calmann-Lévy, 1888–1949. 5 vols.

FRANDON, Ida-Marie. *Autour de 'Germinal'. La Mine et les mineurs.* Geneva, Droz, 1955. 128 pp.

—— 'Valeurs durables dans l'œuvre de Zola.—Art et pensée de Zola d'après *Germinal'*, *Les Cahiers naturalistes*, no. 5 (1956), pp. 214–23.

—— *La Pensée politique d'Émile Zola.* Paris, Champion, 1959. 28 pp.

FRANZÉN, Nils-Olof. *Zola et 'la Joie de vivre'. Genèse du roman, les personnages, les idées.* Stockholm, Almqvist & Wicksell, 1958. 241 pp.

FRASER, Elizabeth M. *Le Renouveau religieux d'après le roman français de 1886 à 1914.* Paris, Les Belles Lettres, 1934. viii + 218 pp.

FRÉVILLE, Jean. *Zola semeur d'orages.* Paris, Éditions sociales, 1952. 162 pp.

GAUTHIER, E. Paul. 'Zola as imitator of Flaubert's style', *Modern Language Notes*, vol. lxxv (1960), pp. 423–7.

—— 'New light on Zola and physiognomy', *P.M.L.A.*, vol. lxxv (1960), pp. 297–308.

GIRARD, Marcel. 'Situation d'Émile Zola', *Revue des Sciences humaines*, fasc. 66 (1952), pp. 137–56.

—— 'Émile Zola ou la joie de vivre', *Aesculape*, vol. xxxiii (1952), pp. 198–203.

—— 'L'univers de *Germinal'*, *Revue des Sciences humaines*, fasc. 69 (1953), pp. 59–76.

—— 'Zola visionnaire', *Montjoie*, vol. i (1953), pp. 6–9.

—— 'Émile Zola et la critique universitaire', *Les Cahiers naturalistes*, no. 1 (1955), pp. 27–33.

—— 'Positions politiques d'Émile Zola jusqu'à l'Affaire Dreyfus', *Revue française de Science politique*, vol. v (1955), pp. 503–28.

GONCOURT, Edmond de. 'Lettres inédites à Émile Zola présentées et commentées par Pierre Cogny', *Les Cahiers naturalistes*, no. 13 (1959), pp. 526–42.

GONCOURT, Edmond and Jules de. *Journal. Mémoires de la vie littéraire.* Texte intégral établi et annoté par Robert Ricatte. Monaco, Éditions de l'Imprimerie Nationale, 1956. 22 vols.

GONCOURT, Jules de. *Lettres de Jules de Goncourt.* Paris, Charpentier, 1885. 328 pp.

GOSSE, Edmund. *French Profiles.* London, Heinemann, 1905. ('The short stories of Zola', pp. 129–52.)

GOURMONT, Remy de. *Épilogues, réflexions sur la vie.* Paris, Mercure de France, 1903. ('Monsieur Zola', pp. 30–34.)

GOURMONT, Remy de. *Épilogues, réflexions sur la vie, 3ᵉ série*. Paris, Mercure de France, 1905. ('M. Émile Zola', pp. 96–104.)

GRANT, Elliott M. 'Studies on Zola's *Son Excellence Eugène Rougon*', *Romanic Review*, vol. xliv (1953), pp. 24–39.

—— 'The composition of *La Curée*', *Romanic Review*, vol. xlv (1954), pp. 29–44.

—— 'The political scene in Zola's *Pot-Bouille*', *French Studies*, vol. viii (1954), pp. 342–7.

—— 'Concerning the sources of *Germinal*', *Romanic Review*, vol. xlix (1958), pp. 168–78.

—— 'The newspapers of *Germinal*: their identity and significance', *Modern Language Review*, vol. lv (1960), pp. 87–89.

—— 'La source historique d'une scène de *Germinal*', *Revue d'Histoire littéraire de la France*, vol. lx (1960), pp. 61–63.

—— 'Marriage or murder: Zola's hesitations concerning Cécile Grégoire', *French Studies*, vol. xv (1961), pp. 41–46.

—— *Zola's 'Germinal'. A Critical and Historical Study*. Leicester University Press, 1962. viii+224 pp.

—— 'The Bishop's role in Zola's *Le Rêve*', *Romanic Review*, vol. lii (1962), pp. 105–11.

—— 'Quelques précisions sur une source de *Germinal*', *Les Cahiers naturalistes*, no. 22 (1962), pp. 249–54.

—— 'L'affaire Poinsot-Jud, Mérimée, et Zola', *Les Cahiers naturalistes*, no. 23 (1963), pp. 313–15.

GRANT, Richard B. 'The Jewish question in Zola's *L'Argent*', *P.M.L.A.*, vol. lxx (1955), pp. 955–67.

—— 'Confusion of meaning in Zola's *La Faute de l'abbé Mouret*', *Symposium*, vol. xiii (1959), pp. 284–9.

—— *Zola's 'Son Excellence Eugène Rougon'*, Durham, N.C., Duke University Press, 1960. 146 pp.

—— 'The problem of Zola's character creation in *L'Argent*', *Kentucky Foreign Language Quarterly*, vol. viii (1961), pp. 58–65.

GREGOR, Ian, and NICHOLAS, Brian. *The Moral and the Story*. London, Faber, 1962. ('The novel as social document: *L'Assommoir*', pp. 63–97.)

GUICHES, Gustave. *Au banquet de la vie*. Paris, Spes, 1925. ('Le Manifeste des Cinq', pp. 216–36.)

GUILLEMIN, Henri. *Zola, légende et vérité*. Paris, Julliard, 1960. 187 pp.

—— *Éclaircissements*. Paris, Gallimard, 1961. ('Judet contre Zola; Zola et l'affaire Dreyfus', pp. 251–85.)

—— *Présentation des 'Rougon-Macquart'*. Paris, Gallimard, 1964. 413 pp.

HALPÉRINE-KAMINSKY, Élie. *Ivan Tourguéneff d'après sa correspondance avec ses amis français*. Paris, Charpentier-Fasquelle, 1901. 359 pp.

HAMILTON, George Heard. *Manet and his Critics*. New Haven, Yale University Press, 1954. ('Manet and Zola, 1866–7', pp. 81–111.)

HARVEY, Lawrence E. 'The cycle myth in *La Terre* of Zola', *Philological Quarterly*, vol. xxxviii (1959), pp. 89–95.

HEMMINGS, F. W. J. 'The genesis of Zola's *Joie de vivre*', *French Studies*, vol. vi (1952), pp. 114–25.
—— 'The origin of the terms *naturalisme*, *naturaliste*', *French Studies*, vol. viii (1954), pp. 109–21.
—— 'Zola on the staff of *Le Gaulois*', *Modern Language Review*, vol. l (1955), pp. 25–29.
—— 'The present position in Zola studies', *French Studies*, vol. x (1956), pp. 97–122.
—— 'Zola, *Le Bien public* and *Le Voltaire*', *Romanic Review*, vol. xlvii (1956), pp. 103–16.
—— 'Zola's apprenticeship to journalism', *P.M.L.A.*, vol. lxxi (1956), pp. 340–54.
—— 'Zola, Manet, and the Impressionists', *P.M.L.A.*, vol. lxxiii (1958), pp. 407–17.
—— 'Zola and *L'Éducation sentimentale*', *Romanic Review*, vol. l (1959), pp. 35–40.
—— 'The secret sources of *La Faute de l'abbé Mouret*', *French Studies*, vol. xiii (1959), pp. 226–39.
—— 'Zola pour ou contre Stendhal?', *Les Cahiers naturalistes*, no. 19 (1961), pp. 107–12.
—— 'Stendhal relu par Zola au temps de "l'Affaire" ', *Stendhal Club*, no. 16 (1962), pp. 302–10.
—— 'Zola par delà la Manche et l'Atlantique (essai bibliographique)', *Les Cahiers naturalistes*, no. 23 (1963), pp. 299–312.
—— 'Les sources d'inspiration de Zola conteur', *Les Cahiers naturalistes*, nos. 24–25 (1963), pp. 29–44.
HOCHE, Jules. *Les Parisiens chez eux*. Paris, Dentu, 1883. ('Zola', pp. 399–413.)
—— 'Le premier roman d'Émile Zola', *La Revue illustrée*, vol. iv (1887), pp. 289–98. (Zola and Louise Solari.)
HUYSMANS, Joris-Karl. *Œuvres complètes*, vol. ii. Paris, Crès, 1928. ('Émile Zola et *l'Assommoir*', pp. 151–92.)
—— *Lettres inédites à Émile Zola* publiées et annotées par Pierre Lambert. Geneva, Droz, 1953. xxxi+153 pp.

JAGMETTI, Antoinette. *'La Bête humaine' d'Émile Zola, étude de stylistique critique*. Geneva, Droz, 1955. 83 pp.
JAMES, Henry. *The House of Fiction*. London, Hart-Davis, 1957. ('Émile Zola', pp. 220–49; 'Nana', pp. 274–80.)
JOSEPHSON, Matthew. *Zola and his Time*. New York, Macaulay, 1928. 558 pp.
JOUVENEL, Bertrand de. *Vie de Zola*. Paris, Librairie Valois, 1931. 366 pp.

KAHN, Maurice. 'Anatole France et Émile Zola', *La Grande Revue*, vol. cxxi (1926), pp. 40–66.
KANES, Martin. *Zola's 'La Bête humaine'. A Study in Literary Creation*. Berkeley and Los Angeles, University of California Press, 1962. 138 pp.

KANES, Martin. 'Zola and Busnach: the temptation of the stage', *P.M.L.A.*, vol. lxxvii (1962), pp. 109–15.

—— '*Germinal*: drama and dramatic structure', *Modern Philology*, vol. lxi (1963), pp. 12–25.

—— 'Zola, Balzac, and "La Fortune des Rogron"', *French Studies*, vol. xviii (1964), pp. 203–12.

—— 'Zola, Pelletan, and *La Tribune*', *P.M.L.A.*, vol. lxxix (1964), pp. 473–83.

KAYSER, Jacques. '*J'accuse!*', *Europe*, no. 25 (1948), pp. 11–21.

—— 'Impressions d'audience', *La Nef*, no. 39 (1948), pp. 55–66.

—— 'Émile Zola et l'opinion publique', *La Nef*, no. 49 (1948), pp. 47–58, and no. 50 (1949), pp. 23–37.

KEINS, Jean-Paul. 'Der historische Wahrheitsgehalt in den Romanen Zolas', *Romanische Forschungen*, vol. xlvi (1932), pp. 361–96.

KERR, Alfred. 'La maison de Zola', *Nouvelles littéraires*, 8 October 1932.

KLEMAN, M. K. *Emil' Zola. Sbornik statey*. Leningrad, Khudozhestvennaya literatura, 1934. 304 pp.

—— 'Iz perepiski E. Zolya s russkimi korrespondentami', *Literaturnoe nasledstvo*, nos. 31–32 (1937), pp. 943–80.

LABORDE, Albert. *Trente-huit années près de Zola. Vie d'Alexandrine Zola*. Paris, Éditeurs Français Réunis, 1963. 246 pp.

LAFARGUE, Paul. *Critiques littéraires*. Paris, Éditions Sociales Internationales, 1936. ('*L'Argent* de Zola', pp. 173–211.)

LALO, Charles. 'Taine et Zola. L'esthétique naturaliste et l'esthétique réaliste', *Revue bleue*, vol. xlix (1911), pp. 214–18, 236–42.

—— 'L'art et la vie. Le complexe de Zola', *Revue des Cours et Conférences*, vol. xxxviii (1937), pp. 508–21.

LANOUX, Armand. *Bonjour, Monsieur Zola*. Paris, Amiot-Dumont, 1954. 398 pp.

LAPP, John C. 'The critical reception of Zola's *La Confession de Claude*', *Modern Language Notes*, vol. lxviii (1953), pp. 457–62.

—— 'Taine et Zola: autour d'une correspondance', *Revue des Sciences humaines*, fasc. 87 (1957), pp. 319–26.

—— 'Zola et la Tentation de Saint Antoine', *Revue des Sciences humaines*, fasc. 92 (1958), pp. 513–18.

—— 'On Zola's habits of revision', *Modern Language Notes*, vol. lxxiii (1958), pp. 603–11.

—— 'The Watcher Betrayed and the Fatal Woman: some recurring patterns in Zola', *P.M.L.A.*, vol. lxxiv (1959), pp. 276–84.

—— 'De nouvelles épreuves corrigées par Zola: *Germinal*', *Les Cahiers naturalistes*, no. 21 (1962), pp. 223–6.

—— *Zola before the 'Rougon-Macquart'*. University of Toronto Press, 1964. vii+171 pp.

LARGUIER, Léo. *Avant le déluge. Souvenirs*. Paris, Grasset, 1929. 257 pp.

LE BLOND, Maurice. *Émile Zola, son évolution, son influence*. Paris, Éditions de Mouvement socialiste, 1903. 28 pp.

—— 'Sur Émile Zola', *Mercure de France*, vol. cvi (1913), pp. 5–19.

—— 'Les projets littéraires d'Émile Zola au moment de sa mort', *Mercure de France*, vol. cxcix (1927), pp. 5–25.

—— *La Publication de 'la Terre'*. Paris, Malfère, 1937. 122 pp.

LE BLOND-ZOLA, Denise. *Émile Zola raconté par sa fille*. Paris, Fasquelle, 1931. 266 pp.

LECERCLE, Jean-Louis. 'De l'art impassible à la littérature militante: *Les Trois Villes* d'Émile Zola', *La Pensée*, no. 46 (1953), pp. 29–38.

LEGOUIS, Émile. '*La Terre* de Zola et *le Roi Lear*', *Revue de Littérature comparée*, vol. xxvii (1953), pp. 417–27.

LEMM, Siegfried. *Zur Entstehungsgeschichte von Émile Zolas Rougon-Macquart und den Quatre Evangiles*. Halle a. S., Niemeyer, 1913. 83 pp.

LEONARD, Frances McNeely. '*Nana*: symbol and action', *Modern Fiction Studies*, vol. ix (1963), pp. 149–58.

LEPELLETIER, Edmond. 'Les débuts de Zola', *Écho de Paris*, 1 October 1902.

—— *Émile Zola, sa vie, son œuvre*. Paris, Mercure de France, 1908. 492 pp.

LEROY, Maxime. 'Le prolétariat vu par Zola dans *l'Assommoir*', *Preuves*, no. 20 (1952), pp. 72–75.

LEVIN, Harry. *The Gates of Horn: a Study of Five French Realists*. New York, Oxford University Press, 1963. ('Zola', pp. 305–71.)

LOLIÉE, Frédéric. 'Persönliche Erinnerungen an Émile Zola', *Deutsche Revue über das gesamte nationale Leben der Gegenwart* (1902), pp. 225–30.

LOQUET, Francis. 'La documentation géographique dans *Germinal*', *Revue des Sciences humaines*, fasc. 79 (1955), pp. 377–85.

LOTE, Georges. 'Zola historien du second Empire', *Revue des Études napoléoniennes*, vol. xiv (1918), pp. 39–87.

—— 'La doctrine et la méthode naturalistes d'après Émile Zola', *Zeitschrift für französische Sprache und Literatur*, vol. li (1928), pp. 193–224, 389–418.

LOUIS, Paul. *Les Types sociaux chez Balzac et Zola*. Paris, Le Monde moderne, 1925. 220 pp.

LUKÁCS, George. *Studies in European Realism*. London, Hillway Publishing Co., 1950. ('The Zola centenary', pp. 85–96.)

MALLARMÉ, Stéphane. *Dix-neuf lettres de Stéphane Mallarmé à Émile Zola*. Paris, Centaine, 1929. 74 pp.

MANDIN, Louis. 'Les origines de *Thérèse Raquin*', *Mercure de France*, vol. ccxcvii (1940), pp. 282–98.

MANN, Heinrich. *Macht und Mensch*. Munich, Kurt Wolff, 1919. ('Zola', pp. 35–131.)

MARTINEAU, Henri. *Le Roman scientifique d'Émile Zola. La Médecine et les Rougon-Macquart*. Paris, Baillière, 1907. 272 pp.

MARTINO, Pierre. *Le Roman réaliste sous le second Empire*. Paris, Hachette, 1913. ('Les premiers romans scientifiques de Zola', pp. 255–86.)

MASSIS, Henri. *Comment Émile Zola composait ses romans*. Paris, Fasquelle, 1906. 344 pp.

MATTHEWS, J. H. 'Note sur la méthode de Zola', *Revue des Sciences humaines*, fasc. 83 (1956), pp. 337–46.

—— *Les Deux Zola*. Geneva, Droz, 1957. 103 pp.

—— 'Zola's *Le Rêve* as an experimental novel', *Modern Language Review*, vol. lii (1957), pp. 187–94.

—— 'The railway in Zola's *La Bête humaine*', *Symposium*, vol. xiv (1960), pp. 53–59.

—— '*Things* in the naturalist novel', *French Studies*, vol. xiv (1960), pp. 212–23.

—— 'L'impressionnisme chez Zola: *le Ventre de Paris*', *Le Français moderne*, vol. xxix (1961), pp. 199–205.

—— 'The art of description in Zola's *Germinal*', *Symposium*, vol. xvi (1962), pp. 267–74.

MAUBLANC, René. 'Actualité de Zola', *La Pensée*, no. 22 (1949), pp. 74–84.

MAUPASSANT, Guy de. *Chroniques, études, correspondance de Guy de Maupassant* recueillies . . . par René Dumesnil. Paris, Gründ, 1938. ('*Les Soirées de Médan*. Comment ce livre a été fait', pp. 20–23; 'Émile Zola', pp. 76–78.)

MELTZER, Charles Henry. 'Personal memories of Zola', *The Bookman*, vol. xvi (1902), pp. 250–2.

MENICHELLI, Gian Carlo. *Bibliographie de Zola en Italie*. Florence, Institut français, 1960. xxxvi+137 pp.

MILNER, George B. 'Zola mis en relief par Cézanne', *Babel*, vol. i (1940), pp. 25–30.

MITTERAND, Henri. 'Un projet inédit d'Émile Zola en 1884-85: le roman des Villes d'Eaux', *Les Cahiers naturalistes*, no. 10 (1958), pp. 401–23.

—— 'Un jeune homme de province à Paris: Émile Zola de 1858 à 1861', *Les Cahiers naturalistes*, no. 11 (1958), pp. 444–53.

—— 'La jeunesse de Zola et de Cézanne: observations nouvelles', *Mercure de France*, vol. cccxxxv (1959), pp. 351–9.

—— 'La publication en feuilleton de *la Fortune des Rougon*', *Mercure de France*, vol. cccxxxvii (1959), pp. 531–6.

—— 'Émile Zola à Marseille et à Bordeaux de septembre à décembre 1870', *Revue des Sciences humaines*, fasc. 98–99 (1960), pp. 257–87.

—— 'Émile Zola et *le Rappel*', *Les Cahiers naturalistes*, no 15 (1960), pp. 589–604.

—— 'La genèse et la publication de *Son Excellence Eugène Rougon*', *Mercure de France*, vol. cccxlii (1961), pp. 669–90.

—— '*Thérèse Raquin* au théâtre', *Revue des Sciences humaines*, fasc. 104 (1961), pp. 489–516.

—— *Zola journaliste. De l'affaire Manet à l'affaire Dreyfus*. Paris, Armand Colin, 1962. 311 pp.

—— 'Quelques aspects de la création littéraire dans l'œuvre d'Émile Zola', *Les Cahiers naturalistes*, nos. 24–25 (1963), pp. 9–20.

MOORE, George. 'My impressions of Zola', *English Illustrated Magazine*, vol. xi (1894), pp. 477–89.

MOREAU, Pierre. 'Le *Germinal* d'Yves Guyot', *Revue d'Histoire littéraire de la France*, vol. liv (1954), pp. 208–13.

NIESS, Robert J. 'Autobiographical elements in Zola's *Joie de vivre*', *P.M.L.A.*, vol. lvi (1941), pp. 1133–49.

—— 'Zola's *La Joie de vivre* and *La Mort d'Olivier Bécaille*', *Modern Language Notes*, vol. lvii (1942), pp. 205–7.

—— 'Zola's *La Joie de vivre* and the opera *Lazare*', *Romanic Review*, vol. xxxiv (1943), pp. 223–7.

—— 'Zola's final revisions of *La Joie de vivre*', *Modern Language Notes*, vol. lviii (1943), pp. 537–9.

—— 'Émile Zola: from fact to fiction', *Modern Language Notes*, vol. lxiii (1948), pp. 407–8.

—— 'Another view of Zola's *L'Œuvre*', *Romanic Review*, vol. xxxix (1948), pp. 282–300.

—— 'Hawthorne and Zola—an influence?', *Revue de Littérature comparée*, vol. xxvii (1953), pp. 446–52. (*Thérèse Raquin*.)

—— 'Henry James and Zola: a parallel', *Revue de Littérature comparée*, vol. xxx (1956), pp. 93–98. (*The Madonna of the Future* and *L'Œuvre*.)

—— 'Antithesis and *reprise* in Zola's *L'Œuvre*', *L'Esprit créateur*, vol. iv (1964), pp. 68–75.

PARTURIER, Maurice. 'Zola et Duranty', *Bulletin du Bibliophile* (1948), pp. 49–73, 97–124.

PATIN, Jacques. 'Une profession de foi naturaliste (lettre inédite de Zola)', *Le Figaro*, 20 June 1931.

PETRICONI, H. *Das Reich des Untergangs*. Hamburg, Hoffmann und Campe, 1958. (*'La Débâcle'*, pp. 37–66.)

PICON, Gaëtan. 'Le "réalisme" d'Émile Zola: du "tel quel" à l'œuvre-objet', *Les Cahiers naturalistes*, no. 22 (1962), pp. 235–40.

PILLET, Alfred. 'Émile Zola', *Germanisch-romanische Monatsschrift*, vol. xix (1931), pp. 200–21.

Présence de Zola. Paris, Fasquelle, 1953. 246 pp. (Essays by various hands.)

PRITCHETT, V. S. *Books in General*. London, Chatto & Windus, 1953. ('Zola', pp. 110–22. On *L'Œuvre* and *L'Assommoir*.)

PSICHARI, Henriette. *Anatomie d'un chef-d'œuvre: 'Germinal'*. Paris, Mercure de France, 1964. 205 pp.

RAPHAËL, Paul. '*La Fortune des Rougon* et la vérité historique', *Mercure de France*, vol. clxvii (1923), pp. 104–18.

RETTÉ, Adolphe. *Le Symbolisme. Anecdotes et souvenirs*. Paris, Vannier, 1903. ('Souvenirs sur Émile Zola', pp. 179–94.)

REUILLARD, Gabriel. 'Zola assassiné?', *Le Monde*, 1 June 1954.

REWALD, John. *Cézanne, sa vie, son œuvre, son amitié pour Zola*. Paris, Albin Michel, 1939. 460 pp.

RHODES, S. A. 'The source of Zola's medical references in *La Débâcle*', *Modern Language Notes*, vol. xlv (1930), pp. 109–11.

RICATTE, Robert. 'A propos de *la Fortune des Rougon*', *Les Cahiers naturalistes*, no. 19 (1961), pp. 97–106.

ROBERT, Guy. 'Une polémique entre Zola et *le Mémorial d'Aix* en 1868', *Arts et Livres*, no. 6 (1946), pp. 5–23.

ROBERT, Guy. 'Zola et le classicisme', *Revue des Sciences humaines*, fasc. 49 (1948), pp. 1–24, and fasc. 50 (1948), pp. 126–53.
—— 'Trois textes inédits d'Émile Zola', *Revue des Sciences humaines*, fasc. 51 (1948), pp. 181–207.
—— *Émile Zola. Principes et caractères généraux de son œuvre*. Paris, Les Belles Lettres, 1952. 205 pp.
—— '*La Terre*' *d'Émile Zola, étude historique et critique*. Paris, Les Belles Lettres, 1952. 490 pp.
ROBERT, Louis de. *De Loti à Proust. Souvenirs et confidences*. Paris, Flammarion, 1928. ('Alphonse Daudet et Émile Zola', pp. 121–49.)
ROD, Édouard. *A propos de 'l'Assommoir'*. Paris, Marpon et Flammarion, 1879. 106 pp.
—— *Les Idées morales du temps présent*. Paris, Perrin, 1891. ('M. Émile Zola', pp. 73–98.)
—— 'The place of Émile Zola in literature', *Contemporary Review*, vol. lxxxii (1902), pp. 617–31.
ROMAINS, Jules. *Saints de notre calendrier*. Paris, Flammarion, 1952. ('Zola et son exemple', pp. 115–29.)
ROOT, Winthrop H. *German Criticism of Zola, 1875–93*. New York, Columbia University Press, 1931. xiv+112 pp.
ROY, Claude. *Descriptions critiques. La Main heureuse*. Paris, Gallimard, 1958. ('Sur *Germinal*', pp. 214–25.)
—— *Descriptions critiques. L'Homme en question*. Paris, Gallimard, 1960. ('Zola', pp. 132–40.)
RUFENER, Helen La Rue. *Biography of a War Novel, Zola's 'La Débâcle'*. New York, King's Crown Press, 1946. ix+125 pp.

SACKVILLE-WEST, Edward. *Inclinations*. London, Secker & Warburg, 1949. ('Zola's *La Débâcle*', pp. 199–204.)
SAINT-GEORGES DE BOUHÉLIER. 'La fatalité dans la mort d'Émile Zola', *Revue bleue*, 5e série, vol. ix (1908), pp. 412–15.
—— 'La mort de Zola', *Le Figaro*, 1 October 1927.
SALVAN, Albert J. *Zola aux États-Unis*. Providence, R.I., Brown University Press, 1943. 218 pp.
SAURAT, Denis. *Perspectives*. Paris, Stock, 1938. ('Zola', pp. 131–9.)
SCHOBER, Rita. 'Observations sur quelques procédés stylistiques de Zola', *Les Cahiers naturalistes*, no. 28 (1964), pp. 149–61.
SCOTT, J. W. 'Réalisme et réalité dans *La Bête humaine*', *Revue d'Histoire littéraire de la France*, vol. lxiii (1963), pp. 635–43.
SEILLIÈRE, Ernest. *Émile Zola*. Paris, Grasset, 1923. ix+358 pp.
SHERARD, Robert Harborough. *Émile Zola, a biographical and critical study*. London, Chatto & Windus, 1893. 288 pp.
—— *Twenty Years in Paris: being some Recollections of a Literary Life*. London, Hutchinson, 1905. 499 pp.
SIMON, Gustave. 'Un souvenir sur Émile Zola', *Le Temps*, 16 June 1924.
SOLARI, Émile. 'Circonstances dans lesquelles Zola composa ses œuvres', *La Grande Revue*, vol. cxiv (1924), pp. 603–28.

Suwala, Halina. 'A propos de quelques sources de *l'Argent*', *Les Cahiers naturalistes*, no. 16 (1960), pp. 651–4.

Tancock, L. W. 'Some early critical work of Émile Zola: *Livres d'aujourd'hui et de demain* (1866)', *Modern Language Review*, vol. xlii (1947), pp. 43–57.

Ternois, René. 'Les amitiés romaines d'Émile Zola', *Revue de Littérature comparée*, vol. xxi (1947), pp. 512–42.

—— *Zola et son temps. Lourdes—Rome—Paris.* Paris, Les Belles Lettres, 1961. 693 pp.

—— 'La naissance de *l'Œuvre*', *Les Cahiers naturalistes*, no. 17 (1961), pp. 1–9.

—— 'Les Zola. Histoire d'une famille vénitienne', *Les Cahiers naturalistes*, no. 18 (1961), pp. 49–70.

—— 'En marge de *Nana*', *Les Cahiers naturalistes*, no. 21 (1962), pp. 218–22.

—— 'Le stoïcisme d'Émile Zola', *Les Cahiers naturalistes*, no. 23 (1963), pp. 289–98.

—— (ed.). Émile Zola. *Mes voyages: Lourdes, Rome.* Paris, Fasquelle, 1958. 302 pp.

Tersen, Émile. 'Sources et sens de *Germinal*', *La Pensée*, no. 95 (1961), pp. 74–89.

Thibaudet, Albert. 'Réflexions sur Zola', *Nouvelle Revue française*, vol. xlv (1935), pp. 906–12.

Tison-Braun, Micheline. *La Crise de l'humanisme.* Paris, Nizet, 1958. ('Zola et l'apostolat humanitaire', pp. 292–313.)

Toulouse, Edmond. *Enquête médico-psychologique sur les rapports de la supériorité intellectuelle avec la névropathie. Émile Zola.* Paris, Société d'Éditions Scientifiques, 1896. xiv+282 pp.

Trilling, Lionel. *A Gathering of Fugitives.* London, Secker & Warburg, 1957. ('In defense of Zola', pp. 12–19.)

Triomphe, Jean. 'Zola collaborateur du *Messager de l'Europe*', *Revue de Littérature comparée*, vol. xvii (1937), pp. 754–65.

Turnell, Martin. *The Art of French Fiction.* London, Hamish Hamilton, 1959. ('Zola', pp. 93–194.)

Varloot, Jean. 'Zola vivant. Le procès du naturalisme. Le réalisme de Zola', *La Pensée*, no. 44 (1952), pp. 111–21, and no. 46 (1953), pp. 17–28.

Vauthier, Gabriel. 'Émile Zola et *la Confession de Claude*', *La Révolution de 1848*, vol. xxiii (1925), pp. 626–30.

Vauzat, Guy. 'Nana et Blanche d'Antigny', *La Grande Revue*, vol. cxl (1933), pp. 443–56.

Verhaeren, Émile. *Impressions, 2ᵉ série.* Paris, Mercure de France, 1927. ('Zola: *L'Argent*', pp. 195–202.)

Vicaire, Gabriel. 'L'esthétique d'Émile Zola', *Revue des Deux Mondes*, vol. xxi (1924), pp. 810–31.

VINCHON, Jean. 'Zola dîne avec les Goncourt', *Aesculape*, vol. xxxiv (1953), pp. 1–7.

VISSIÈRE, Jean-Louis. 'L'art de la phrase dans *l'Assommoir*', *Les Cahiers naturalistes*, no. 11 (1958), pp. 455–64.

—— 'Politique et prophétie dans *Germinal*', *Les Cahiers naturalistes*, no. 20 (1962), pp. 166–7.

VIZETELLY, Ernest Alfred. *With Zola in England*. London, Chatto & Windus, 1899. xvi+218 pp.

—— 'Some recollections of Émile Zola', *Pall Mall Magazine*, vol. xxix (1903), pp. 63–76.

—— *Émile Zola, Novelist and Reformer: an Account of his Life and Work*. London, Bodley Head, 1904. x+560 pp.

WALKER, Philip. 'Prophetic myths in Zola', *P.M.L.A.*, vol. lxxiv (1959), pp. 444–52.

—— 'Zola's use of color imagery in *Germinal*', *P.M.L.A.*, vol. lxxvii (1962), pp. 442–9.

—— 'Zola's art of characterization in *Germinal*', *L'Esprit créateur*, vol. iv (1964), pp. 60–67.

WALTER, Rodolphe. 'Zola et ses amis à Bennecourt (1866)', *Les Cahiers naturalistes*, no. 17 (1961), pp. 19–35.

—— 'Deux lettres inédites d'Émilie Zola à Gabrielle-Alexandrine Meley et à Émile Zola', *Les Cahiers naturalistes*, no. 22 (1962), pp. 280–3.

—— 'Émile Zola et Claude Monet', *Les Cahiers naturalistes*, no. 26 (1964), pp. 51–61.

WEINSTEIN, Sophie R. 'The genesis of Zola's *La Confession de Claude*', *Modern Language Notes*, vol. liii (1938), pp. 196–8.

WEISKE, Fritz. 'Zolas Stellung zum Katholizismus nach seinen Romanen *Lourdes, Rome, Paris*', *Germanisch-romanische Monatsschrift*, vol. xxiv (1936), pp. 127–44.

WENGER, Jared. 'The art of the flashback: violent techniques in *Les Rougon-Macquart*', *P.M.L.A.*, vol. lvii (1942), pp. 1137–59.

—— 'Character-types of Scott, Balzac, Dickens, Zola', *P.M.L.A.*, vol. lxii (1947), pp. 213–32.

WEST, Anthony. *Principles and Persuasions*. London, Eyre & Spottiswoode, 1958. ('Émile Zola', pp. 126–31.)

WILSON, Angus. *Émile Zola. An Introductory Study of his Novels*. London, Secker & Warburg, 1952. 148 pp.

XAU, Fernand. *Émile Zola*. Paris, Marpon et Flammarion, 1880. 68 pp.

ZÉVAES, Alexandre. 'La première chronique d'Émile Zola', *Nouvelles littéraires*, 14 May 1932.

—— 'A propos de *la Confession de Claude*. Émile Zola et le parquet impérial', *Nouvelles littéraires*, 3 March 1934.

—— 'Émile Zola et Jules Guesde', *Commune*, no. 42 (1937), pp. 689–95.

—— *A la gloire de . . . Zola*. Paris, Éditions de la *Revue critique*, 1945. 315 pp.

—— *Le Cinquantenaire de 'J'accuse'*. Paris, Fasquelle, 1948. 164 pp.

INDEX

PRINTED IN GREAT BRITAIN
AT THE UNIVERSITY PRESS, OXFORD
BY VIVIAN RIDLER
PRINTER TO THE UNIVERSITY